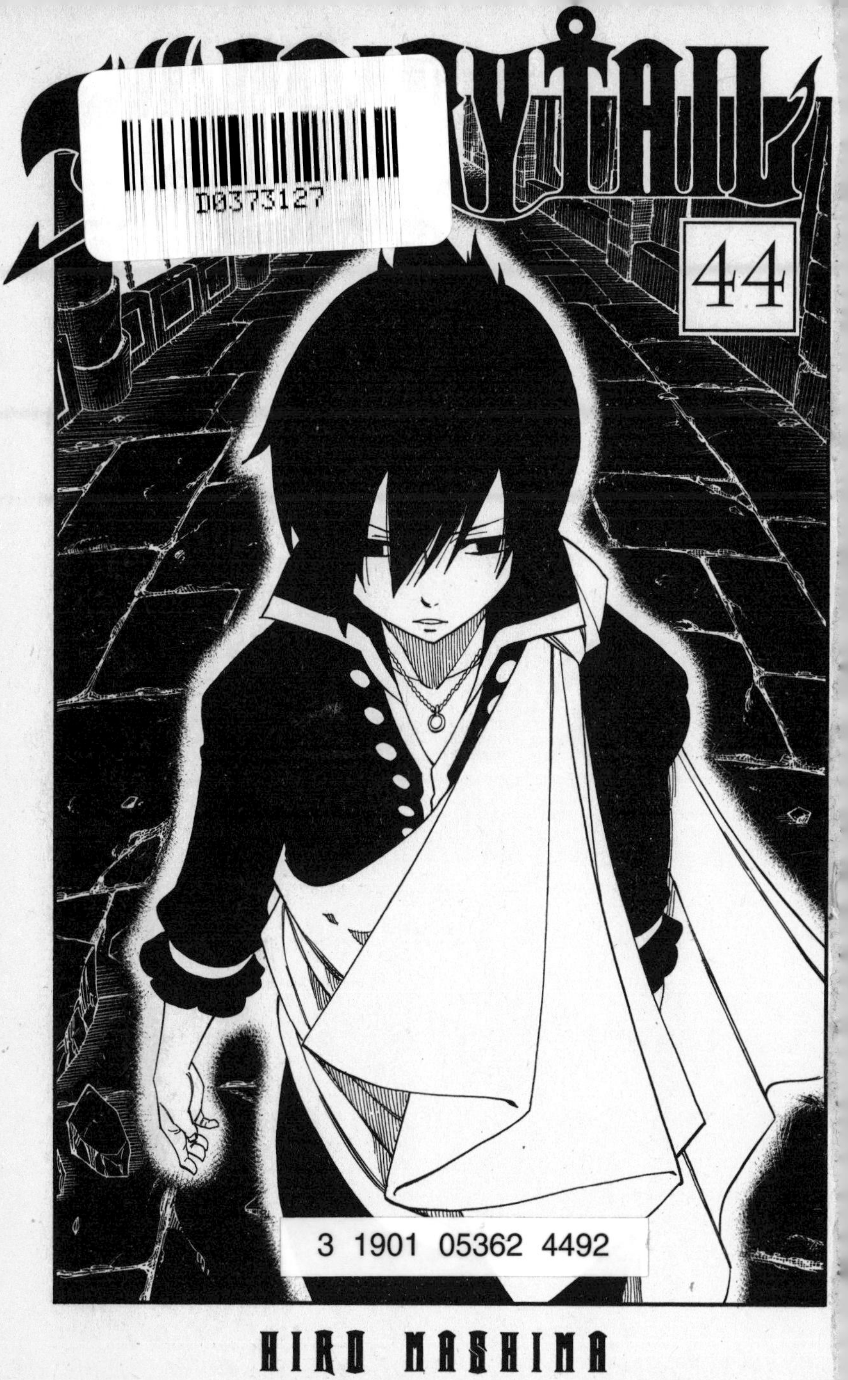

44

HIRO MASHIMA

FAIRY TAIL
VOL. 44 CONTENTS
FA FA FA FA FA!

FAIRY TAIL

Chapter 370: Devil Reincarnation

MERMAID HEEL

Name: Beth Vanderwood   Age: 16

Magic:
Vegetable Magic

Likes: Dislikes:
Vegetables   **Garden pests**

Remarks

An immigrant from the western continent. She also serves as the nutritionist for Mermaid Heel. Vegetable magic is magic that makes fruits and vegetables grow from the ground and attack one's opponent. These fruits and vegetables are edible, but they aren't nutritious, and they taste awful.

She thinks the key to growing good vegetables is to put one's heart into it, so she has established a farm as a side business as well.

She's noticed that Millianna treats Kagura like an older sister, but she doesn't know that Millianna is actually older than Kagura.

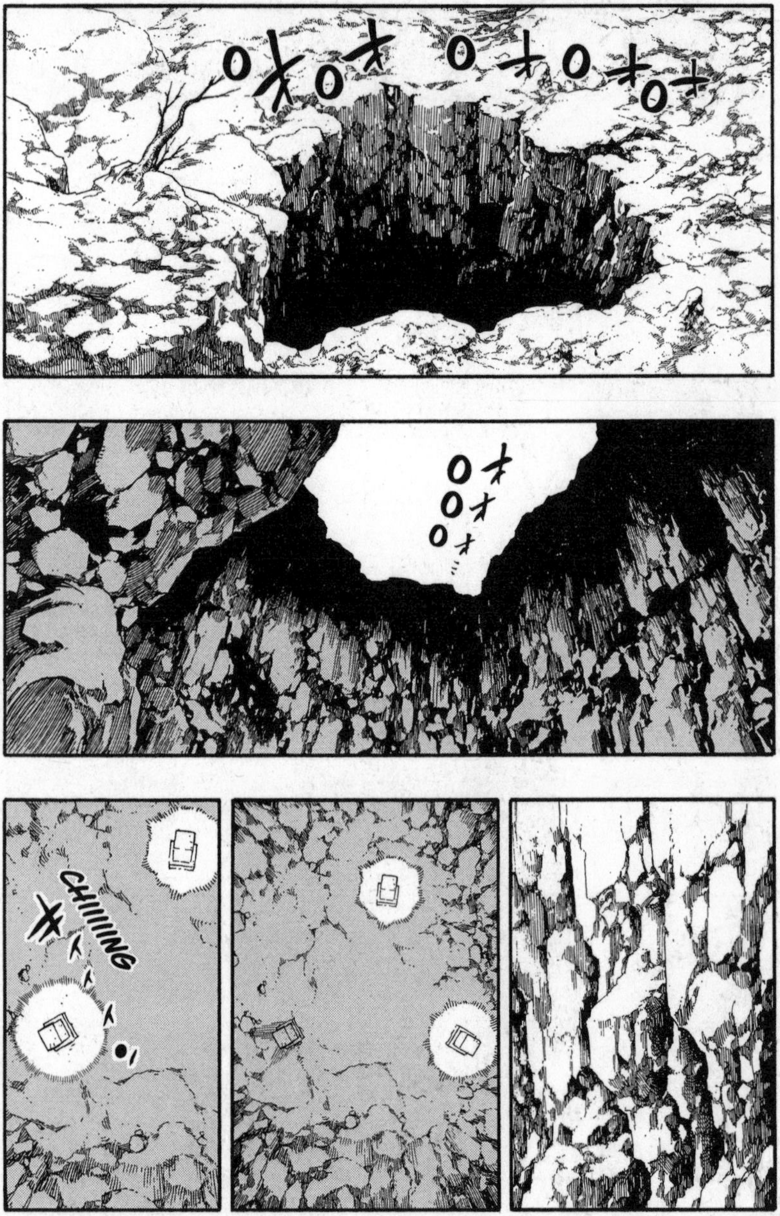
CHIIIIING

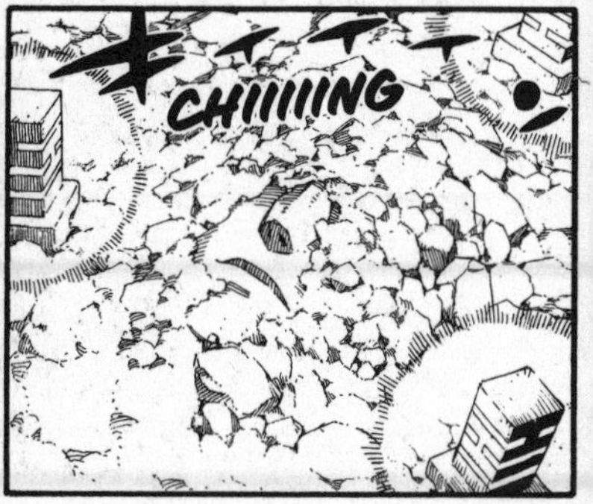
CHIIIIING

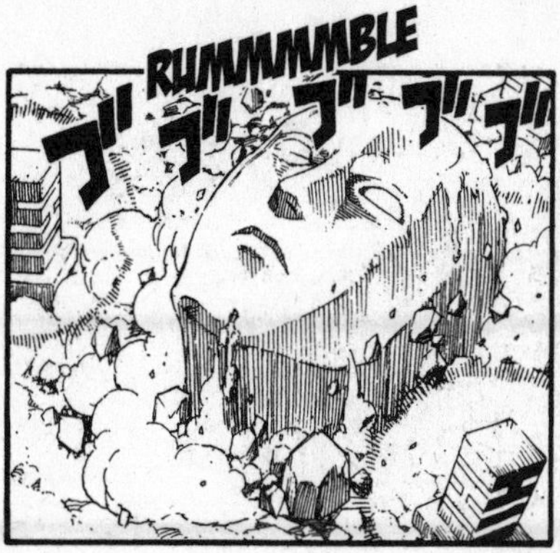
RUMMMMBLE
ゴゴゴゴゴ

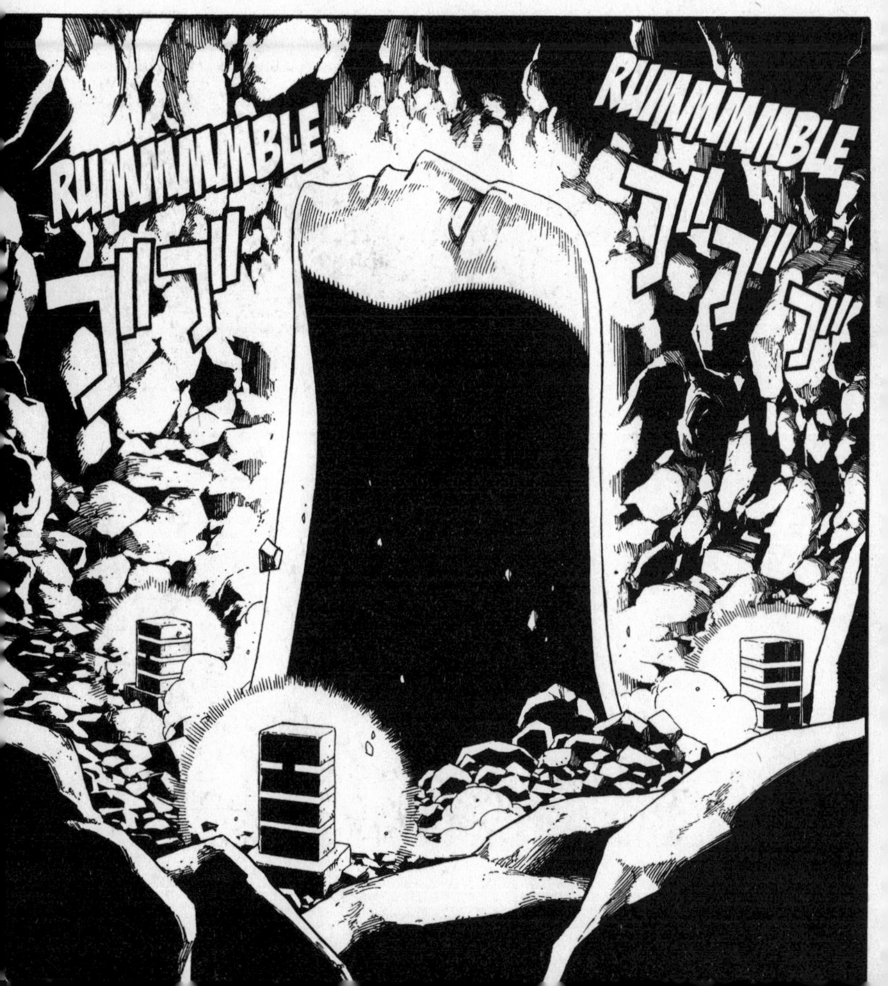
RUMMMMBLE
ゴゴゴ
RUMMMMBLE
ゴゴ

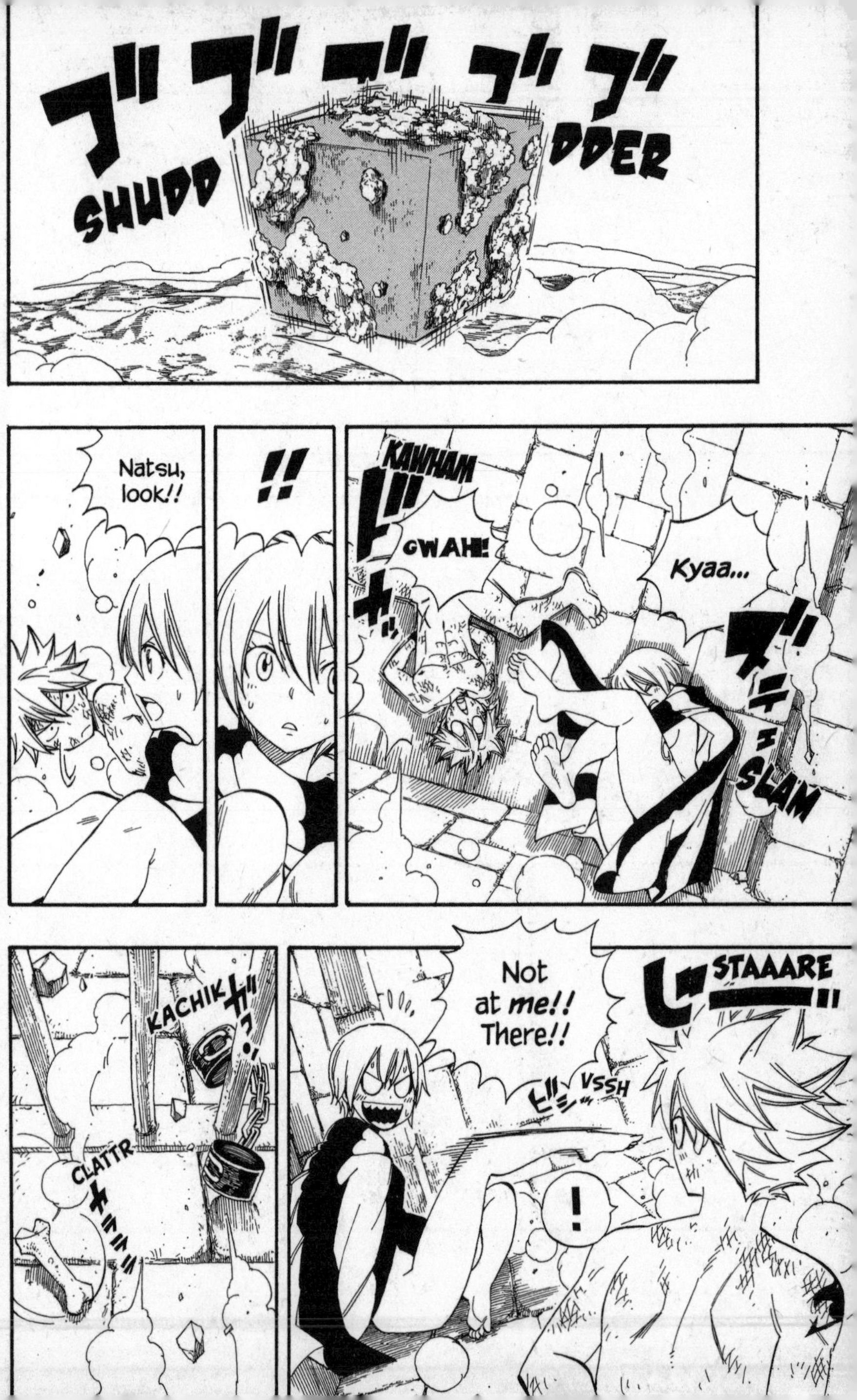

SHUDD
DDER
KAWHAM
GWAH!
Kyaa...
SLAM
!!
Natsu, look!!
STAAARE
Not at *me!!* There!!
VSSH
!
KACHIK
CLATTR

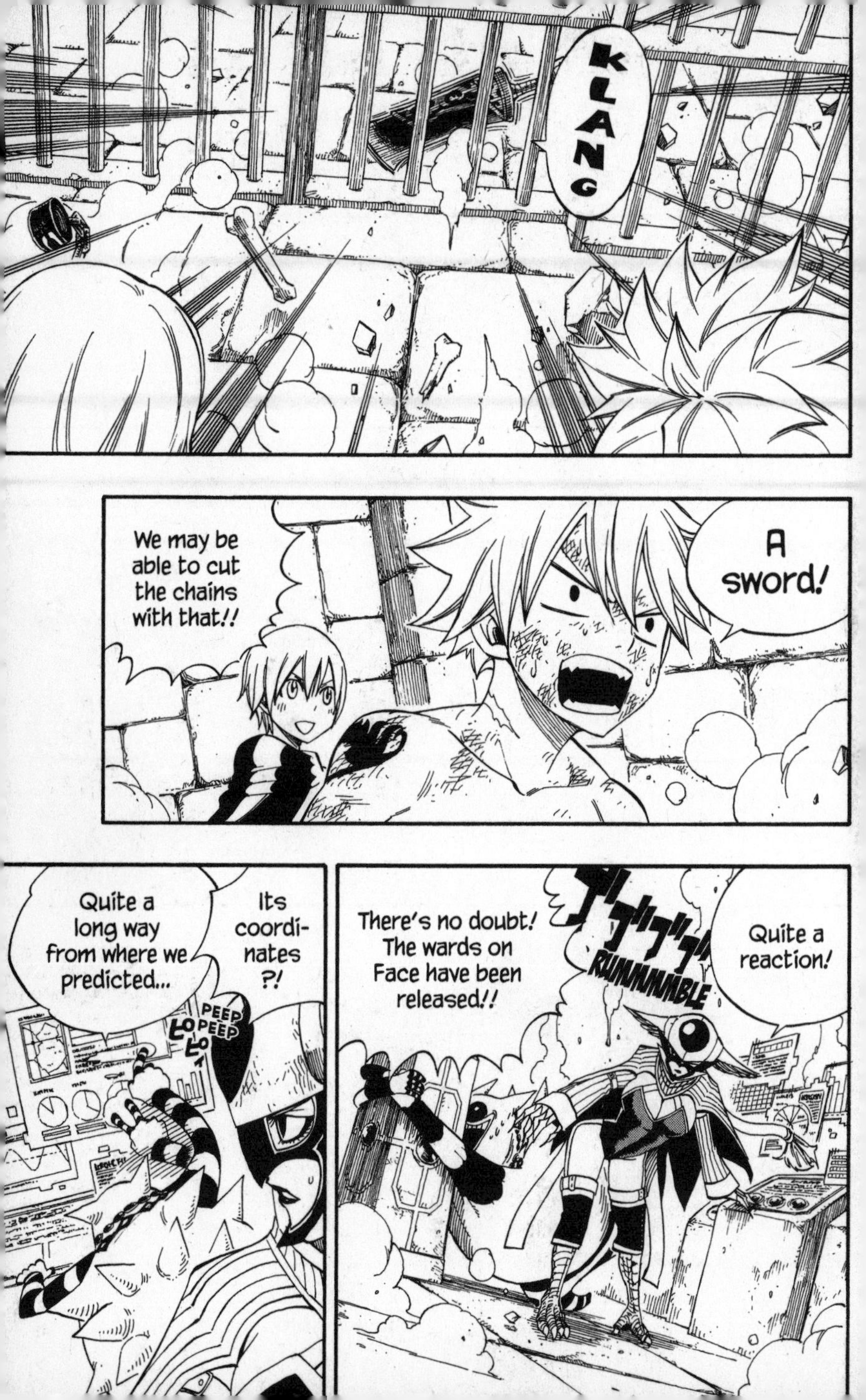
KLANG
A sword!
We may be able to cut the chains with that!!
Quite a reaction!
RUMMMMBLE
There's no doubt! The wards on Face have been released!!
Its coordinates?!
Quite a long way from where we predicted...
PEEP PEEP

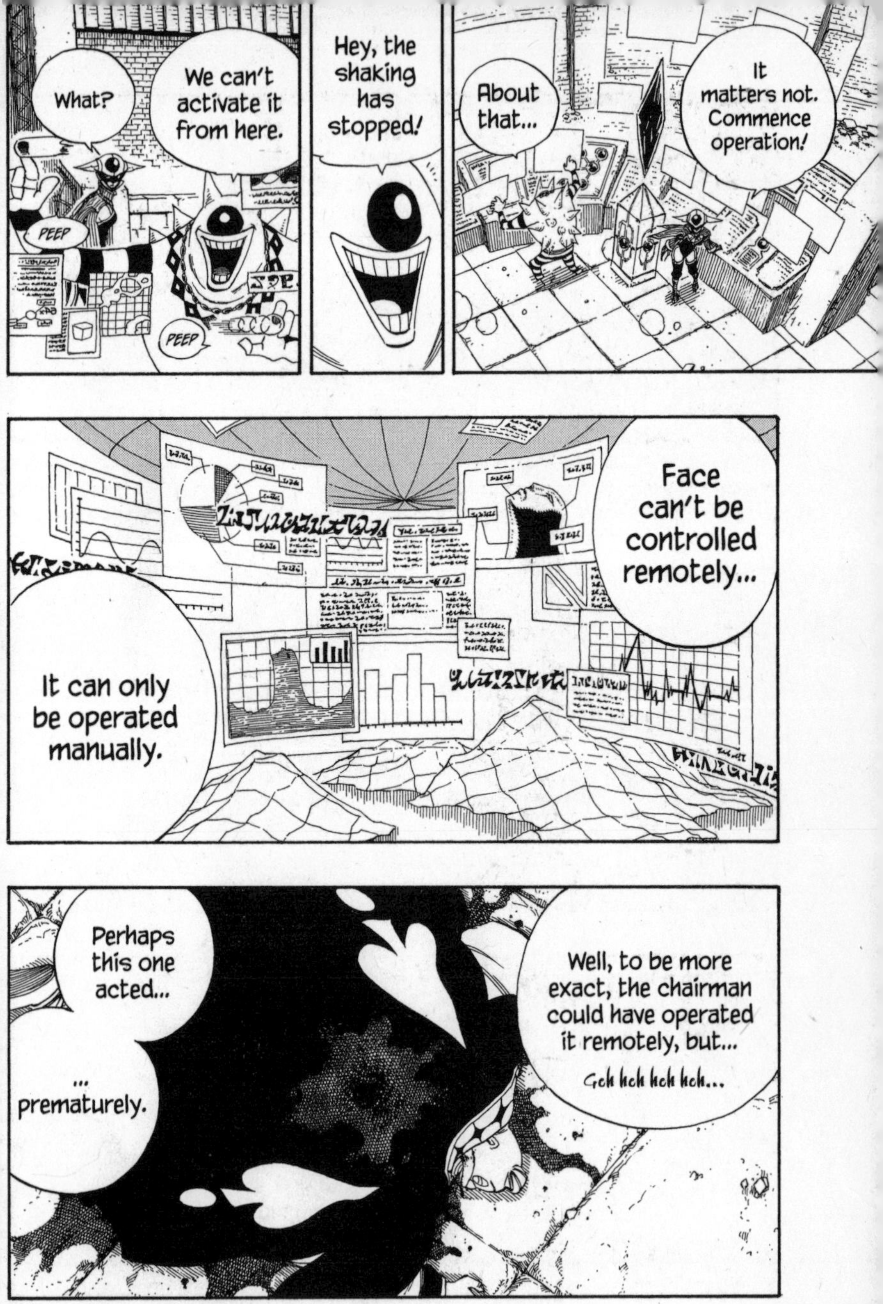
It matters not. Commence operation!
About that...
Hey, the shaking has stopped!
We can't activate it from here.
What?
PEEP
PEEP
Face can't be controlled remotely...
It can only be operated manually.
Well, to be more exact, the chairman could have operated it remotely, but...
Geh heh heh heh...
Perhaps this one acted...
... prematurely.

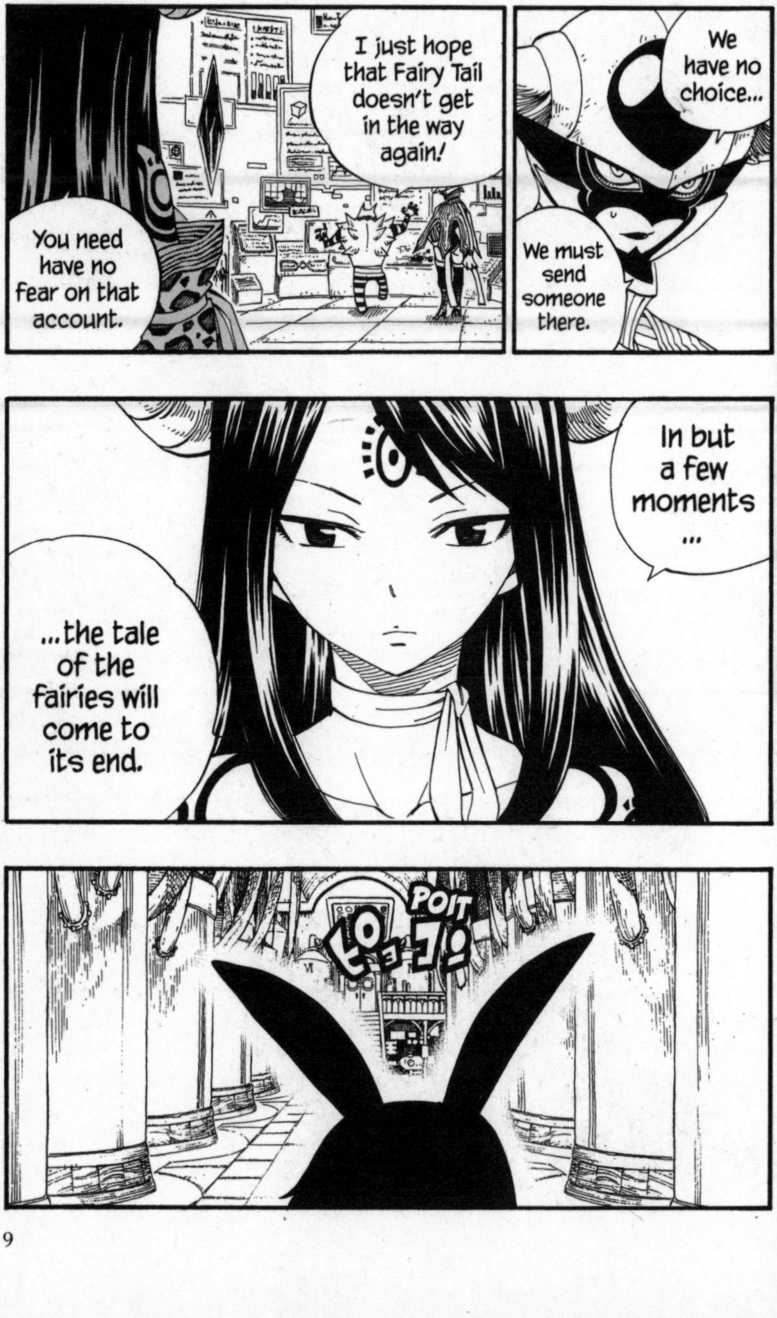
We have no choice...
We must send someone there.
I just hope that Fairy Tail doesn't get in the way again!
You need have no fear on that account.
In but a few moments ...
...the tale of the fairies will come to its end.
POIT

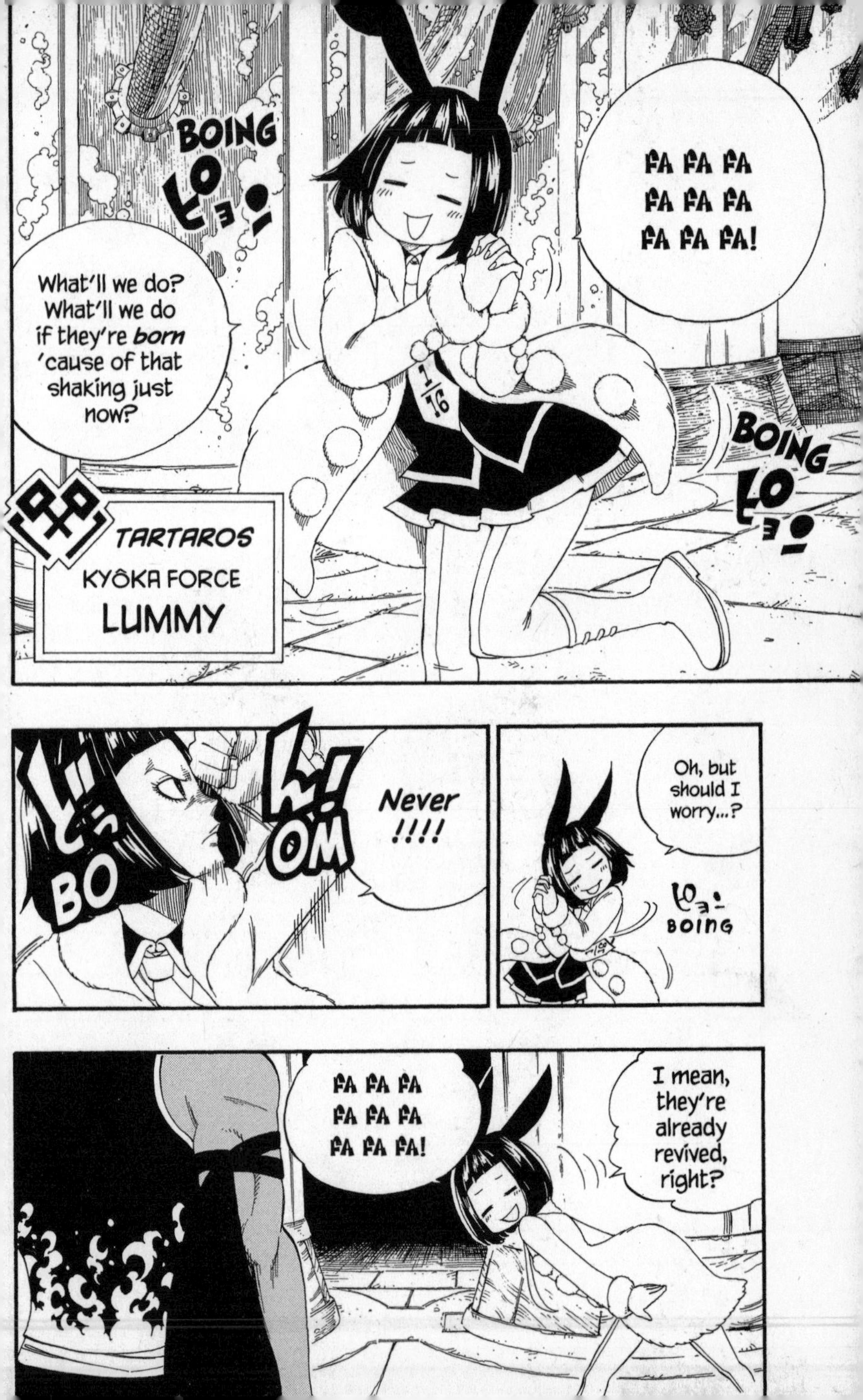
FA FA FA FA FA FA FA FA FA!
BOING
BOING
What'll we do? What'll we do if they're *born* 'cause of that shaking just now?
TARTAROS
KYÔKA FORCE
LUMMY
Oh, but should I worry...?
BOING
Never !!!!
BOOM
I mean, they're already revived, right?
FA FA FA FA FA FA FA FA FA!

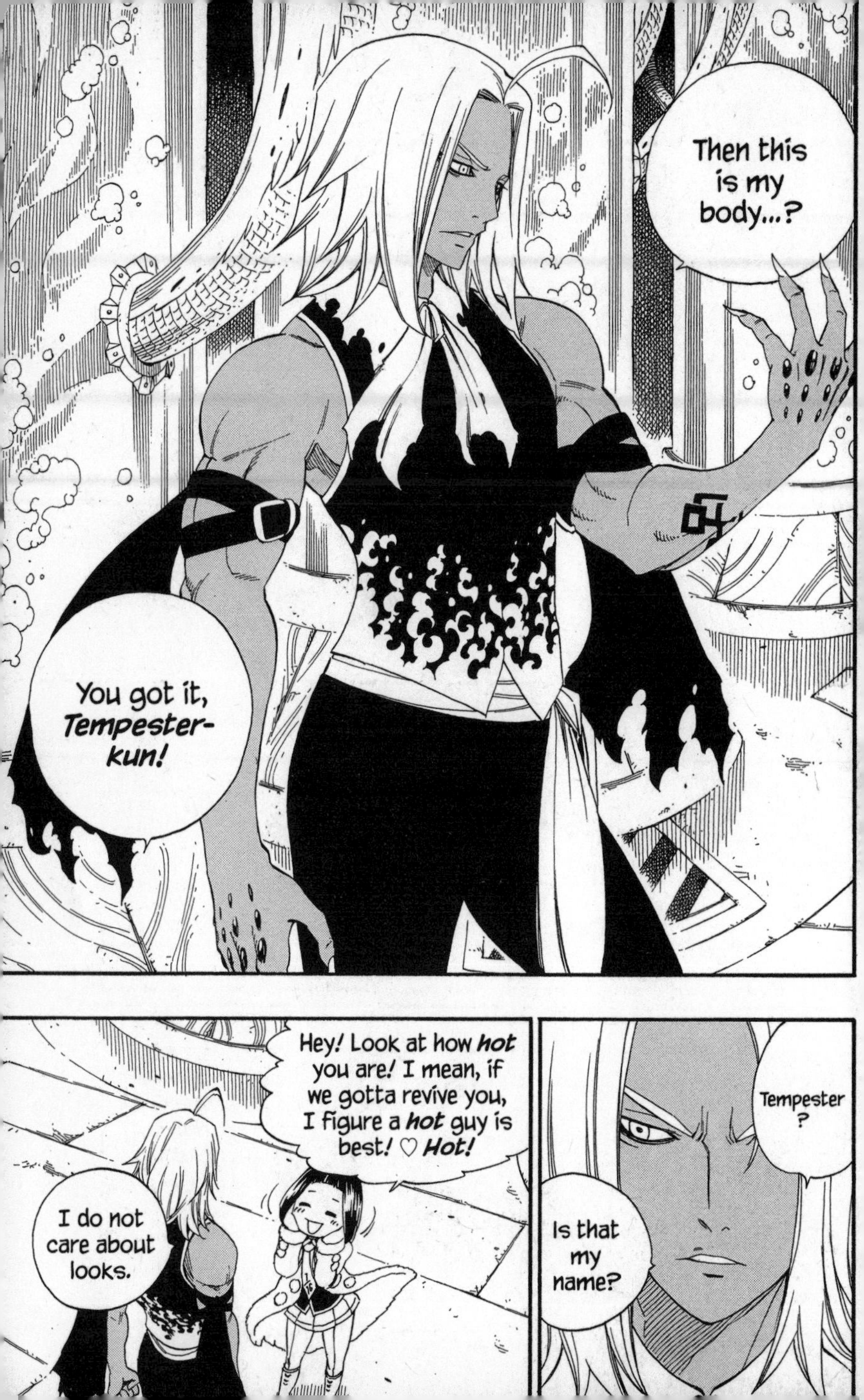
Then this is my body...?
You got it, *Tempester-kun!*
Tempester?
Is that my name?
Hey! Look at how ***hot*** you are! I mean, if we gotta revive you, I figure a ***hot*** guy is best! ♡ ***Hot!***
I do not care about looks.

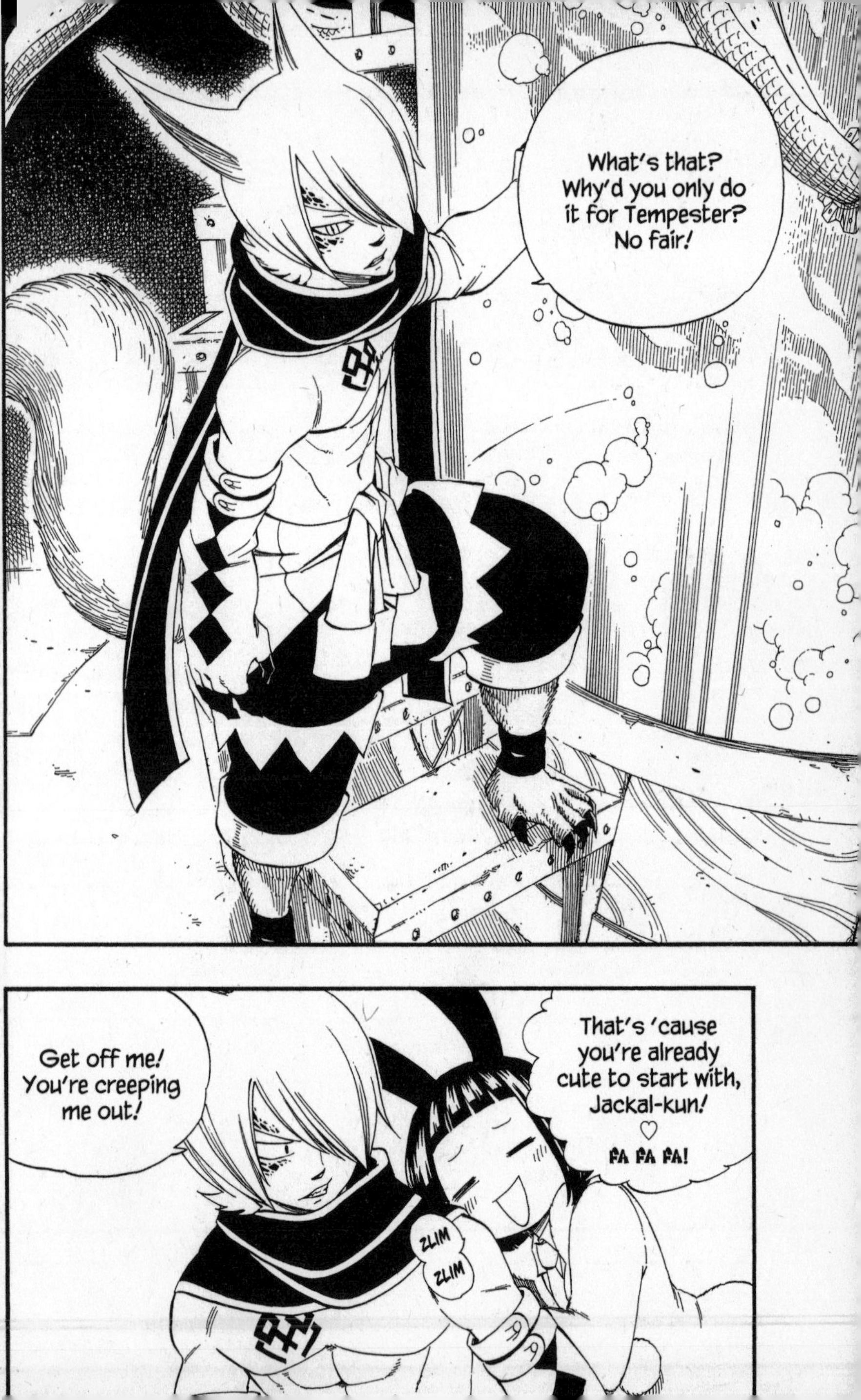
What's that? Why'd you only do it for Tempester? No fair!
That's 'cause you're already cute to start with, Jackal-kun! ♡
FA FA FA!
Get off me! You're creeping me out!
ZLIM
ZLIM

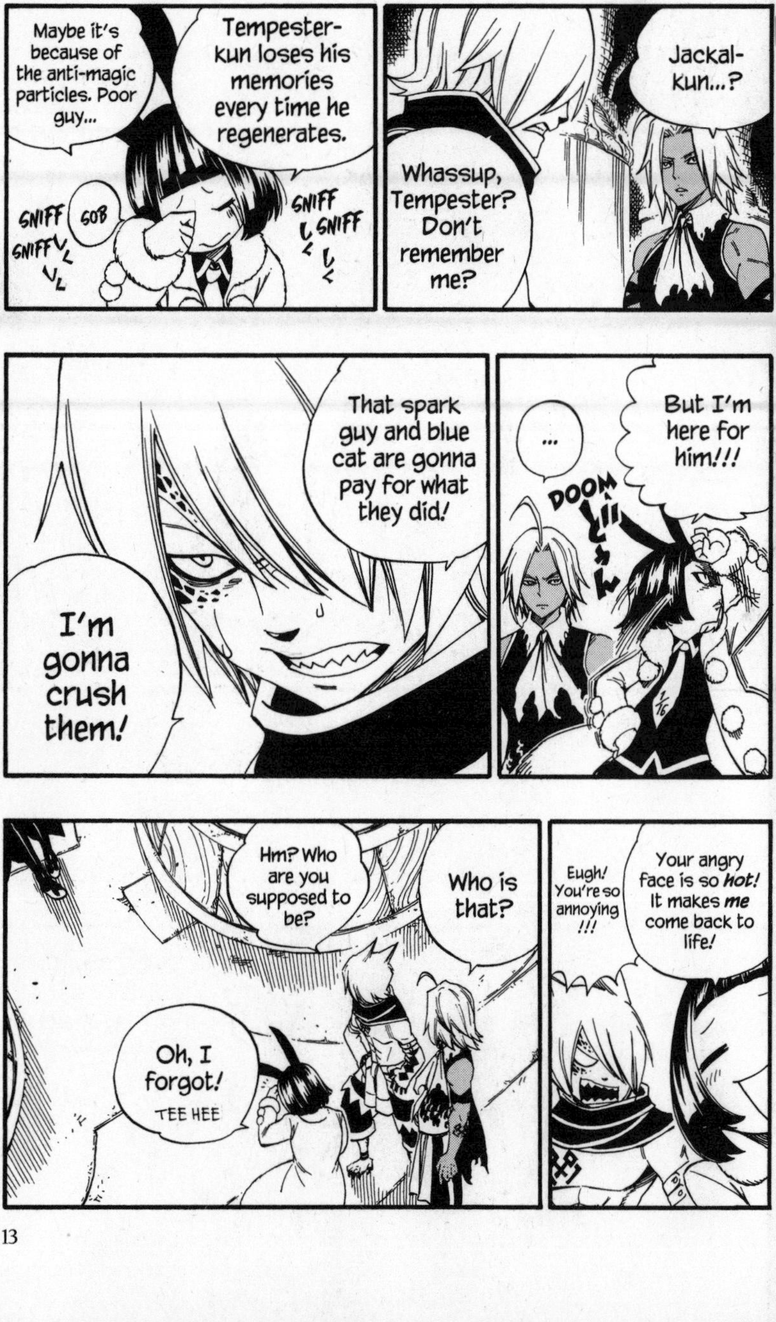

Jackal-kun...?
Whassup, Tempester? Don't remember me?
Tempester-kun loses his memories every time he regenerates.
Maybe it's because of the anti-magic particles. Poor guy...
SNIFF SNIFF
SOB
SNIFF SNIFF
But I'm here for him!!!
...
DOOM
That spark guy and blue cat are gonna pay for what they did!
I'm gonna crush them!
Your angry face is so *hot*! It makes *me* come back to life!
Eugh! You're so annoying!!!
Who is that?
Hm? Who are you supposed to be?
Oh, I forgot!
TEE HEE

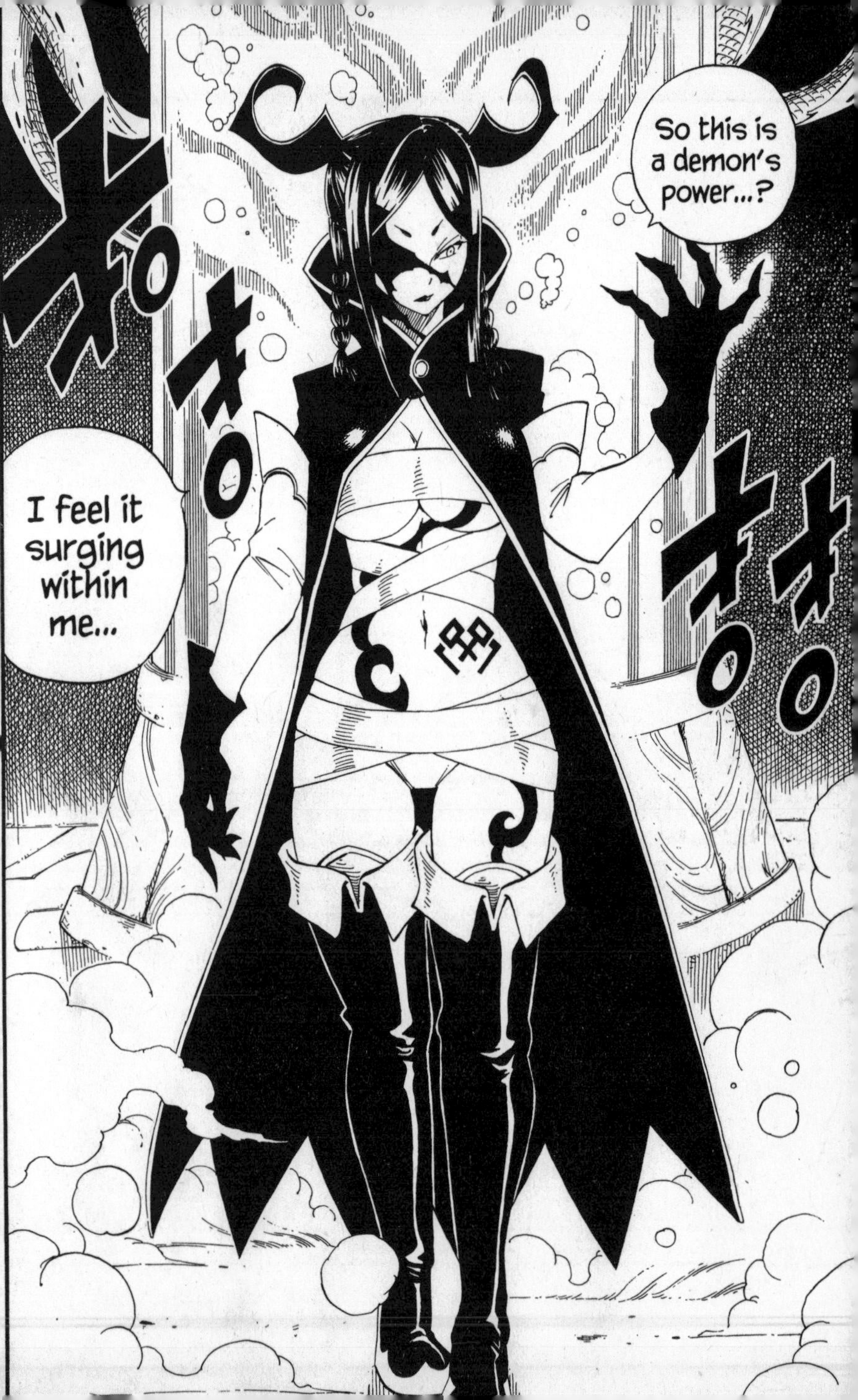
So this is a demon's power...?
I feel it surging within me...

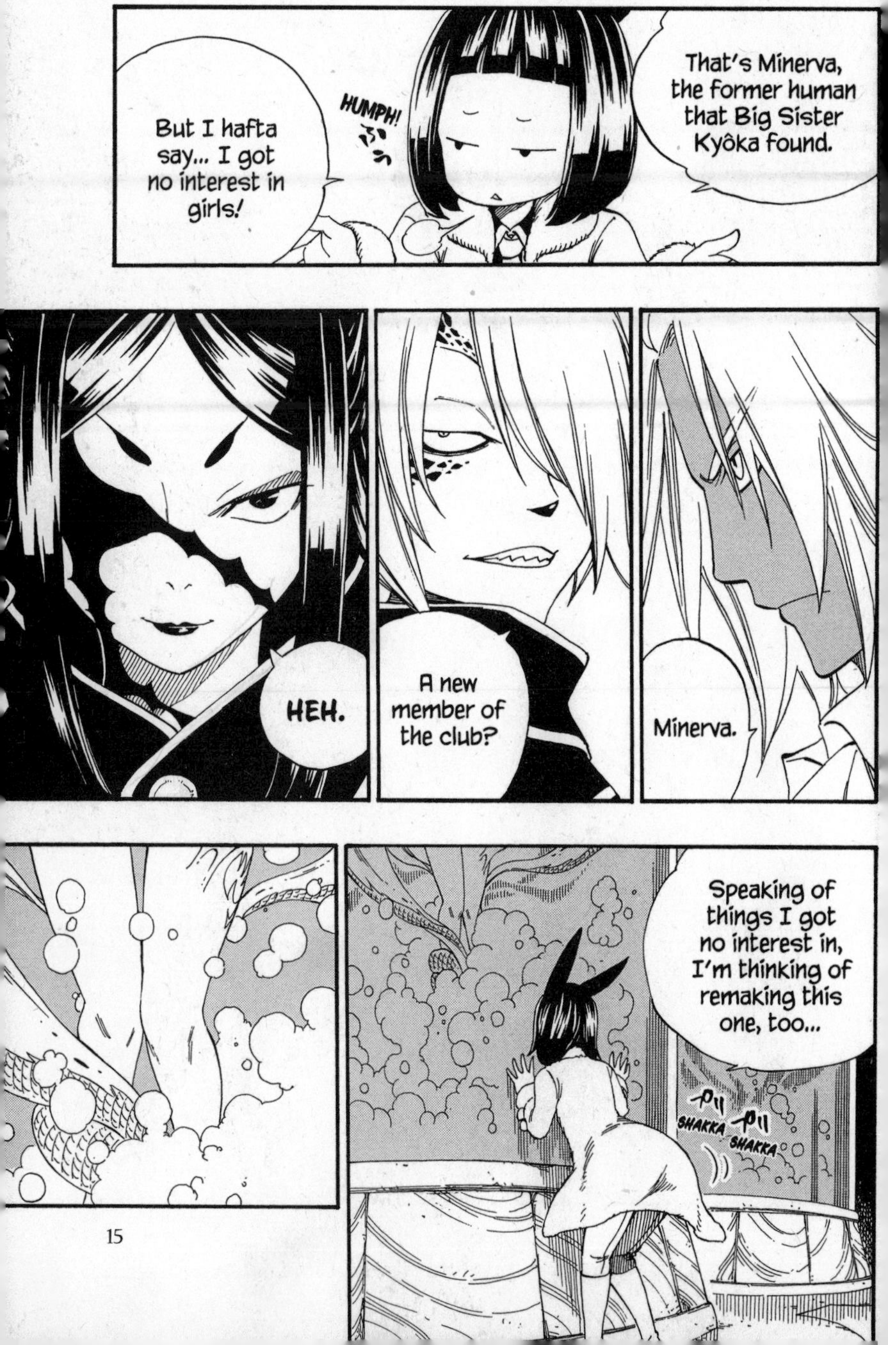
That's Minerva, the former human that Big Sister Kyôka found.
HUMPH!
But I hafta say... I got no interest in girls!
Minerva.
A new member of the club?
HEH.
Speaking of things I got no interest in, I'm thinking of remaking this one, too...
SHAKKA SHAKKA

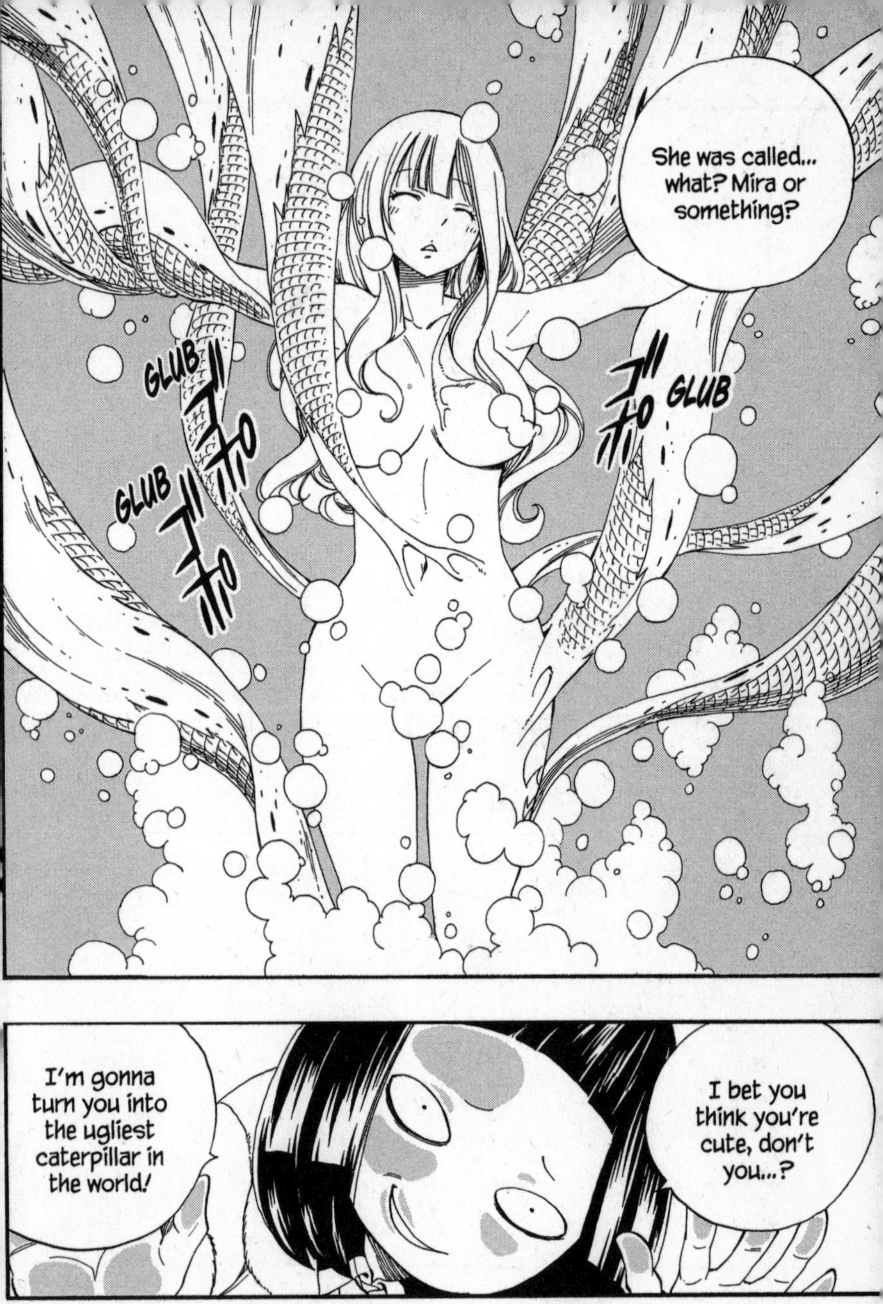
She was called... what? Mira or something?
GLUB
GLUB
GLUB
I bet you think you're cute, don't you...?
I'm gonna turn you into the ugliest caterpillar in the world!

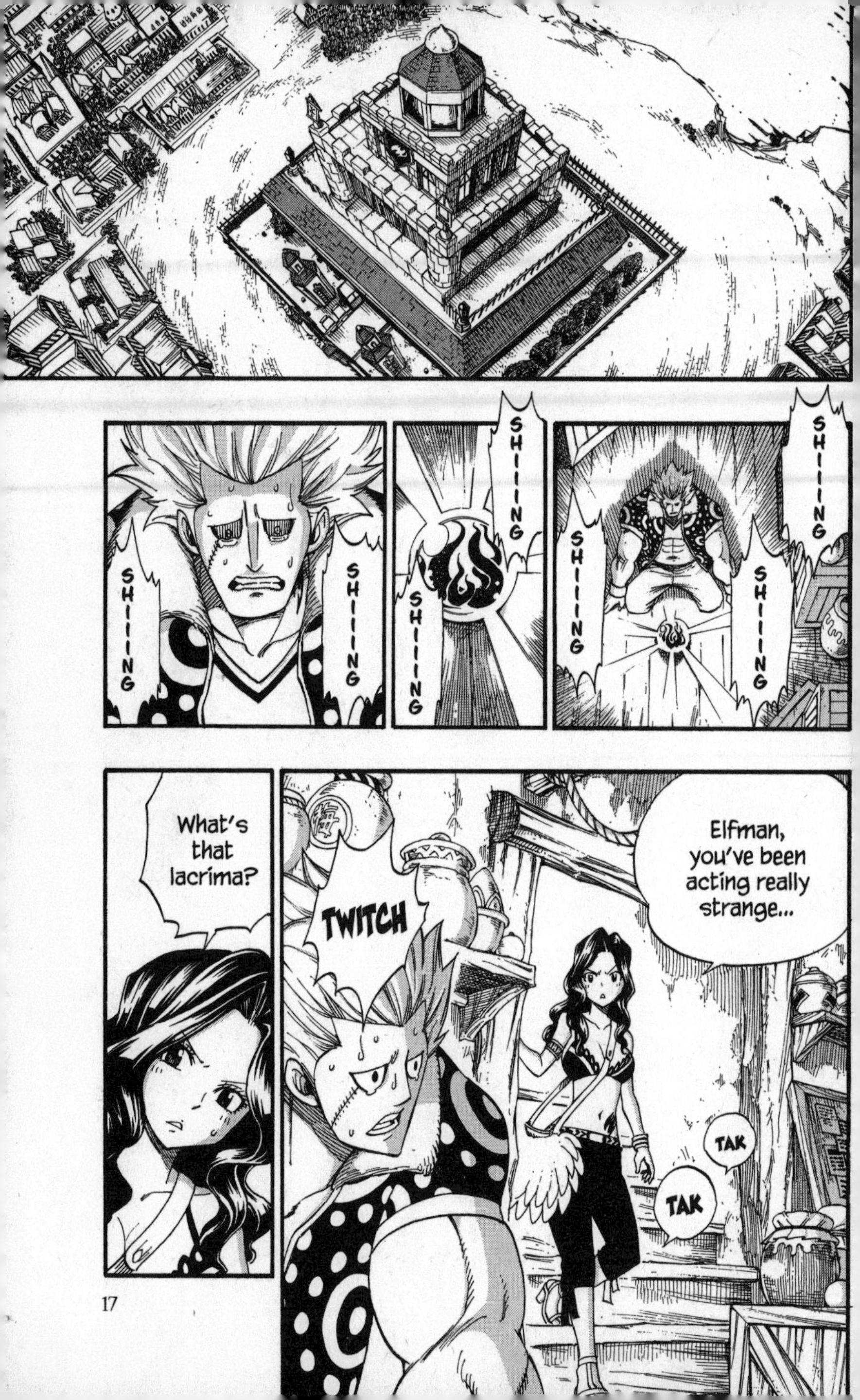
SHIIIING
SHIIIING
SHIIIING
SHIIIING
SHIIIING
SHIIIING
Elfman, you've been acting really strange...
TWITCH
TAK
TAK
What's that lacrima?

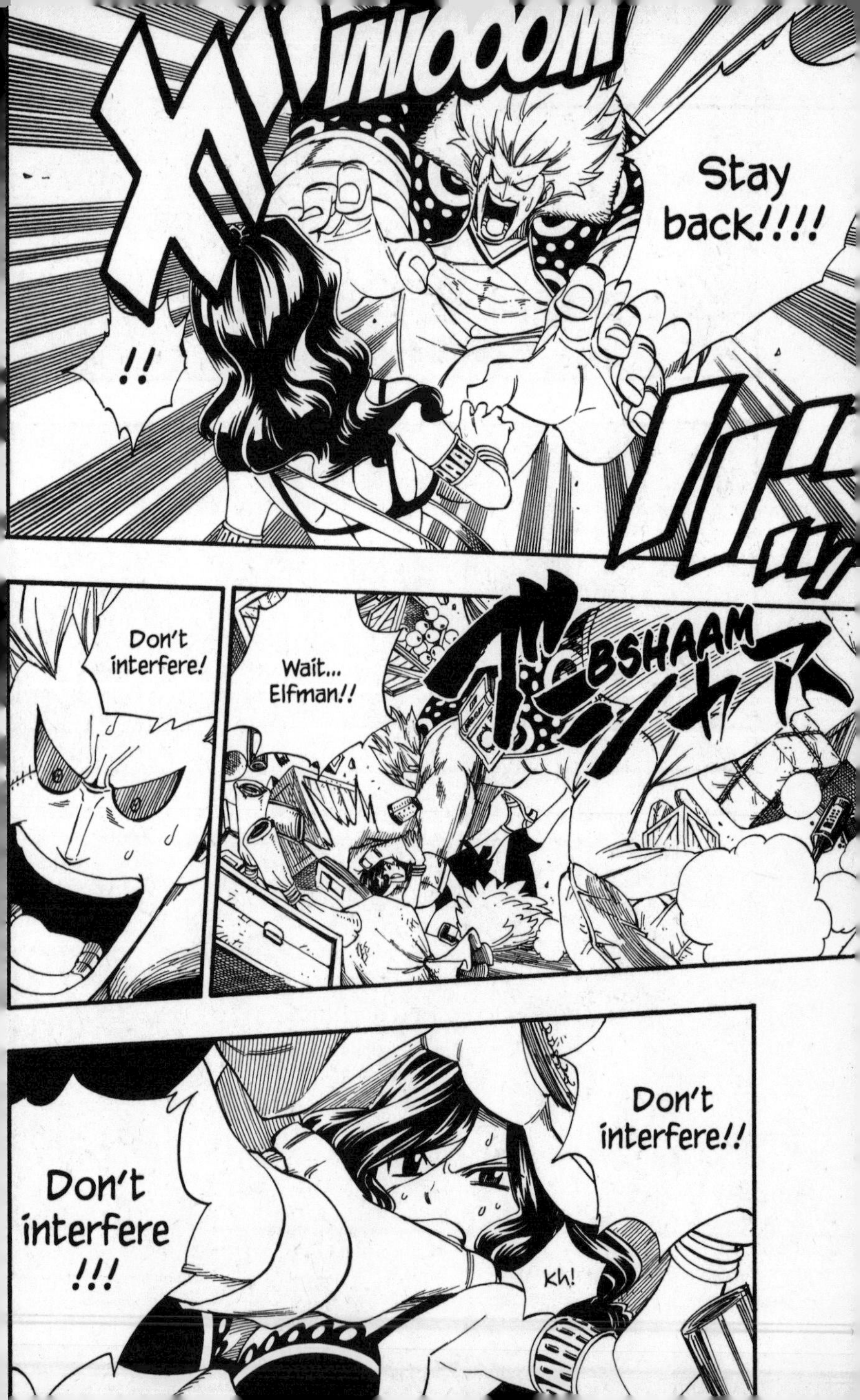
WOOOM
Stay back!!!!
!!
BSHAAM
Wait... Elfman!!
Don't interfere!
Don't interfere!!
kh!
Don't interfere !!!

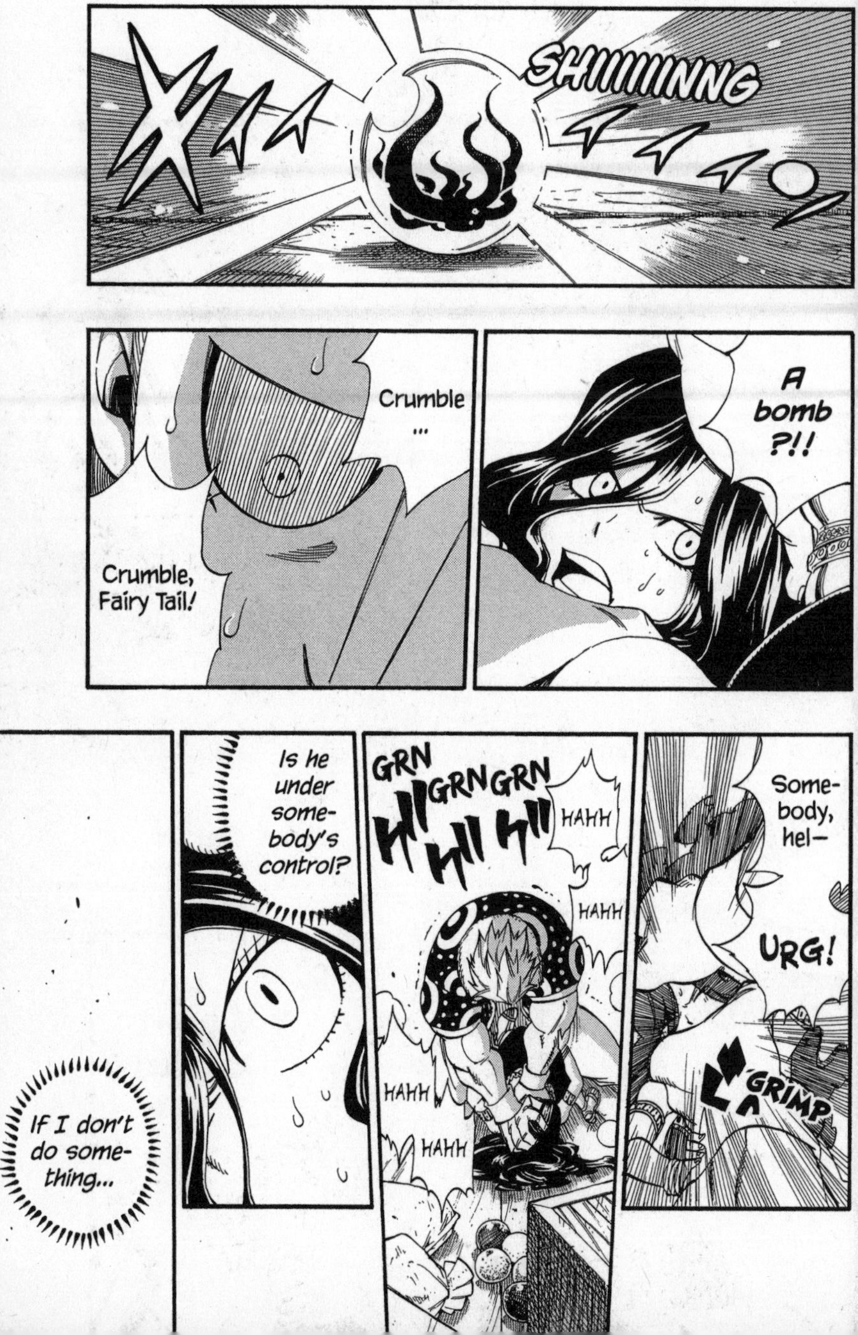
SHIIIIIINNG
A bomb?!!
Crumble...
Crumble, Fairy Tail!
Some-body, hel—
URG!
GRIMP
GRN GRNGRN
HAHH
HAHH
HAHH
HAHH
Is he under some-body's control?
If I don't do some-thing...

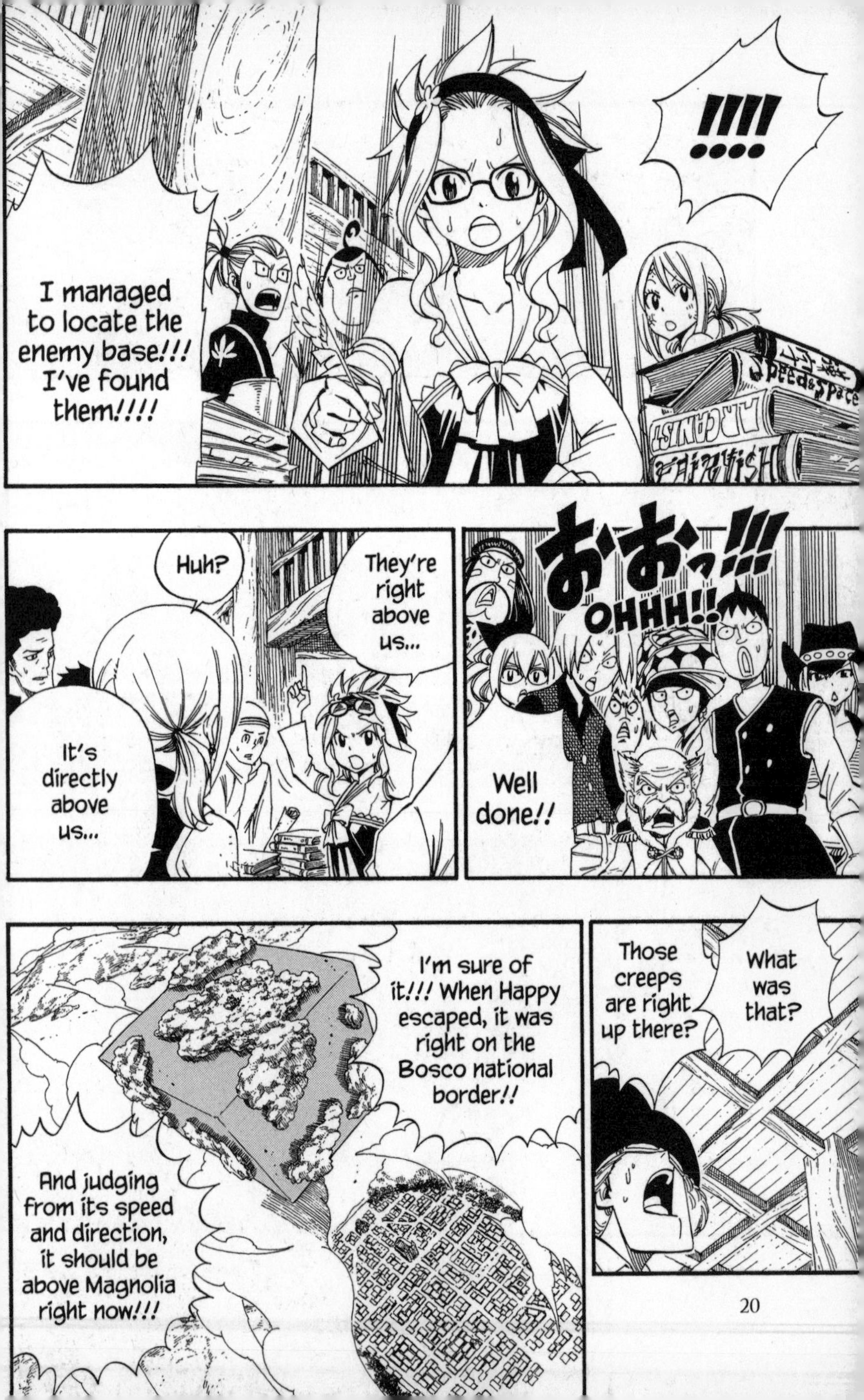
!!!!
••••
I managed to locate the enemy base!!! I've found them!!!!
おおっ!!!
OHHH!!
Well done!!
They're right above us...
Huh?
It's directly above us...
What was that?
Those creeps are right up there?
I'm sure of it!!! When Happy escaped, it was right on the Bosco national border!!
And judging from its speed and direction, it should be above Magnolia right now!!!

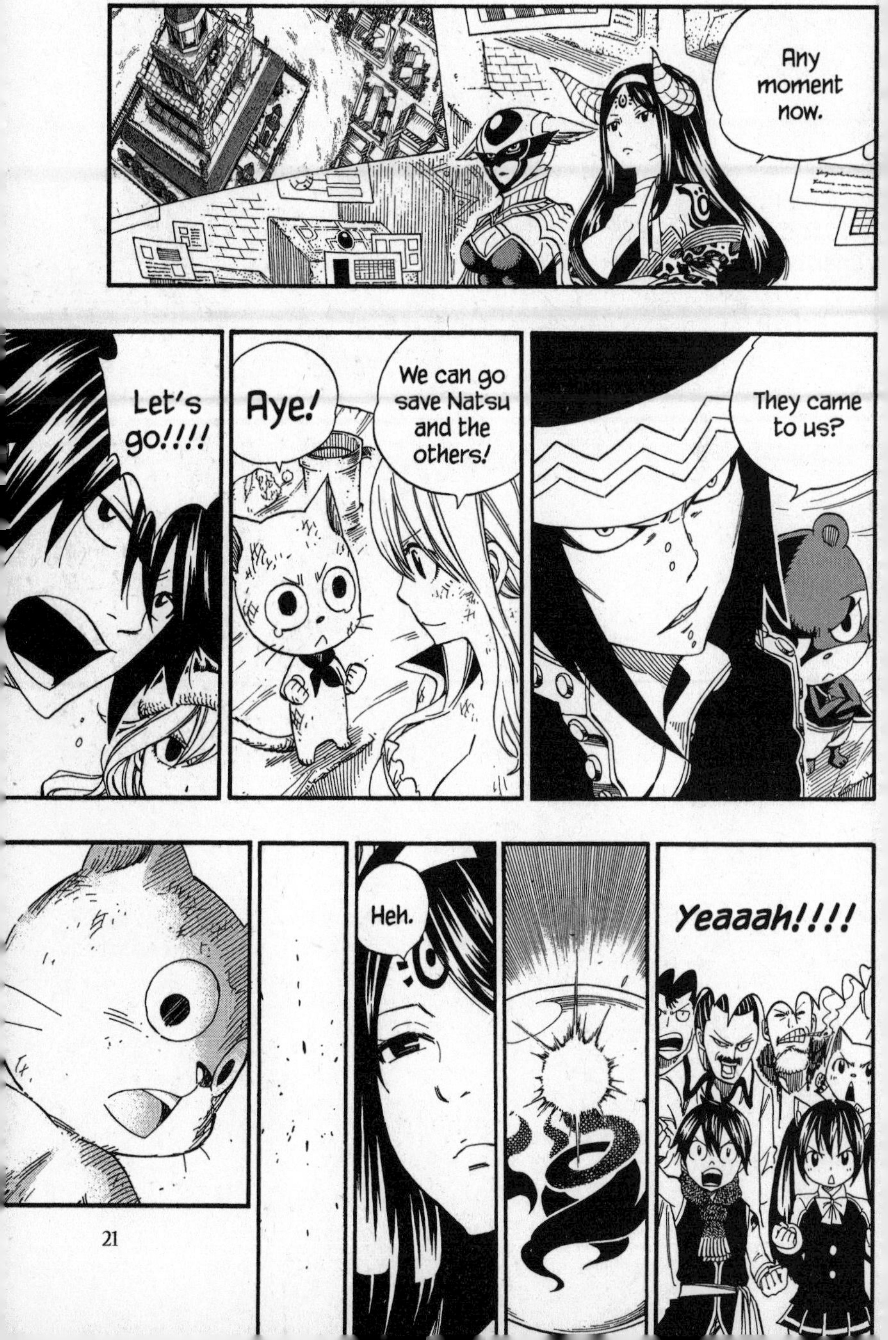
Any moment now.
They came to us?
We can go save Natsu and the others!
Aye!
Let's go!!!!
Yeaaah!!!!
Heh.

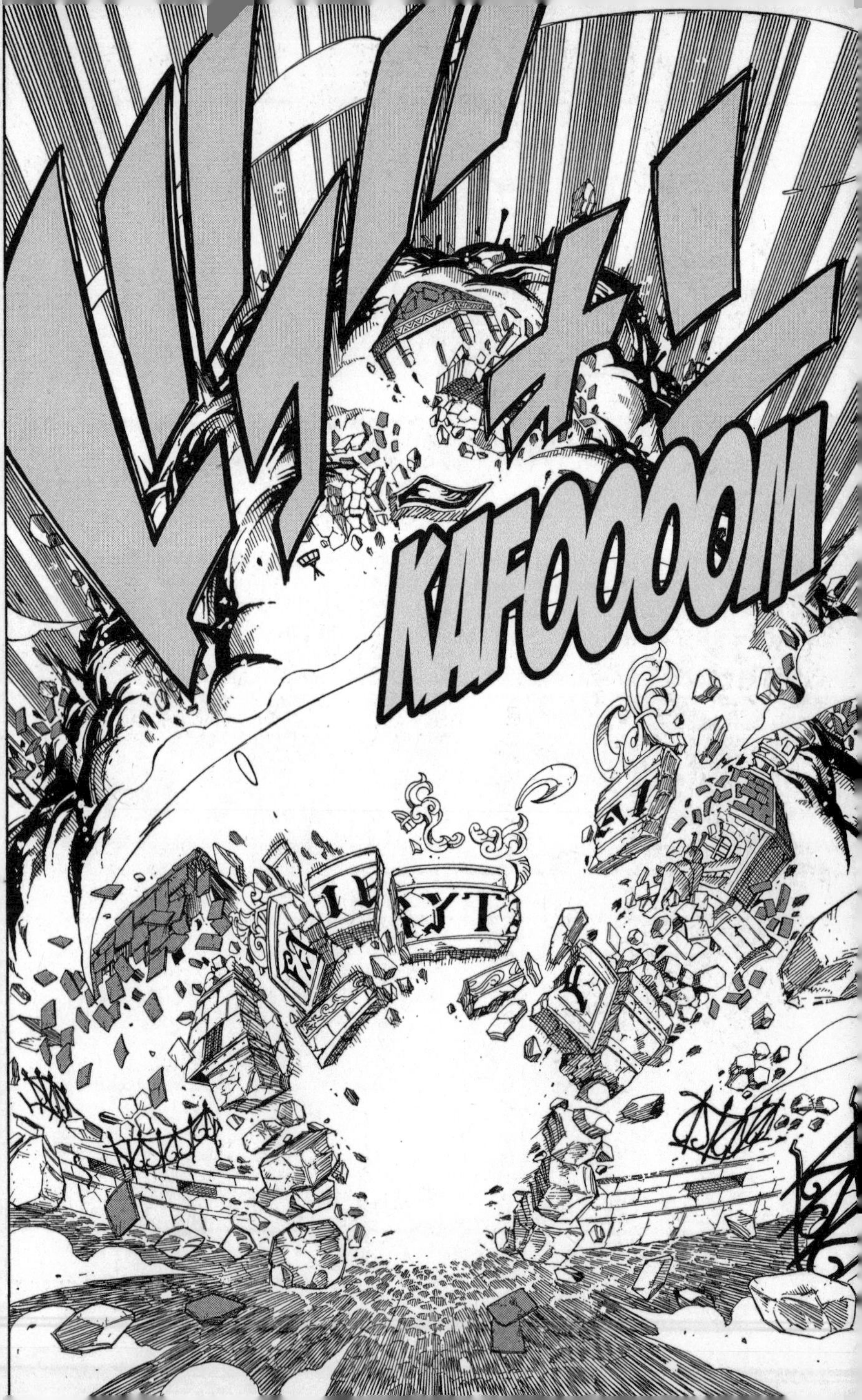
KAFOOOOM

FAIRY TAIL

Quattro Cerberus

Name: Bacchus Glowe   **Age:** 28

Magic:
Drunk Pigua Quan

Likes: **Dislikes:**

Liquor   Mornings

Remarks

The ace of Quattro Cerberus. Seven years ago, he was strong enough to go one-on-one against Erza. His strength hasn't diminished any, but during the Games, he lost to Elfman, and now he's on a serious training journey to get even better.

He and Cana are still drinking buddies, and every now and then, they drink a liquor barrel dry together.

There is also a band of thieves who call themselves Bacchus, but he has nothing to do with them now.

Chapter 371:
Tartaros Arc, Part 2:
Song of the Sky Dragon

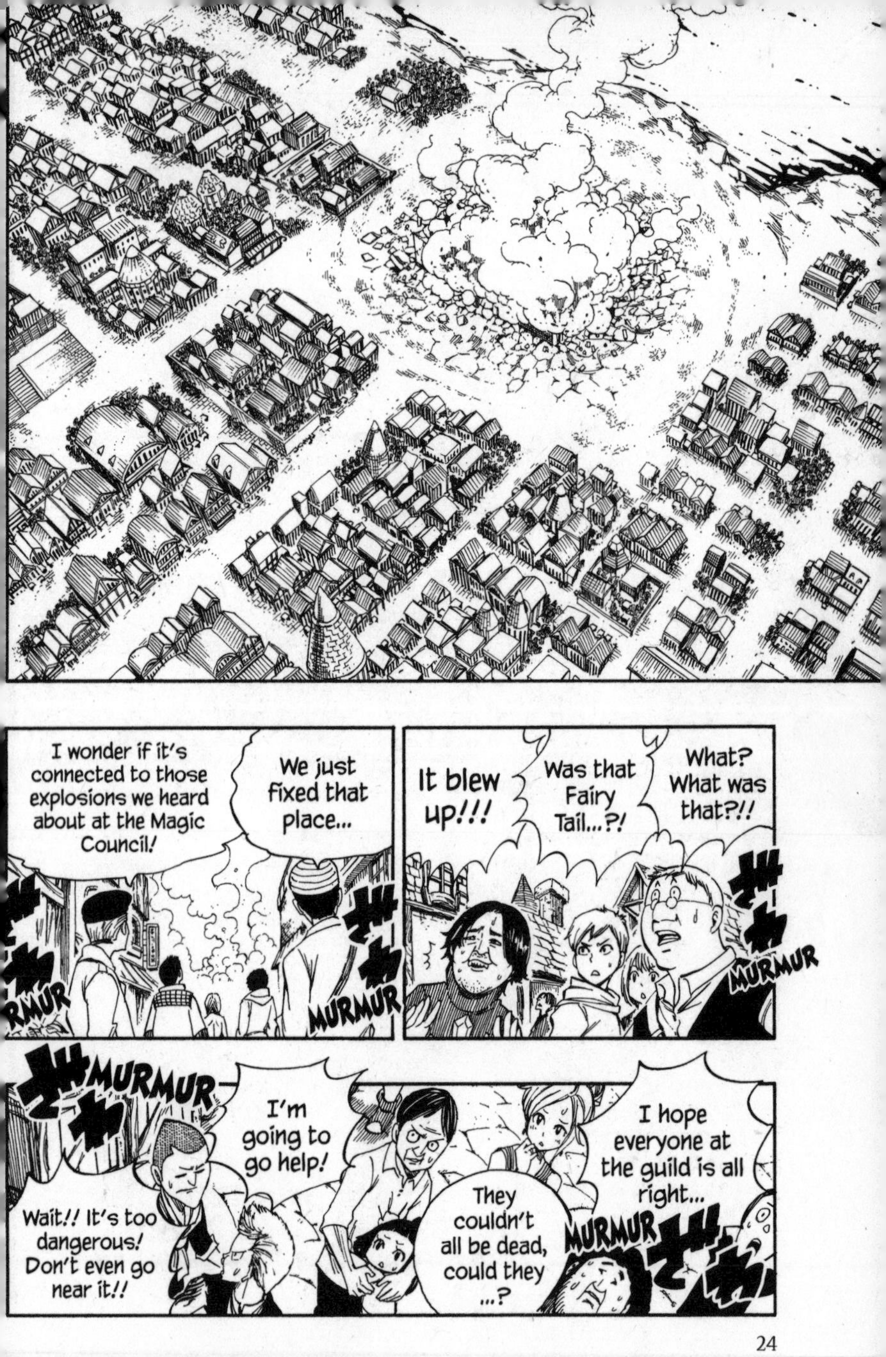
What? What was that?!!
Was that Fairy Tail...?!
It blew up!!!
MURMUR
We just fixed that place...
I wonder if it's connected to those explosions we heard about at the Magic Council!
MURMUR
I hope everyone at the guild is all right...
MURMUR
They couldn't all be dead, could they ...?
I'm going to go help!
Wait!! It's too dangerous! Don't even go near it!!
MURMUR

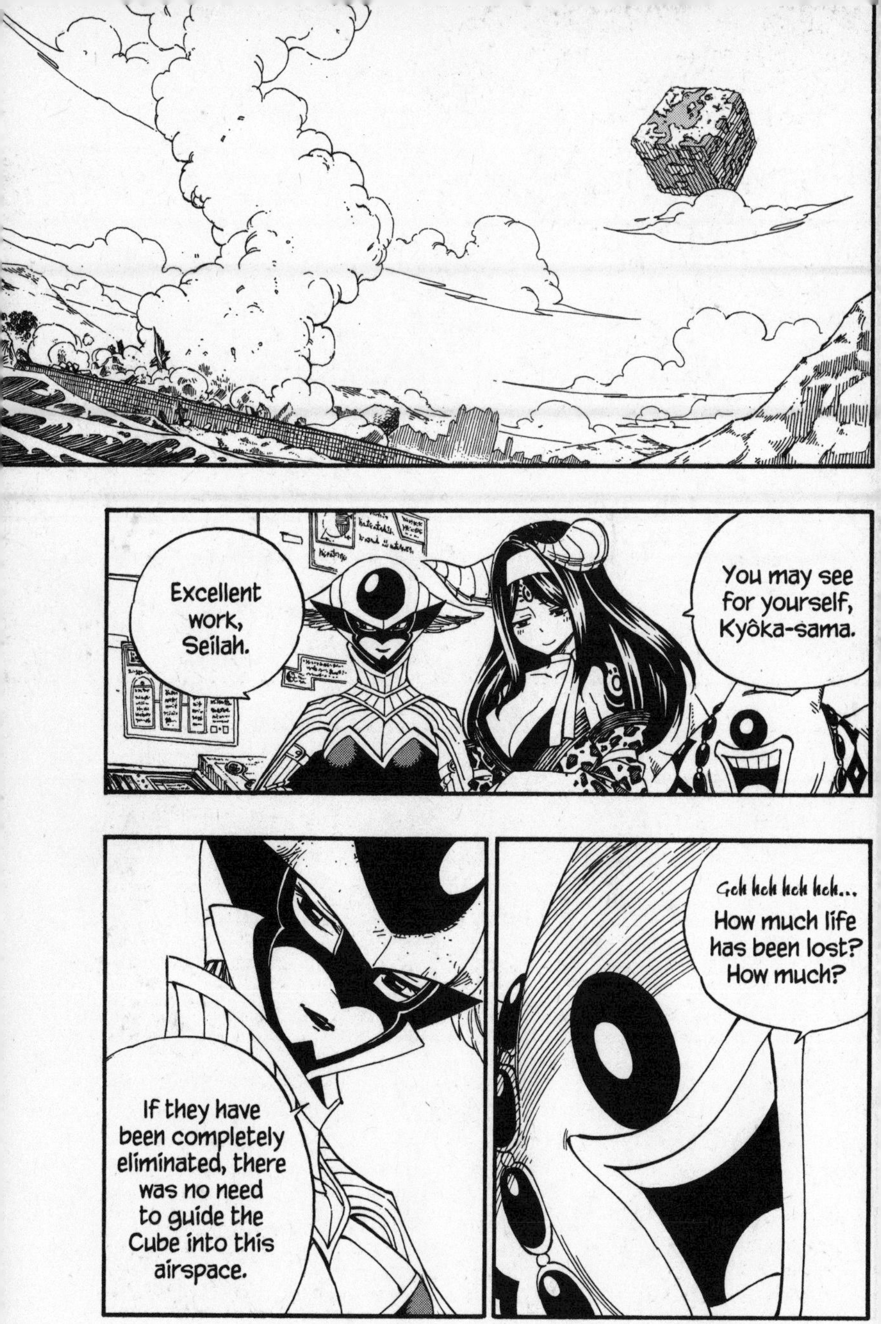
You may see for yourself, Kyôka-sama.
Excellent work, Seilah.
Geh heh heh heh...
How much life has been lost? How much?
If they have been completely eliminated, there was no need to guide the Cube into this airspace.

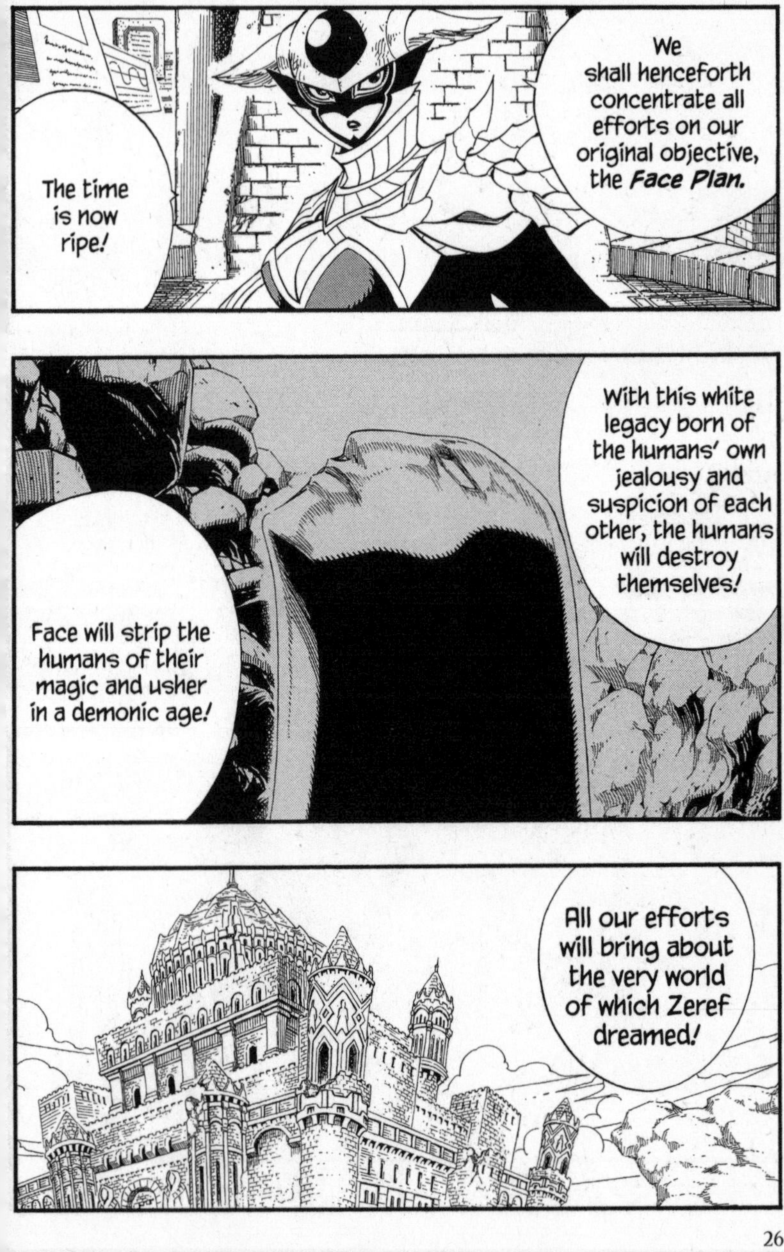
We shall henceforth concentrate all efforts on our original objective, the *Face Plan.*
The time is now ripe!
With this white legacy born of the humans' own jealousy and suspicion of each other, the humans will destroy themselves!
Face will strip the humans of their magic and usher in a demonic age!
All our efforts will bring about the very world of which Zeref dreamed!

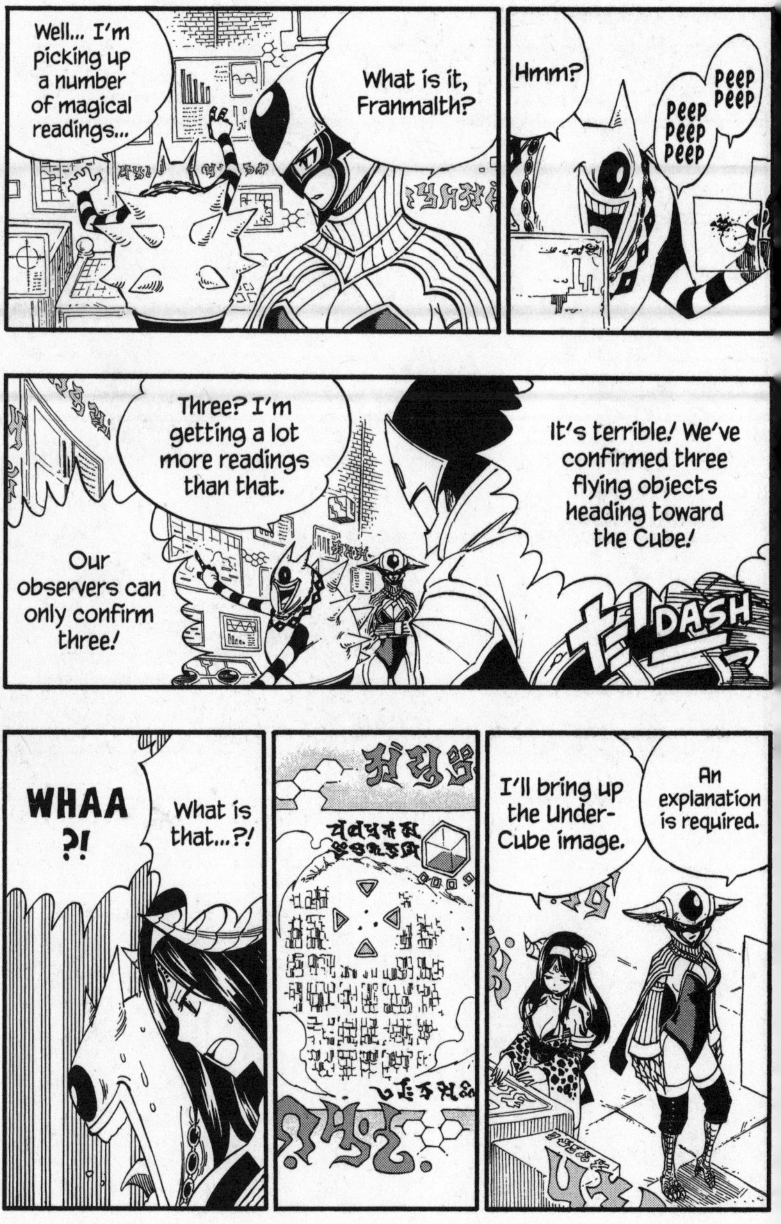
PEEP PEEP
PEEP PEEP PEEP
Hmm?
What is it, Franmalth?
Well... I'm picking up a number of magical readings...
It's terrible! We've confirmed three flying objects heading toward the Cube!
Our observers can only confirm three!
Three? I'm getting a lot more readings than that.
DASH
An explanation is required.
I'll bring up the Under-Cube image.
What is that...?!
WHAA ?!

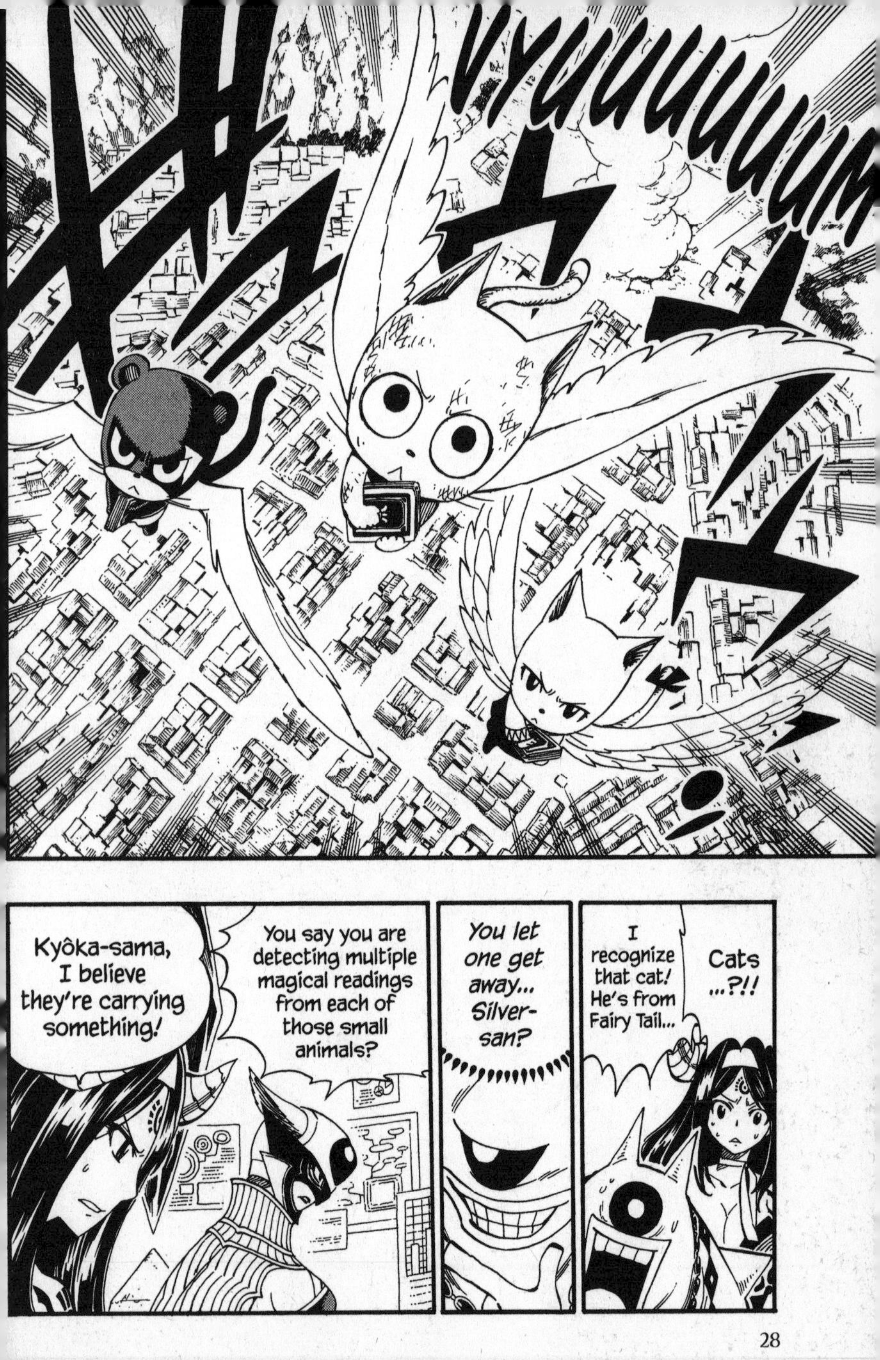
VYUUUUUUUM
Cats ...?!!
I recognize that cat! He's from Fairy Tail...
You let one get away... Silver-san?
You say you are detecting multiple magical readings from each of those small animals?
Kyôka-sama, I believe they're carrying something!

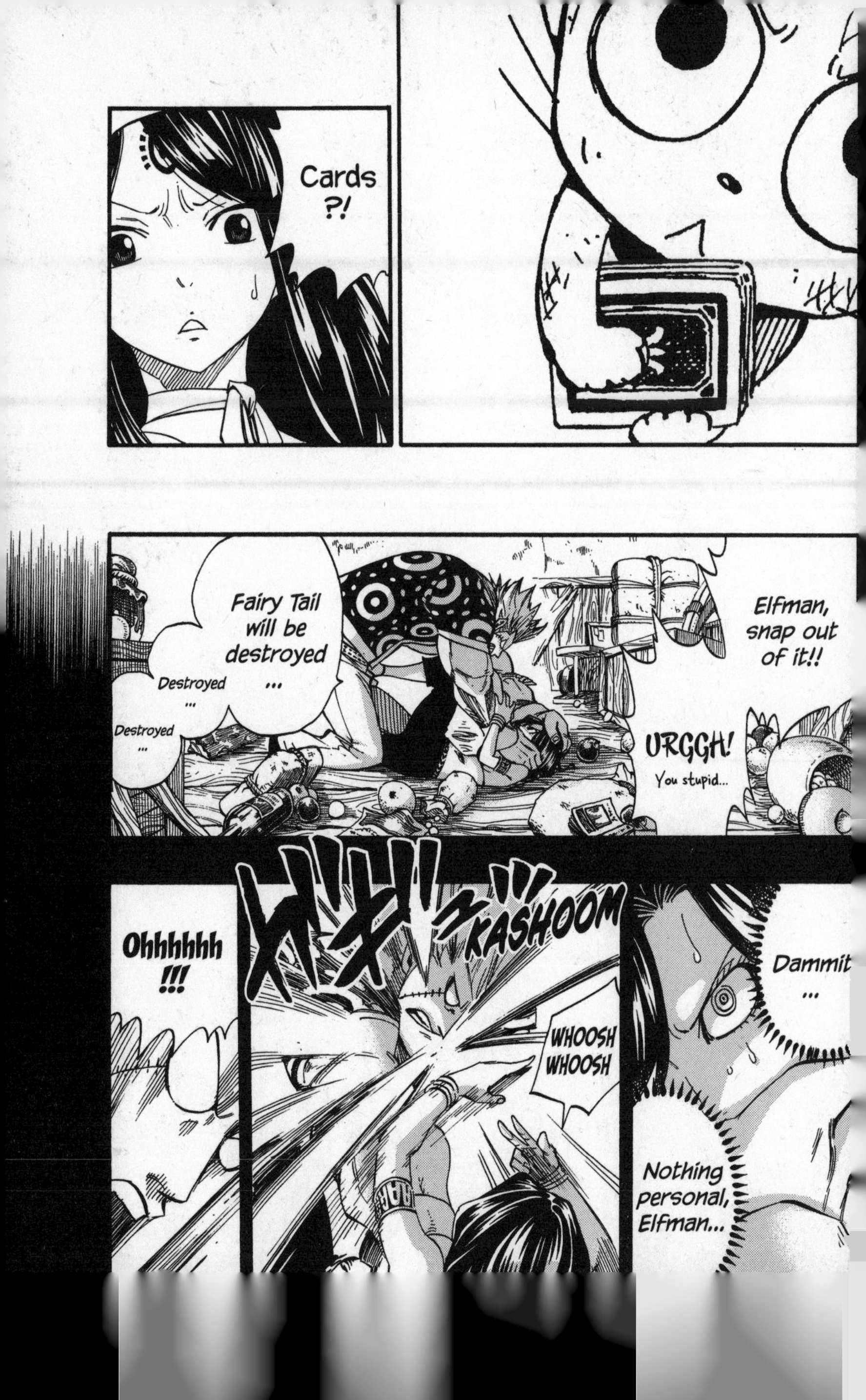
Cards ?!
Elfman, snap out of it!!
URGGH!
You stupid...
Fairy Tail will be destroyed ...
Destroyed ...
Destroyed ...
Dammit ...
Nothing personal, Elfman...
KASHOOM
WHOOSH WHOOSH
Ohhhhhh !!!

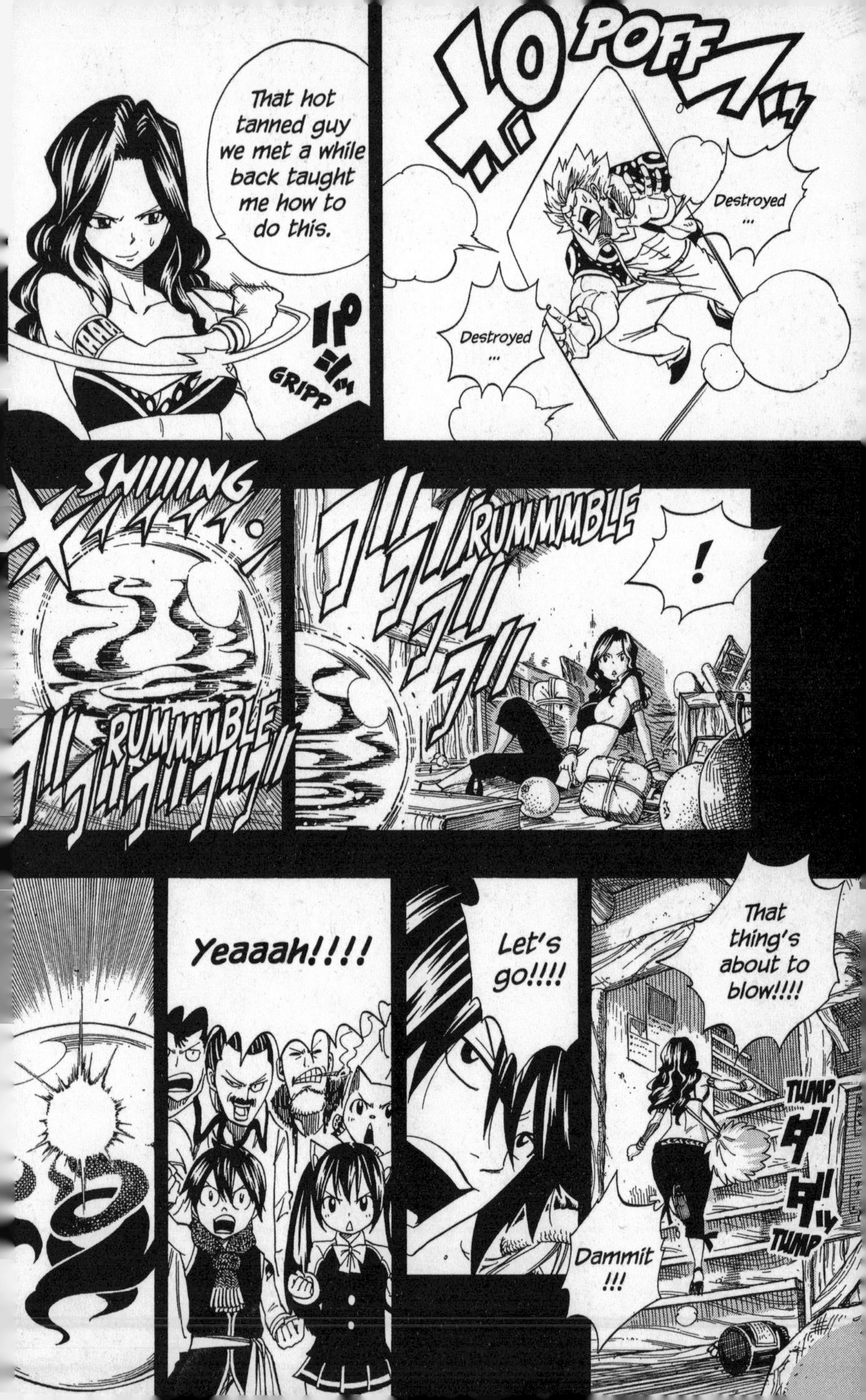
POFF
Destroyed ...
Destroyed ...
That hot tanned guy we met a while back taught me how to do this.
GRIPP
RUMMMBLE
!
SHIIIING
RUMMMBLE
That thing's about to blow!!!!
TUMP
TUMP
Let's go!!!!
Dammit !!!
Yeaaah!!!!

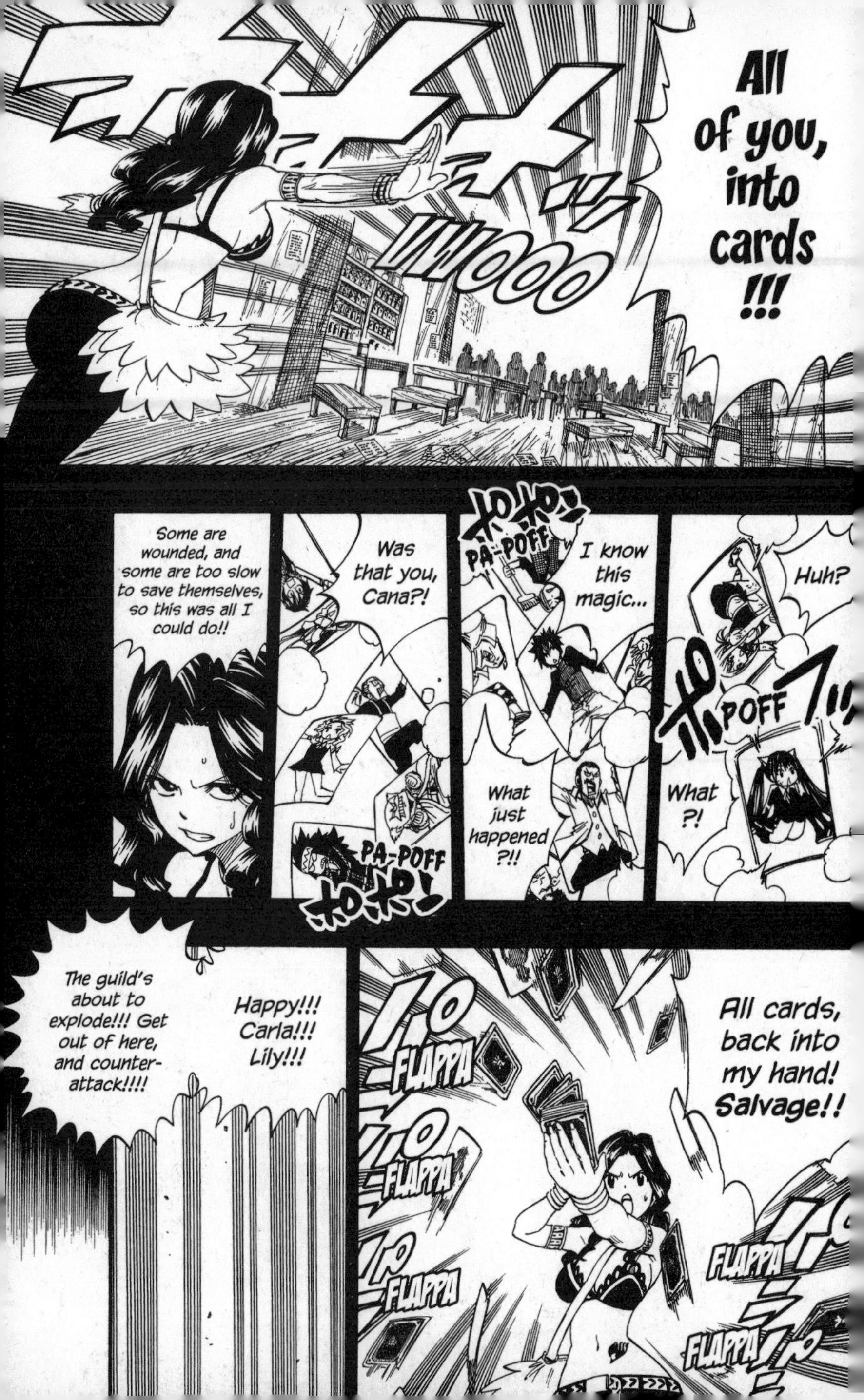
All of you, into cards!!!
WOOO
Huh?
POFF
What?!
I know this magic...
PA-POFF
What just happened?!!
Was that you, Cana?!
PA-POFF
Some are wounded, and some are too slow to save themselves, so this was all I could do!!
All cards, back into my hand! Salvage!!
FLAPPA
FLAPPA
FLAPPA
FLAPPA
FLAPPA
Happy!!! Carla!!! Lily!!!
The guild's about to explode!!! Get out of here, and counter-attack!!!!

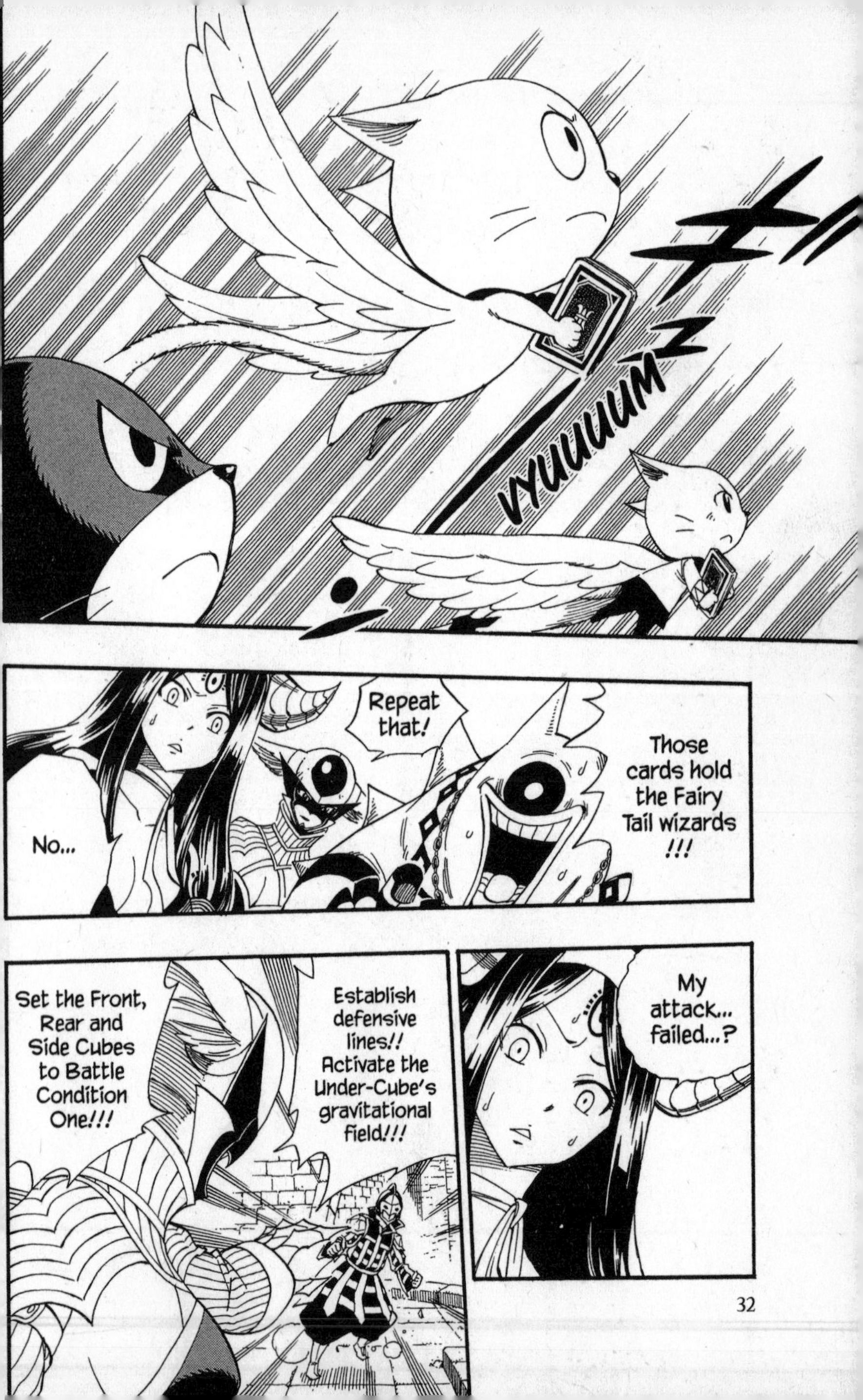
VYUUUUM
Those cards hold the Fairy Tail wizards !!!
Repeat that!
No...
My attack... failed...?
Establish defensive lines!! Activate the Under-Cube's gravitational field!!!
Set the Front, Rear and Side Cubes to Battle Condition One!!!

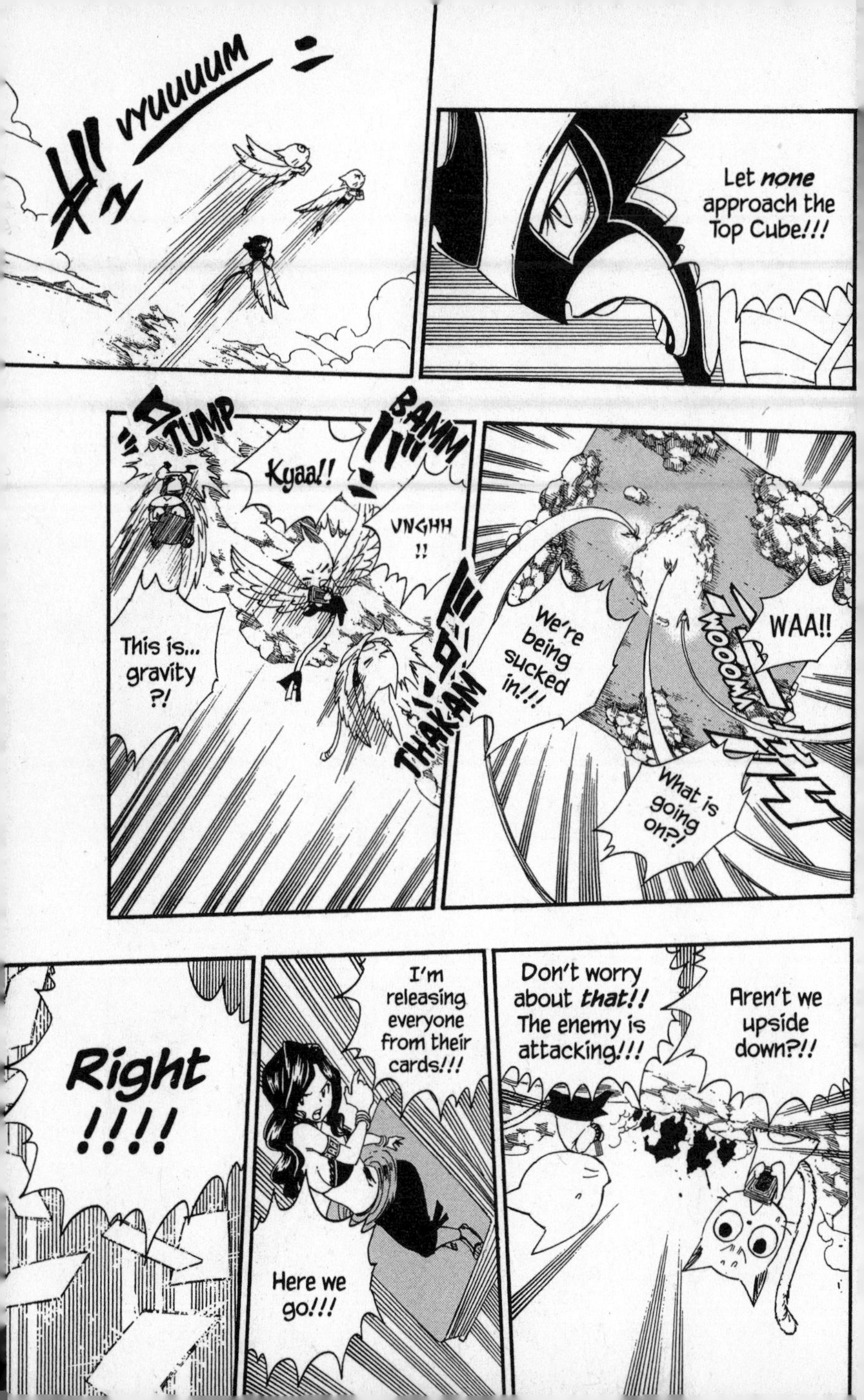
Let none approach the Top Cube!!!
VYUUUUM
BAMM
Kyaa!!
UNGHH!!
TUMP
This is... gravity?!
THAKAM
WAA!!
WOOOM
We're being sucked in!!!
What is going on?!
Aren't we upside down?!!
Don't worry about that!! The enemy is attacking!!!
I'm releasing everyone from their cards!!!
Here we go!!!
Right!!!!

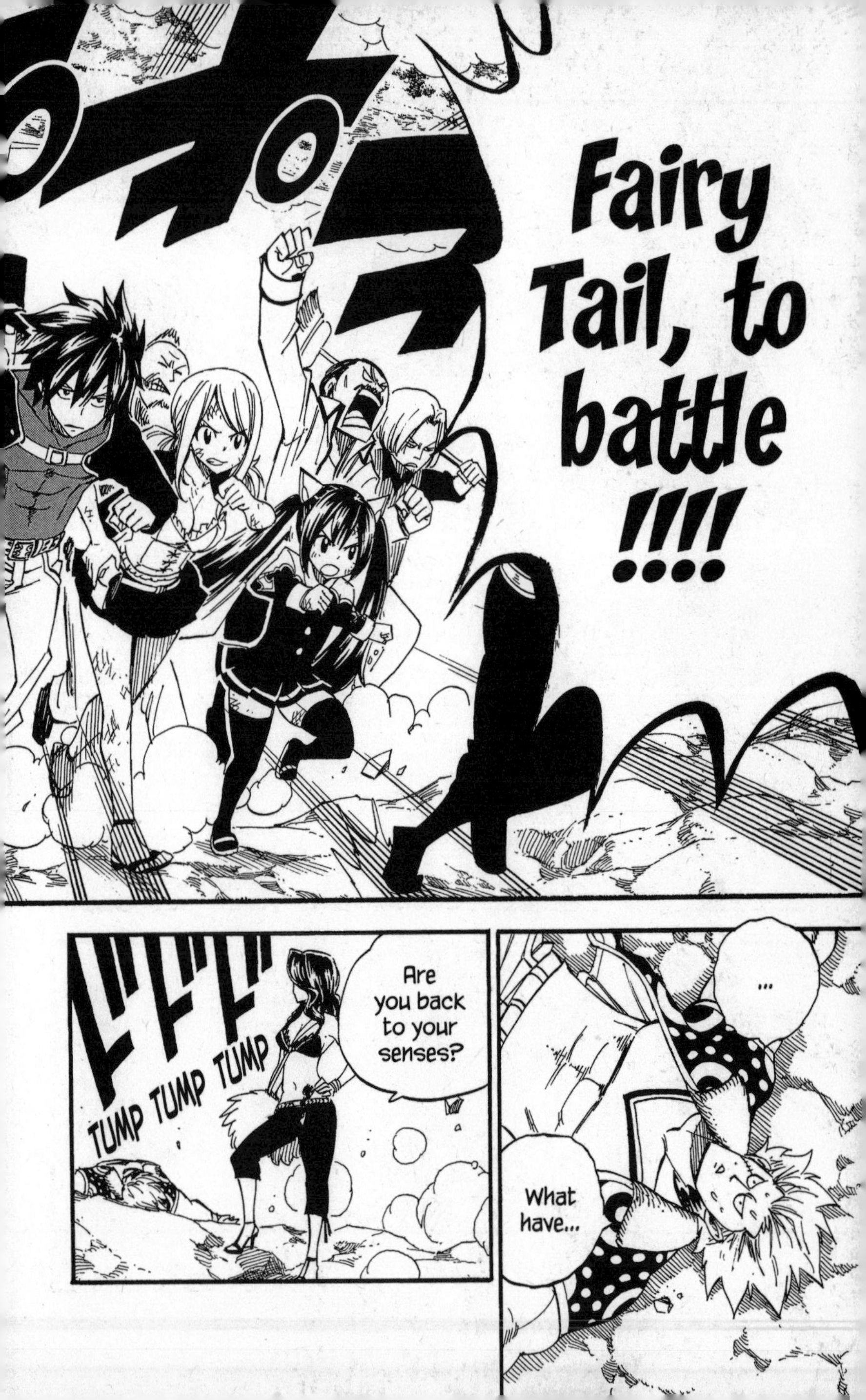
Fairy Tail, to battle!!!!
...
What have...
Are you back to your senses?
TUMP TUMP TUMP

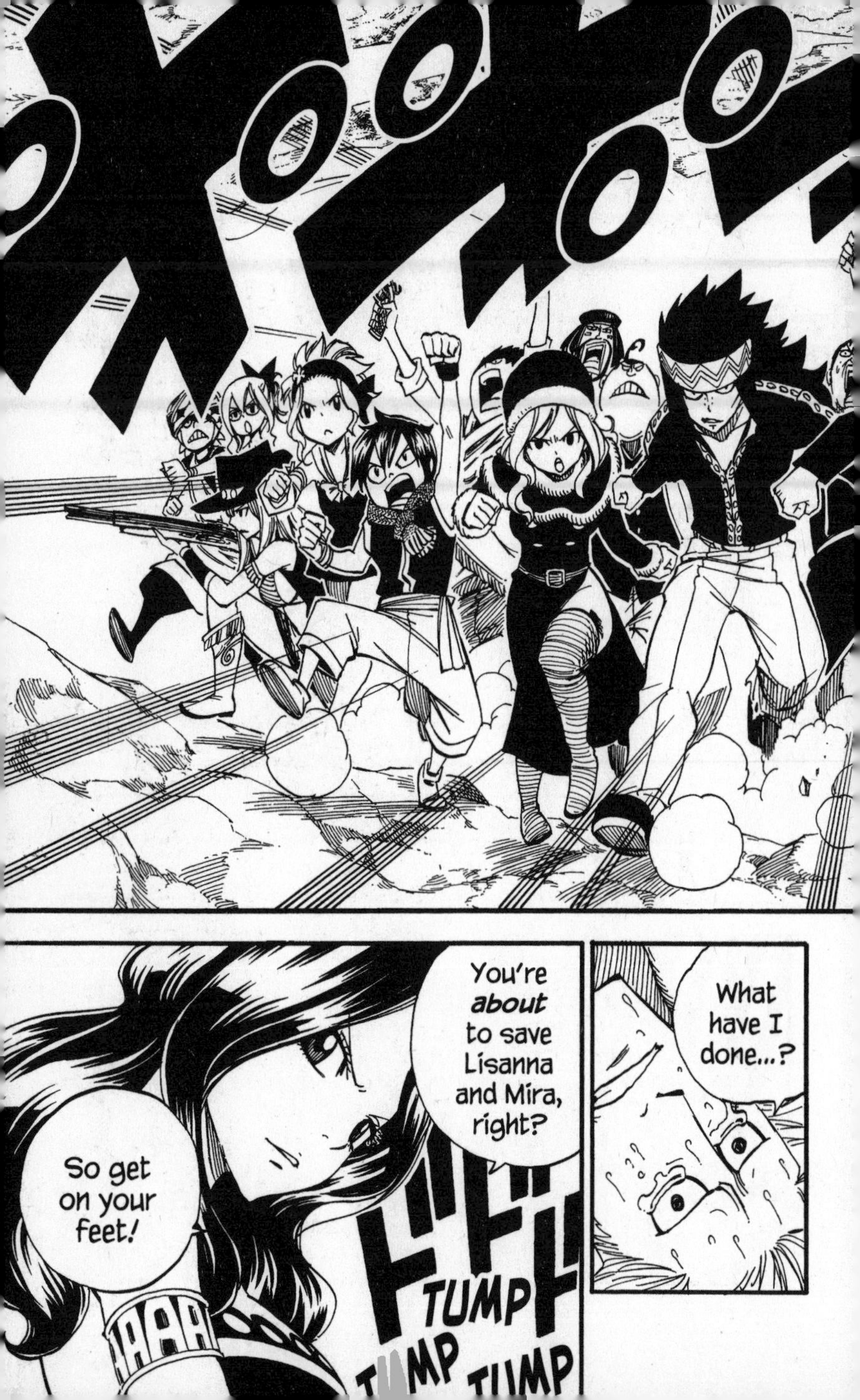
What have I done...?
You're *about* to save Lisanna and Mira, right?
So get on your feet!
TUMP
TUMP
TUMP

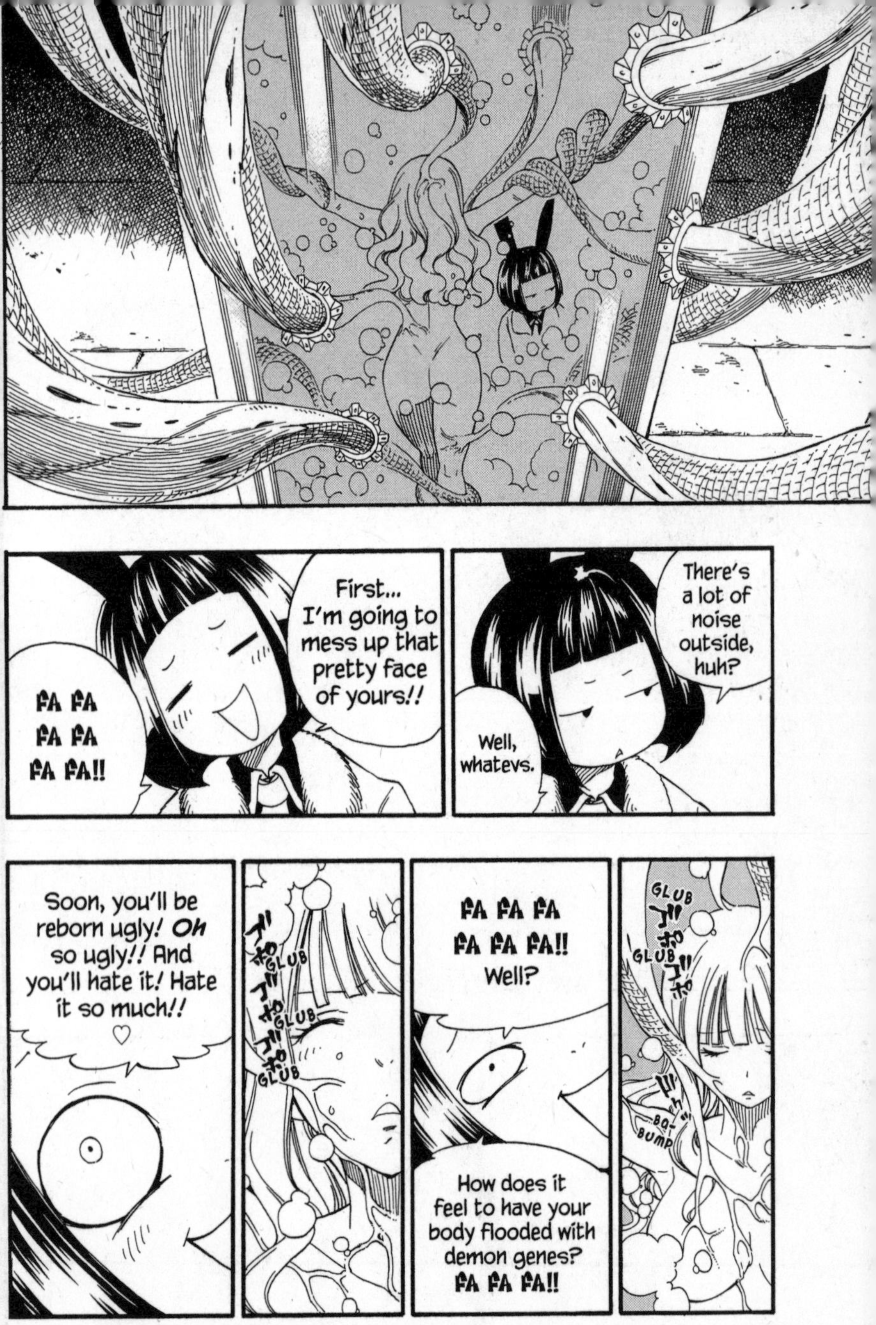

There's a lot of noise outside, huh?
Well, whatevs.
First... I'm going to mess up that pretty face of yours!!
FA FA FA FA FA FA!!
GLUB
GLUB
BA-BUMP
FA FA FA FA FA FA!! Well?
How does it feel to have your body flooded with demon genes? FA FA FA!!
GLUB
GLUB
GLUB
Soon, you'll be reborn ugly! *Oh* so ugly!! And you'll hate it! Hate it so much!! ♡

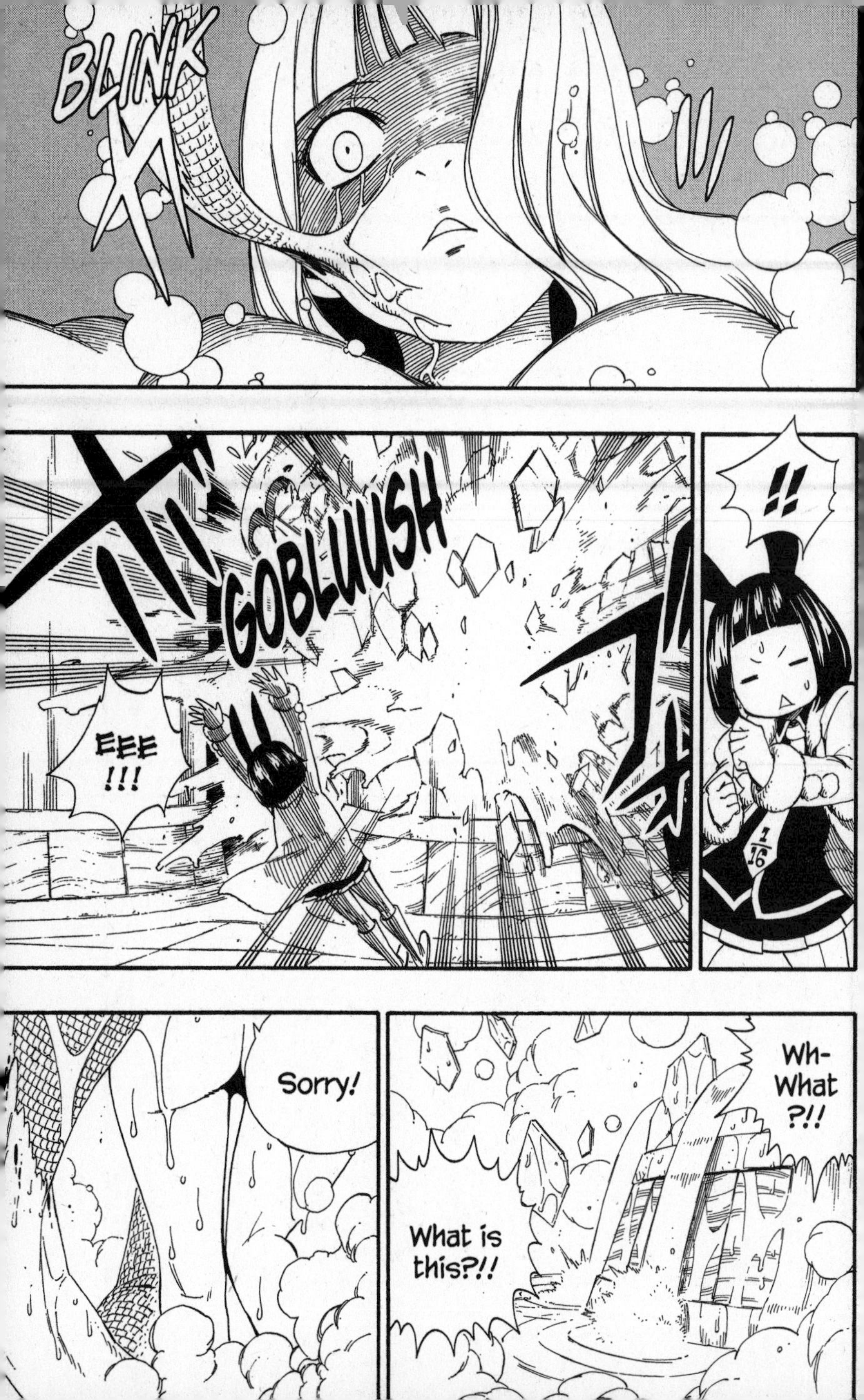
BLINK
!!
GOBLUUSH
EEE!!!
Wh-What?!!
What is this?!!
Sorry!

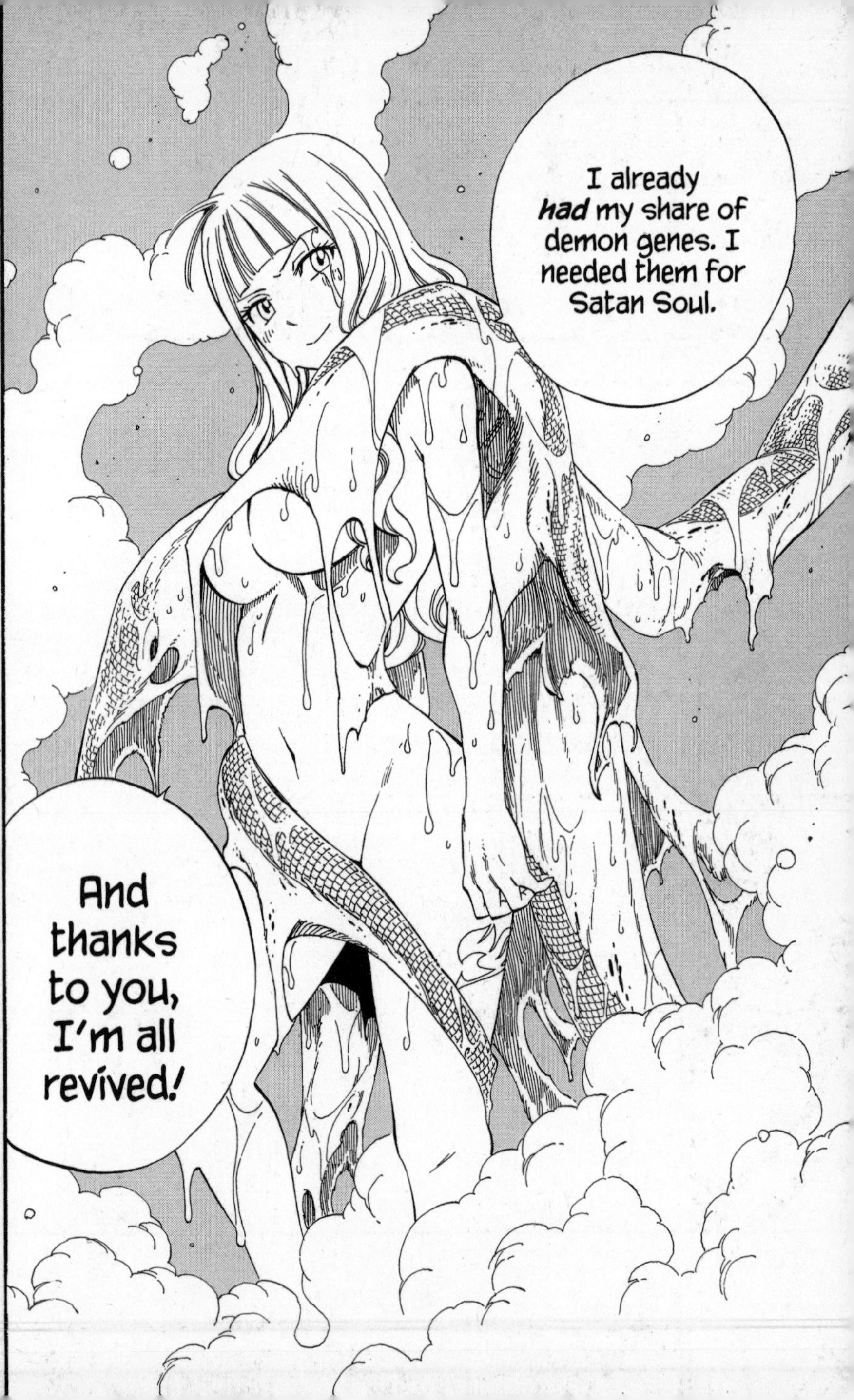
I already *had* my share of demon genes. I needed them for Satan Soul.
And thanks to you, I'm all revived!

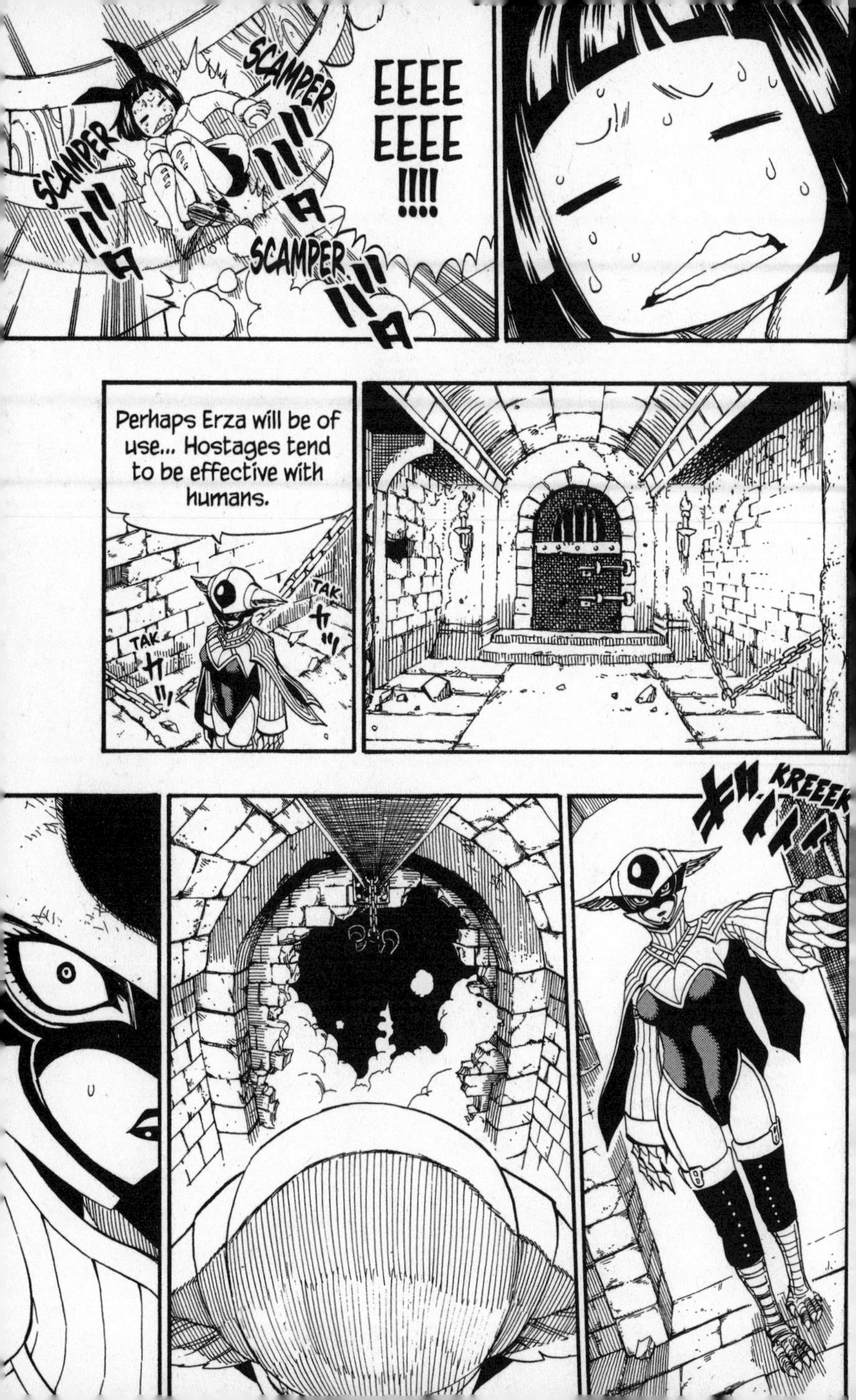

EEEE EEEE!!!!
SCAMPER
SCAMPER
SCAMPER
Perhaps Erza will be of use... Hostages tend to be effective with humans.
TAK
TAK
KREEEK

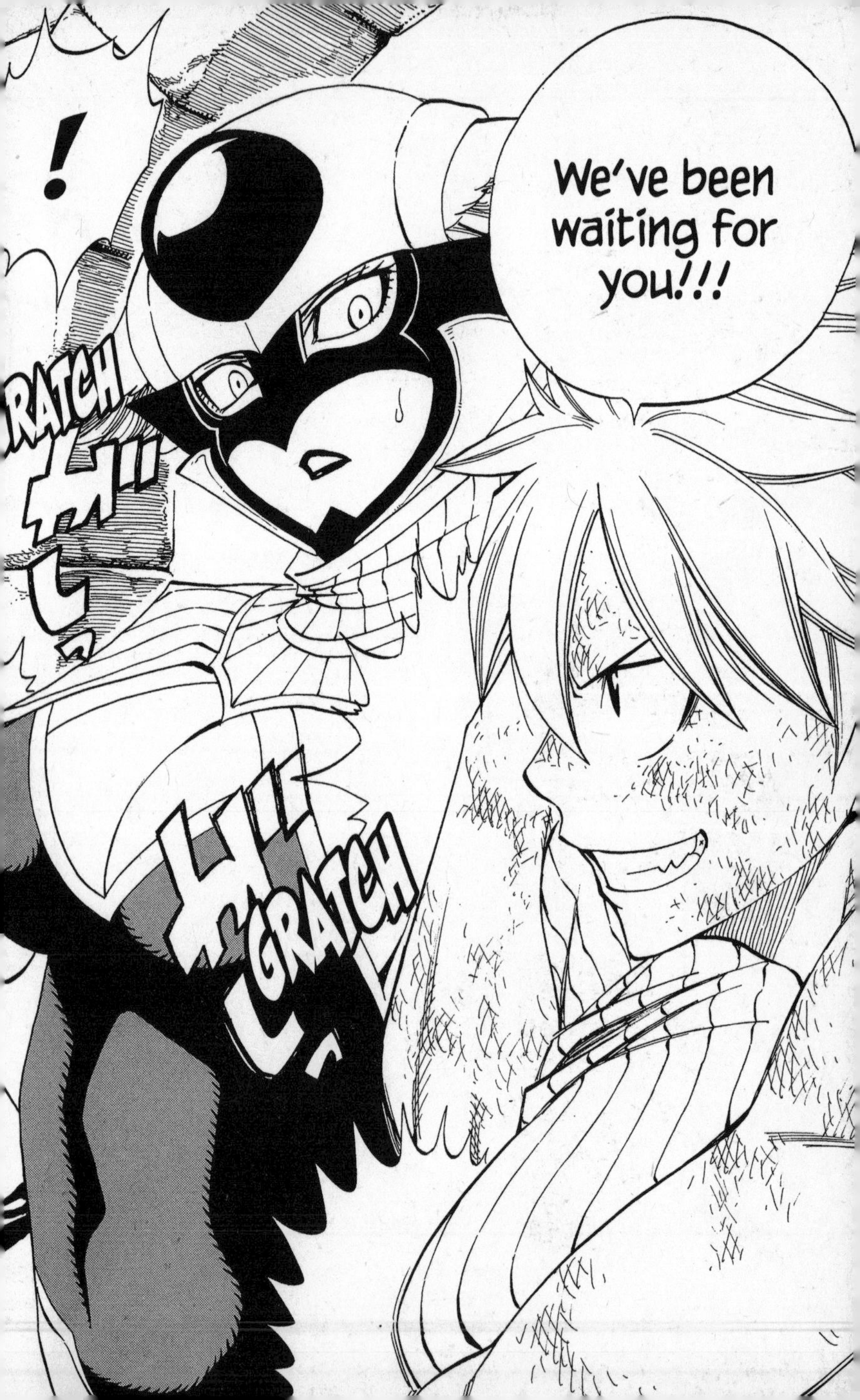
We've been waiting for you!!!
!
RATCH
GRATCH

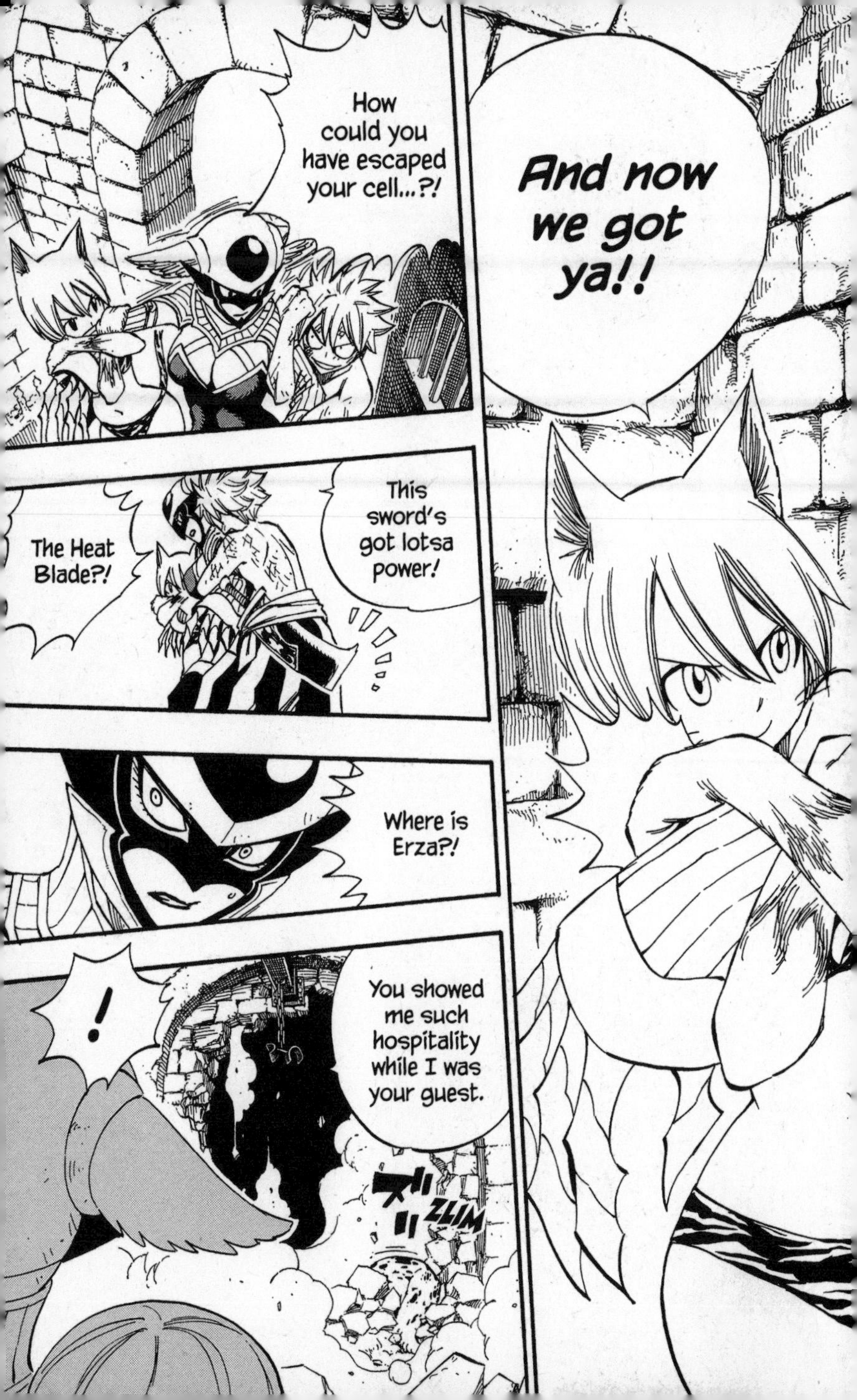

And now we got ya!!
How could you have escaped your cell...?!
This sword's got lotsa power!
The Heat Blade?!
Where is Erza?!
You showed me such hospitality while I was your guest.
!
ZLIM

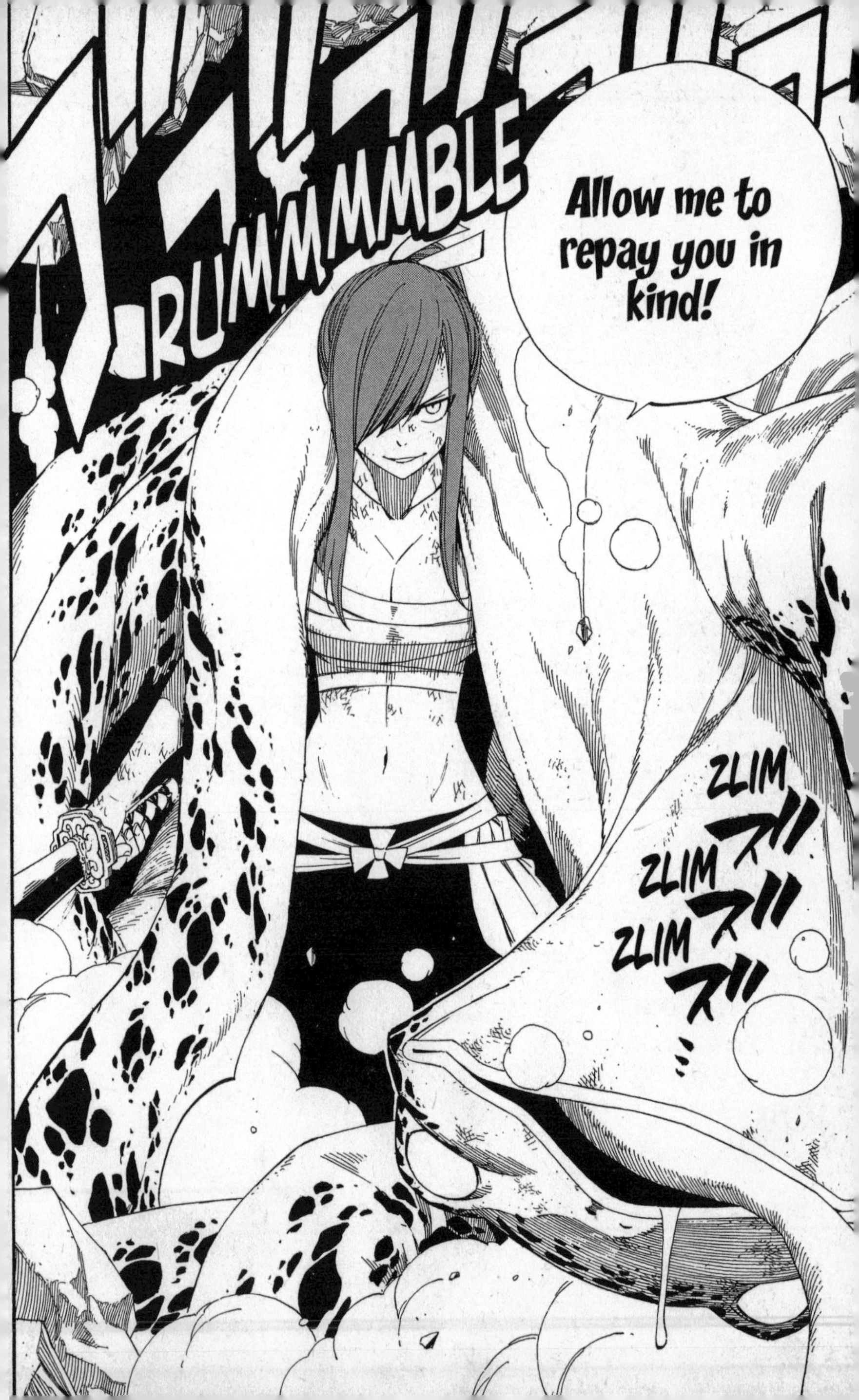
RUMMMMBLE
Allow me to repay you in kind!
ZLIM
ZLIM
ZLIM

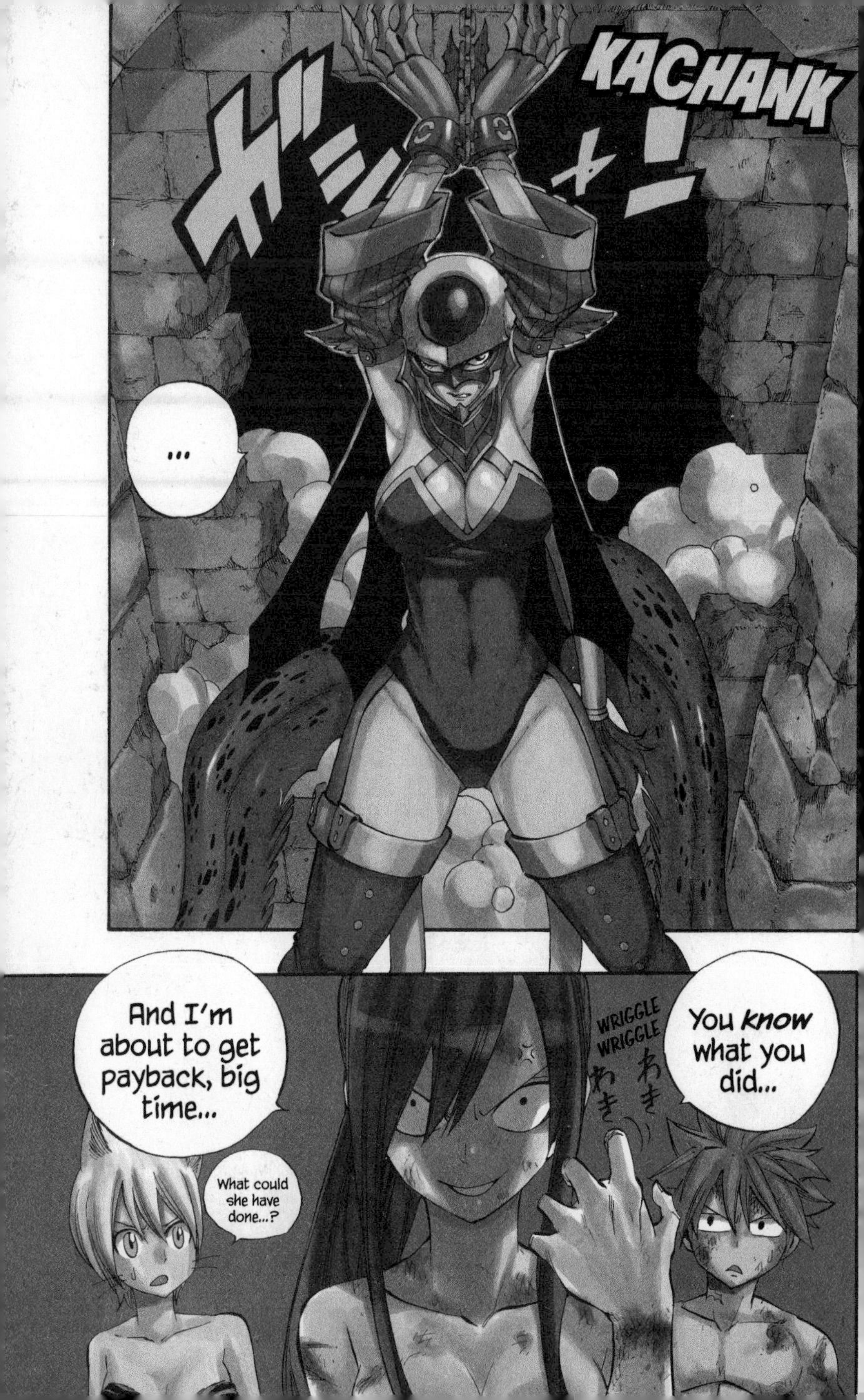
KACHANK
...
You *know* what you did...
WRIGGLE WRIGGLE
わき わき
And I'm about to get payback, big time...
What could she have done...?

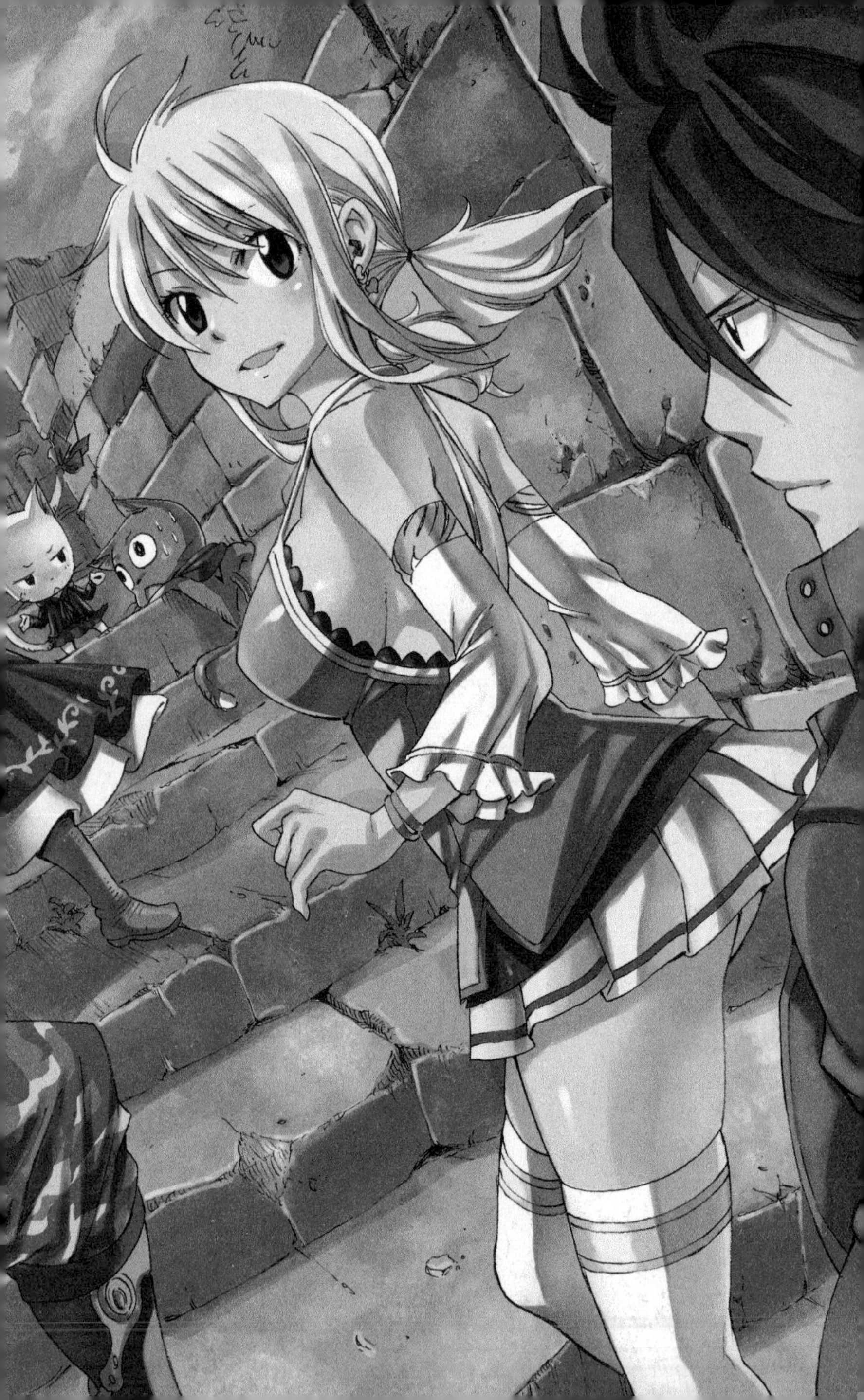

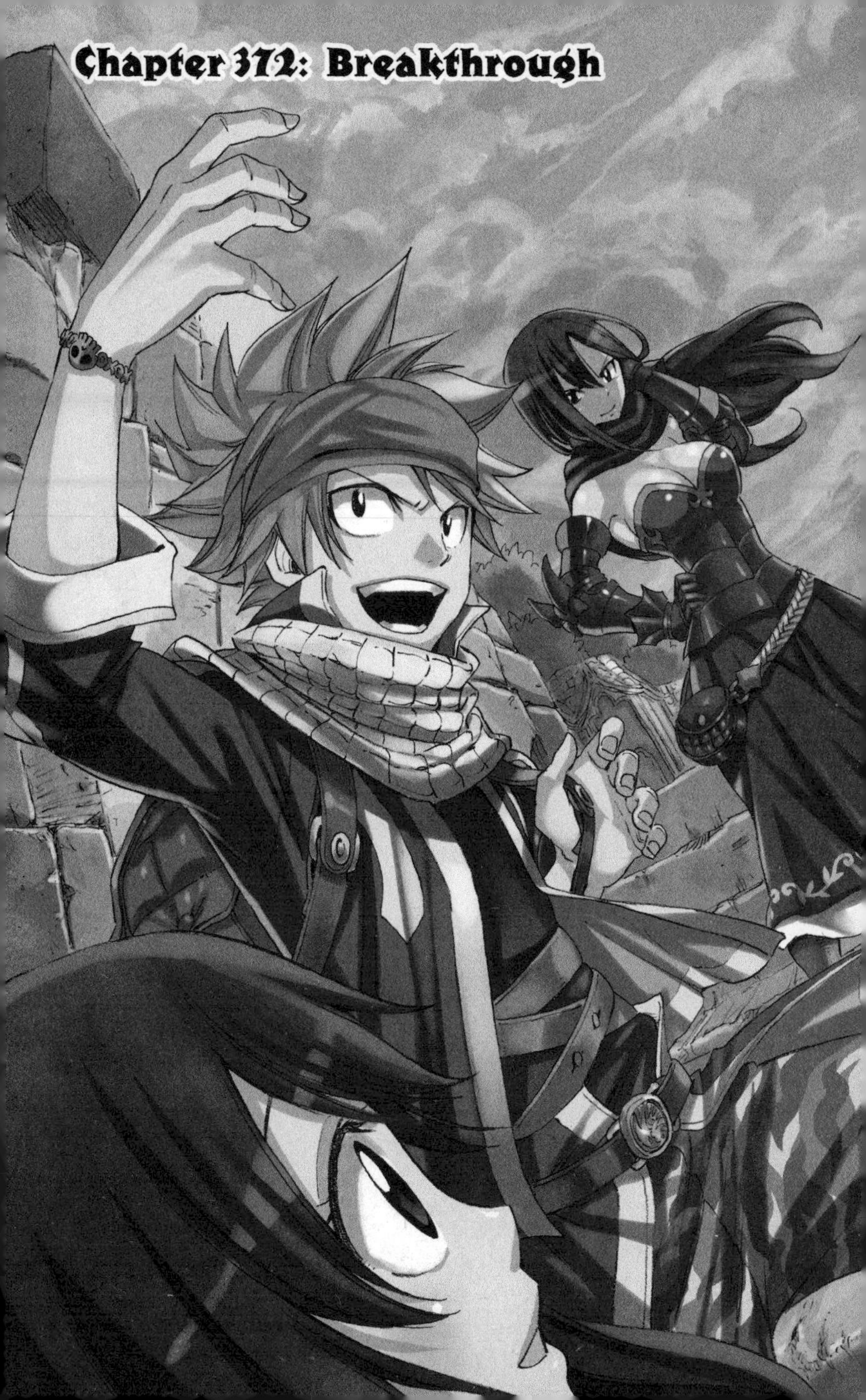
Chapter 372: Breakthrough

The Fairy Tail Guild is looking for illustrations! Please send in your art on a postcard or at postcard size, and do it in black pen, okay? Those chosen to be published will get a signed mini poster! ♪ Make sure you write your real name and address on the back of your illustration!

FAIRY TAIL GUILD d'ART PART 1

Saitama Prefecture, Minori Chiba

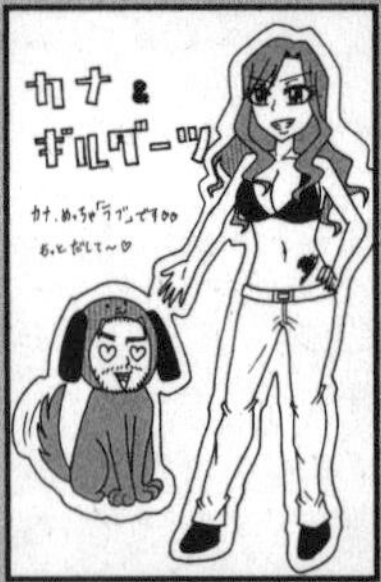
カナ & ギルダーツ

▲ Wa ha ha! What is this?! (Laughs) That doggy Gildarts is just the best!!

▼ Seilah, Tartaros's beauty. Just how much power does she have?

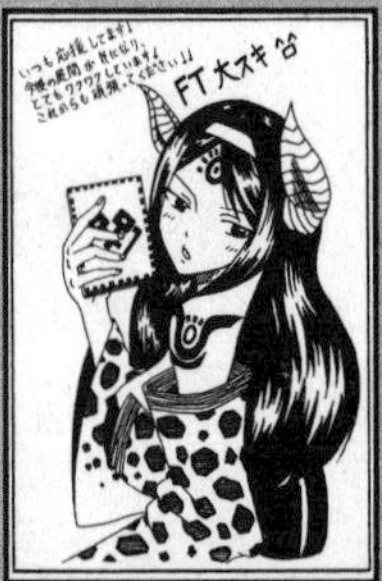
FT大スキ☆

Tokyo, Hisato Uematsu

▼ Nine Demon Gates Unite!! The fight begins now!!

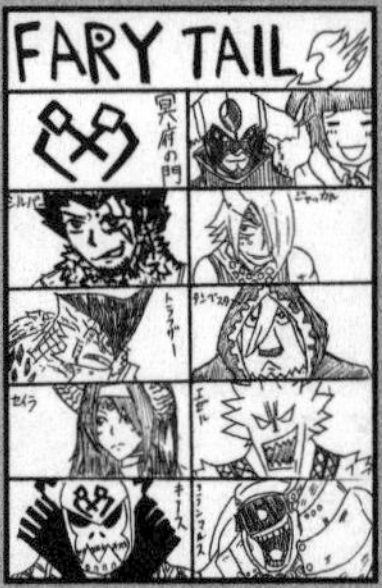
FARY TAIL

Gunma Prefecture, Kyousuke Yoshinaga

Fukuoka Prefecture, Wakagi

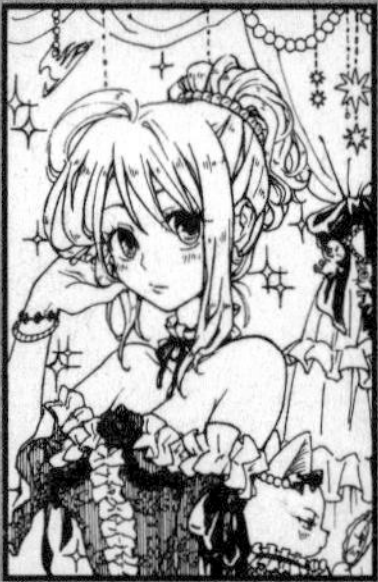

▲ Very well drawn!! And with Lucy and Carla!! You'd think they'd go together, but it's a rare pairing.

Tochigi Prefecture, Miki Abe

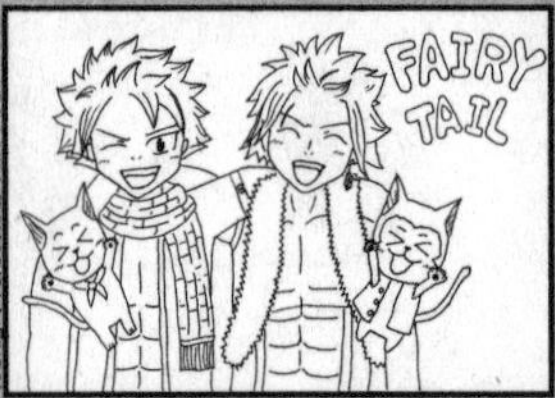
FAIRY TAIL

◀ Natsu and Sting! You know, someday I'd like to draw the two of them working together.

REJECTION CORNER

Th- This battle has the lowest stakes I've ever seen... ▶

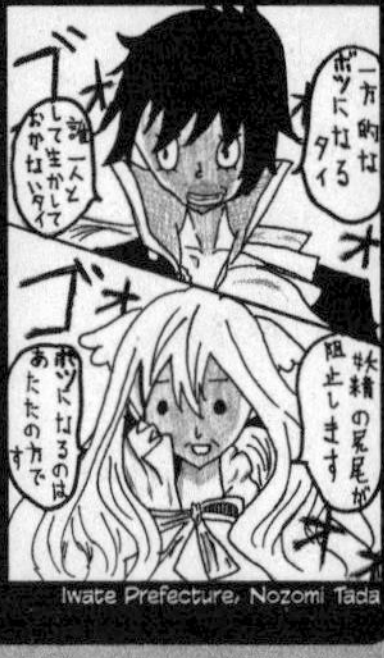

Iwate Prefecture, Nozomi Tada

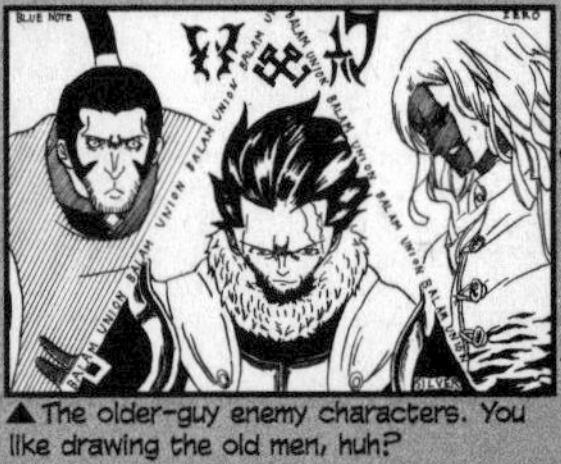

Kanagawa Prefecture, Ryan

▲ The older-guy enemy characters. You like drawing the old men, huh?

By sending in letters or postcards, you give us permission to give your name, address, postal code, and any other information you include to the artist as-is. Please keep that in mind.

Send to Hiro Mashima, Kodansha Comics 451 Park Ave. South, 7th Floor New York, NY 10016

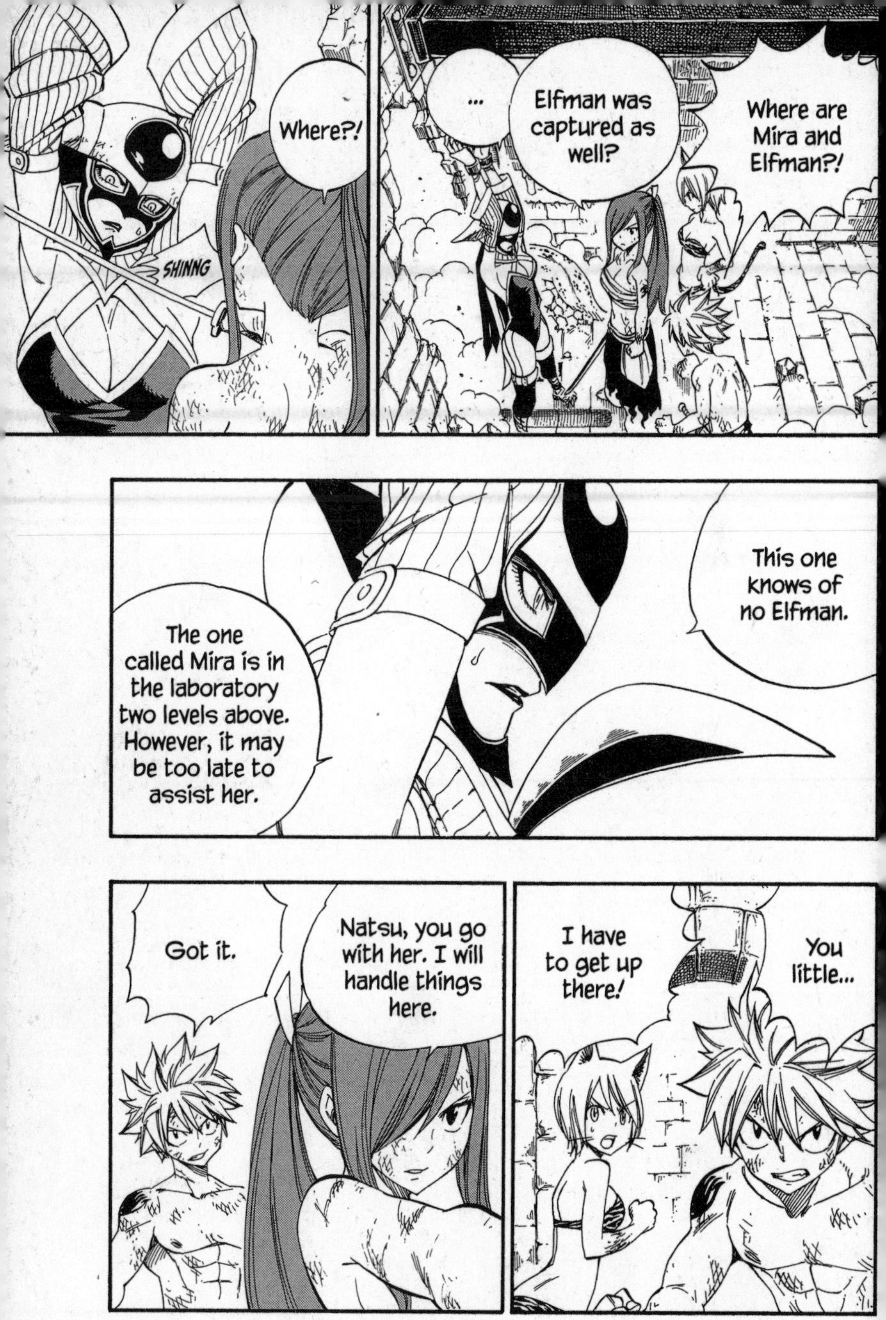
Where are Mira and Elfman?!
Elfman was captured as well?
...
Where?!
SHINNG
This one knows of no Elfman.
The one called Mira is in the laboratory two levels above. However, it may be too late to assist her.
You little...
I have to get up there!
Natsu, you go with her. I will handle things here.
Got it.

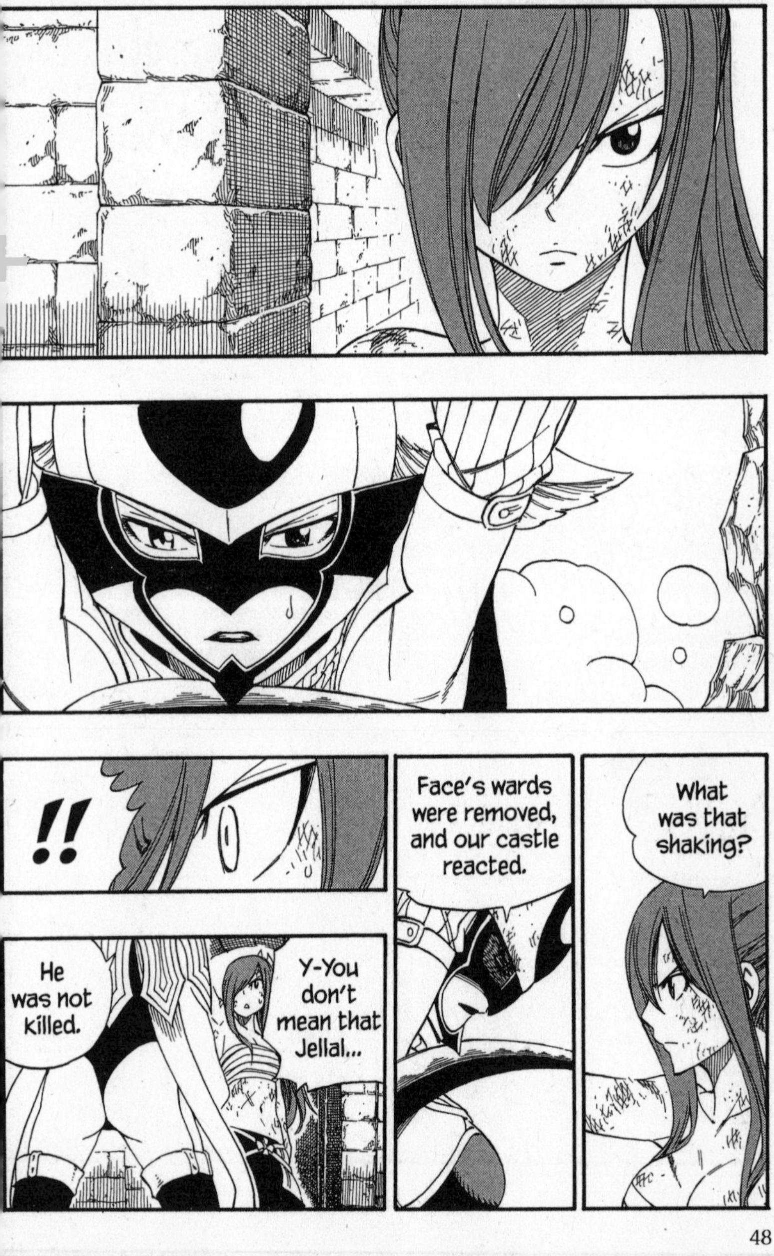
What was that shaking?
Face's wards were removed, and our castle reacted.
!!
Y-You don't mean that Jellal...
He was not killed.

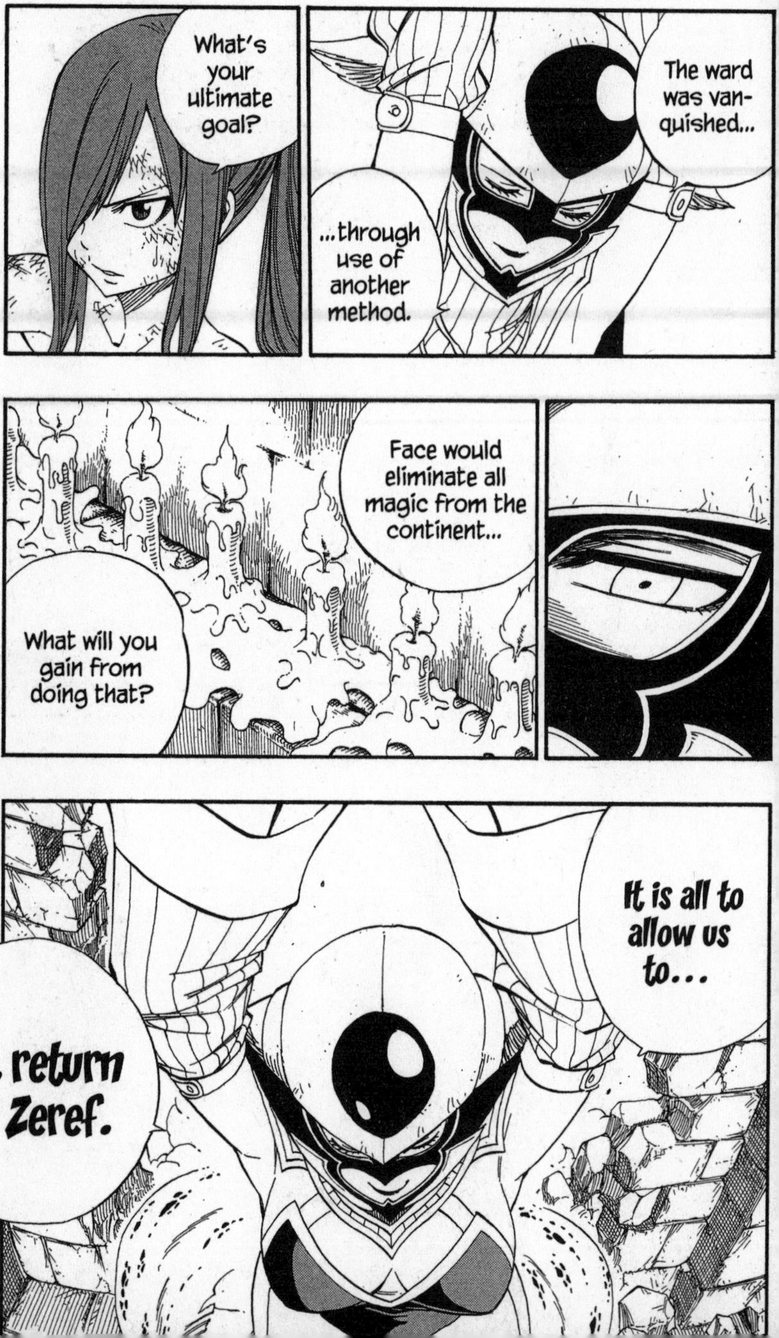
The ward was van-quished...
...through use of another method.
What's your ultimate goal?
Face would eliminate all magic from the continent...
What will you gain from doing that?
It is all to allow us to...
...return to Zeref.

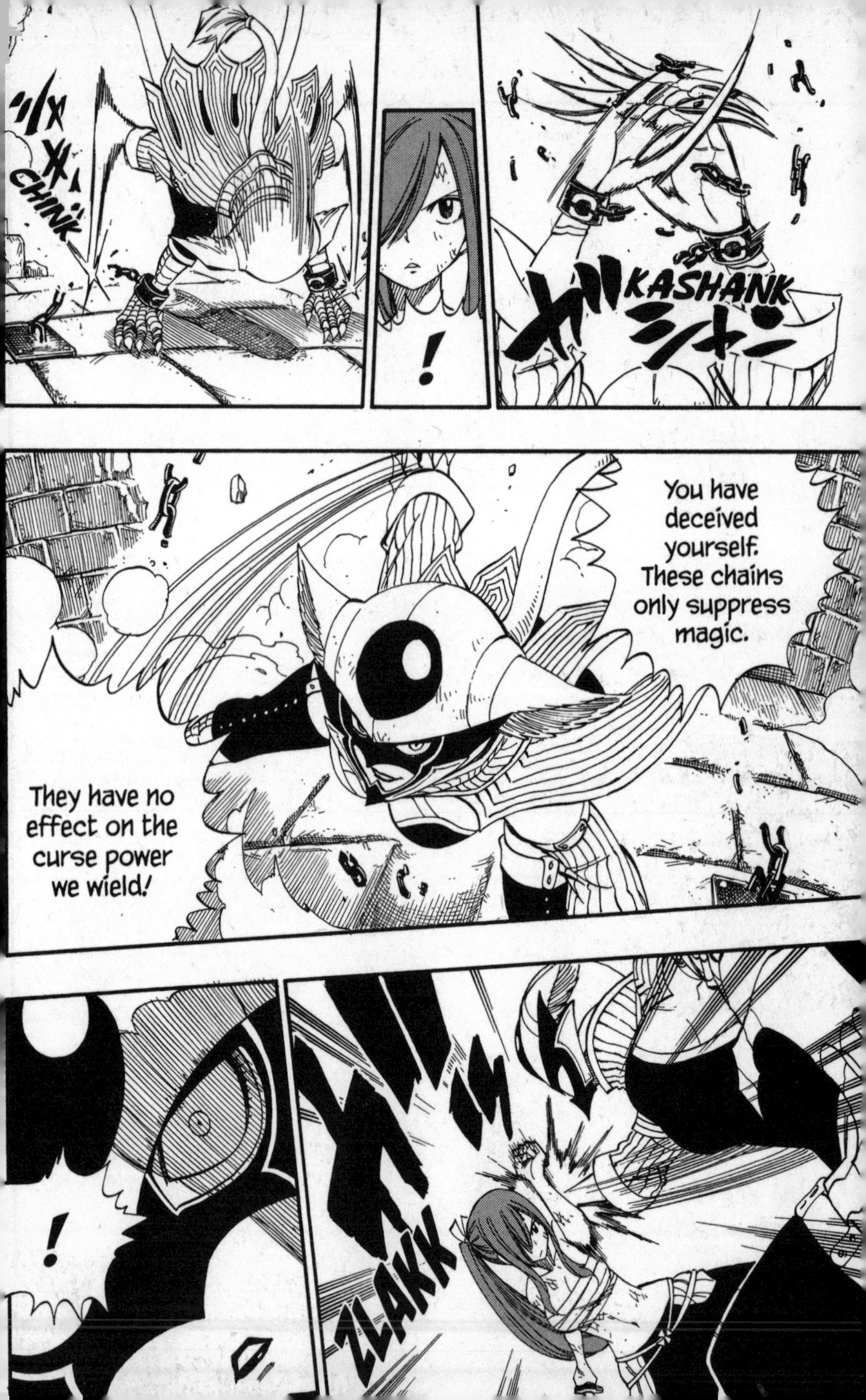
KASHANK
!
CHINK
You have deceived yourself. These chains only suppress magic.
They have no effect on the curse power we wield!
ZLAKK
!

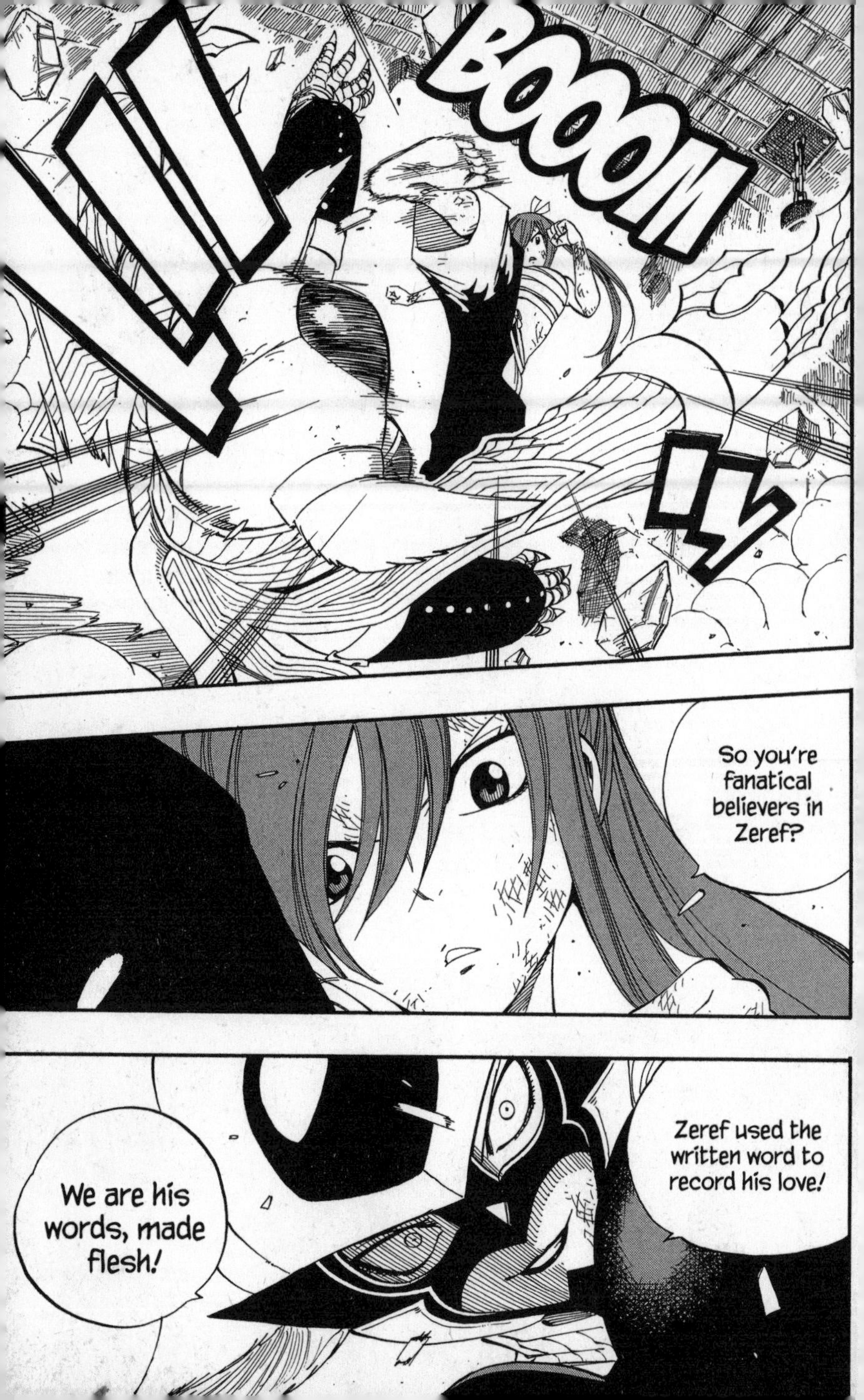
BOOOM
So you're fanatical believers in Zeref?
Zeref used the written word to record his love!
We are his words, made flesh!

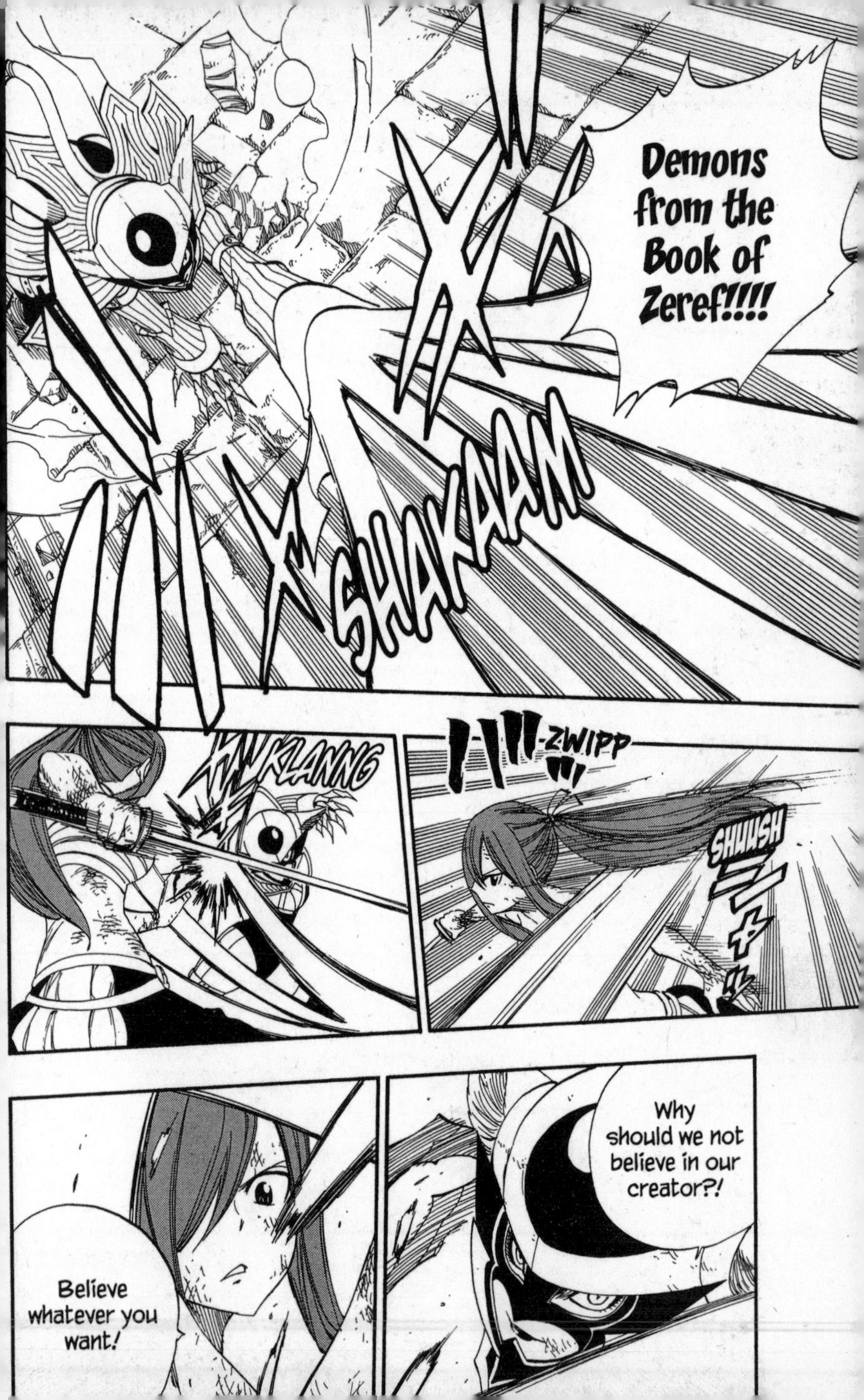
Demons from the Book of Zeref!!!!
SHAKAAM
ZWIPP
SHUUSH
KLANNG
Why should we not believe in our creator?!
Believe whatever you want!

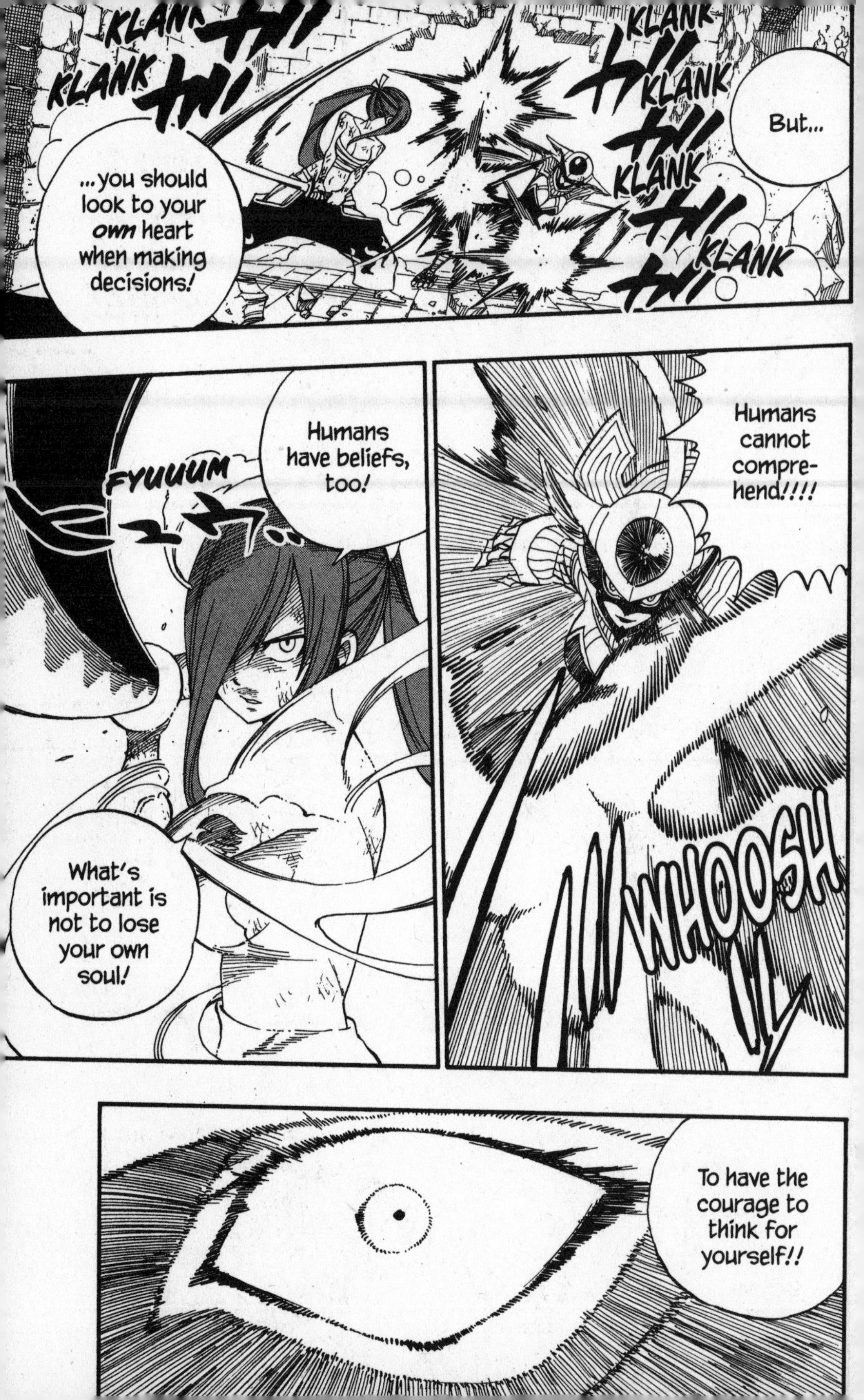
KLANK
KLANK
KLANK
KLANK
KLANK
KLANK
But...
...you should look to your *own* heart when making decisions!
Humans cannot compre-hend!!!!
WHOOSH
Humans have beliefs, too!
FYUUUM
What's important is not to lose your own soul!
To have the courage to think for yourself!!

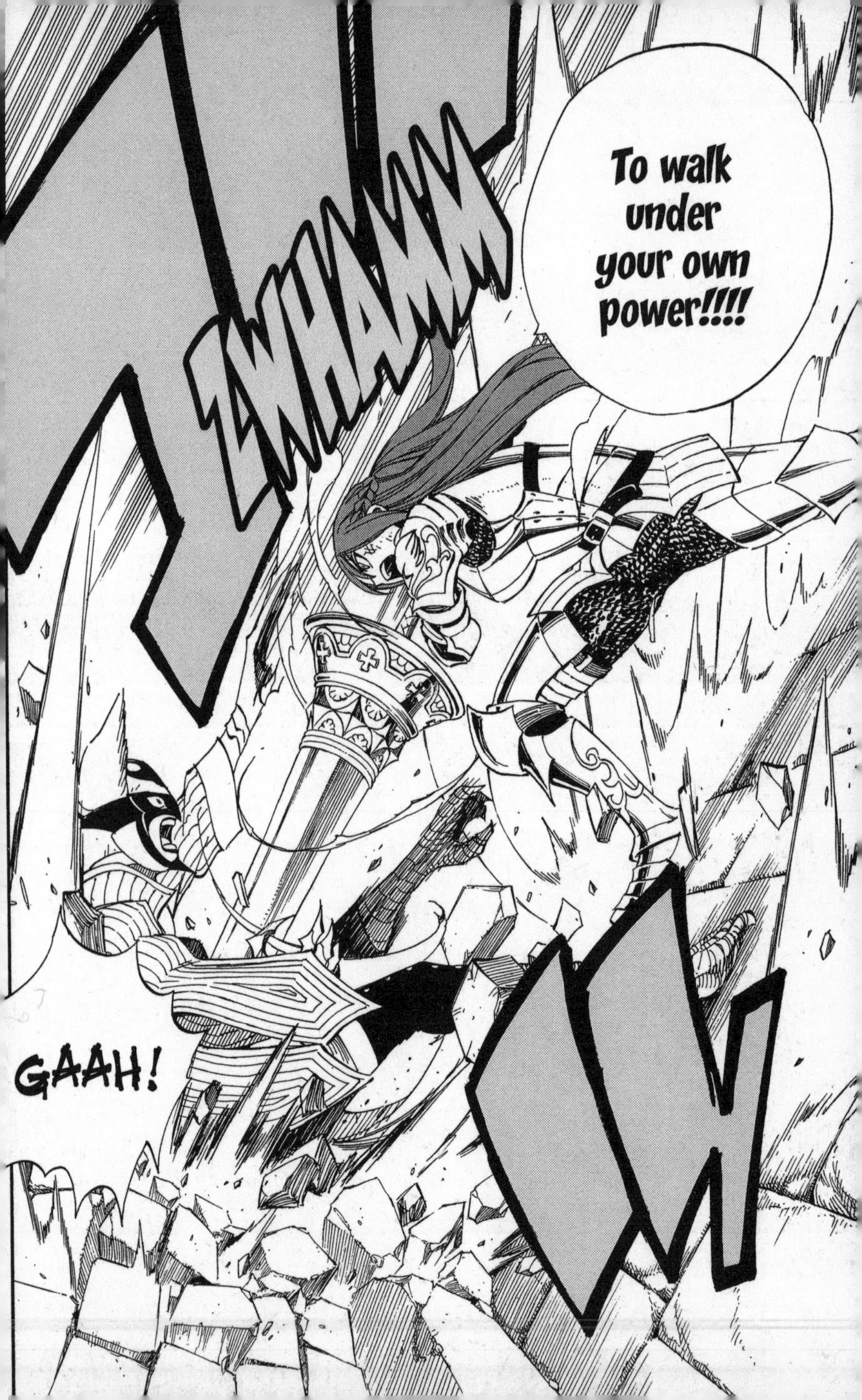
To walk under your own power!!!!
ZWHAMM
GAAH!

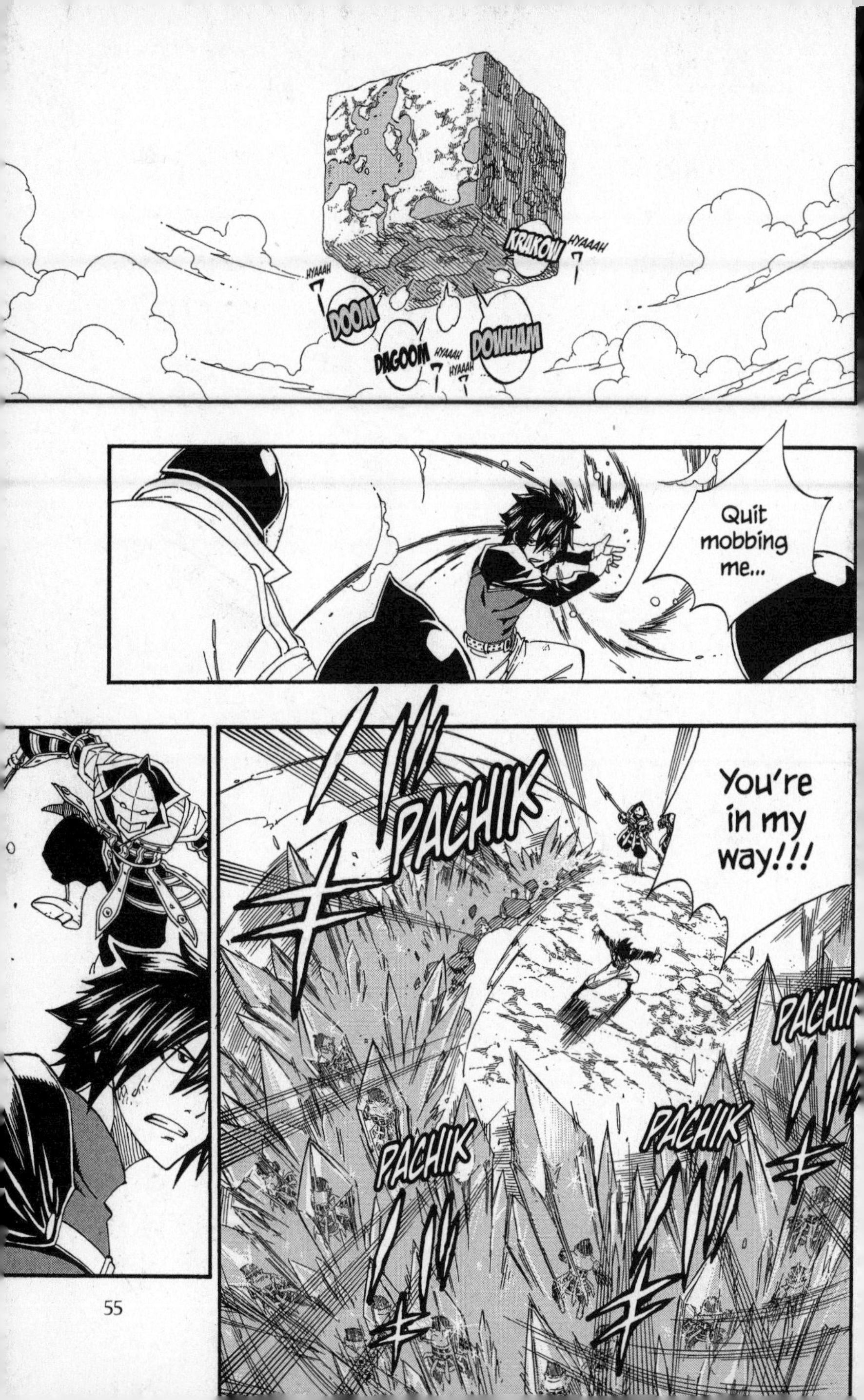
KRAKOW
HYAAAH
DOWHAM
HYAAAH
HYAAAH
DAGOOM
DOOM
HYAAAH
Quit mobbing me...
You're in my way!!!
PACHIK
PACHIK
PACHIK
PACHIK

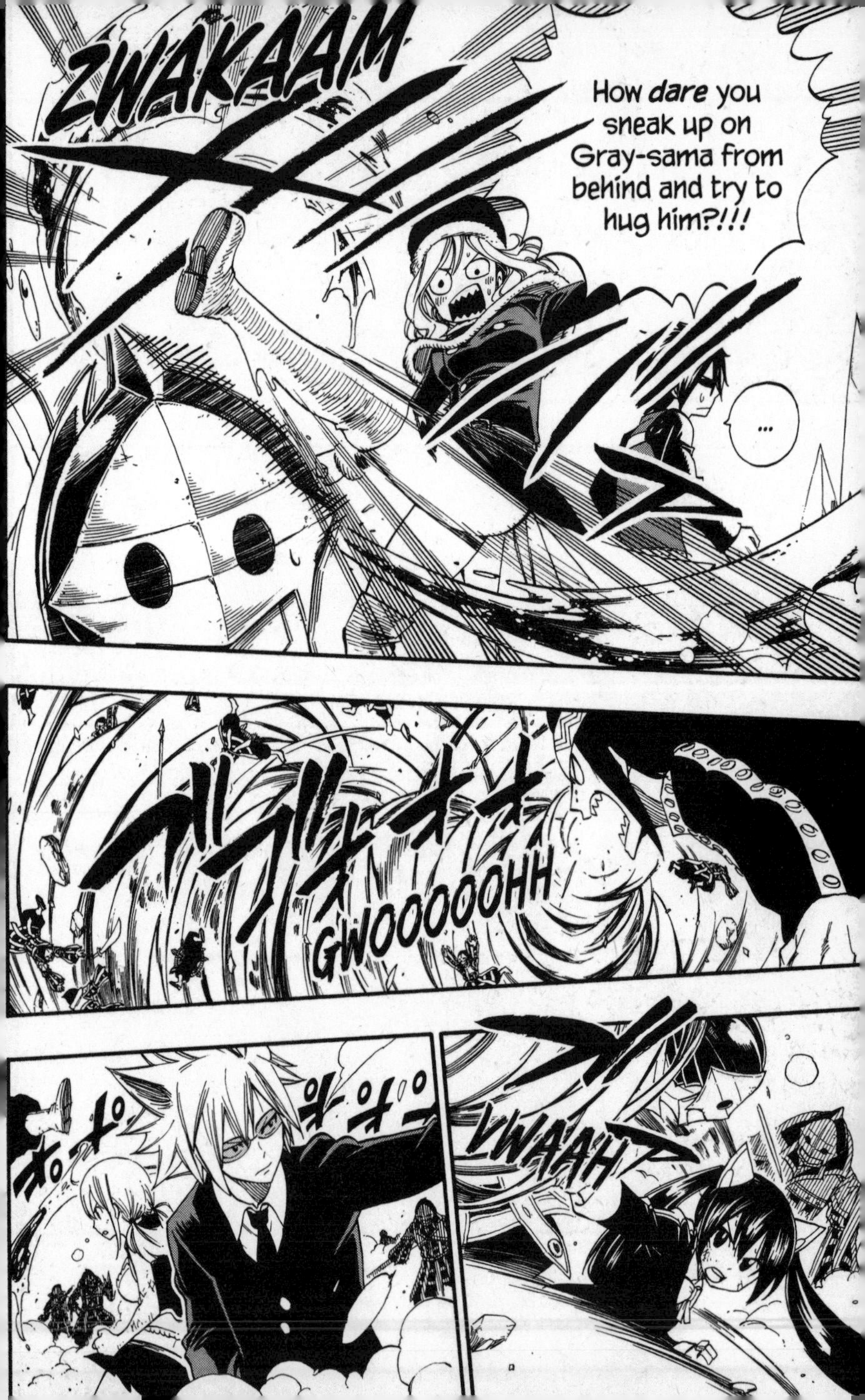
How dare you sneak up on Gray-sama from behind and try to hug him?!!!
ZWAKAAM
...
GWOOOOOOHH
VWAAH

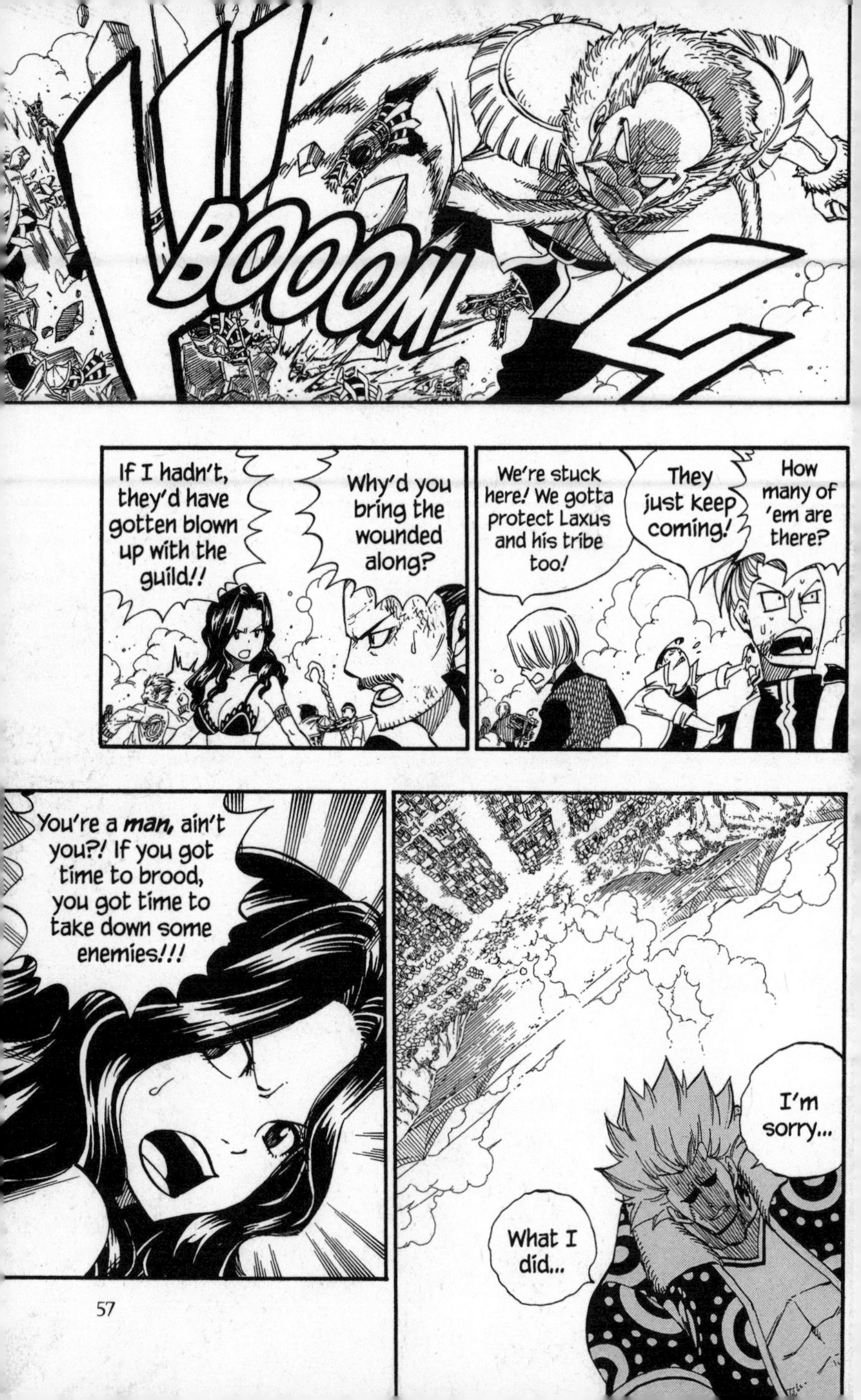
BOOOM
How many of 'em are there?
They just keep coming!
We're stuck here! We gotta protect Laxus and his tribe too!
Why'd you bring the wounded along?
If I hadn't, they'd have gotten blown up with the guild!!
I'm sorry...
What I did...
You're a *man*, ain't you?! If you got time to brood, you got time to take down some enemies!!!

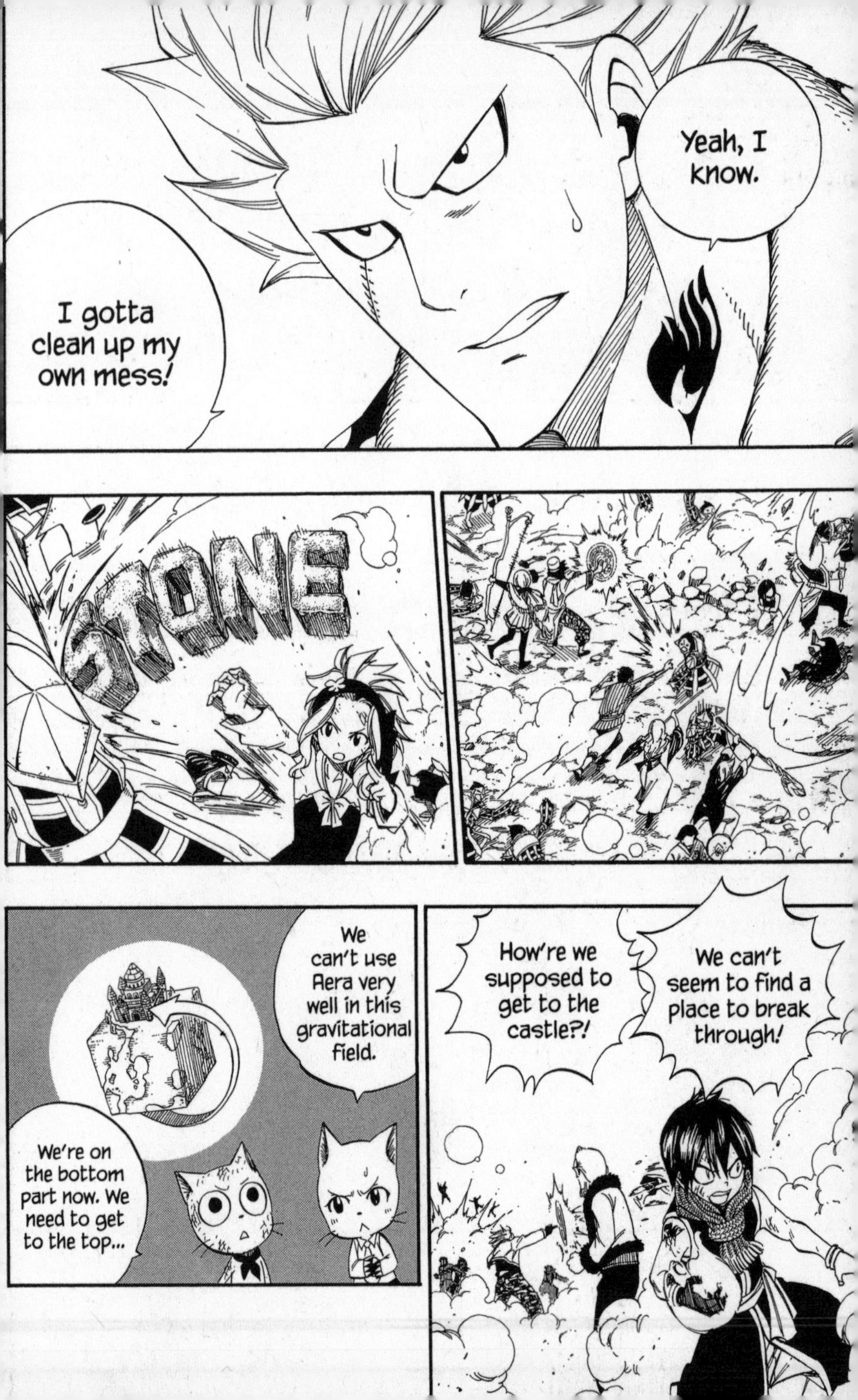
Yeah, I know.
I gotta clean up my own mess!
STONE
We can't seem to find a place to break through!
How're we supposed to get to the castle?!
We can't use Aera very well in this gravitational field.
We're on the bottom part now. We need to get to the top...

While we're wasting our efforts here...

...Erza and the others are...

But how...?

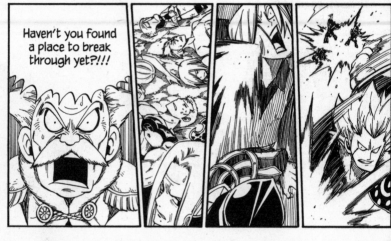

Haven't you found a place to break through yet?!!!

GWUMP...

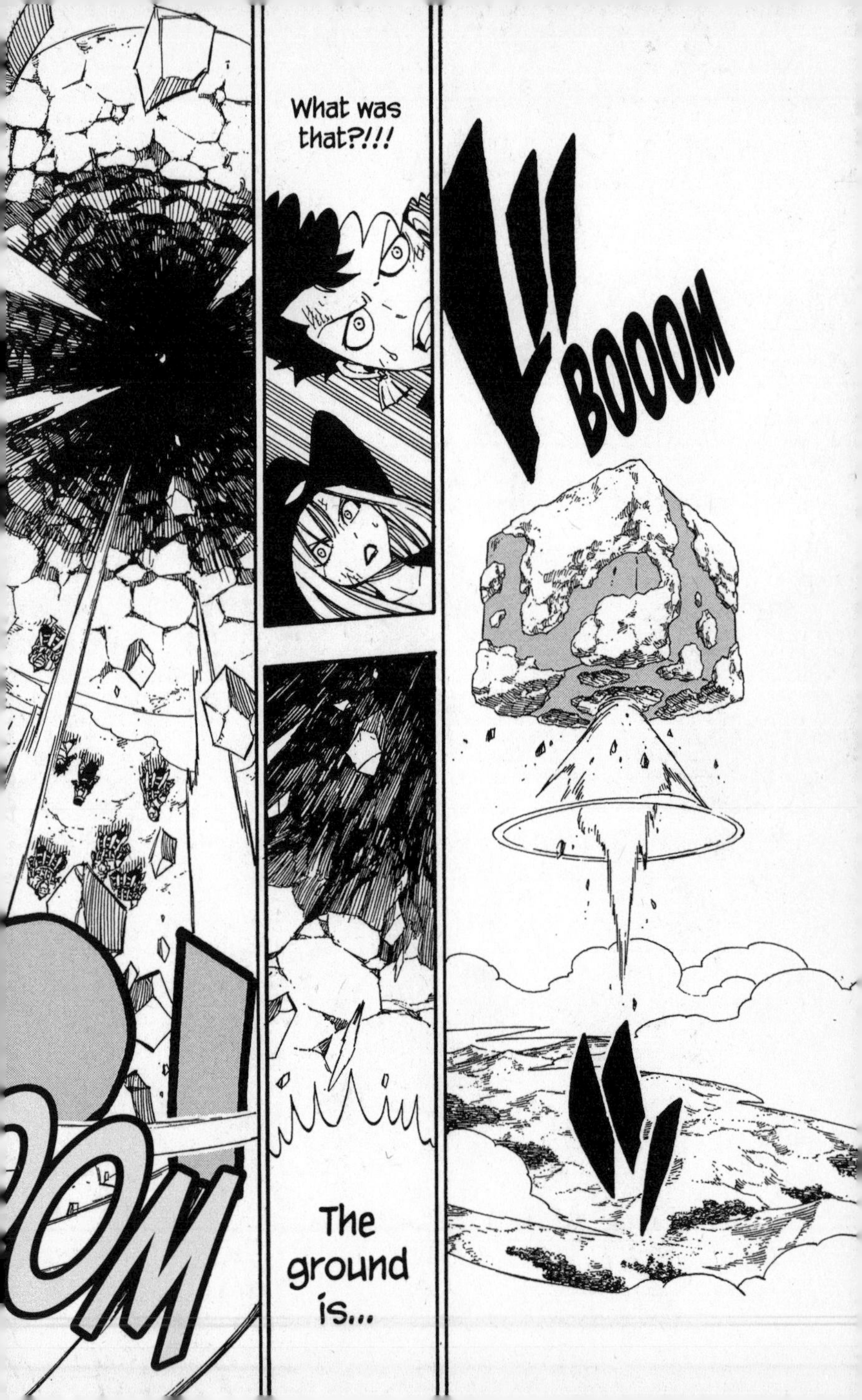
BOOOM
What was that?!!!
The ground is...
OOM

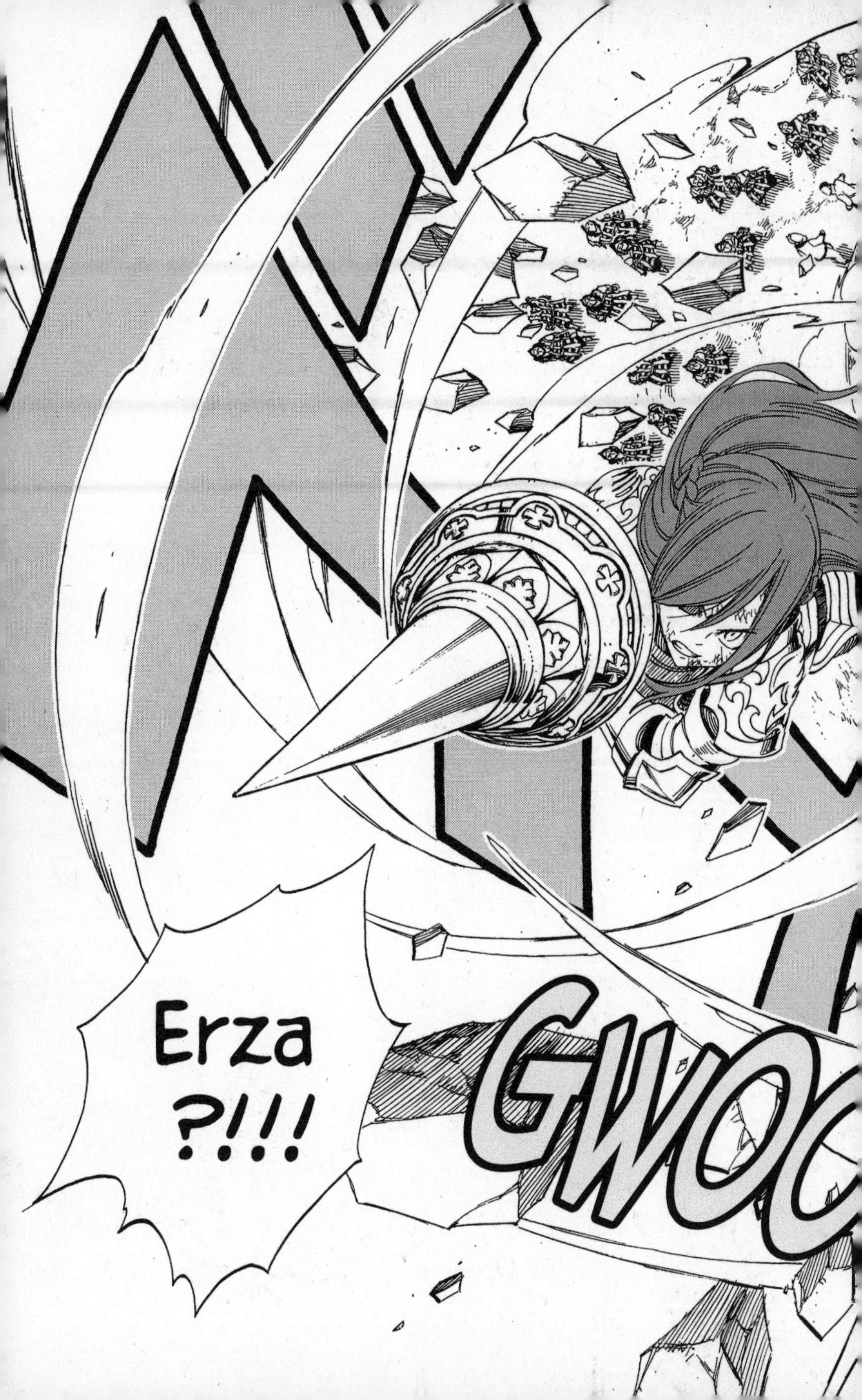
Erza ?!!!
GWOO

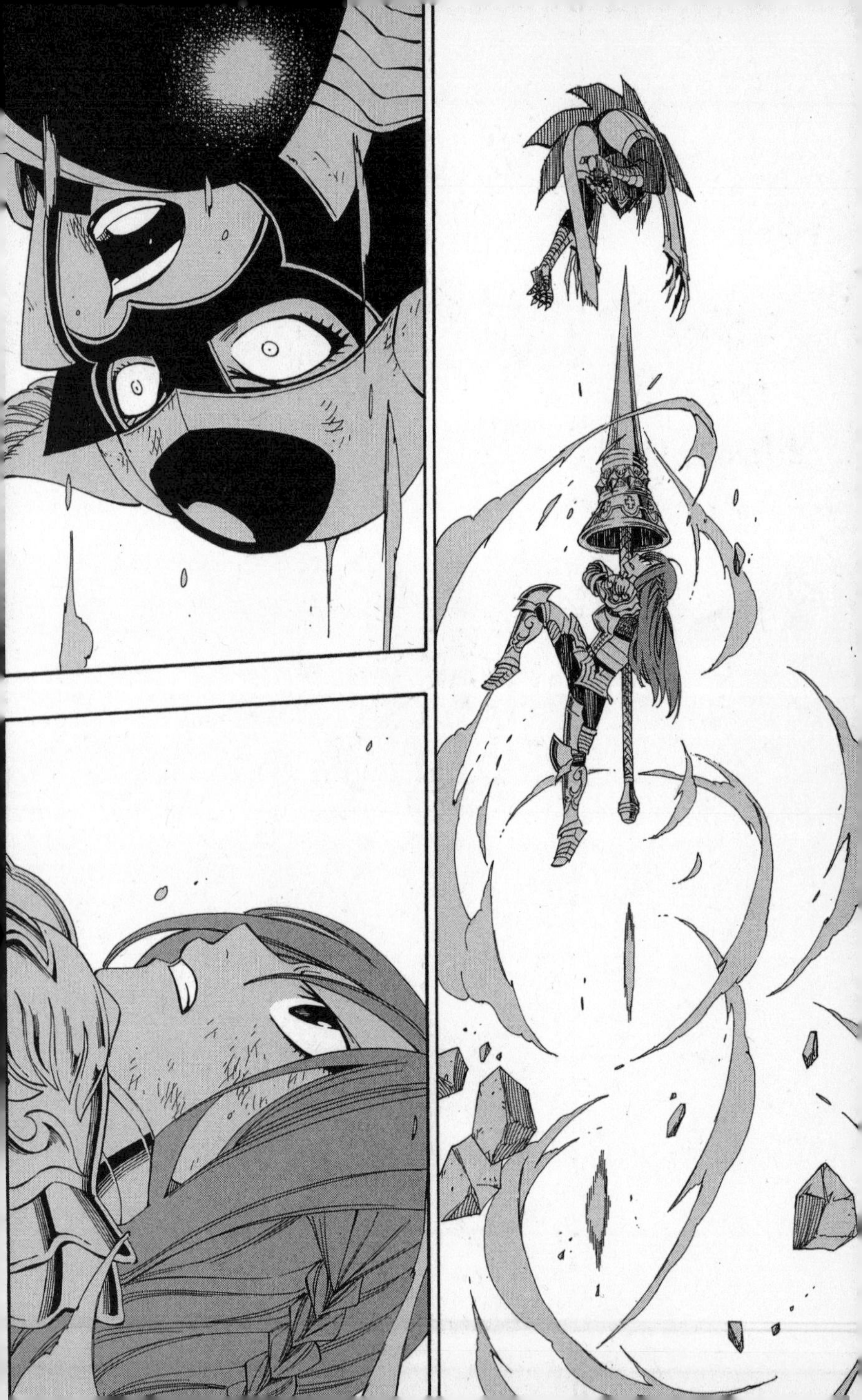

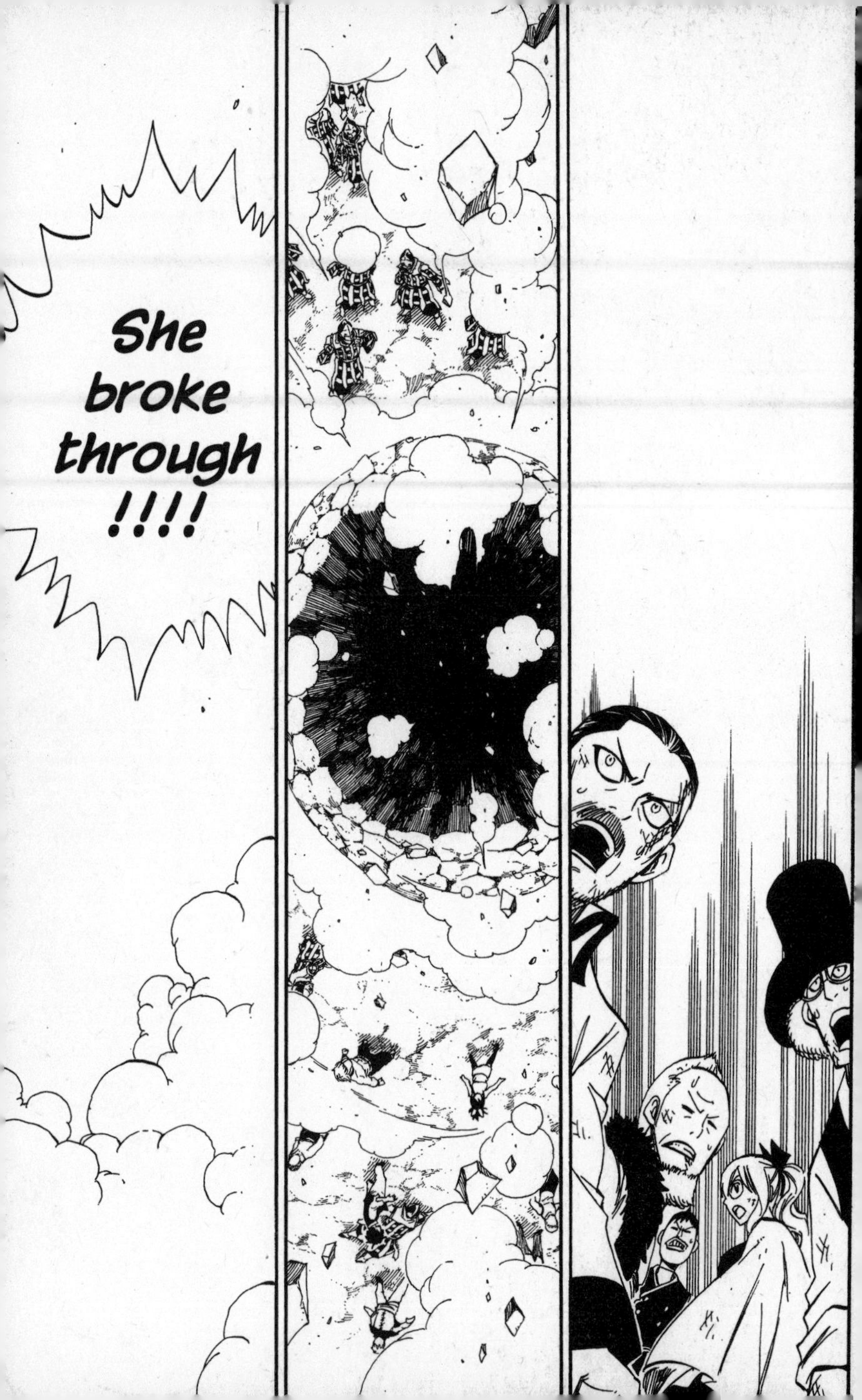
She broke through !!!!

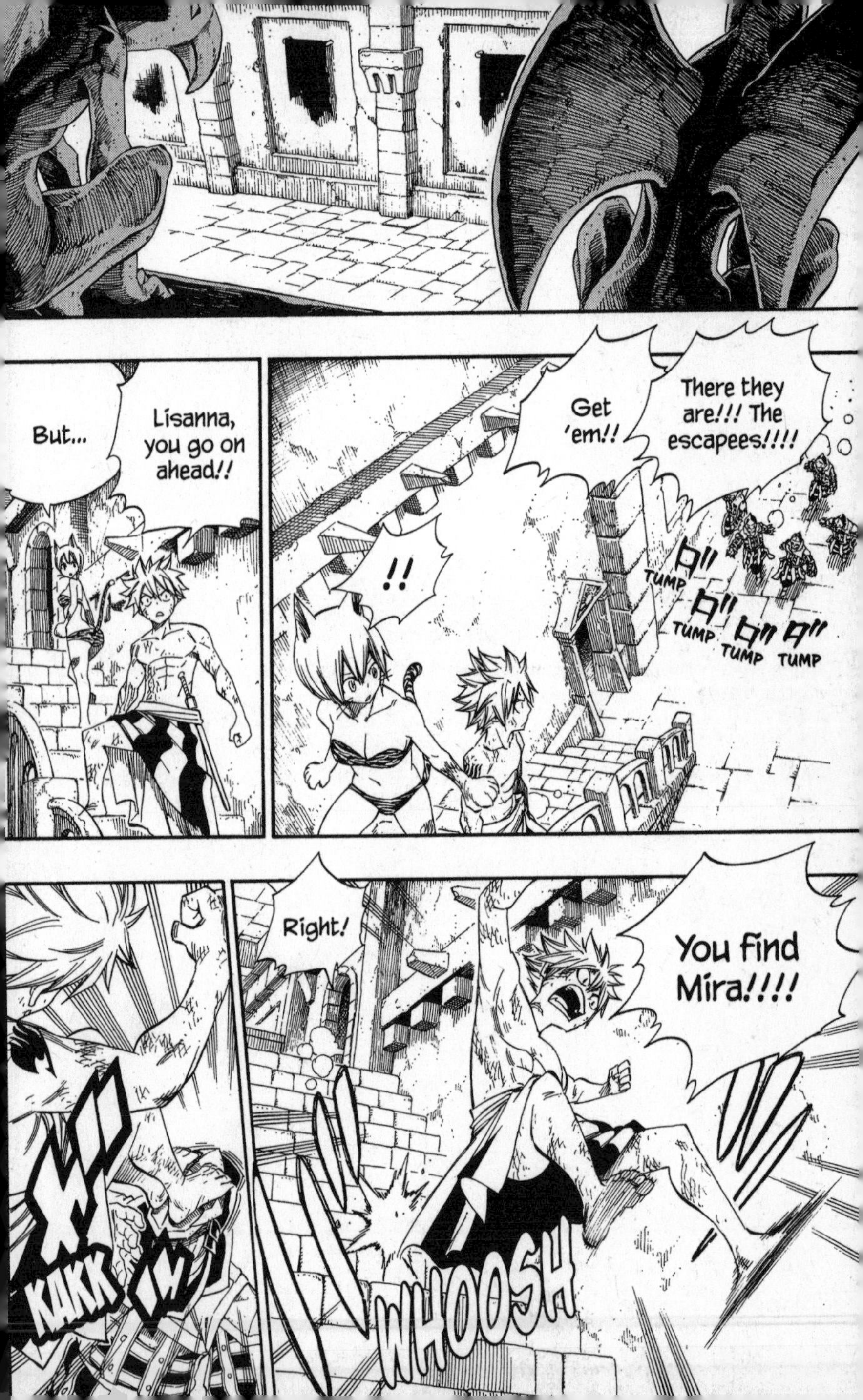
There they are!!! The escapees!!!!
Get 'em!!
TUMP
TUMP
TUMP
TUMP
!!
Lisanna, you go on ahead!!
But...
You find Mira!!!!
Right!
WHOOSH
KAKK

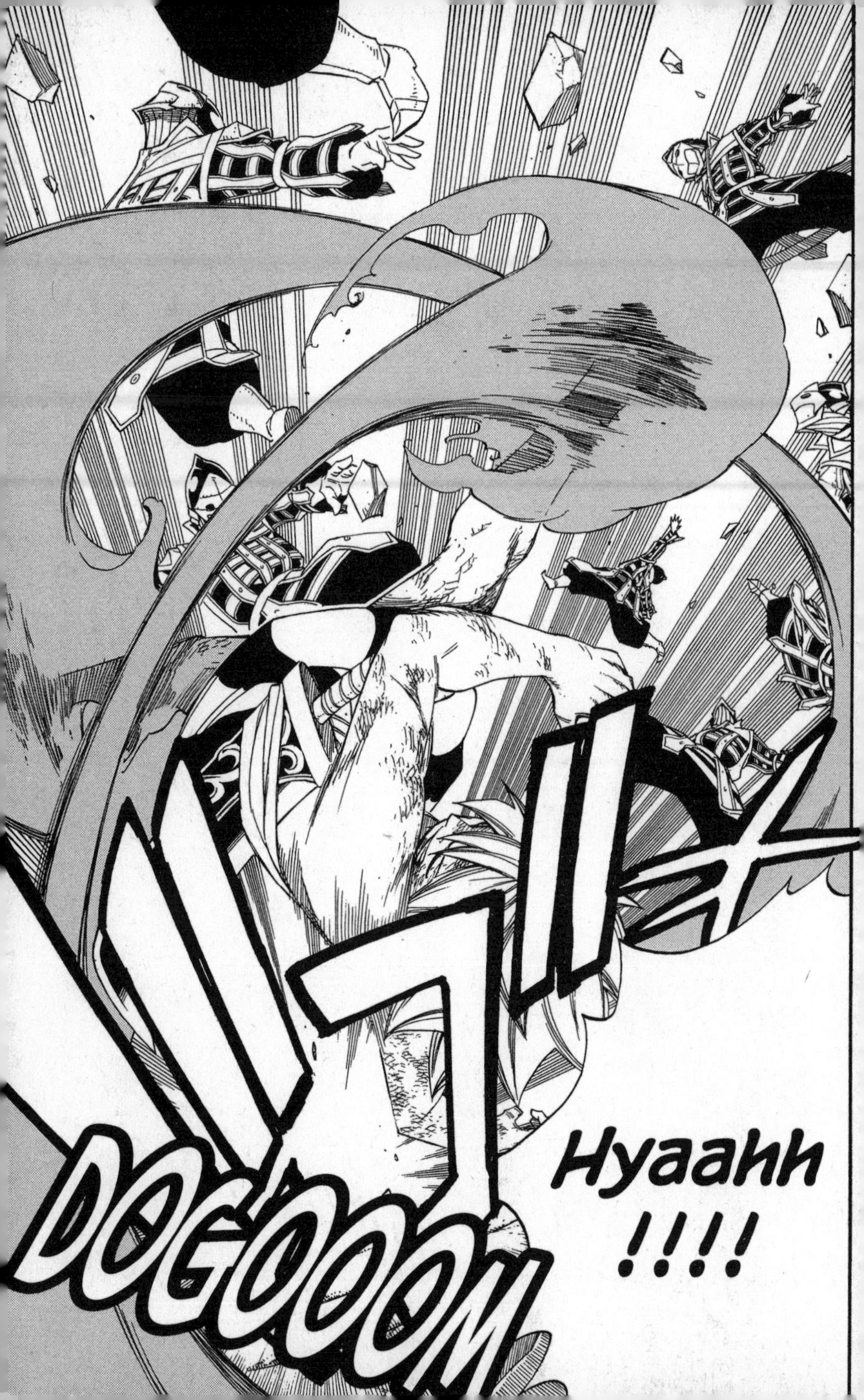
DOGOOOM
Hyaahh
!!!!

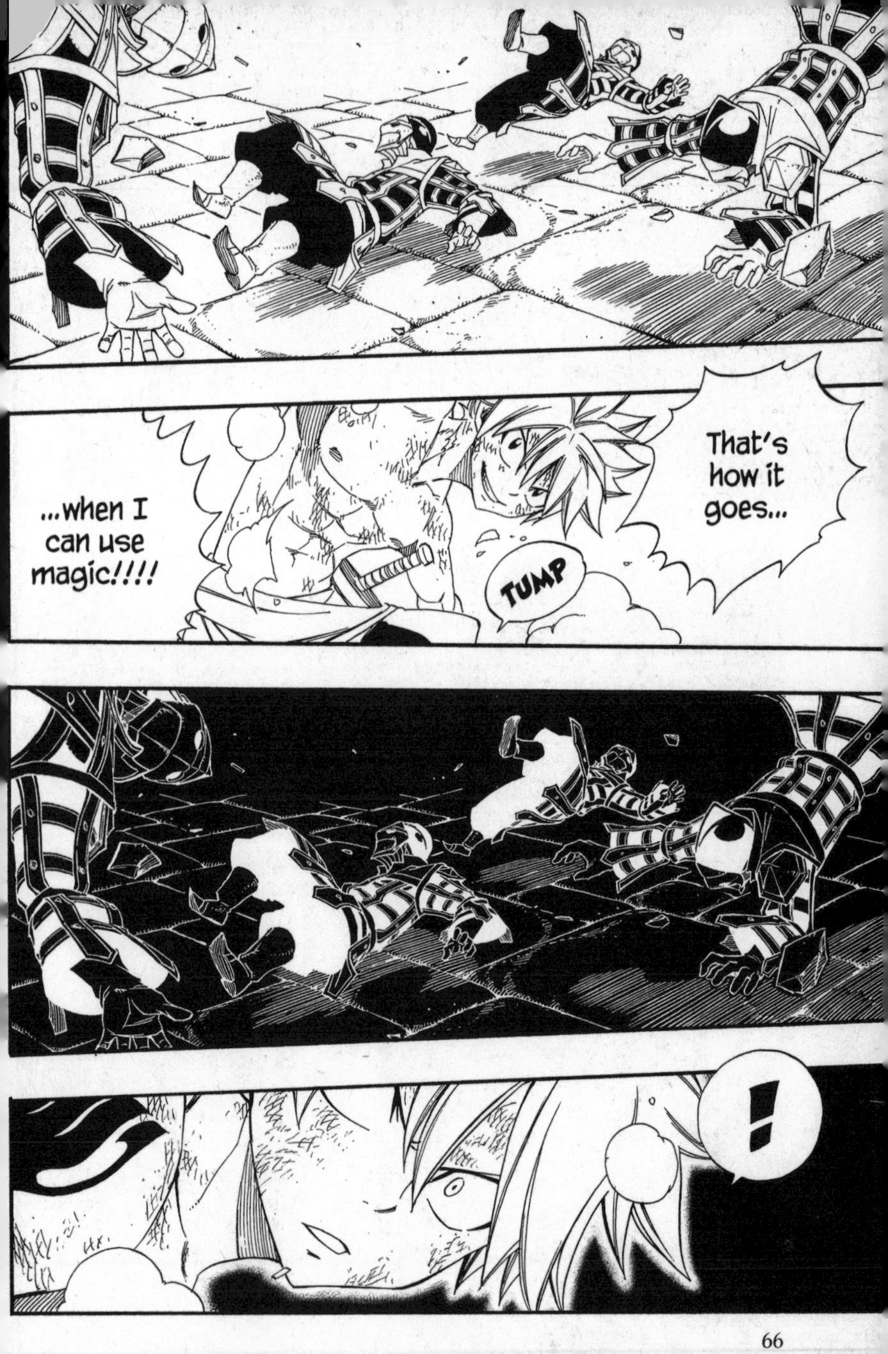
That's how it goes...
TUMP
...when I can use magic!!!!
!

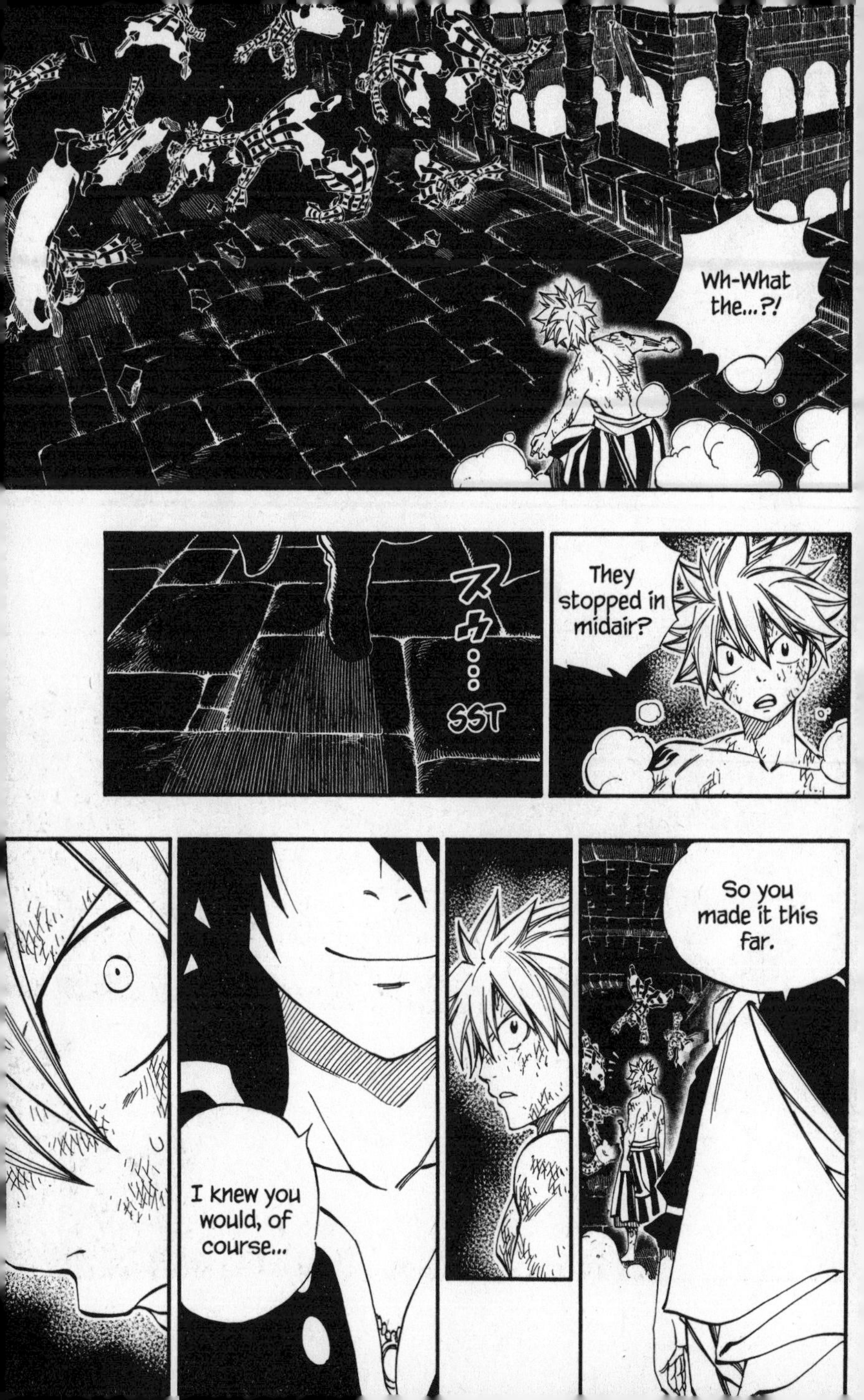
Wh-What the...?!
They stopped in midair?
スゥ…
SST
So you made it this far.
I knew you would, of course...

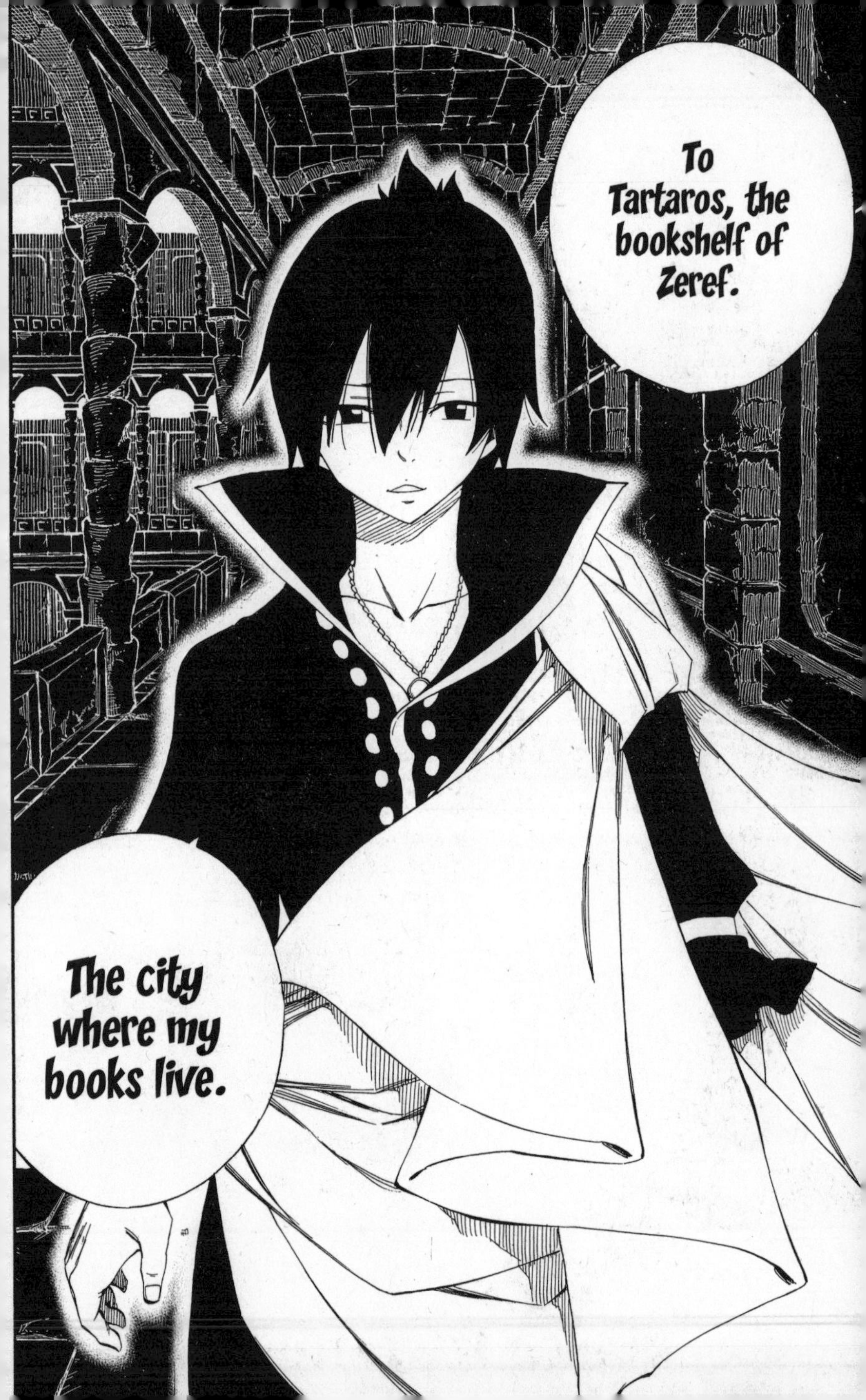
To Tartaros, the bookshelf of Zeref.
The city where my books live.

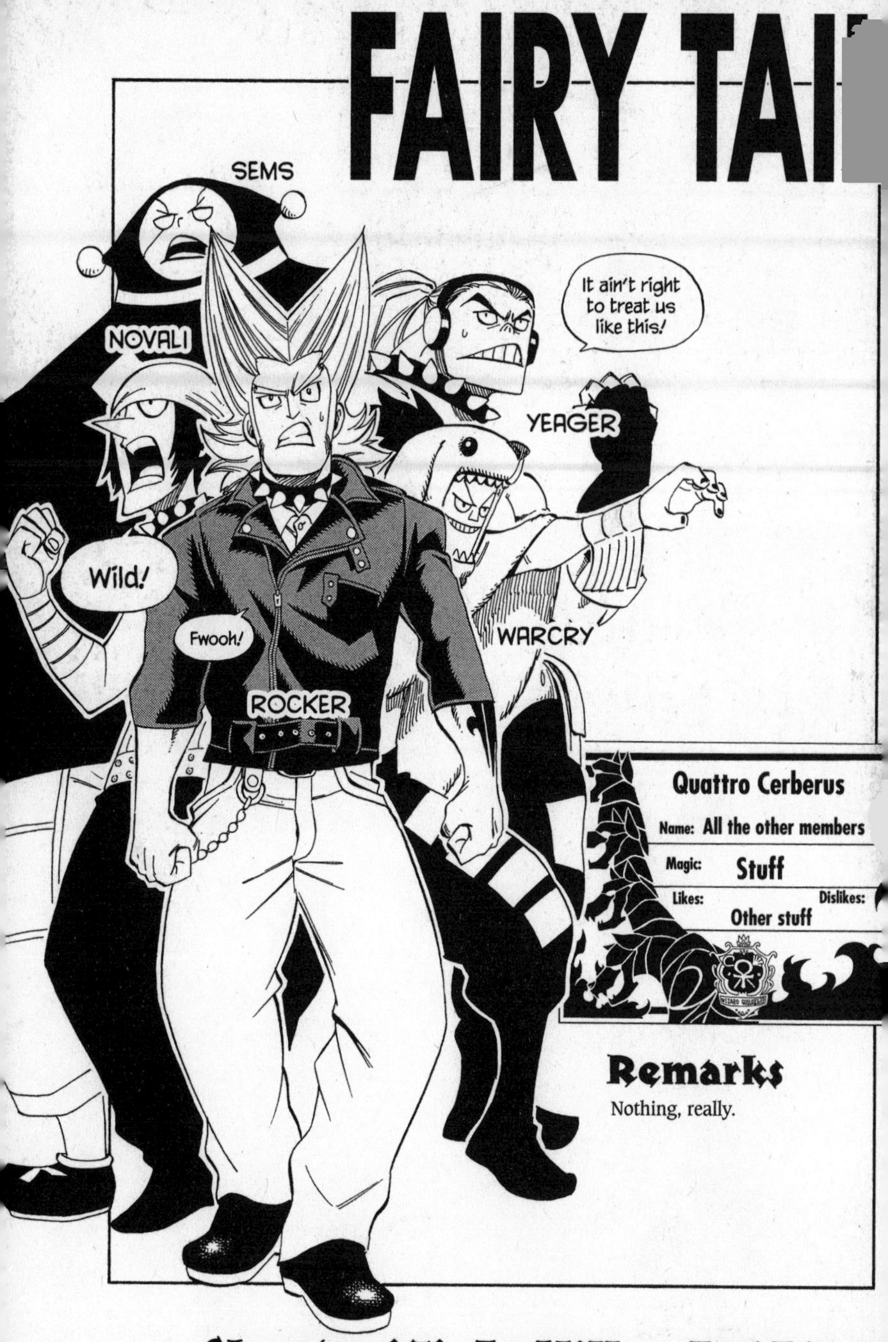

Chapter 373: To Kill or Let Live

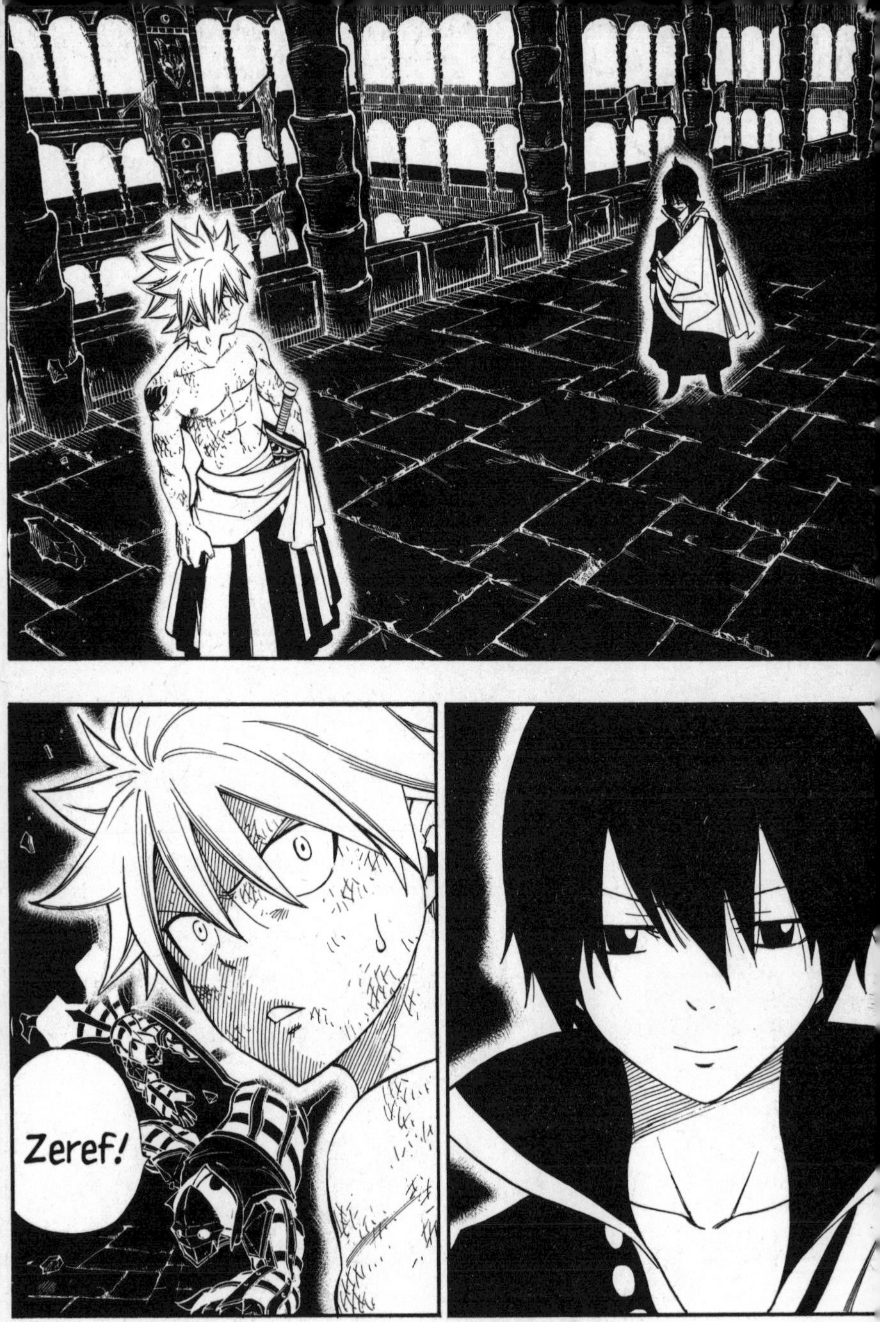
Zeref!

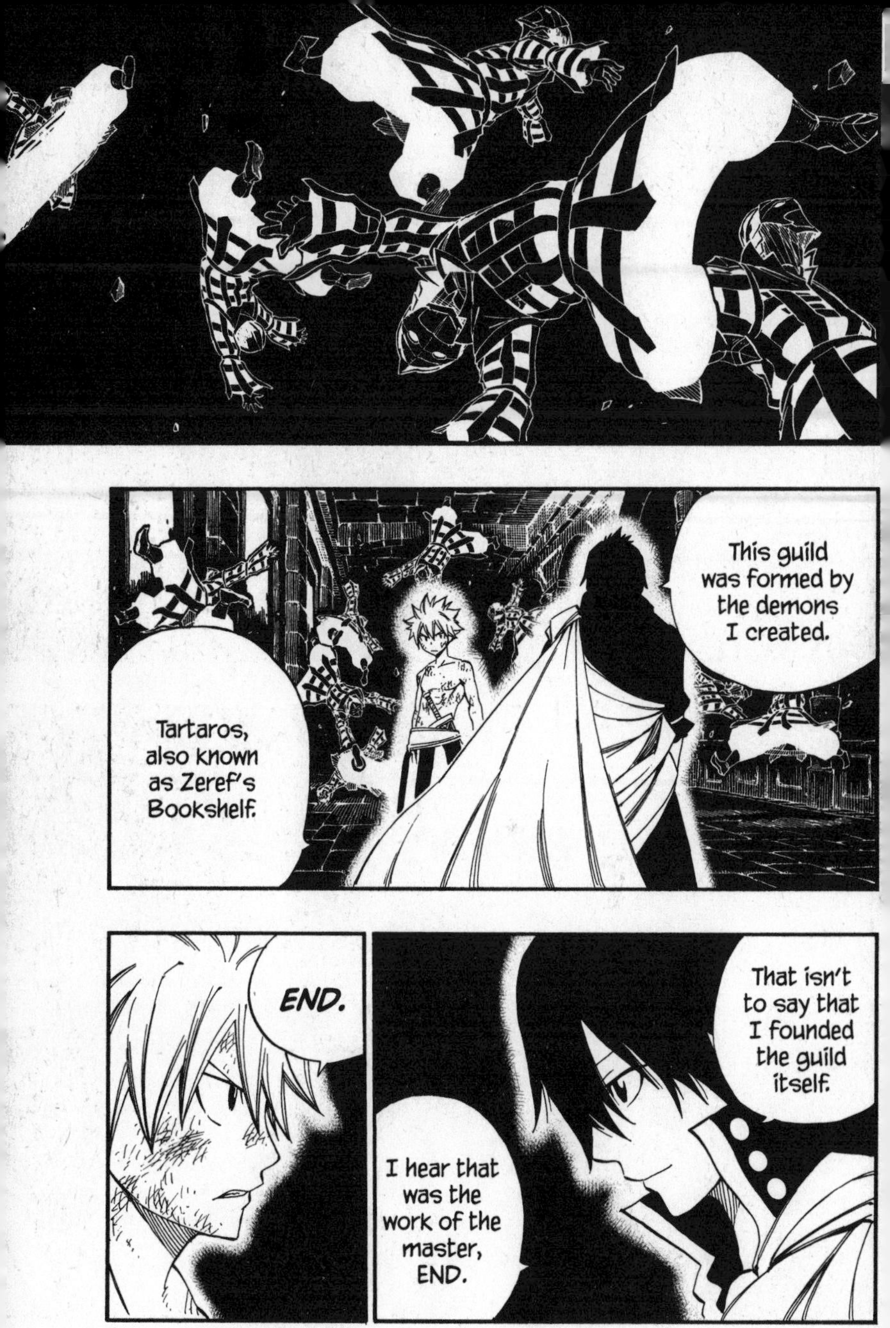
This guild was formed by the demons I created.
Tartaros, also known as Zeref's Bookshelf.
That isn't to say that I founded the guild itself.
I hear that was the work of the master, END.
END.

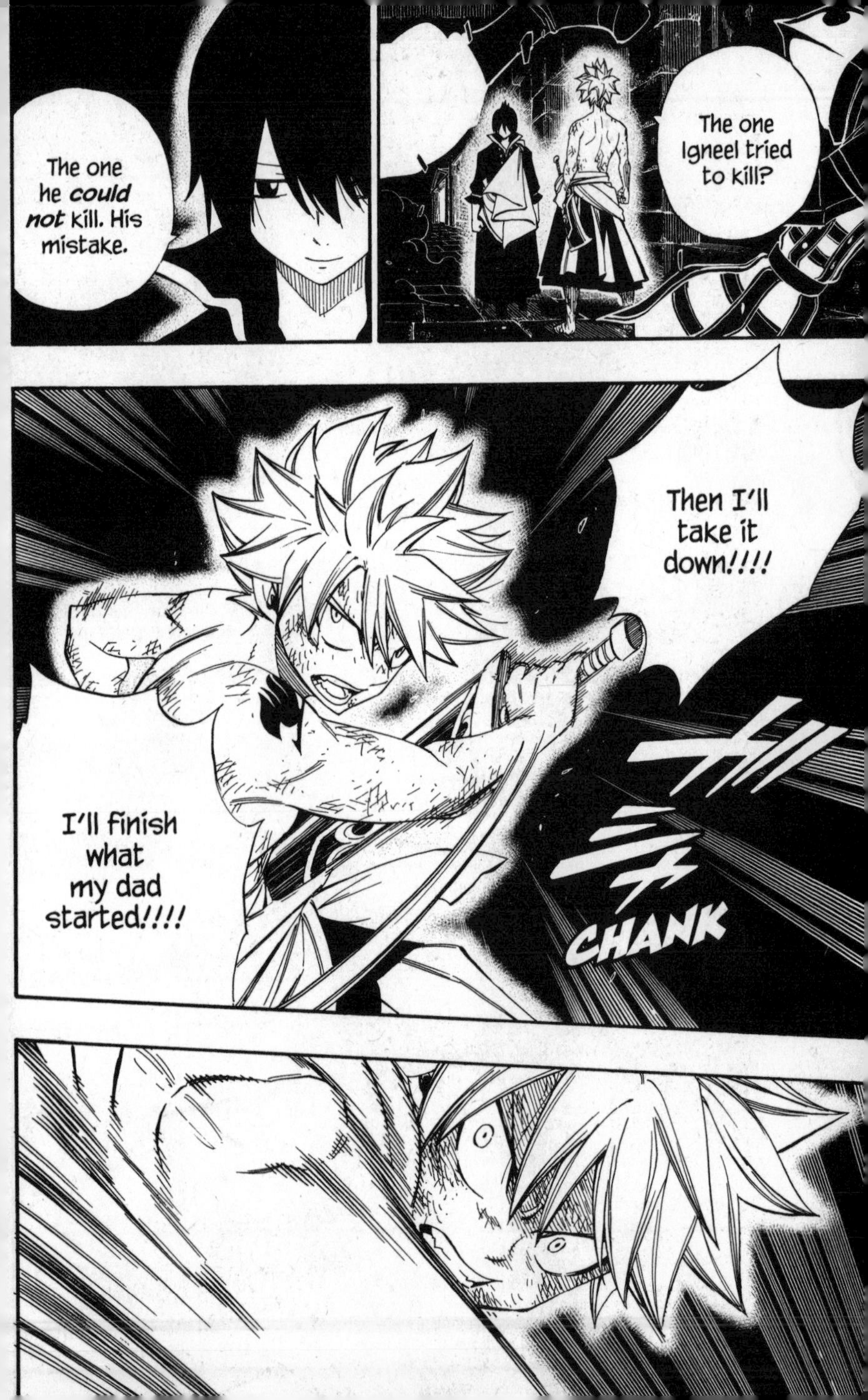
The one Igneel tried to kill?
The one he *could not* kill. His mistake.
Then I'll take it down!!!!
I'll finish what my dad started!!!!
CHANK

I believe you could.

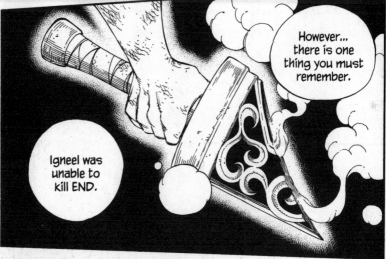

However... there is one thing you must remember.

Igneel was unable to kill END.

END was the most powerful demon I created.

Huh?

The time will come when you will need to make a decision.

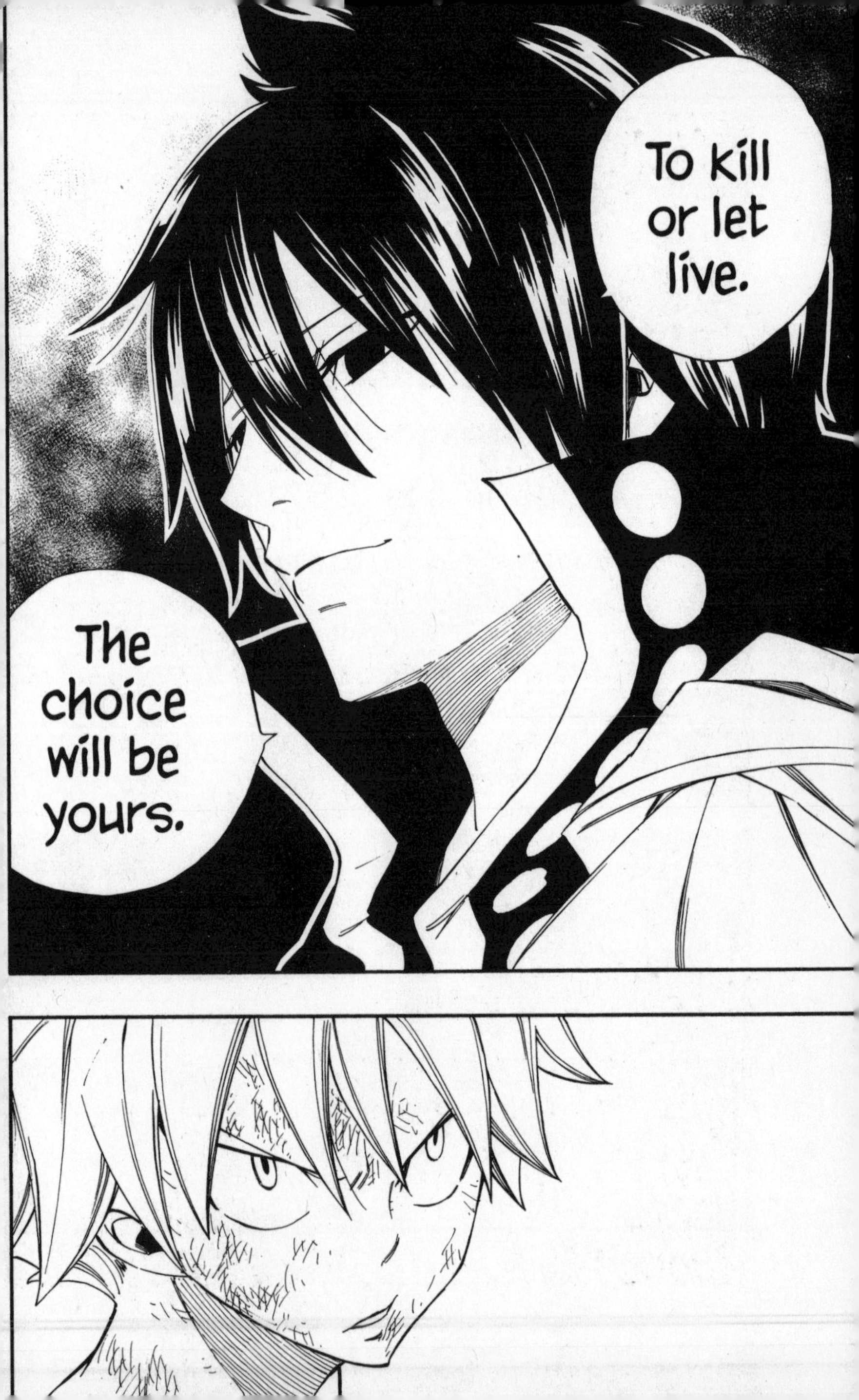
To kill or let live.
The choice will be yours.

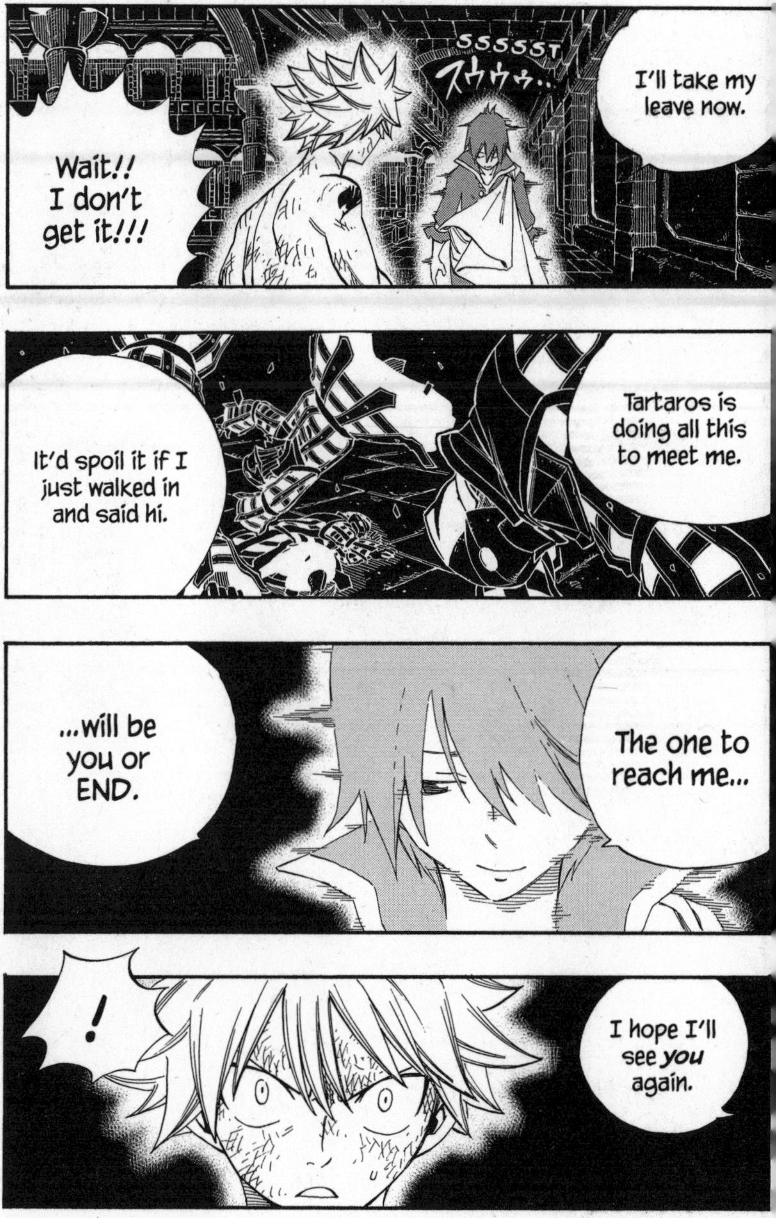
I'll take my leave now.
SSSSST
スウウウ…
Wait!! I don't get it!!!
Tartaros is doing all this to meet me.
It'd spoil it if I just walked in and said hi.
The one to reach me...
...will be you or END.
I hope I'll see *you* again.
!

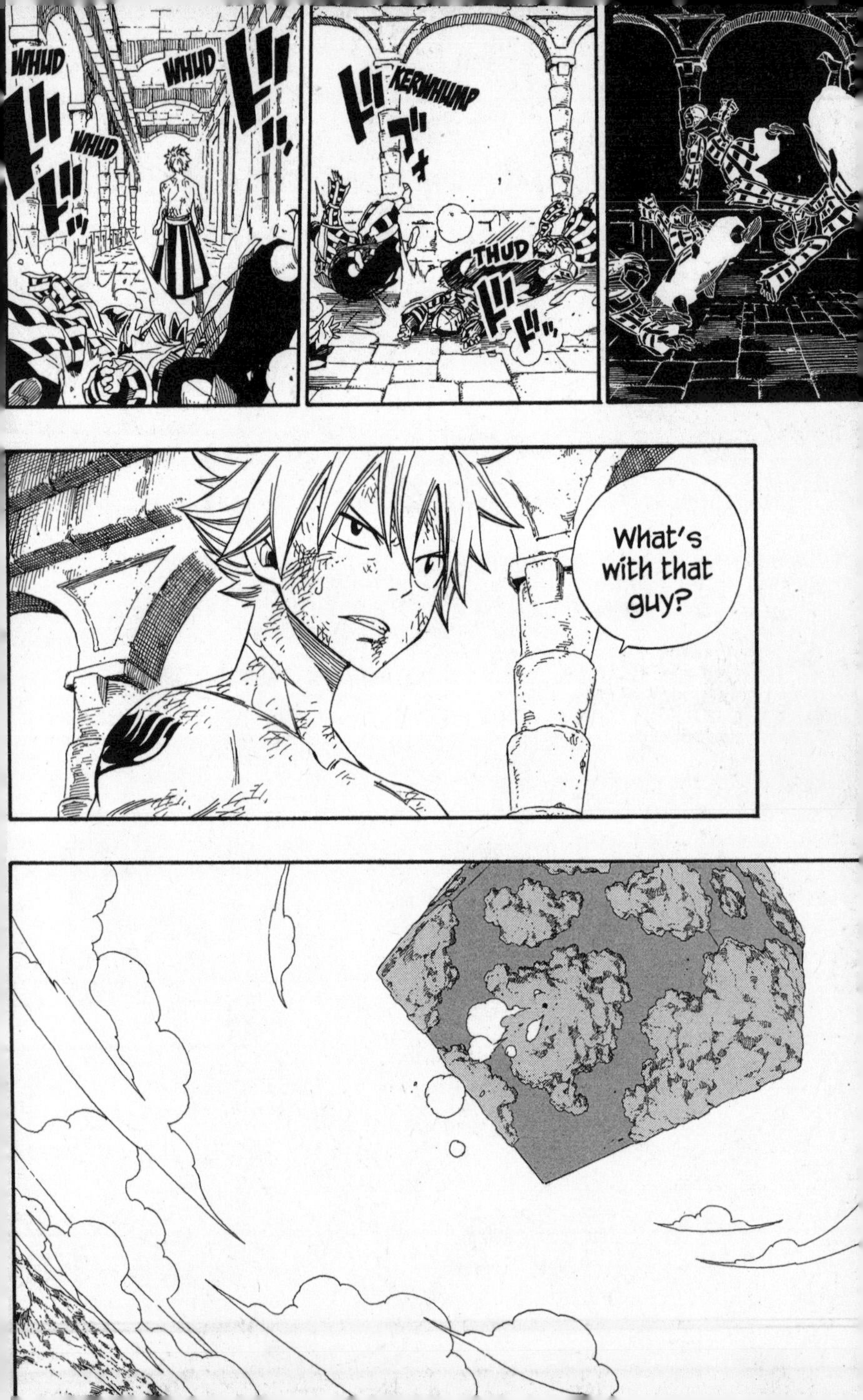
KERWHUMP
THUD
WHUD
WHUD
WHUD
What's with that guy?

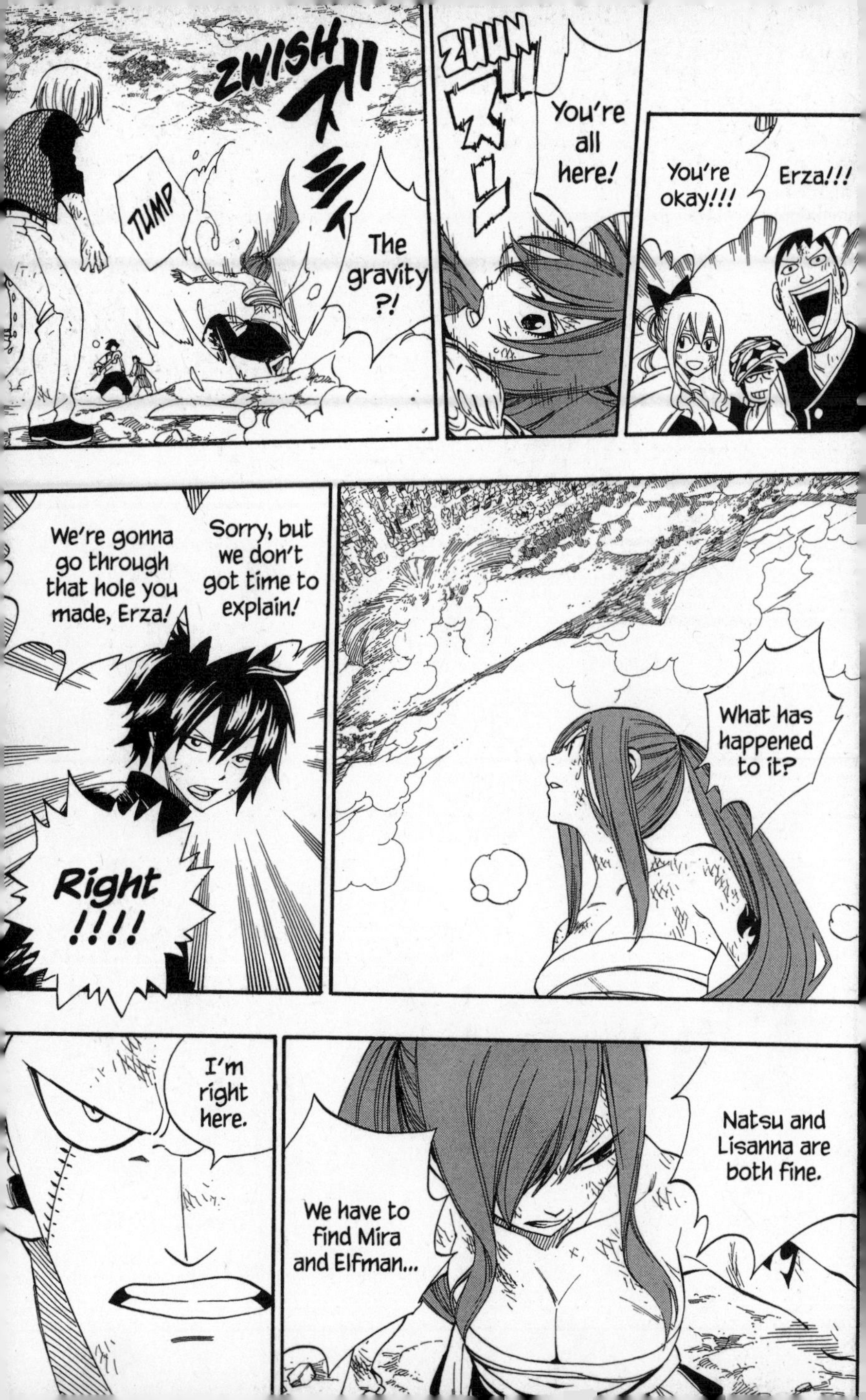
Erza!!!
You're okay!!!
ZUUN
You're all here!
ZWISH
The gravity?!
TUMP
What has happened to it?
Sorry, but we don't got time to explain!
We're gonna go through that hole you made, Erza!
Right!!!!
Natsu and Lisanna are both fine.
We have to find Mira and Elfman...
I'm right here.

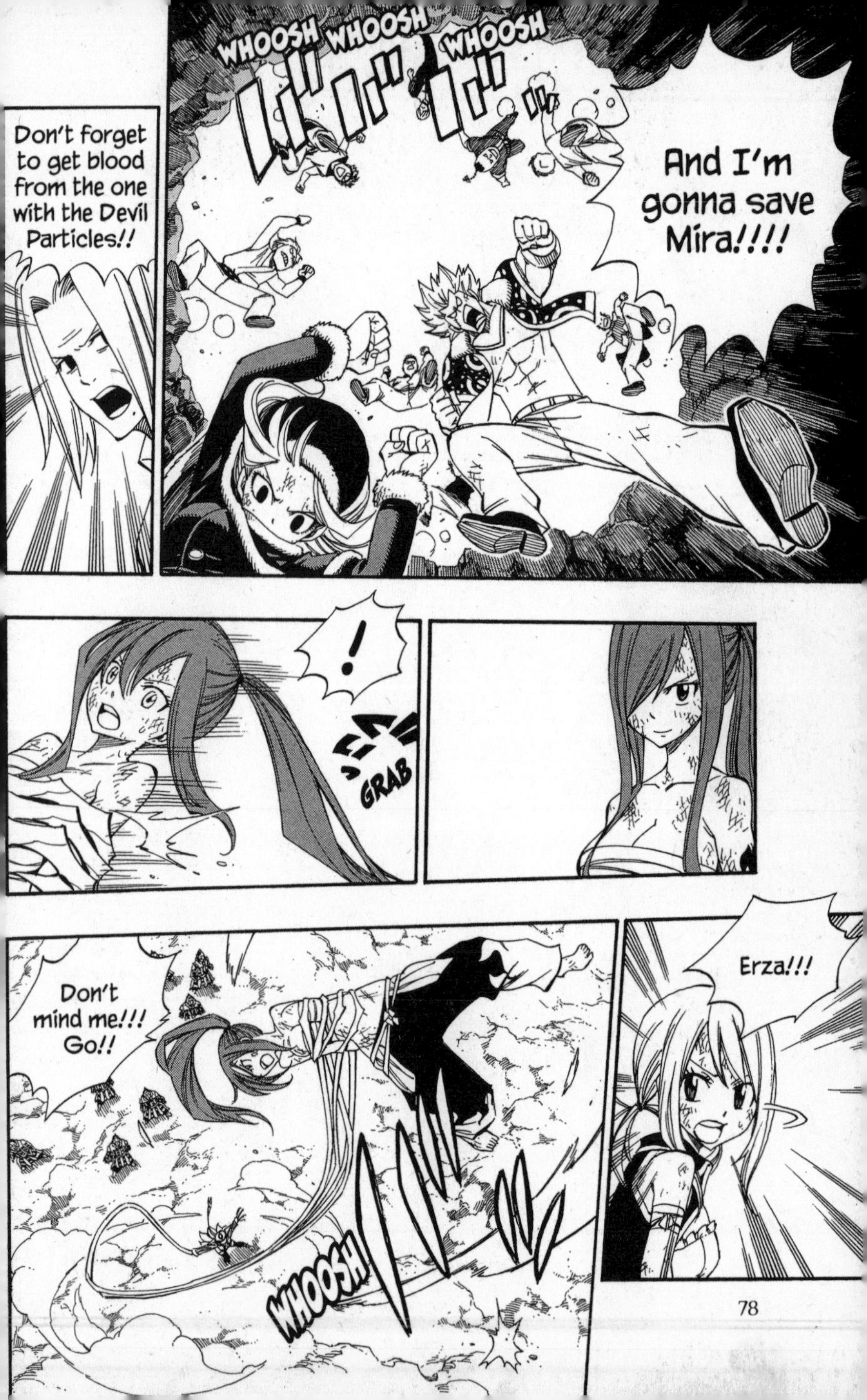
WHOOSH WHOOSH WHOOSH
And I'm gonna save Mira!!!!
Don't forget to get blood from the one with the Devil Particles!!
!
GRAB
Erza!!!
Don't mind me!!! Go!!
WHOOSH

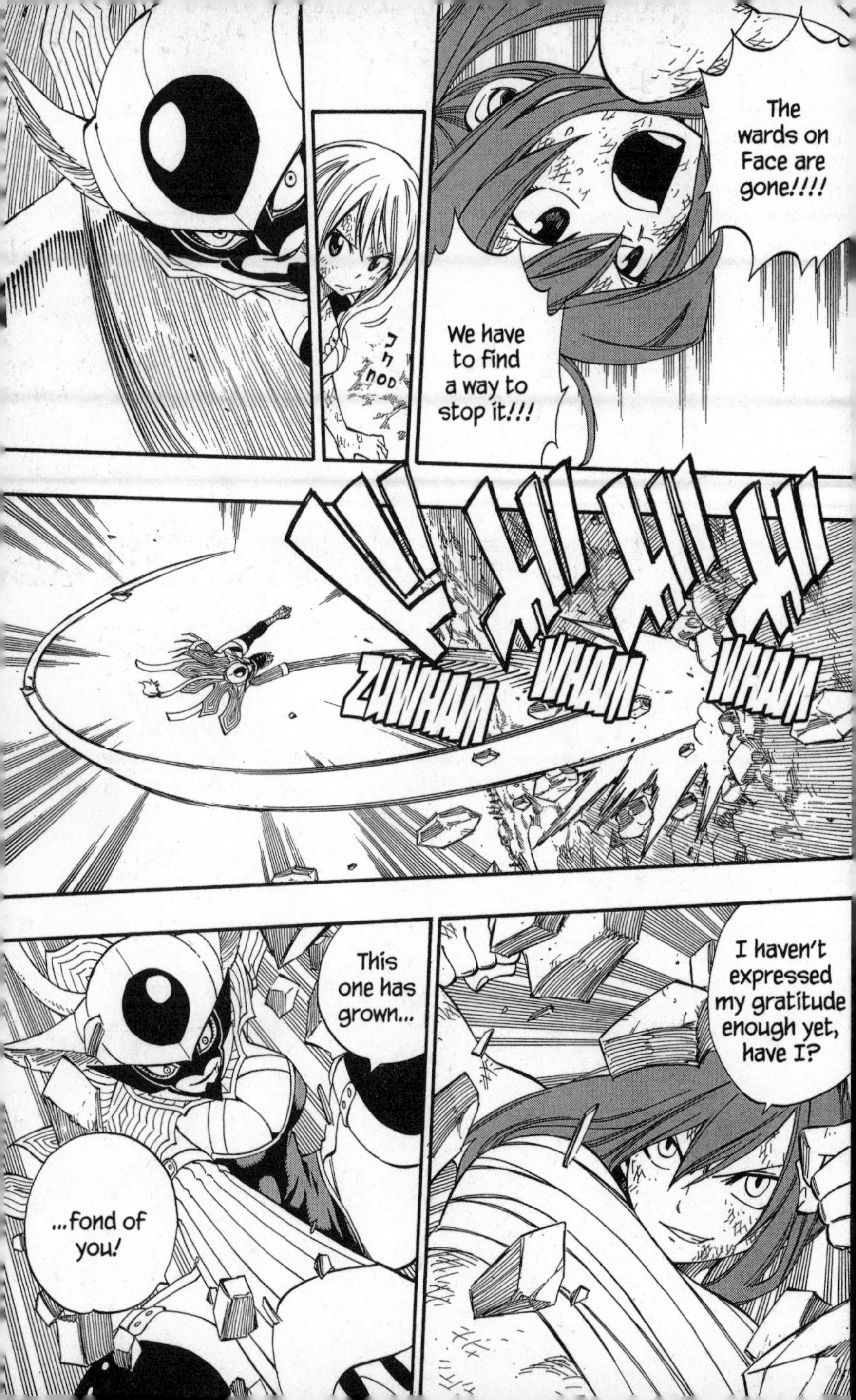

The wards on Face are gone!!!!
We have to find a way to stop it!!!
NOD
WHAM
WHAM
ZUWHAM
I haven't expressed my gratitude enough yet, have I?
This one has grown...
...fond of you!

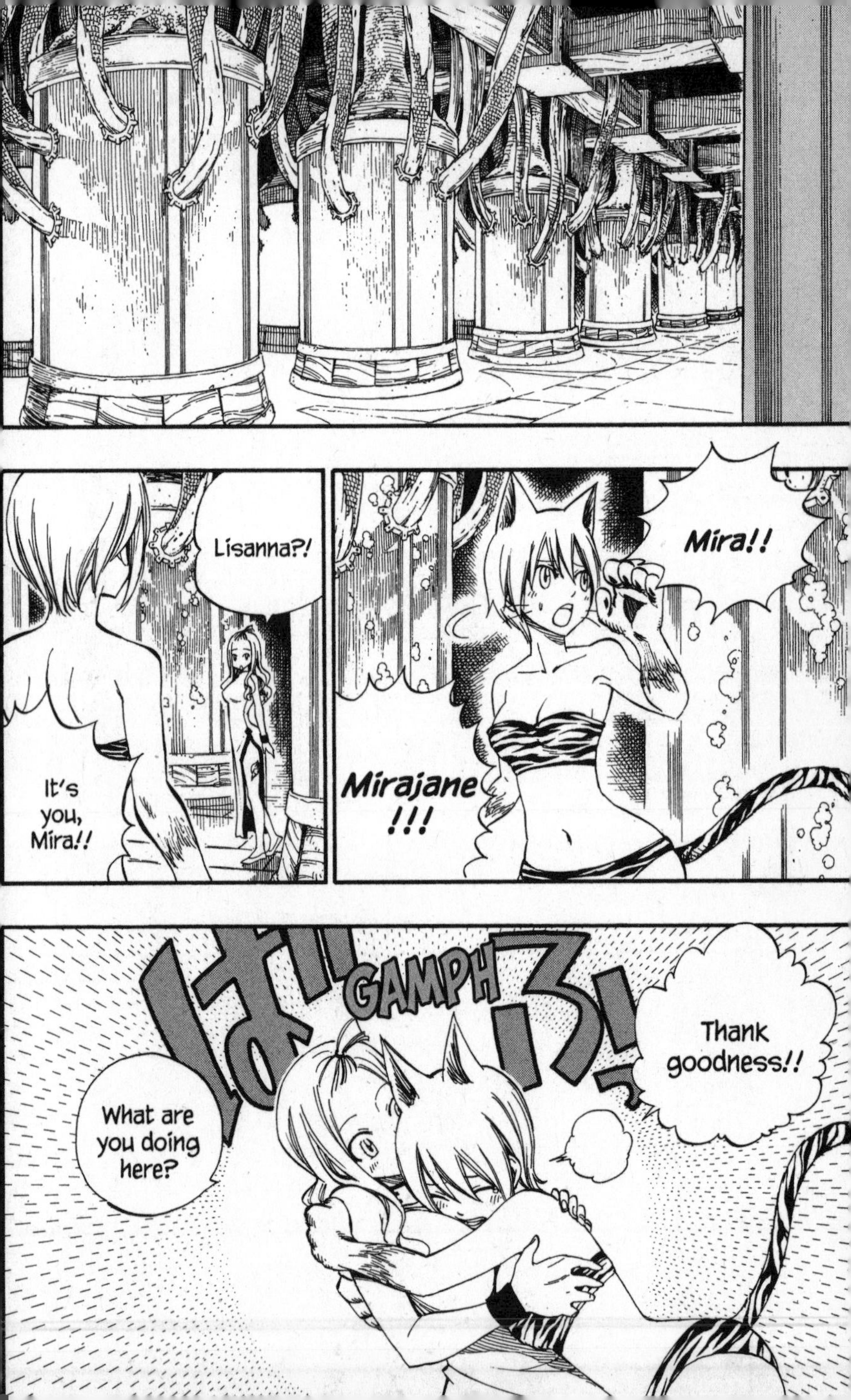
Mira!!
Mirajane!!!
Lisanna?!
It's you, Mira!!
GAMPH
Thank goodness!!
What are you doing here?

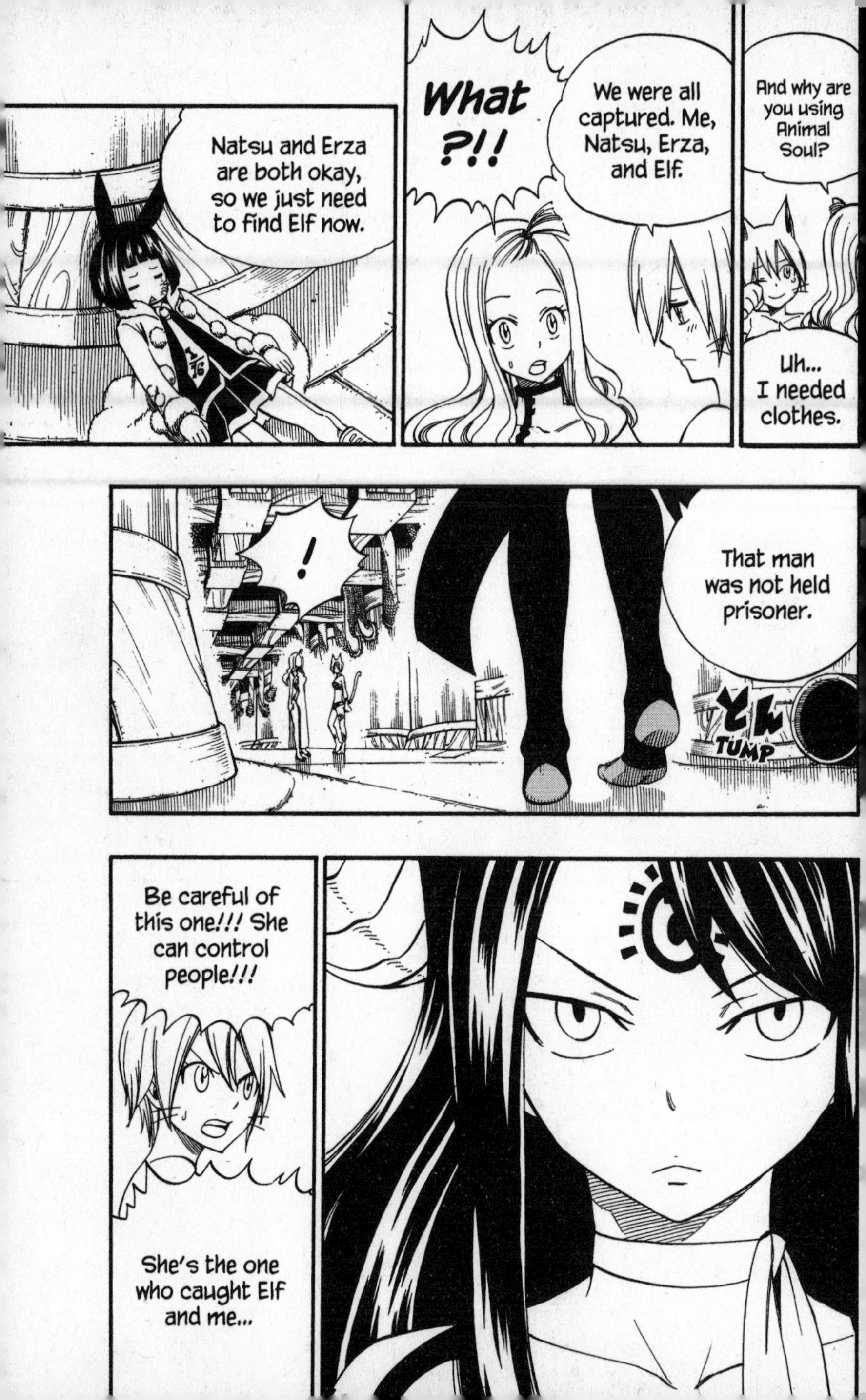
And why are you using Animal Soul?
Uh... I needed clothes.
We were all captured. Me, Natsu, Erza, and Elf.
What?!!
Natsu and Erza are both okay, so we just need to find Elf now.
That man was not held prisoner.
TUMP
!
Be careful of this one!!! She can control people!!!
She's the one who caught Elf and me...

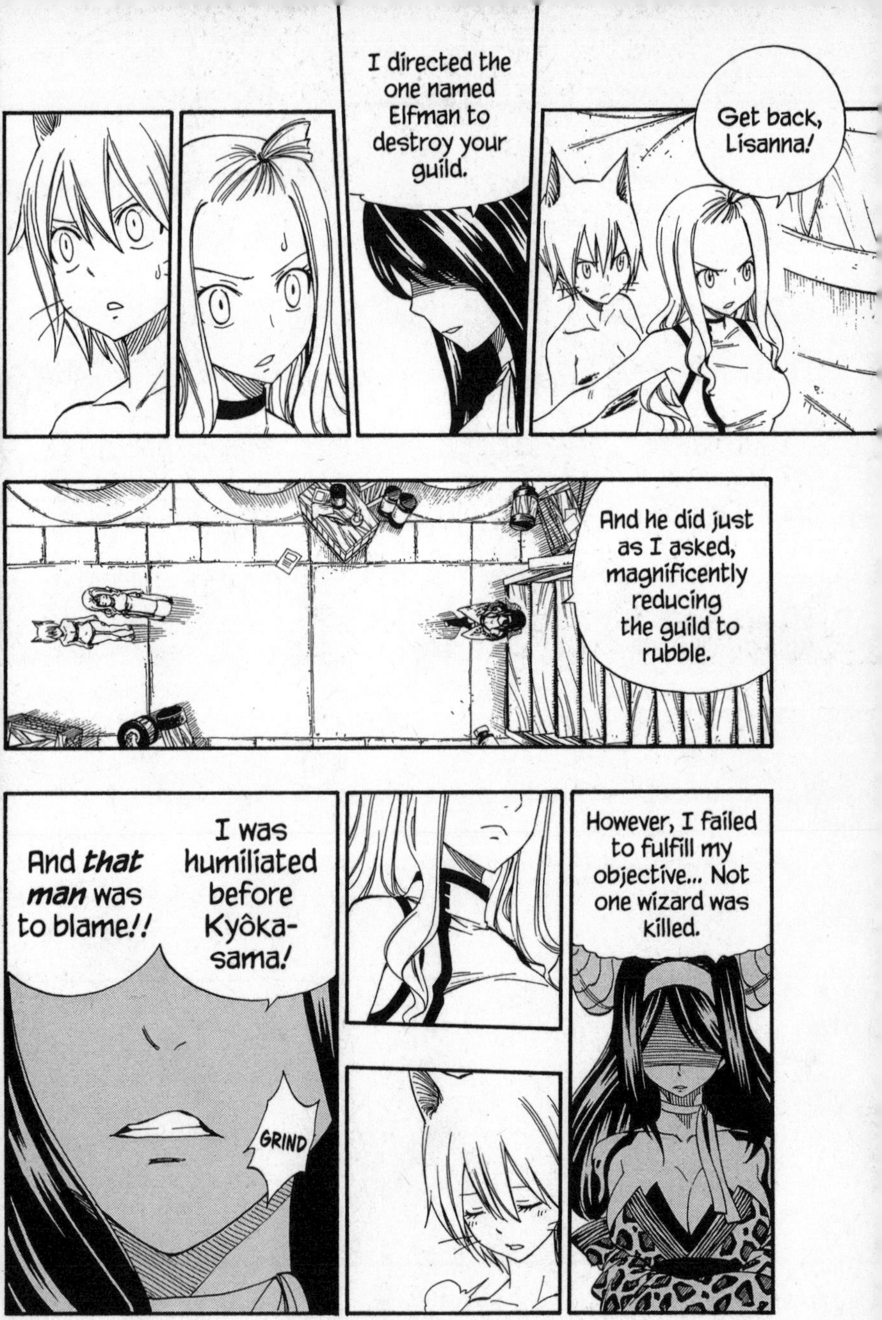
Get back, Lisanna!
I directed the one named Elfman to destroy your guild.
And he did just as I asked, magnificently reducing the guild to rubble.
However, I failed to fulfill my objective... Not one wizard was killed.
I was humiliated before Kyôka-sama!
And *that man* was to blame!!
GRIND

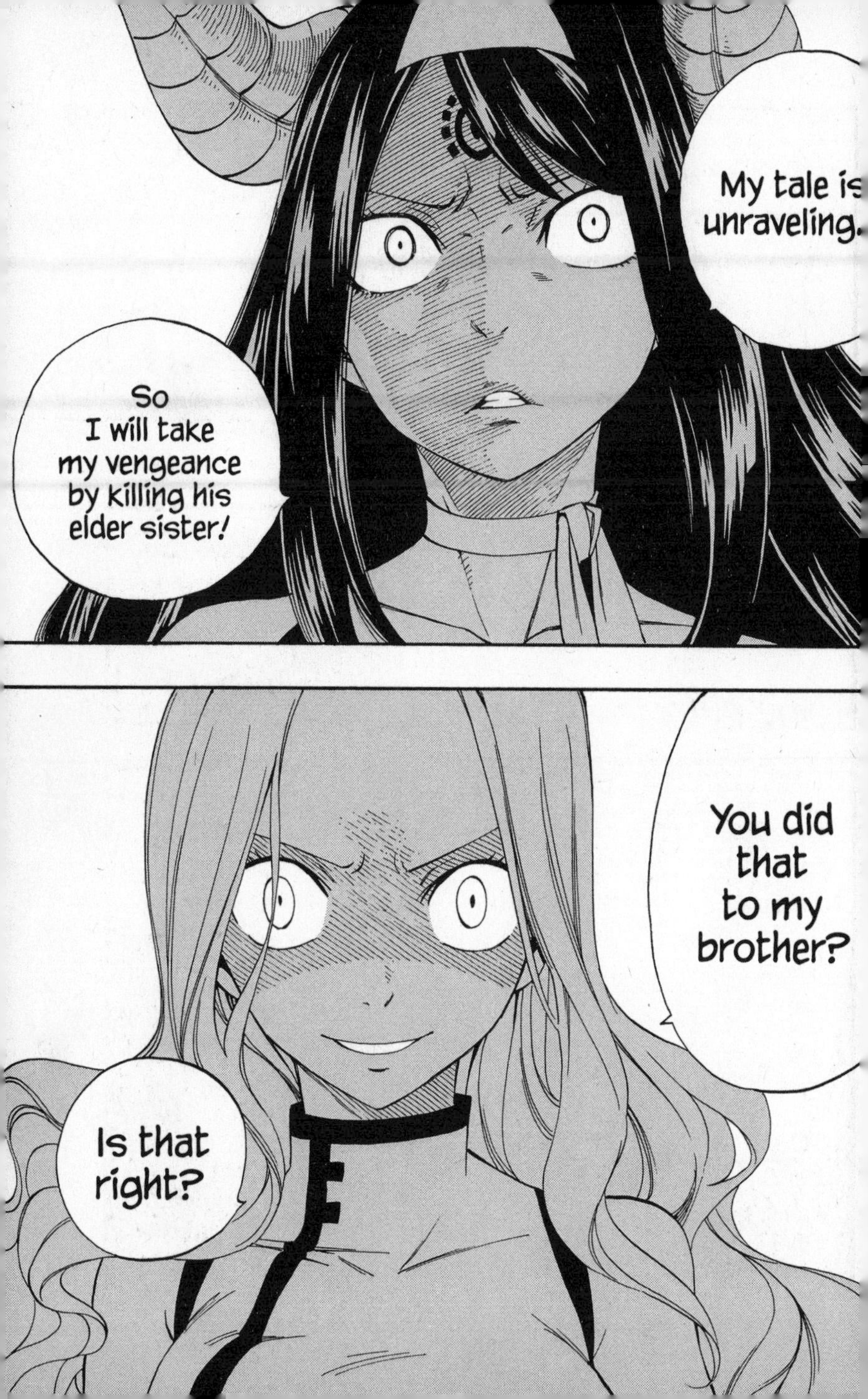
My tale is unraveling.
So I will take my vengeance by killing his elder sister!
You did that to my brother?
Is that right?

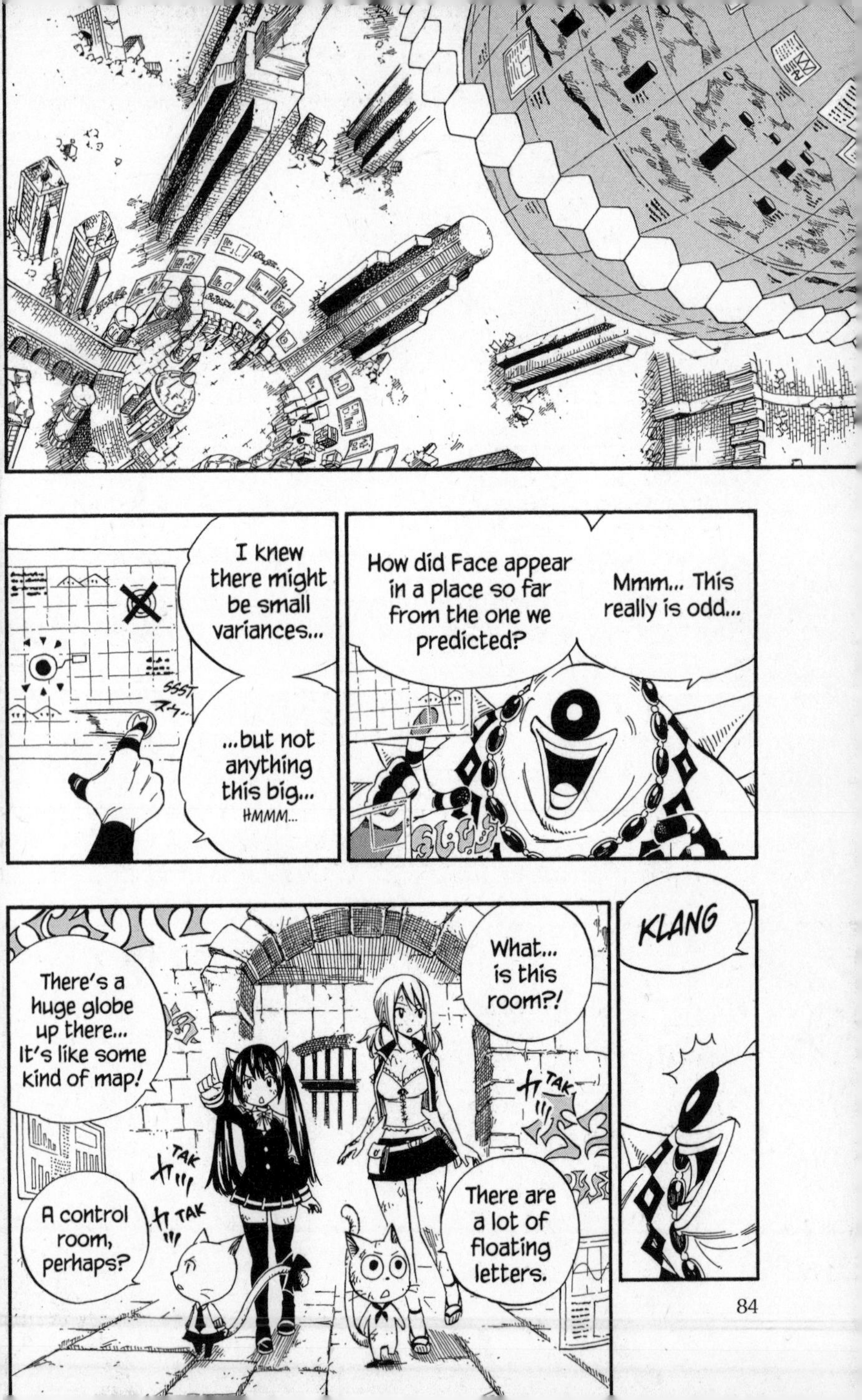

Mmm... This really is odd...
How did Face appear in a place so far from the one we predicted?
I knew there might be small variances...
SSST
...but not anything this big...
HMMM...
KLANG
What... is this room?!
TAK
There's a huge globe up there... It's like some kind of map!
TAK
There are a lot of floating letters.
TAK
A control room, perhaps?

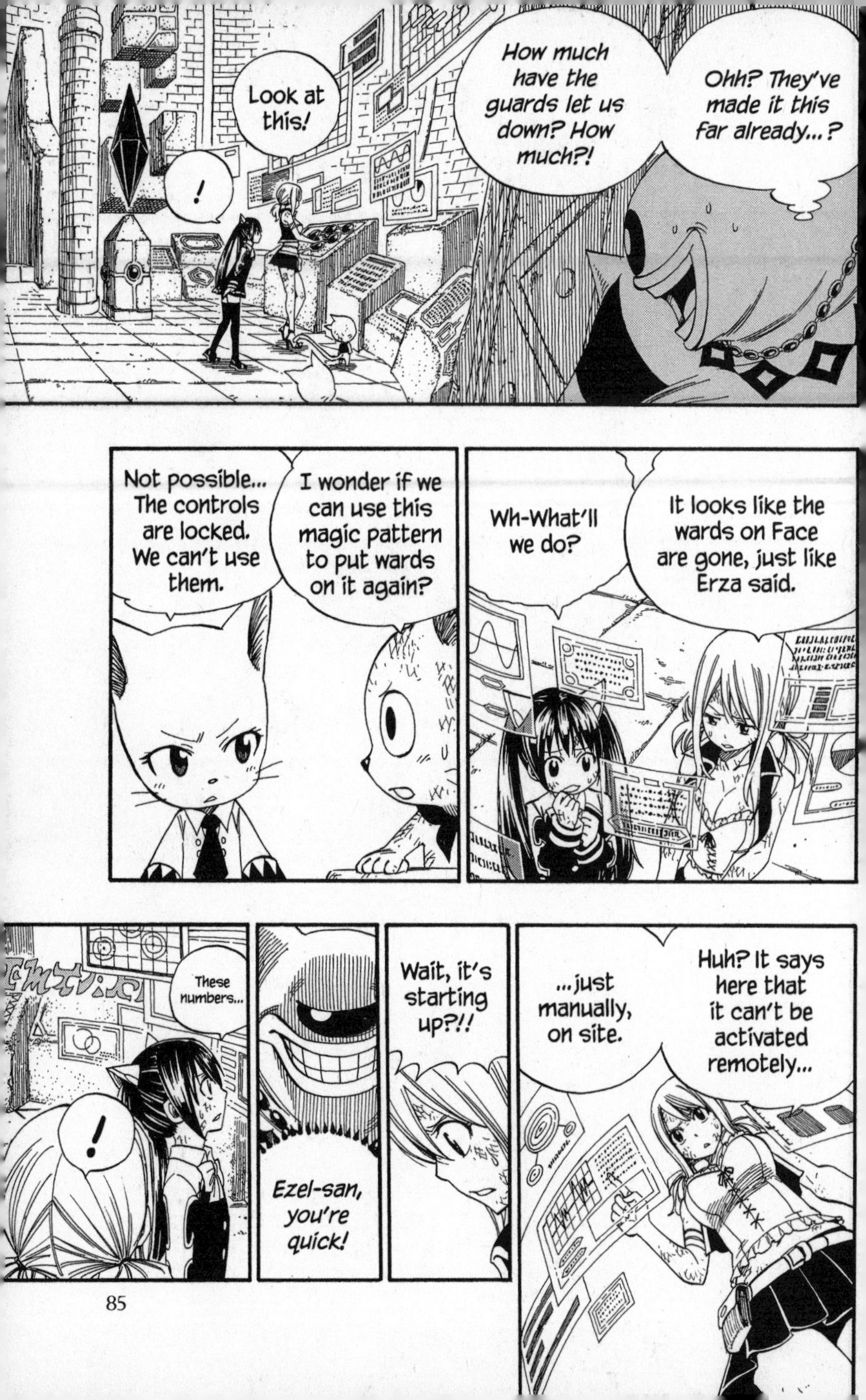
Ohh? They've made it this far already...?
How much have the guards let us down? How much?!
Look at this!
!
It looks like the wards on Face are gone, just like Erza said.
Wh-What'll we do?
I wonder if we can use this magic pattern to put wards on it again?
Not possible... The controls are locked. We can't use them.
Huh? It says here that it can't be activated remotely...
...just manually, on site.
Wait, it's starting up?!!
Ezel-san, you're quick!
These numbers...
!

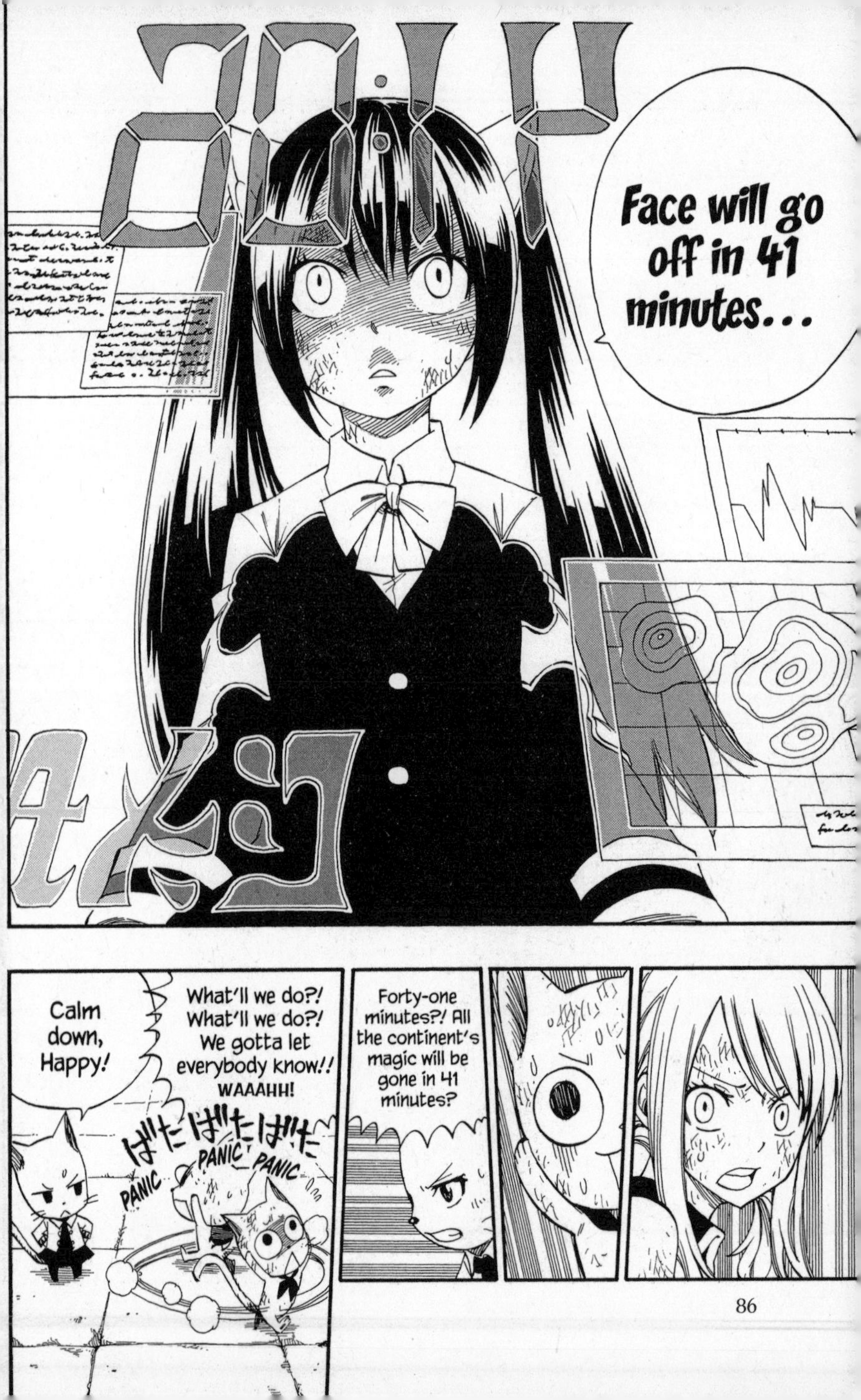
Face will go off in 41 minutes...
Forty-one minutes?! All the continent's magic will be gone in 41 minutes?
What'll we do?! What'll we do?! We gotta let everybody know!! WAAAHH!
Calm down, Happy!
ばたばたばた
PANIC PANIC PANIC

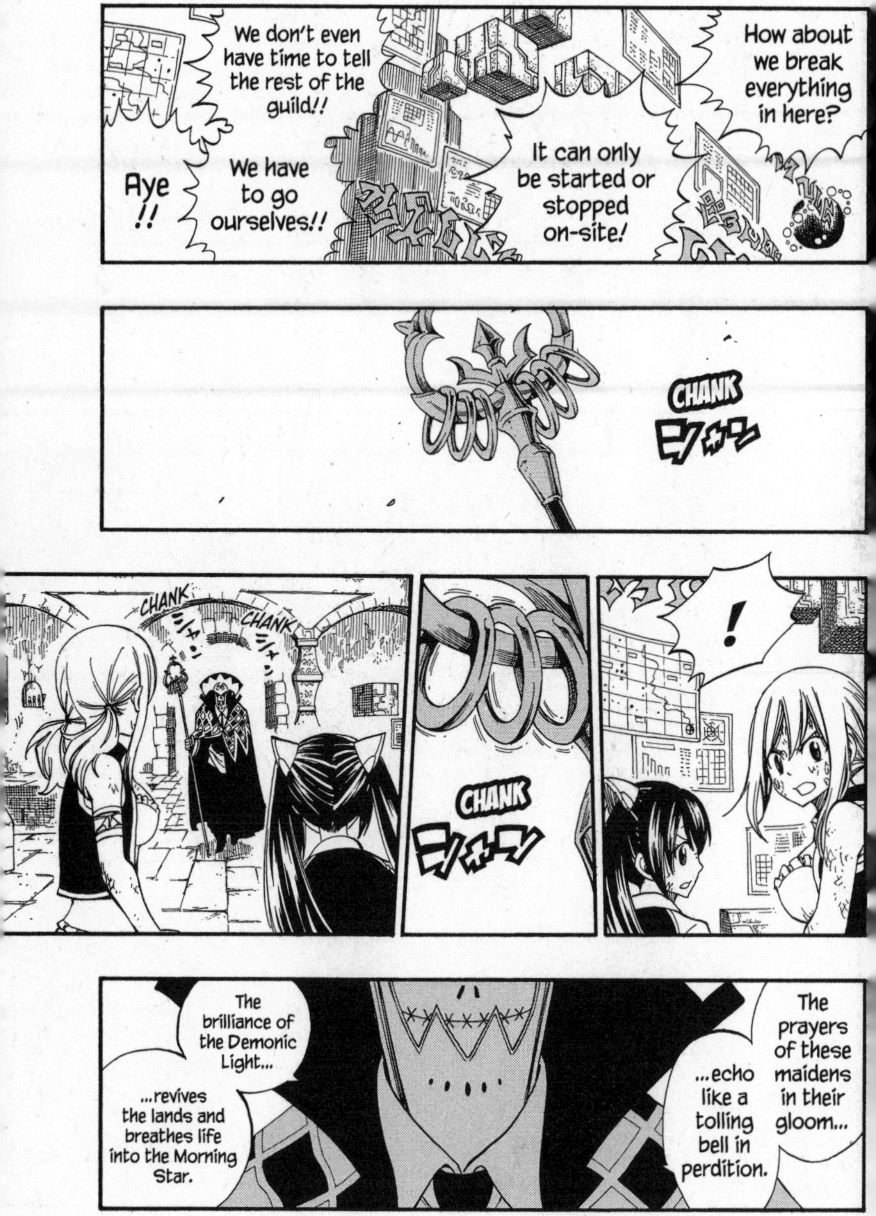
How about we break everything in here?
It can only be started or stopped on-site!
We don't even have time to tell the rest of the guild!!
We have to go ourselves!!
Aye!!
CHANK
!
CHANK
CHANK
CHANK
The prayers of these maidens in their gloom...
...echo like a tolling bell in perdition.
The brilliance of the Demonic Light...
...revives the lands and breathes life into the Morning Star.

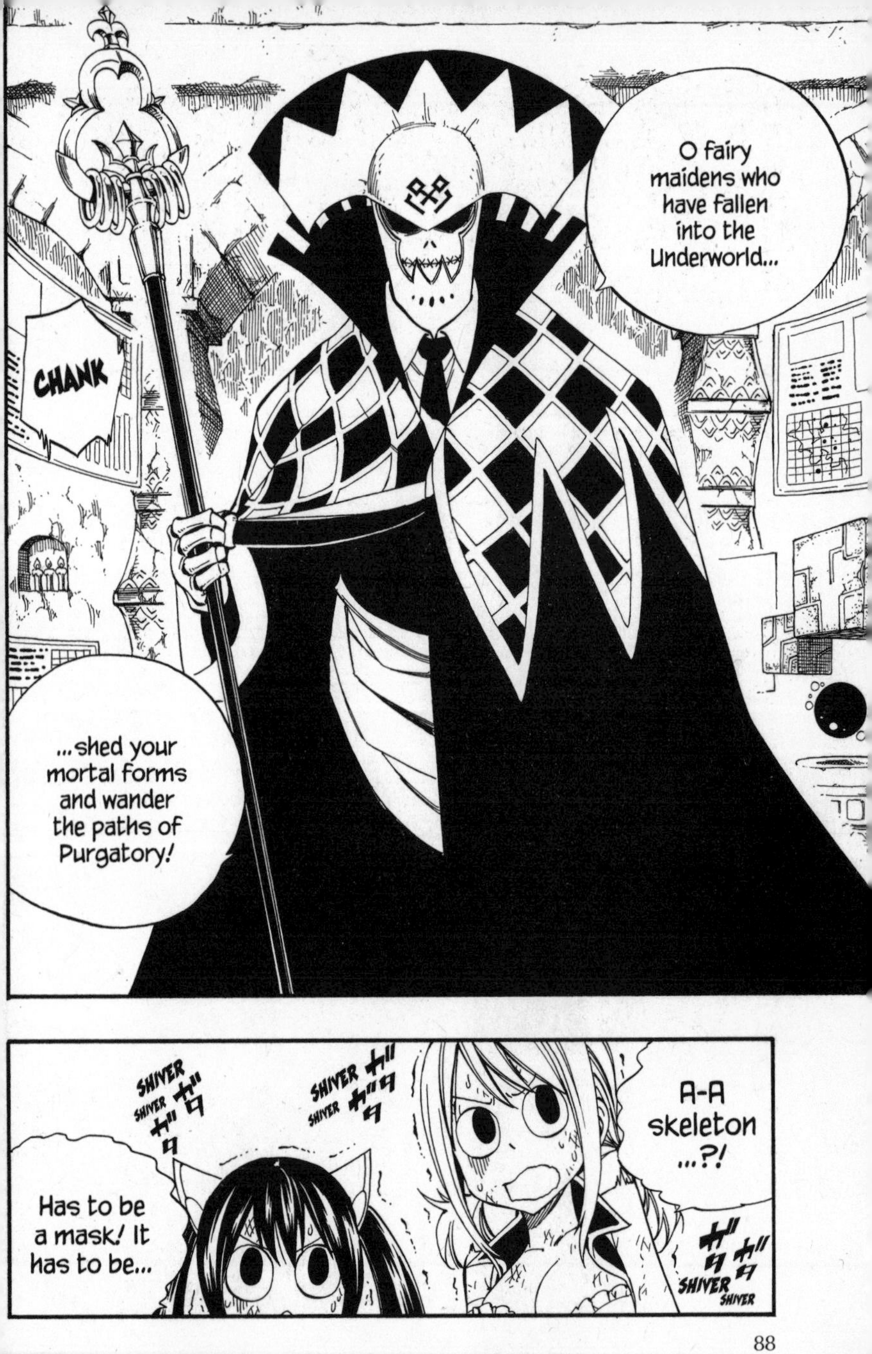
O fairy maidens who have fallen into the Underworld...
CHANK
...shed your mortal forms and wander the paths of Purgatory!
A-A skeleton ...?!
SHIVER SHIVER
SHIVER SHIVER
SHIVER SHIVER
Has to be a mask! It has to be...

フェアリーテイル

Chapter 374: Revolution

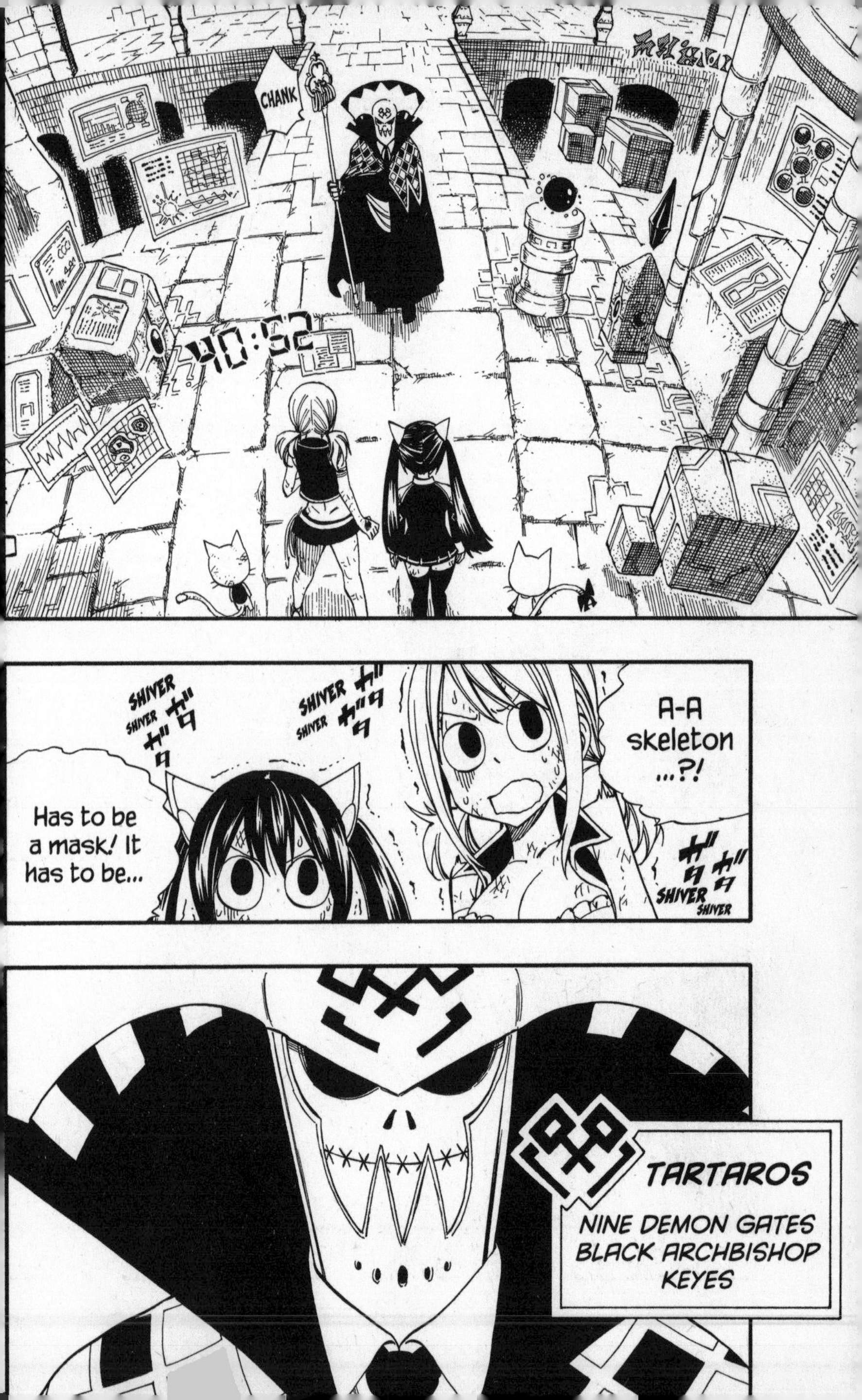
CHANK
40:52
A-A skeleton ...?!
SHIVER SHIVER
SHIVER SHIVER
SHIVER SHIVER
Has to be a mask! It has to be...
TARTAROS
NINE DEMON GATES BLACK ARCHBISHOP KEYES

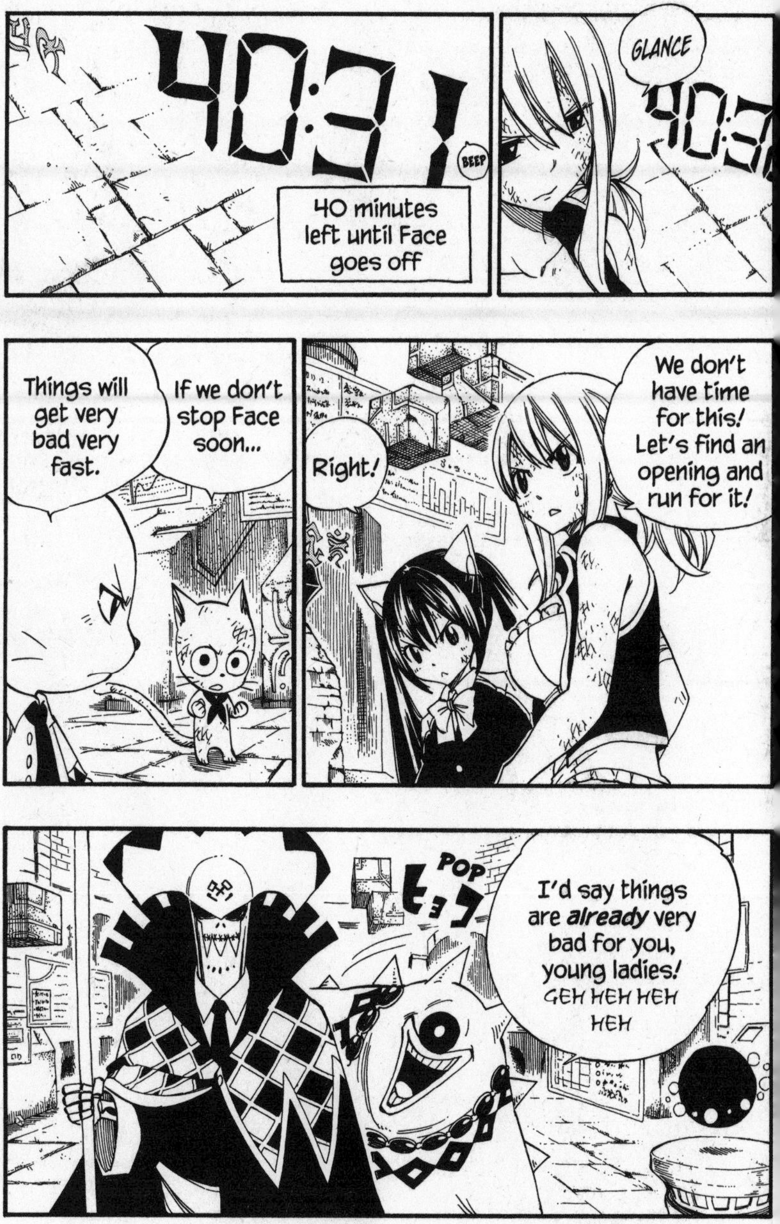
GLANCE
40:31
BEEP
40 minutes left until Face goes off
We don't have time for this! Let's find an opening and run for it!
Right!
If we don't stop Face soon...
Things will get very bad very fast.
POP
I'd say things are *already* very bad for you, young ladies! GEH HEH HEH HEH

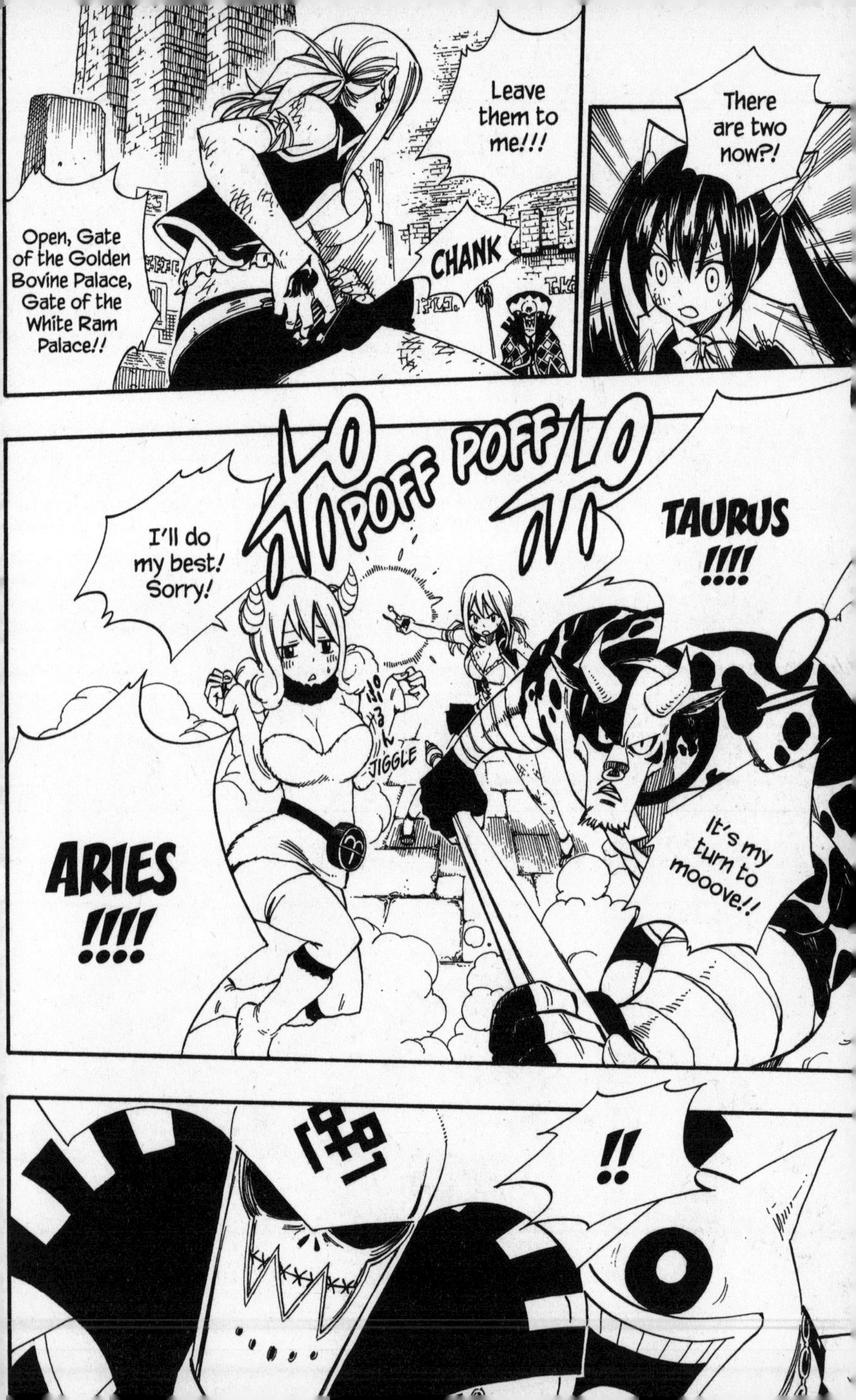
There are two now?!
Leave them to me!!!
CHANK
Open, Gate of the Golden Bovine Palace, Gate of the White Ram Palace!!
POFF POFF
TAURUS !!!!
I'll do my best! Sorry!
It's my turn to mooove!!
JIGGLE
ARIES !!!!
!!

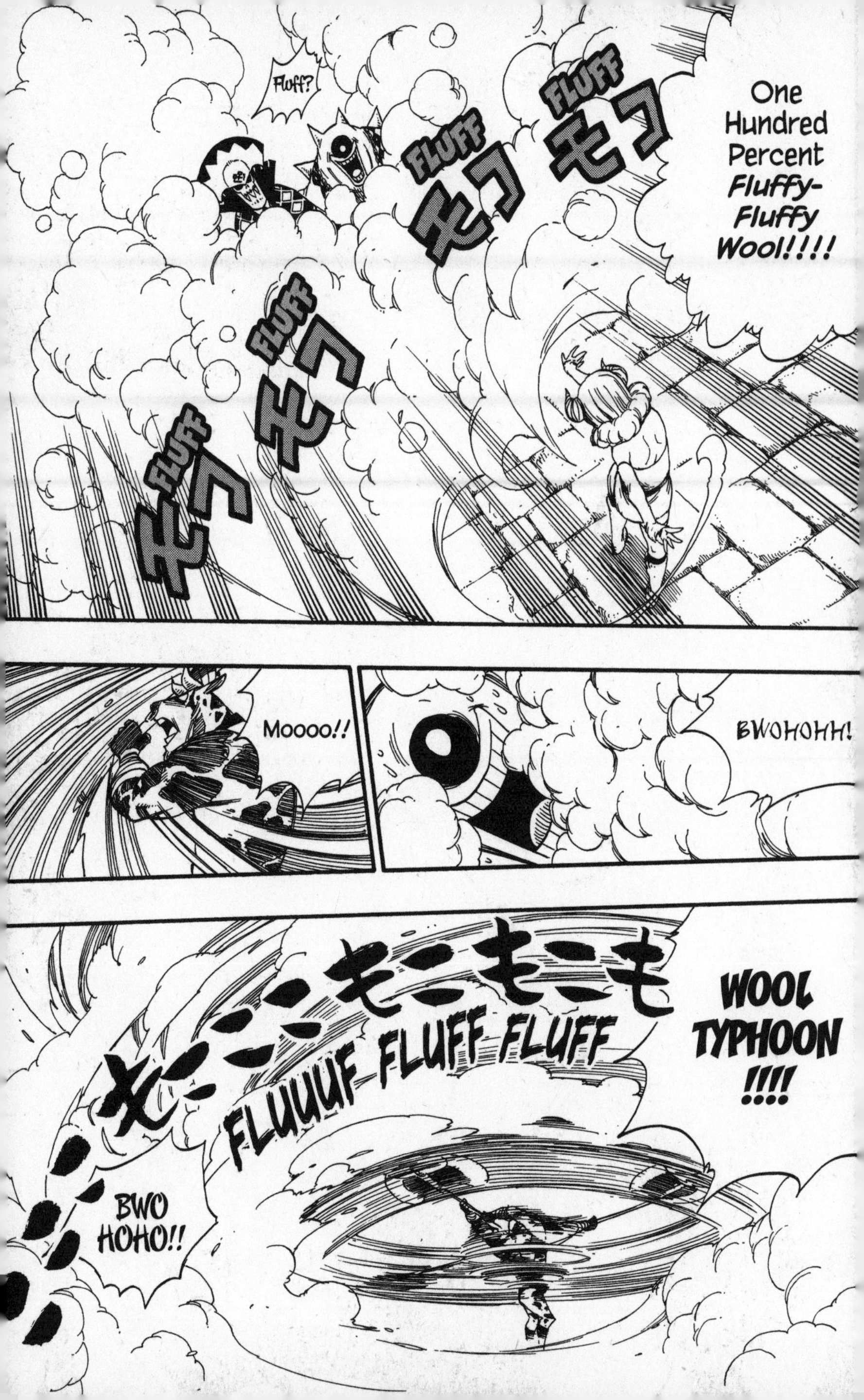
One Hundred Percent Fluffy-Fluffy Wool!!!!
Fluff?
FLUFF FLUFF
FLUFF FLUFF
BWOHOHH!
Moooo!!
WOOL TYPHOON!!!!
FLUUUF FLUFF FLUFF
BWO HOHO!!

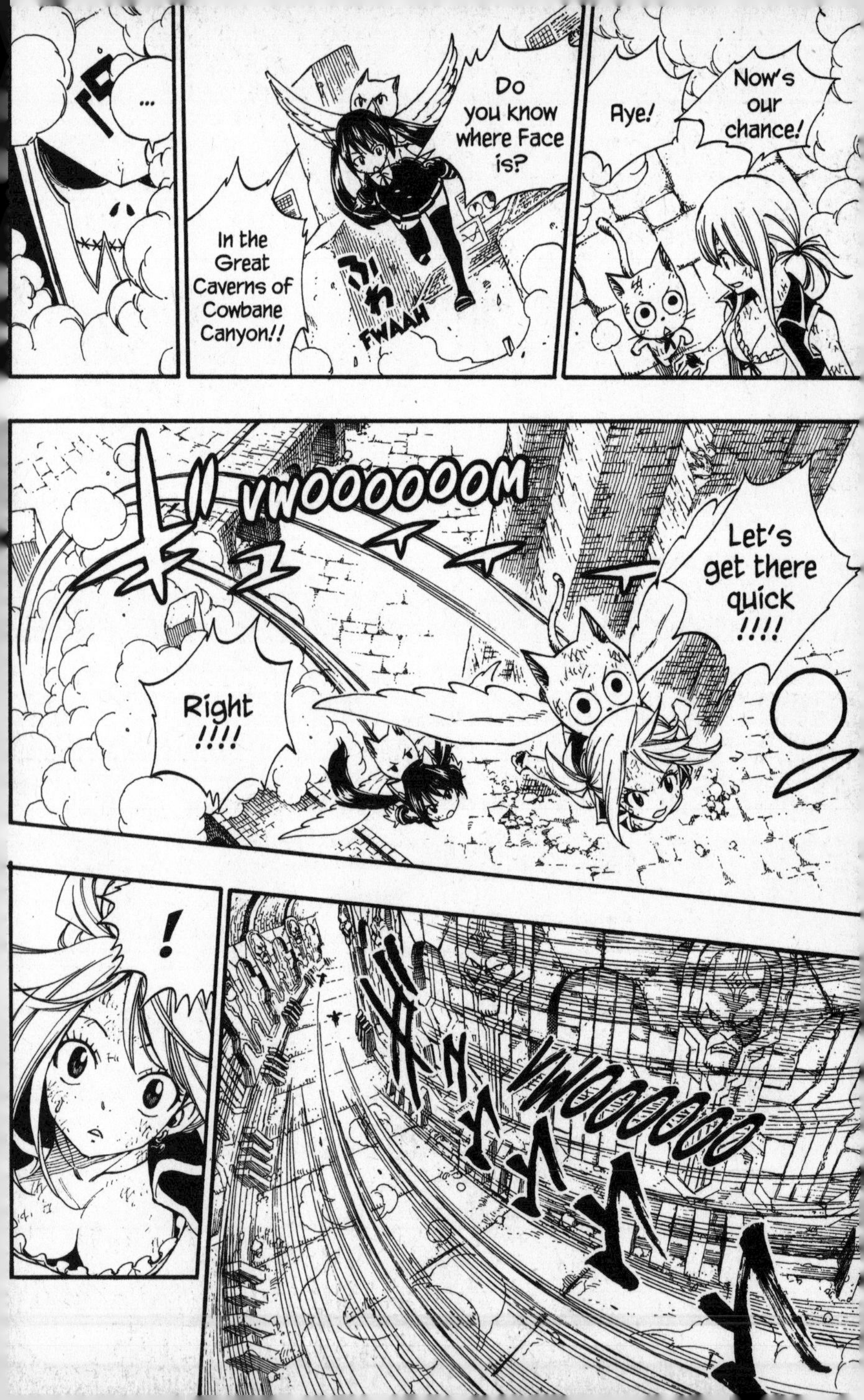
Now's our chance!
Aye!
Do you know where Face is?
ふわ
FWAAH
In the Great Caverns of Cowbane Canyon!!
...
Let's get there quick !!!!
VWOOOOOOOM
Right !!!!
VWOOOOOO
!

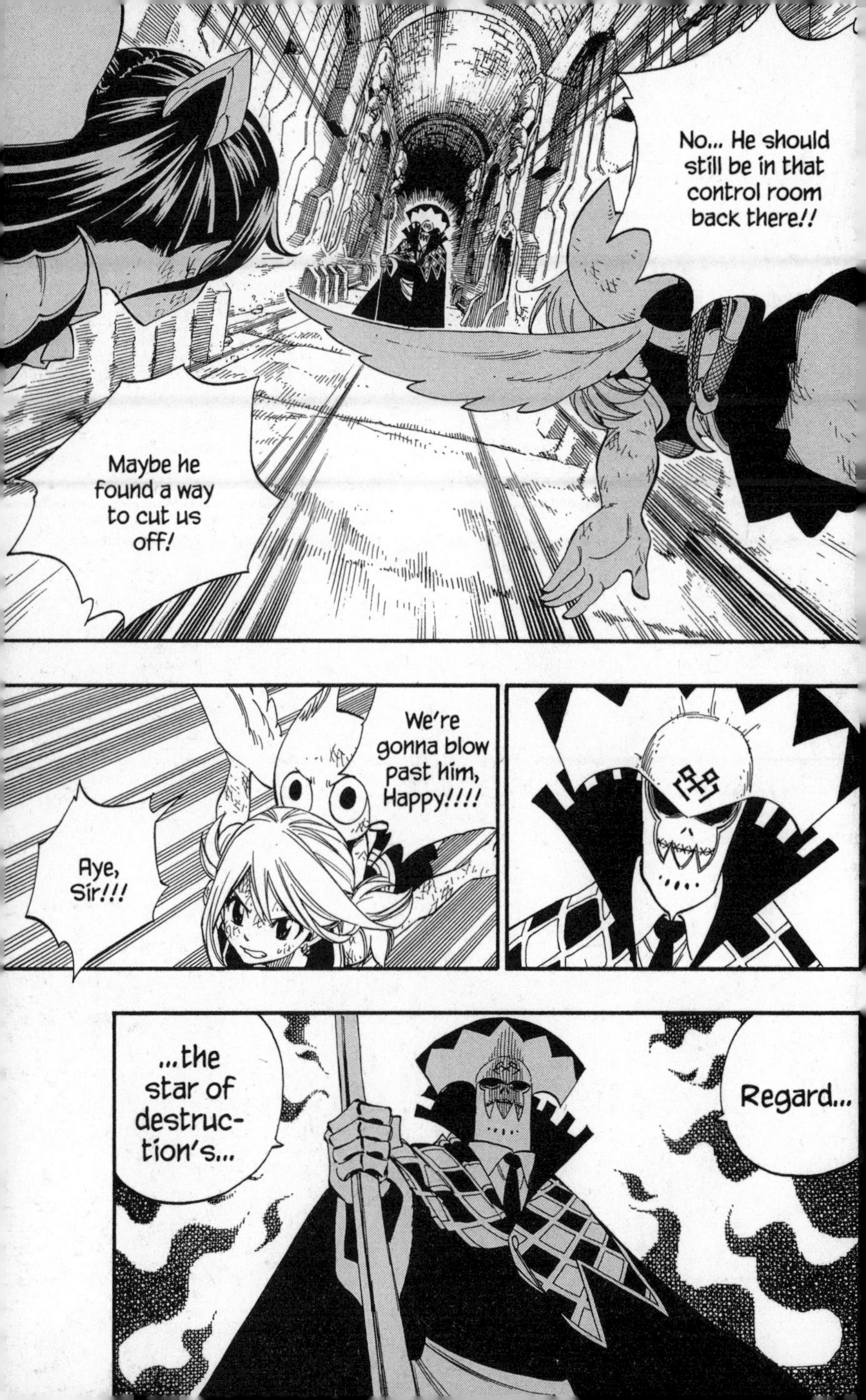
No... He should still be in that control room back there!!
Maybe he found a way to cut us off!
We're gonna blow past him, Happy!!!!
Aye, Sir!!!
Regard...
...the star of destruction's...

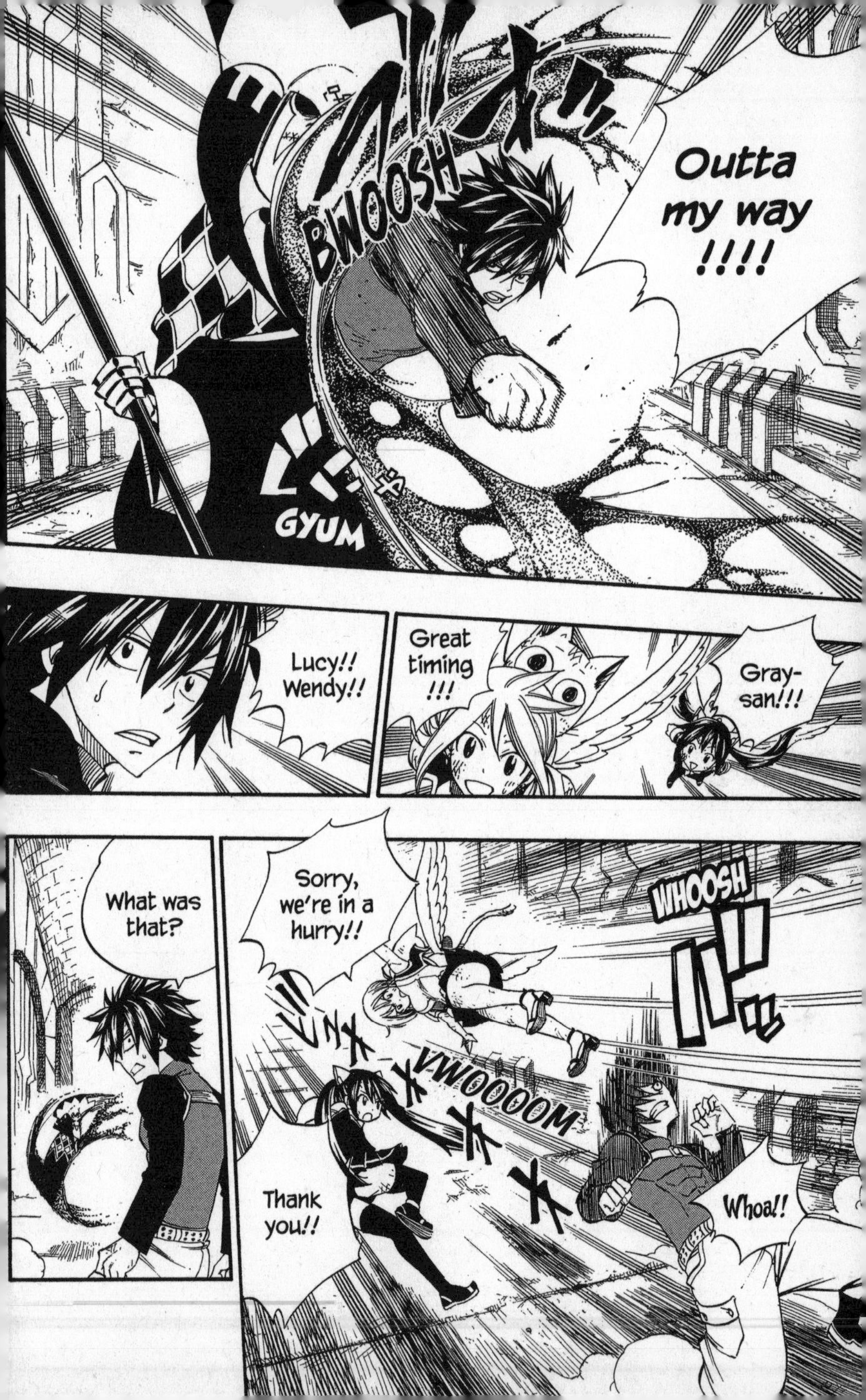
Outta my way !!!!
BWOOSH
GYUM
Gray-san!!!
Great timing !!!
Lucy!! Wendy!!
WHOOSH
Sorry, we're in a hurry!!
VWOOOOM
Whoa!!
Thank you!!
What was that?

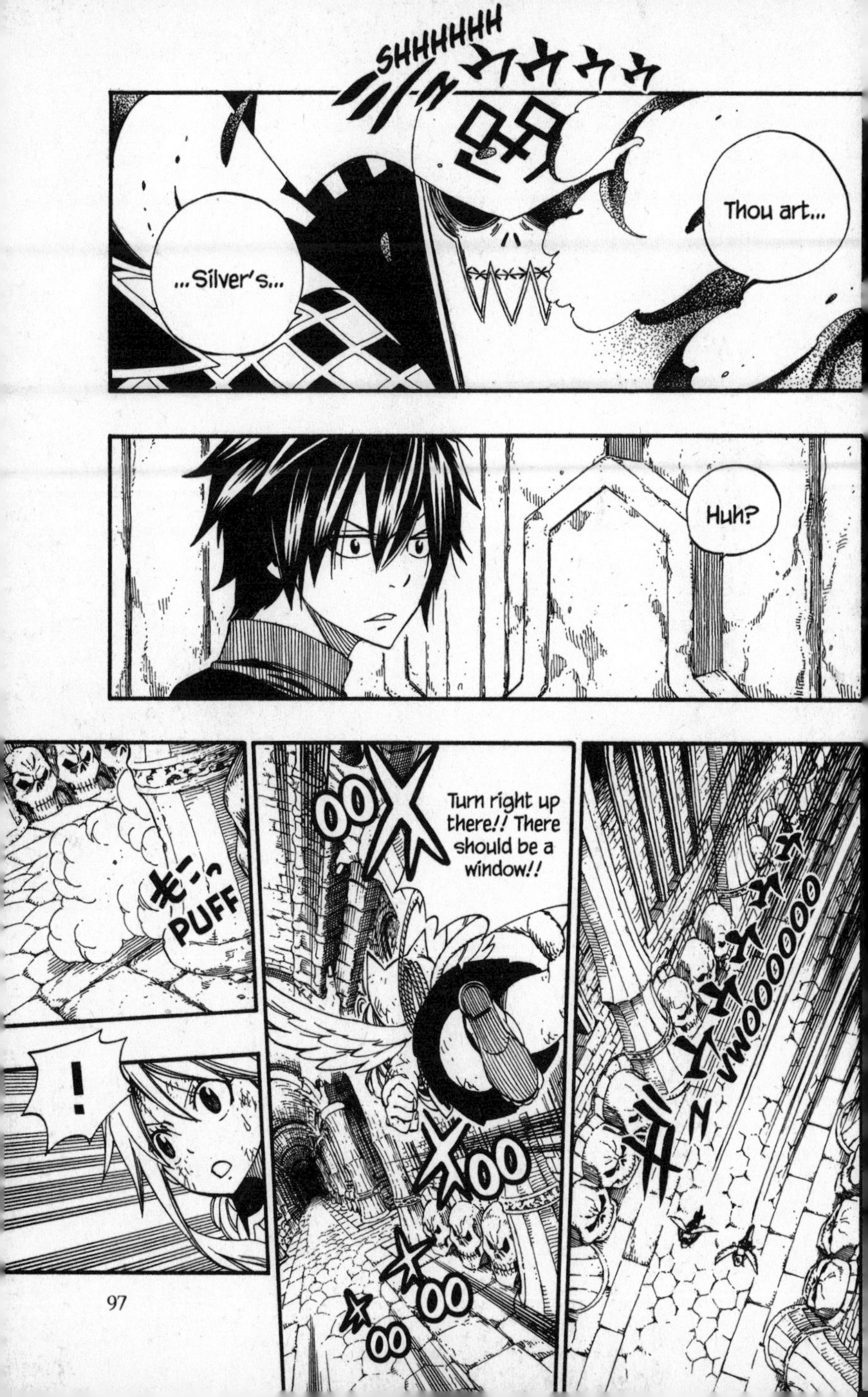
SHHHHHH
Thou art...
...Silver's...
Huh?
VWOOOOOO
OO
Turn right up there!! There should be a window!!
OO
OO
OO
PUFF
!

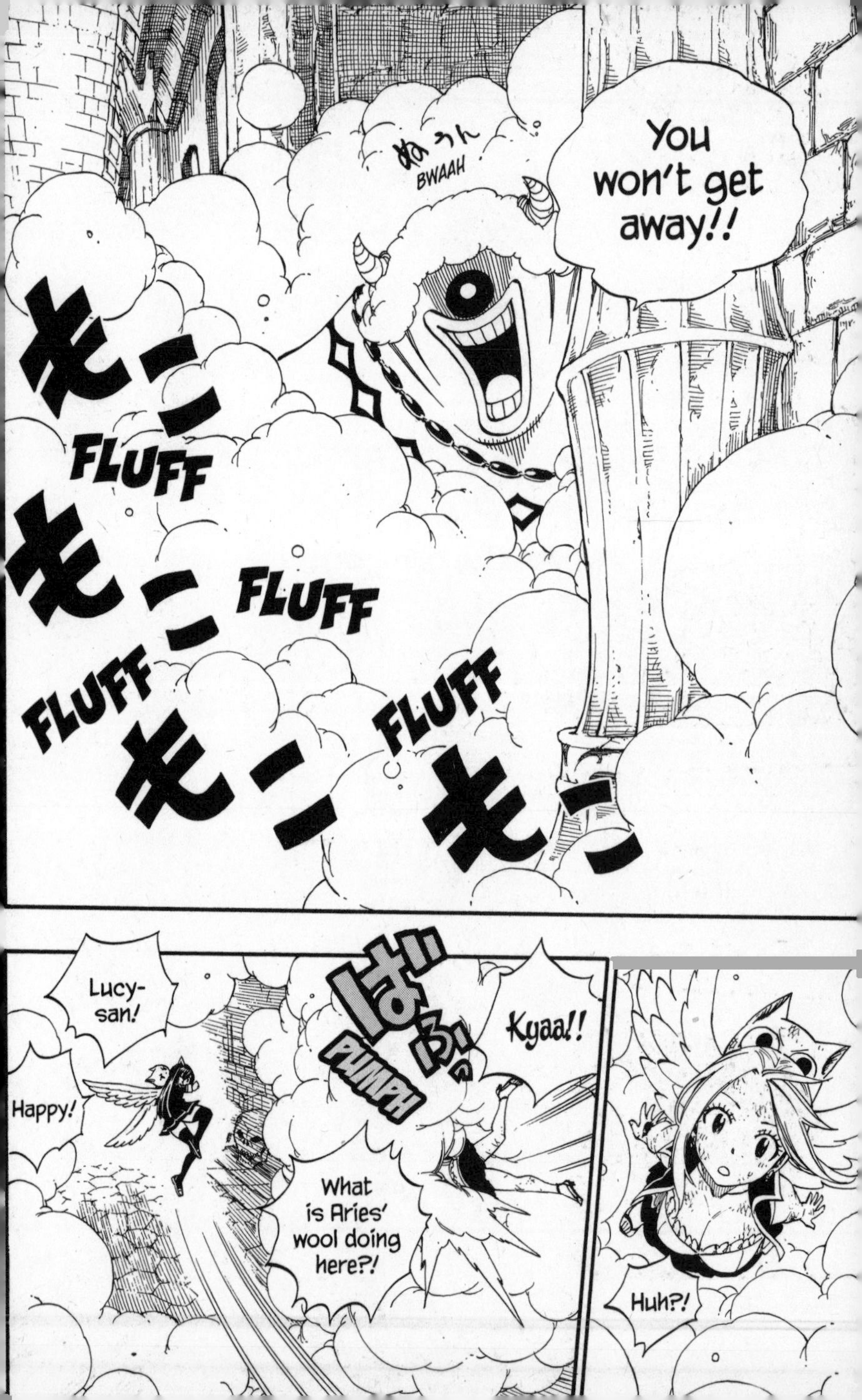

You won't get away!!
ぬうん
BWAAH
もこ
FLUFF
もこ
FLUFF
FLUFF
もこ
FLUFF
もこ
Huh?!
Kyaa!!
ばふっ
PUMPH
What is Aries' wool doing here?!
Lucy-san!
Happy!

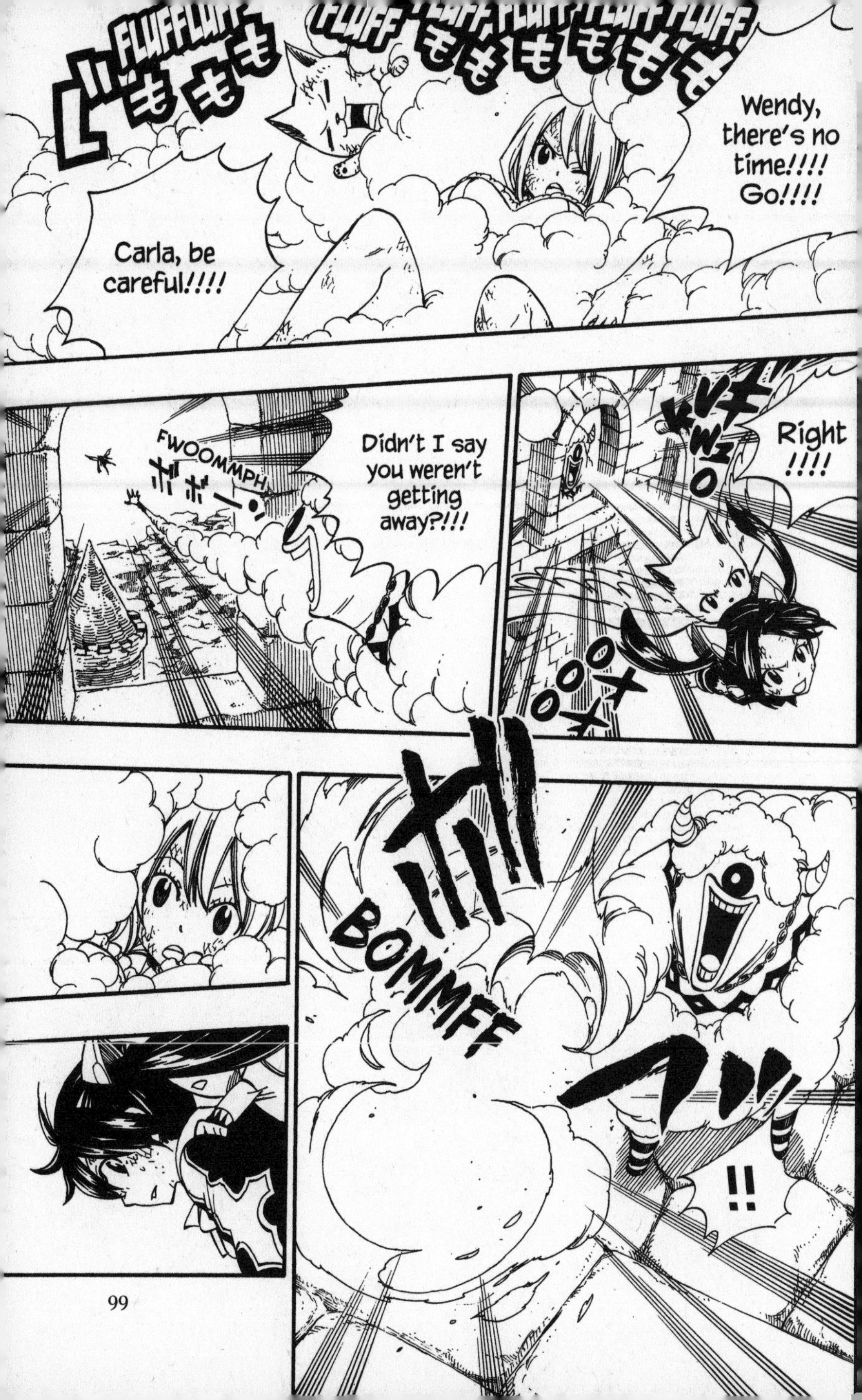

Wendy, there's no time!!!! Go!!!!
FLUFF
FLUFFLUFF
Carla, be careful!!!!
Right!!!!
Didn't I say you weren't getting away?!!!
FWOOMMPH
BOMMFF
!!

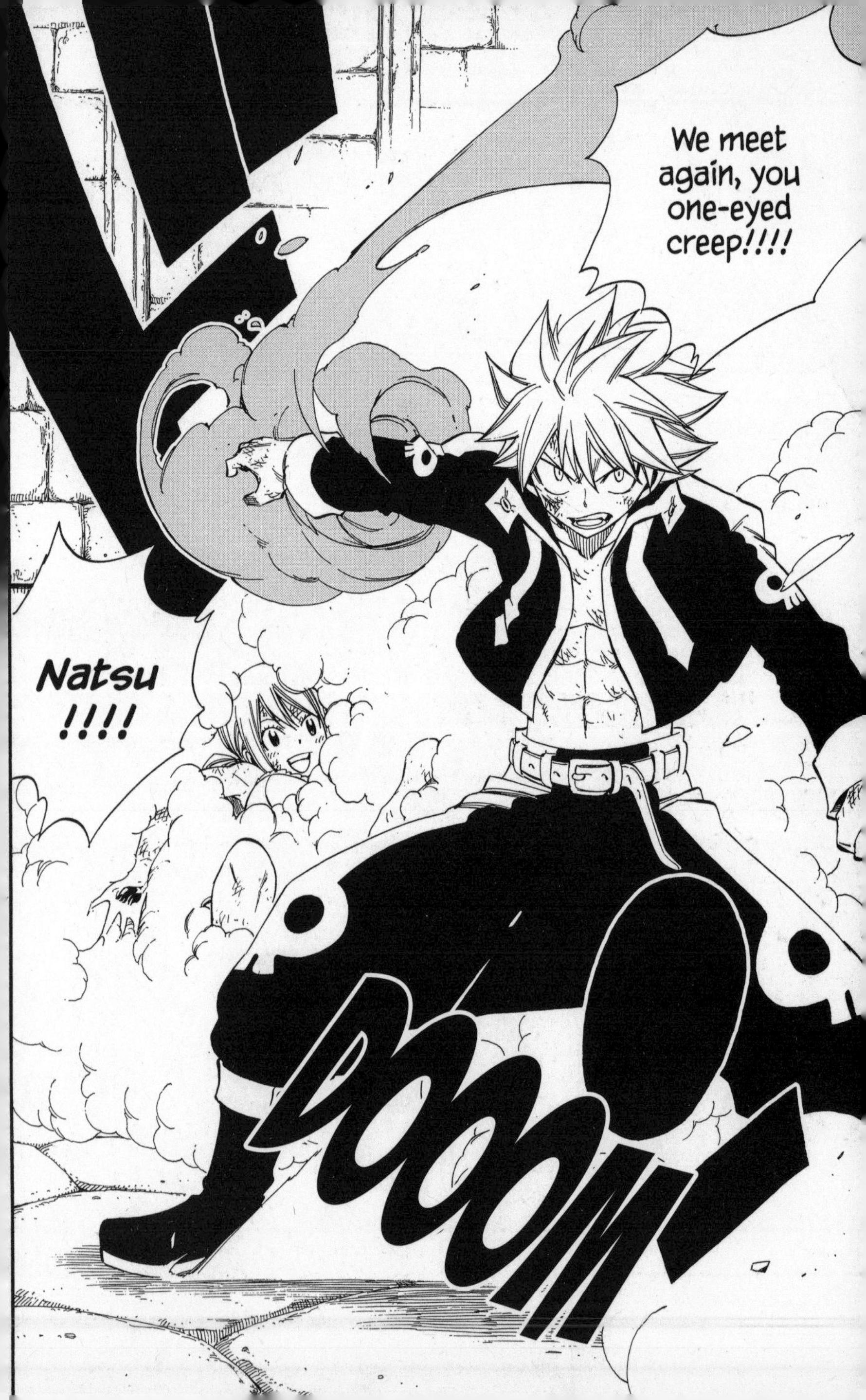
We meet again, you one-eyed creep!!!!
Natsu !!!!
BOOOM

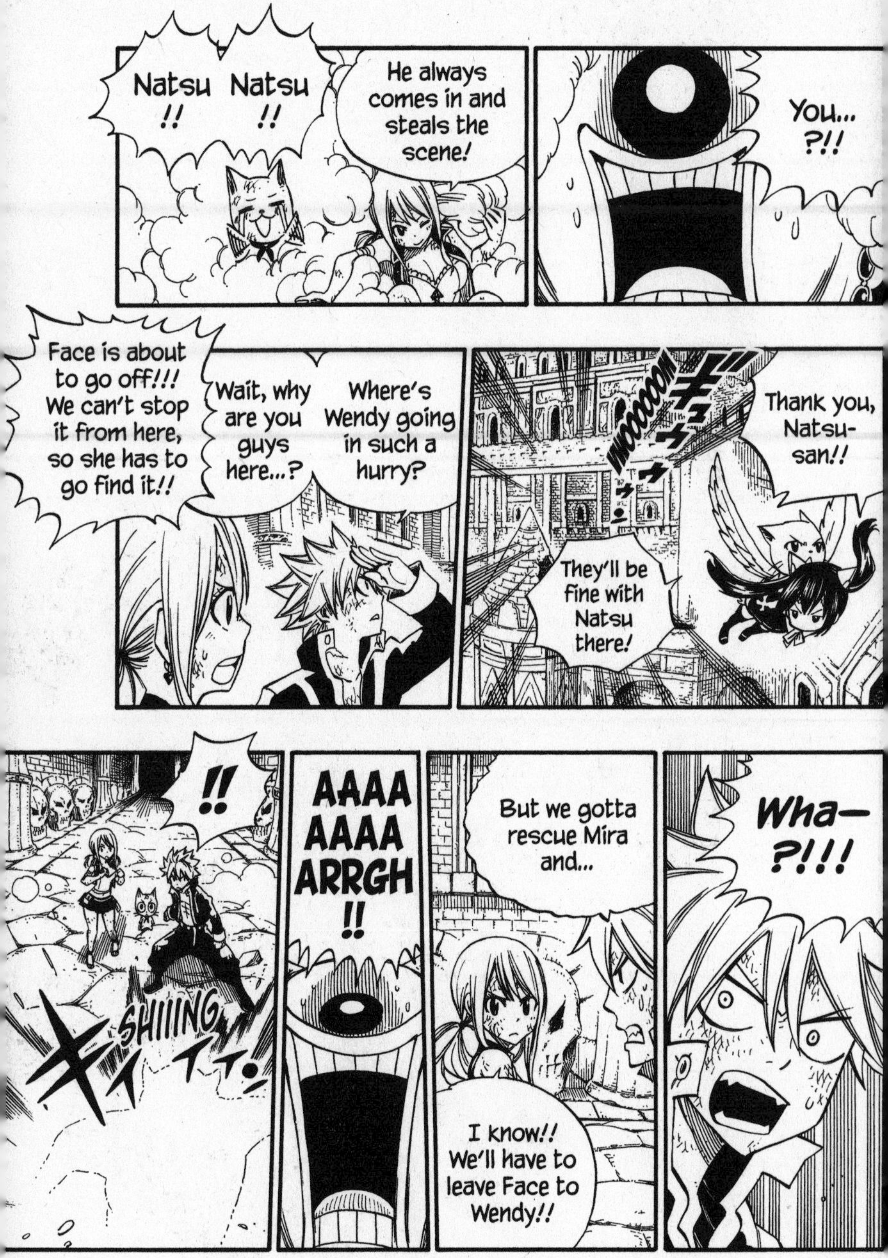
You...?!!
He always comes in and steals the scene!
Natsu!! Natsu!!
Thank you, Natsu-san!!
WOOOOOOOM
They'll be fine with Natsu there!
Where's Wendy going in such a hurry?
Wait, why are you guys here...?
Face is about to go off!!! We can't stop it from here, so she has to go find it!!
Wha-?!!!
But we gotta rescue Mira and...
I know!! We'll have to leave Face to Wendy!!
AAAA AAAA ARRGH!!
!!
SHIIING

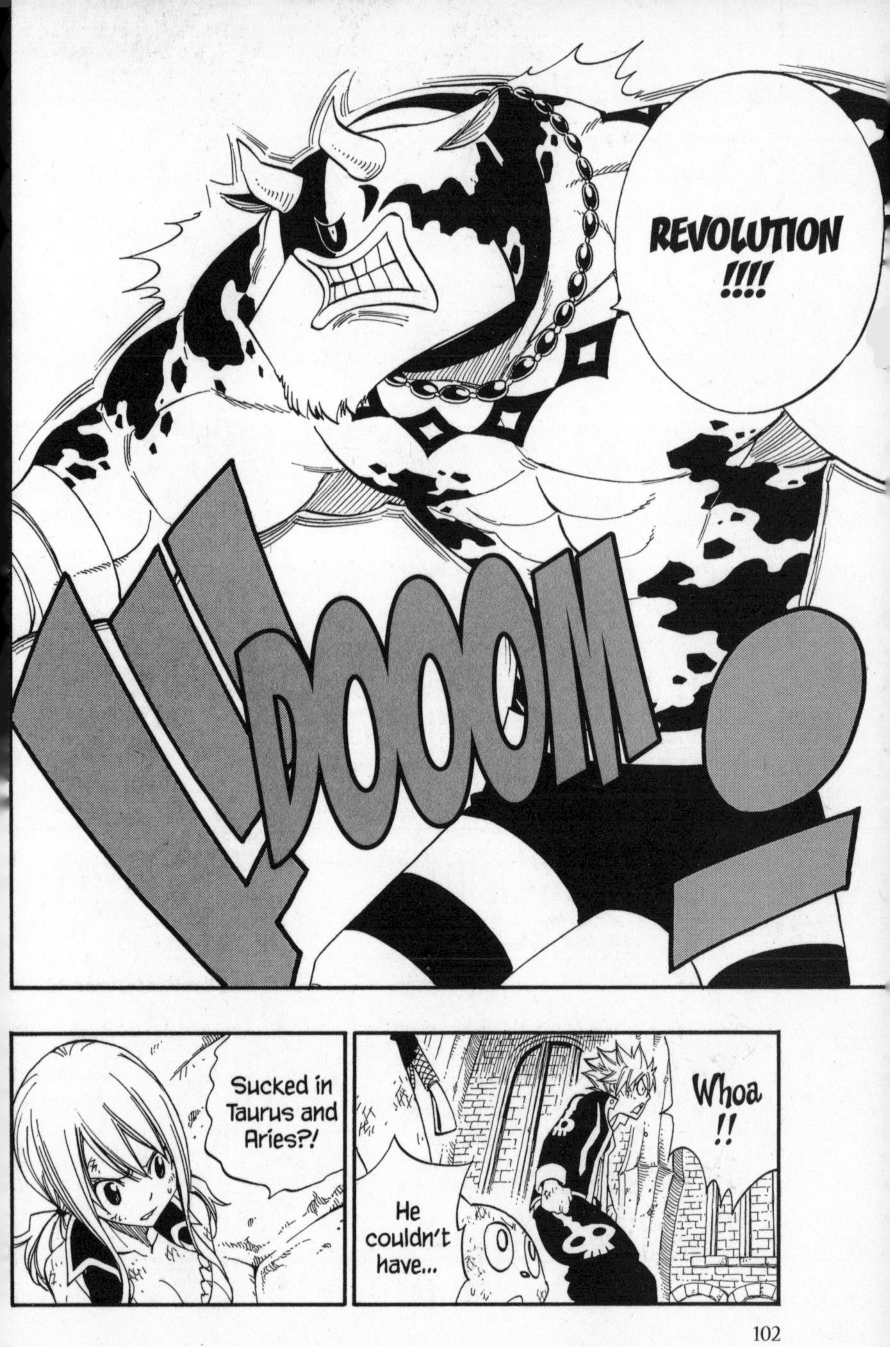
REVOLUTION !!!!
DOOOM
Whoa !!
He couldn't have...
Sucked in Taurus and Aries?!

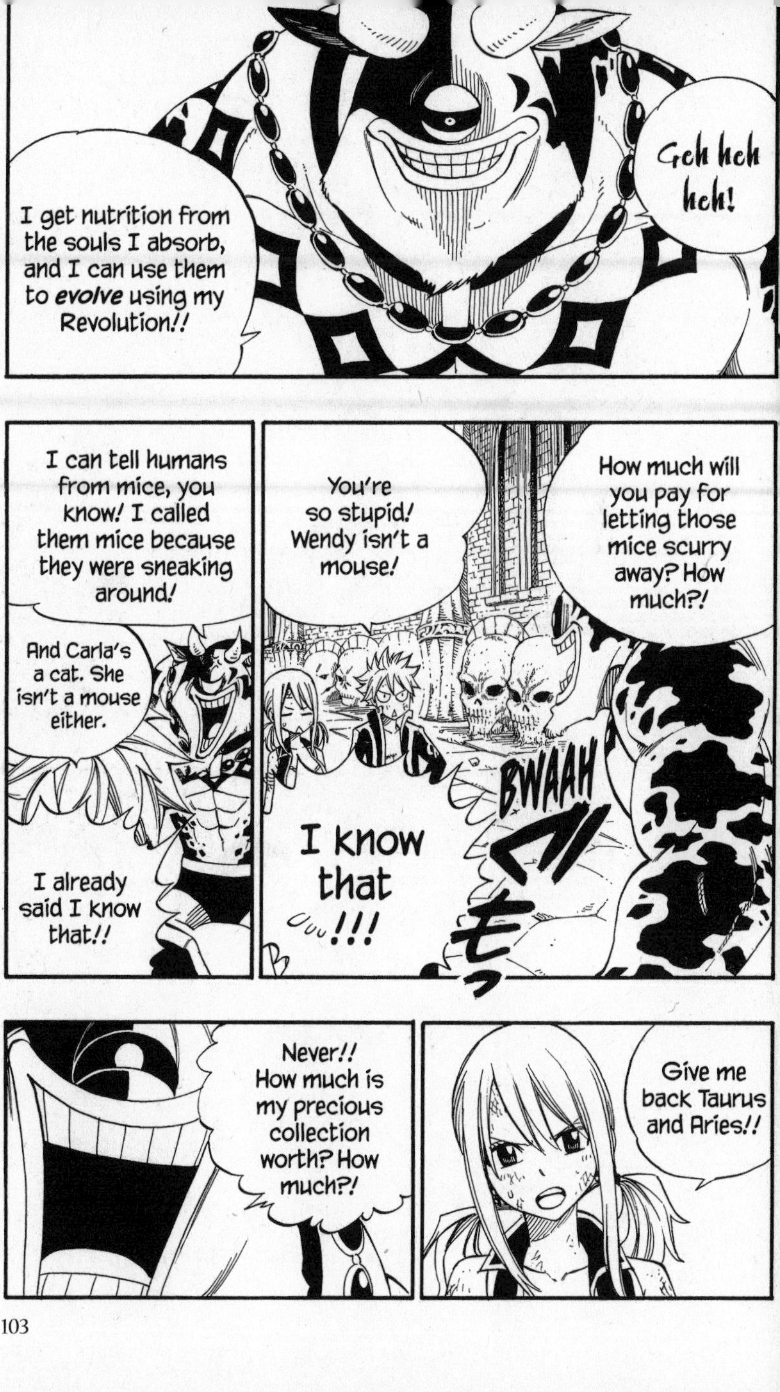
Geh heh heh!
I get nutrition from the souls I absorb, and I can use them to *evolve* using my Revolution!!
How much will you pay for letting those mice scurry away? How much?!
You're so stupid! Wendy isn't a mouse!
BWAAH
I know that!!!
I can tell humans from mice, you know! I called them mice because they were sneaking around!
And Carla's a cat. She isn't a mouse either.
I already said I know that!!
Give me back Taurus and Aries!!
Never!! How much is my precious collection worth? How much?!

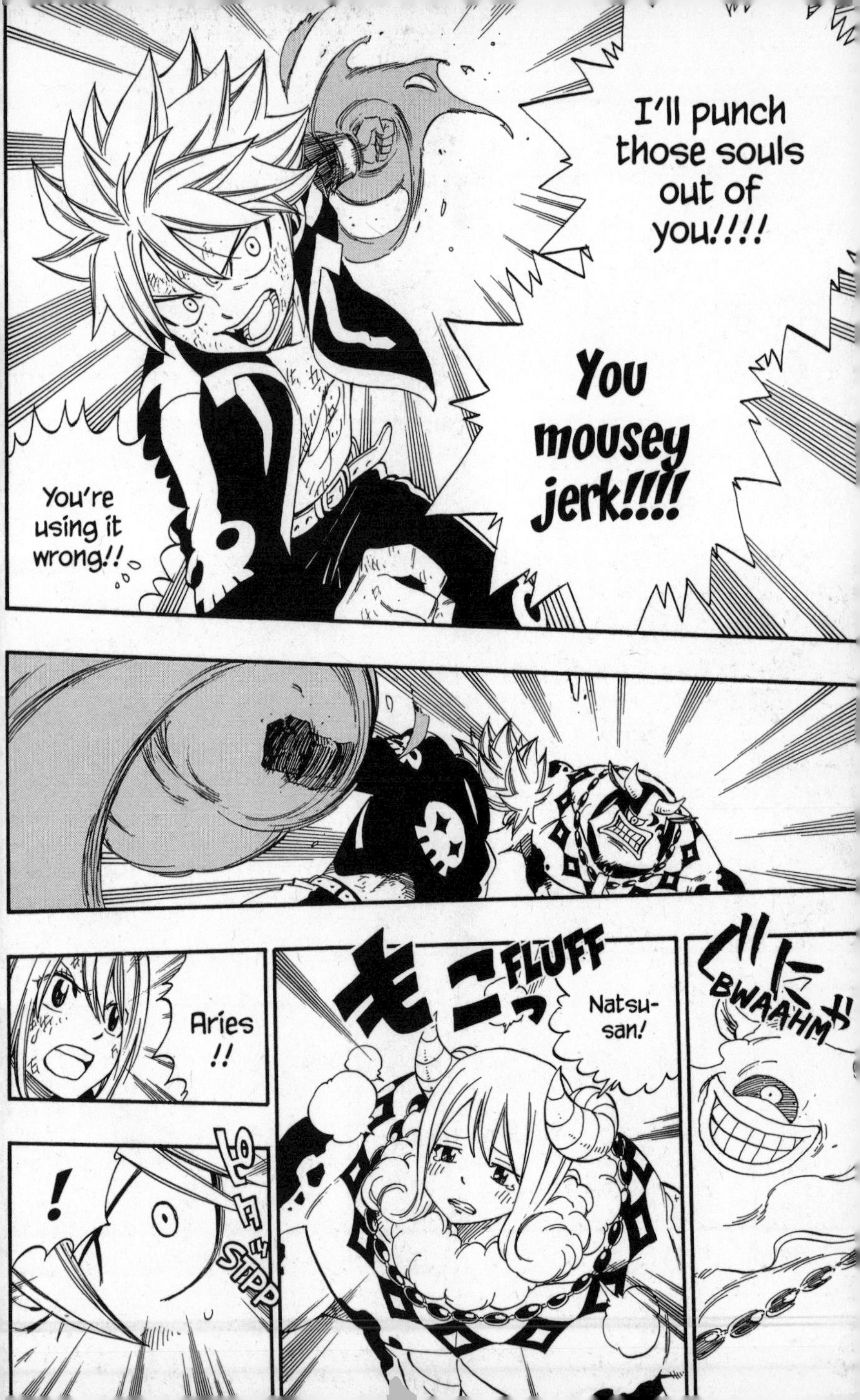
I'll punch those souls out of you!!!!
You mousey jerk!!!!
You're using it wrong!!
BWAAHM
FLUFF
Natsu-san!
Aries!!
!
STIPP

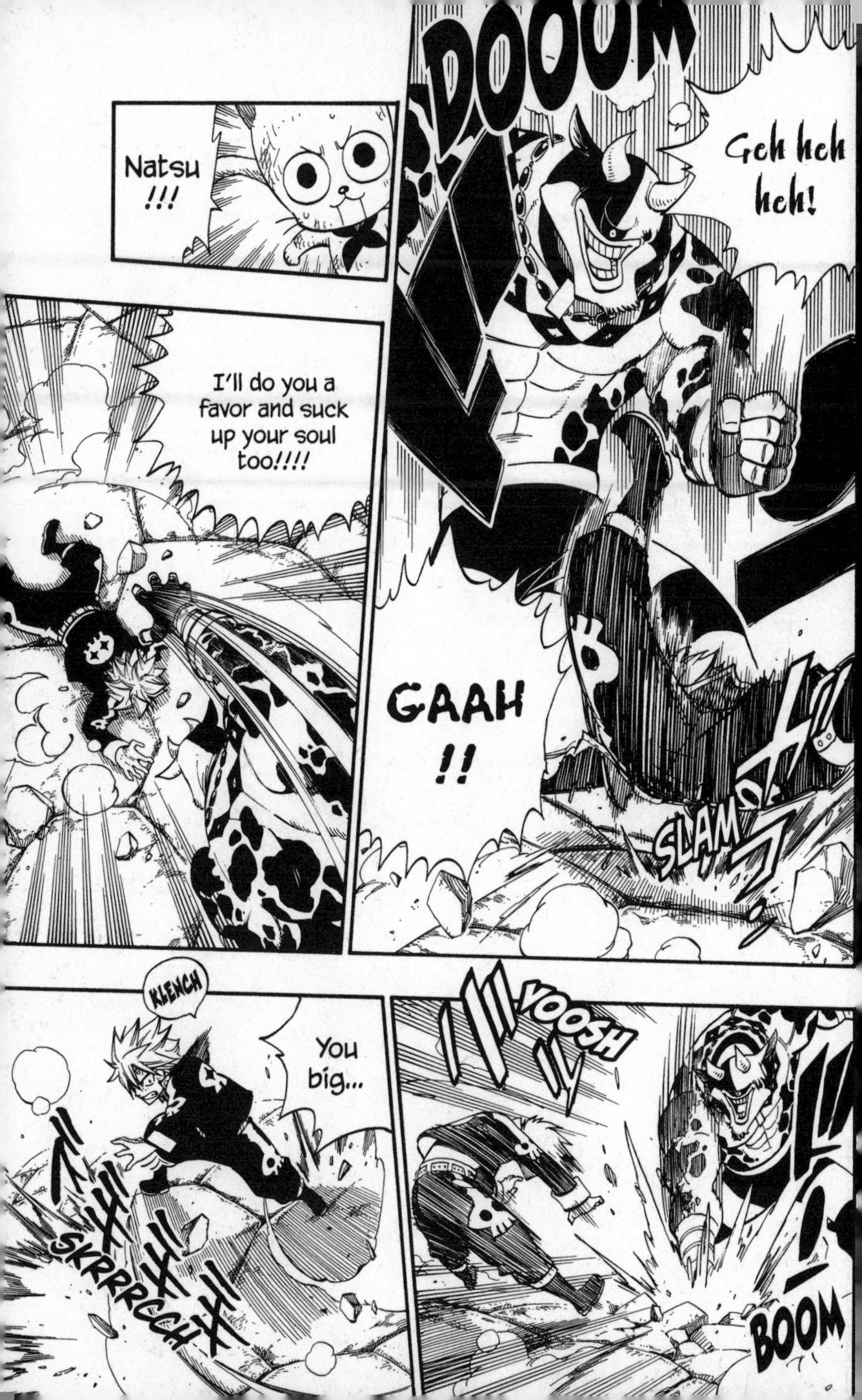
DOOOM
Geh heh heh!
GAAH!!
SLAM
Natsu!!!
I'll do you a favor and suck up your soul too!!!!
VOOSH
BOOM
KLENCH
You big...
SKRRRCH

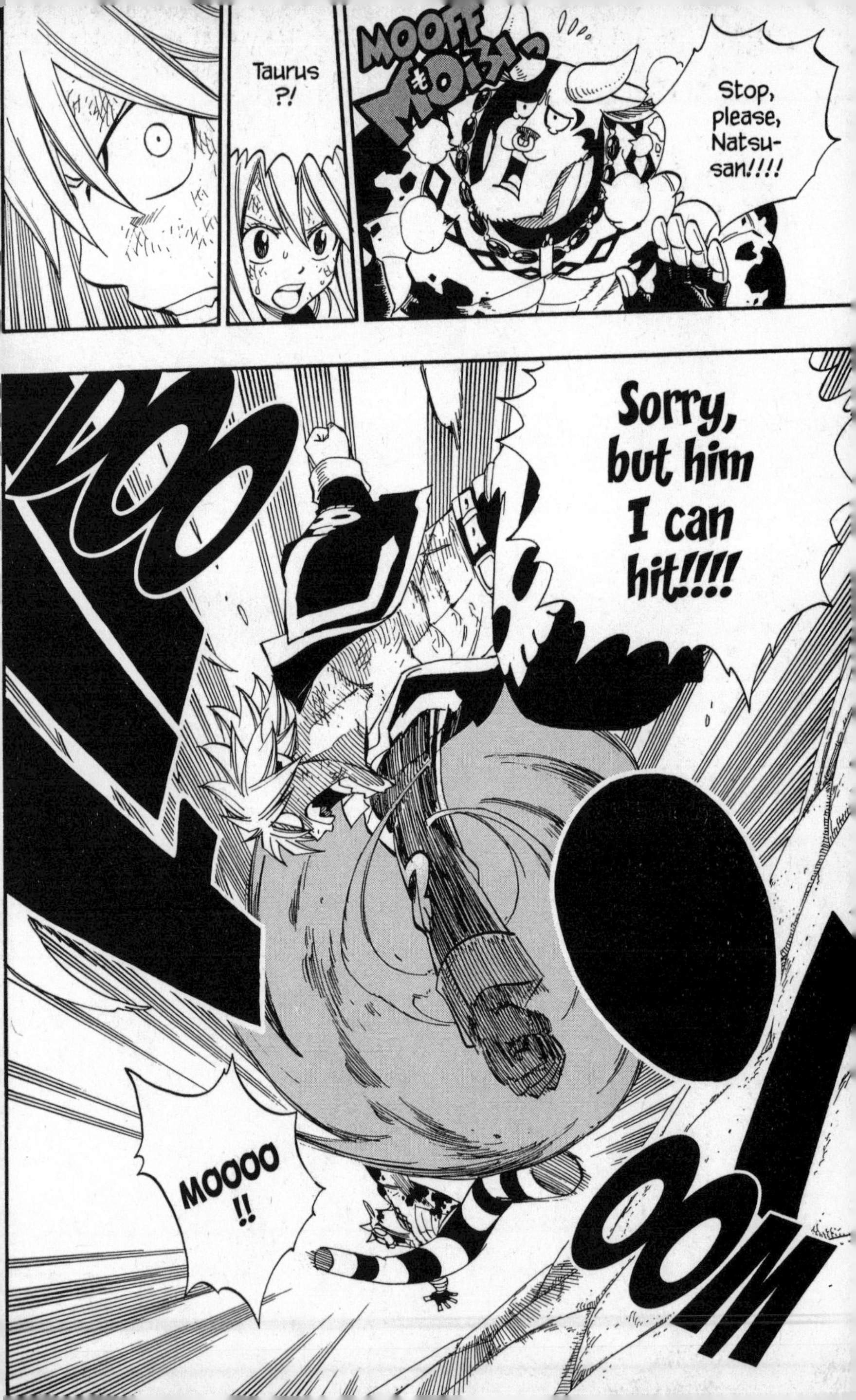
MOOFF
Stop, please, Natsu-san!!!!
Taurus ?!
Sorry, but him I can hit!!!!
MOOOO !!

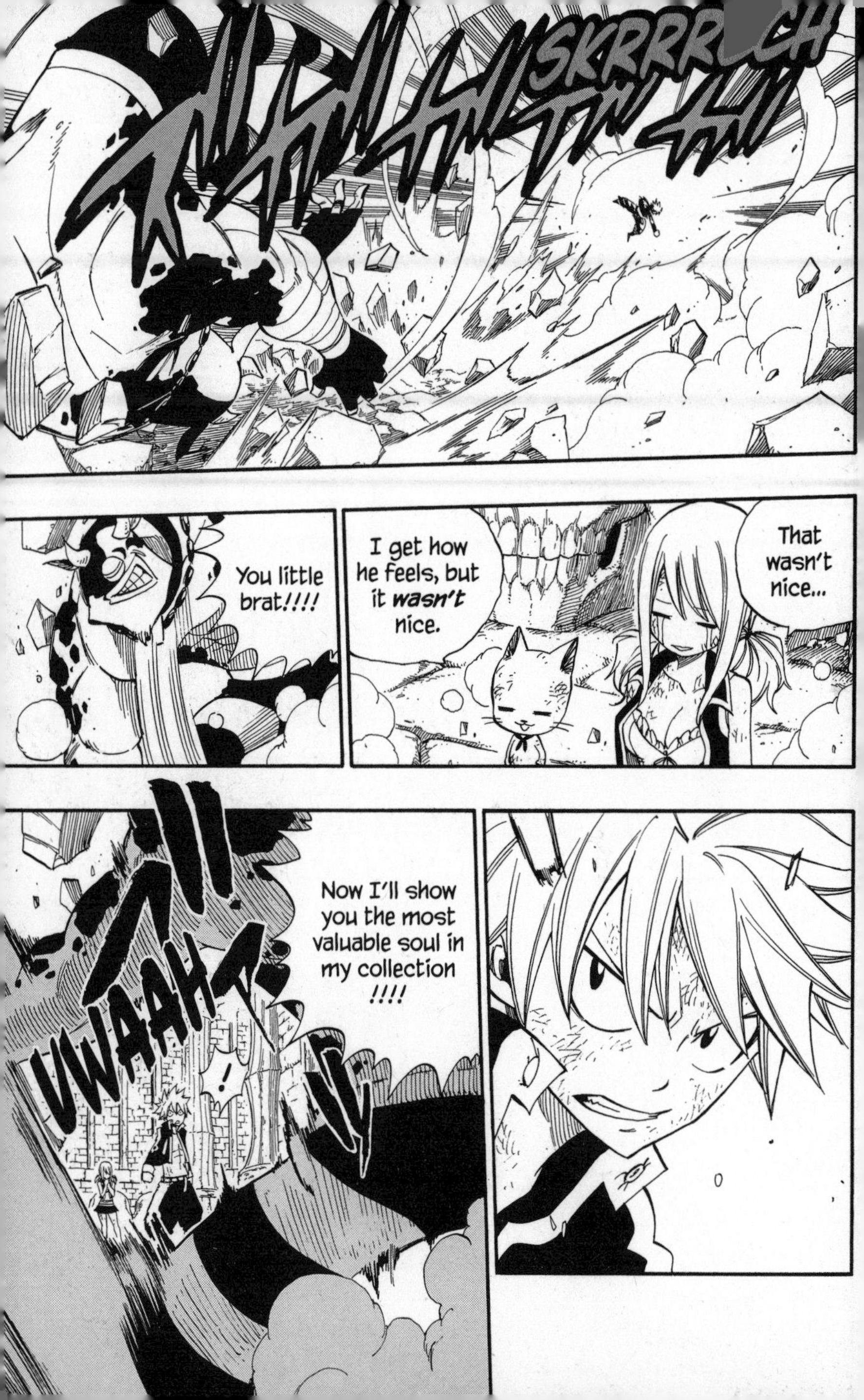
SKRRR CH
That wasn't nice...
I get how he feels, but it wasn't nice.
You little brat!!!!
Now I'll show you the most valuable soul in my collection!!!!
UWAAH-!!
!

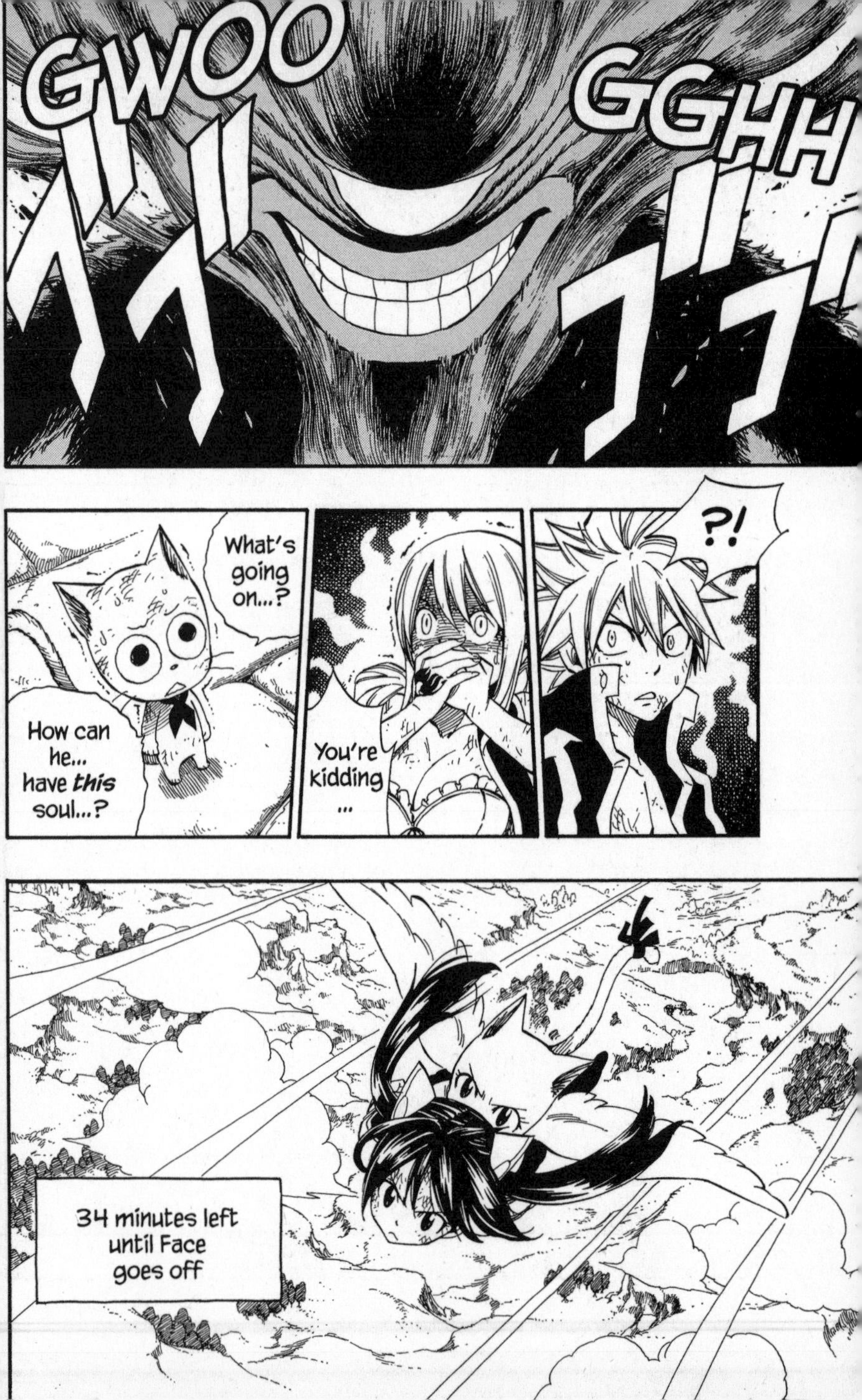
GWOO
GGHH
?!
You're kidding ...
What's going on...?
How can he... have *this* soul...?
34 minutes left until Face goes off

FAIRY TAIL

フェアリーテイル

Chapter 375: Herculean Madness

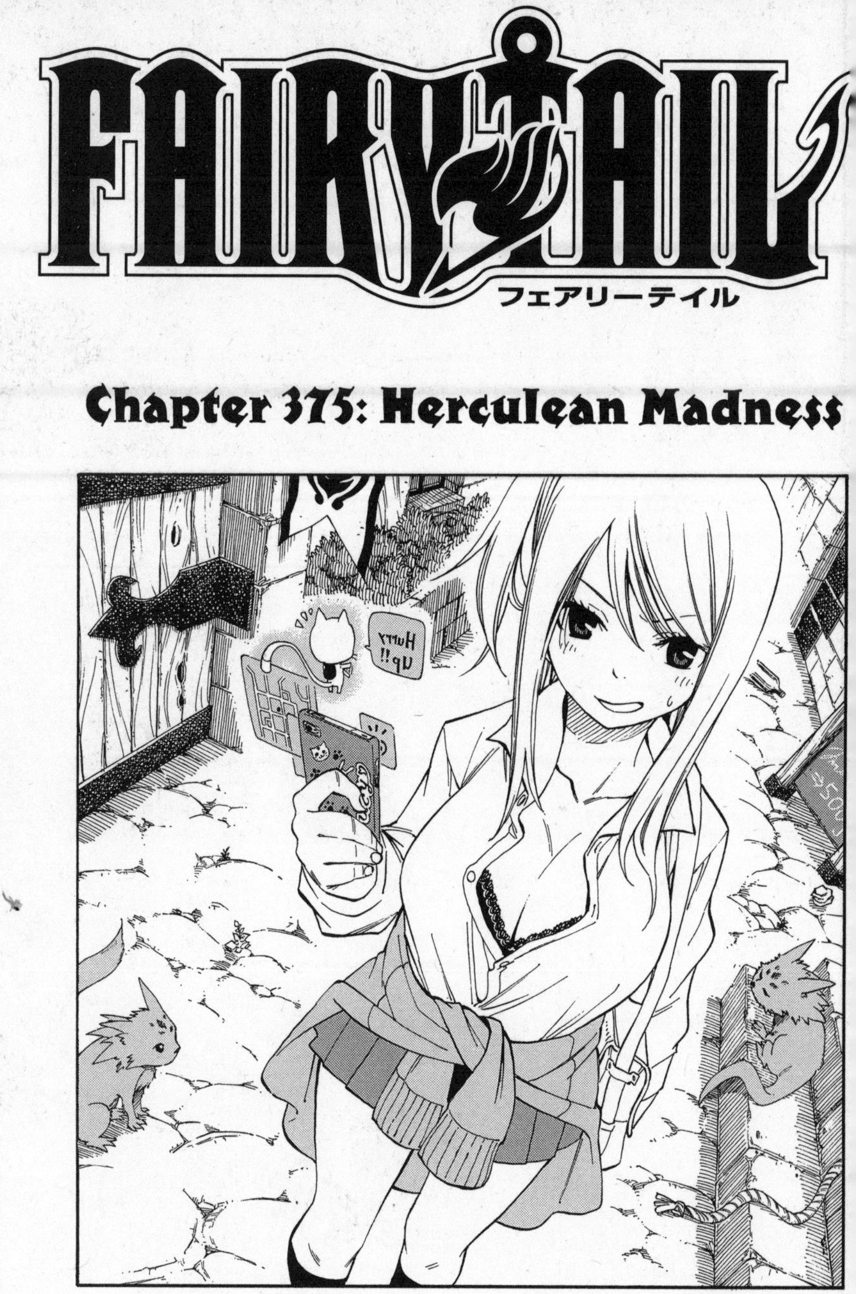
Hurry Up!!

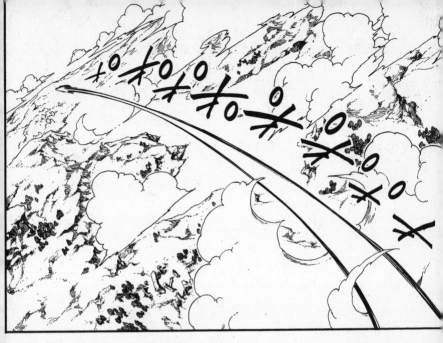

We've got to hurry, Carla!! Faster!!

I know!! But one thing...

How are we supposed to shut down Face?

If Natsu-san were here, *he'd* find a way!!

I don't know...

...but we have to!

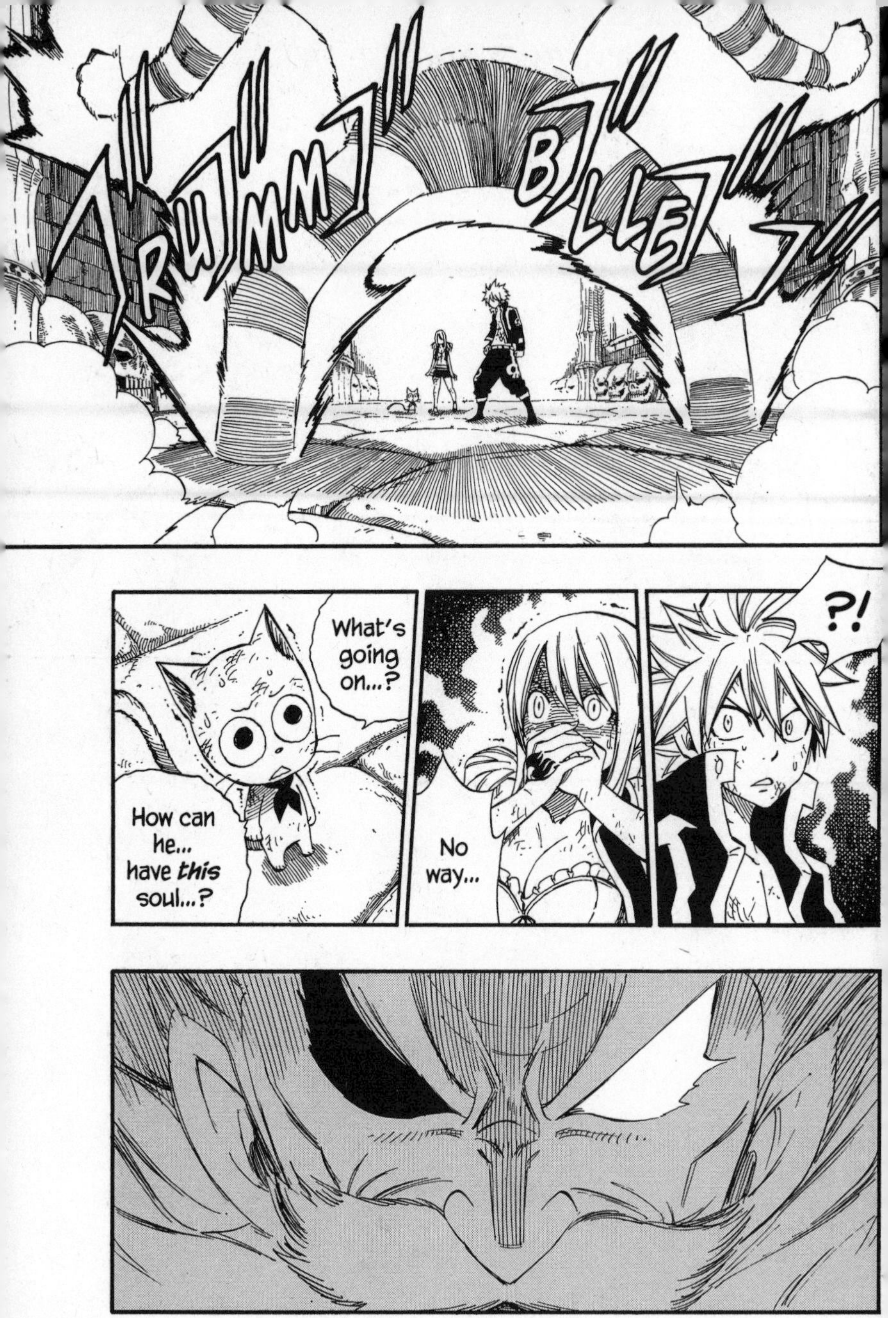
RUMMBLLE
?!
No way...
What's going on...?
How can he... have *this* soul...?

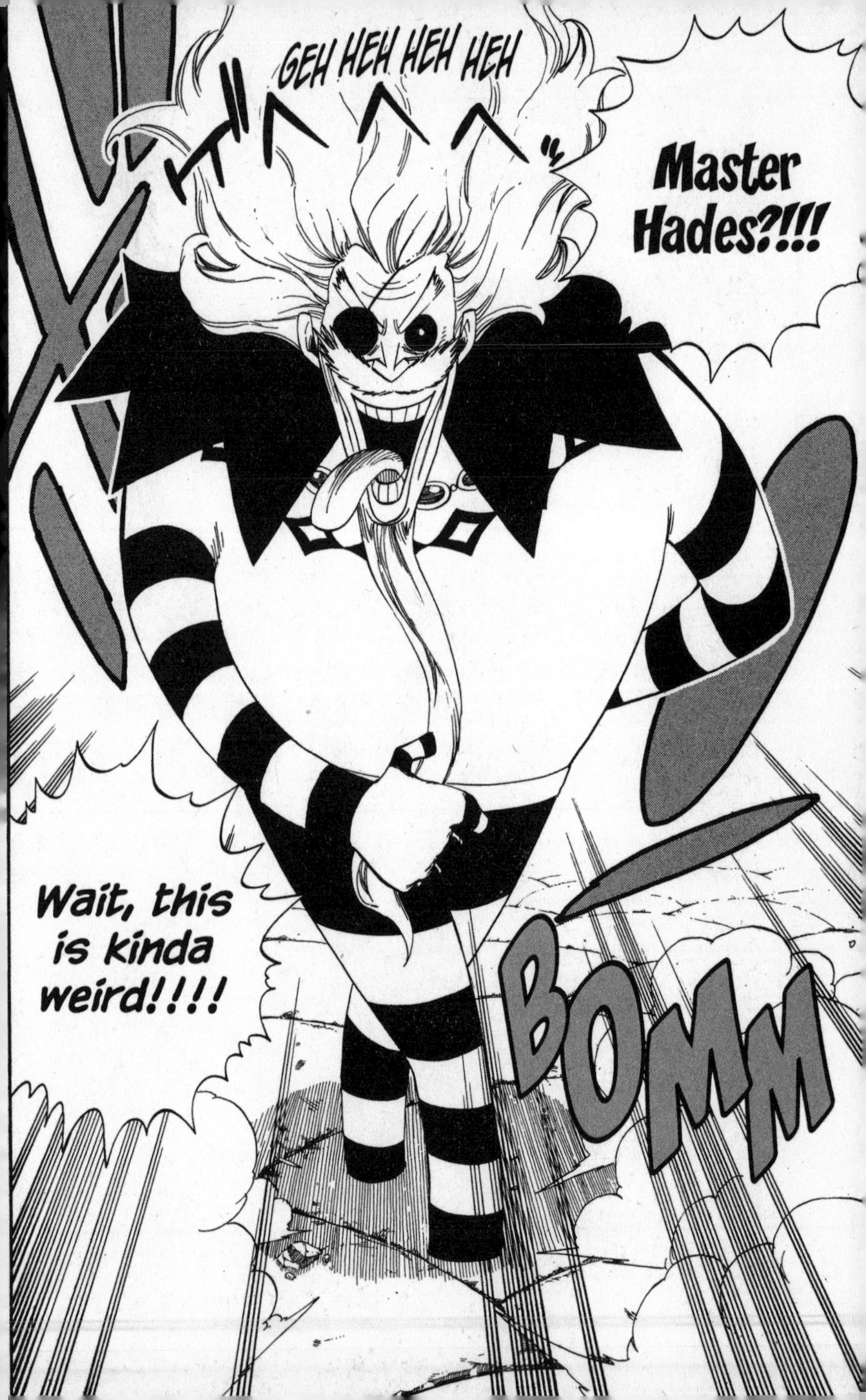
Master Hades?!!!
GEH HEH HEH HEH
Wait, this is kinda weird!!!!
BOMM

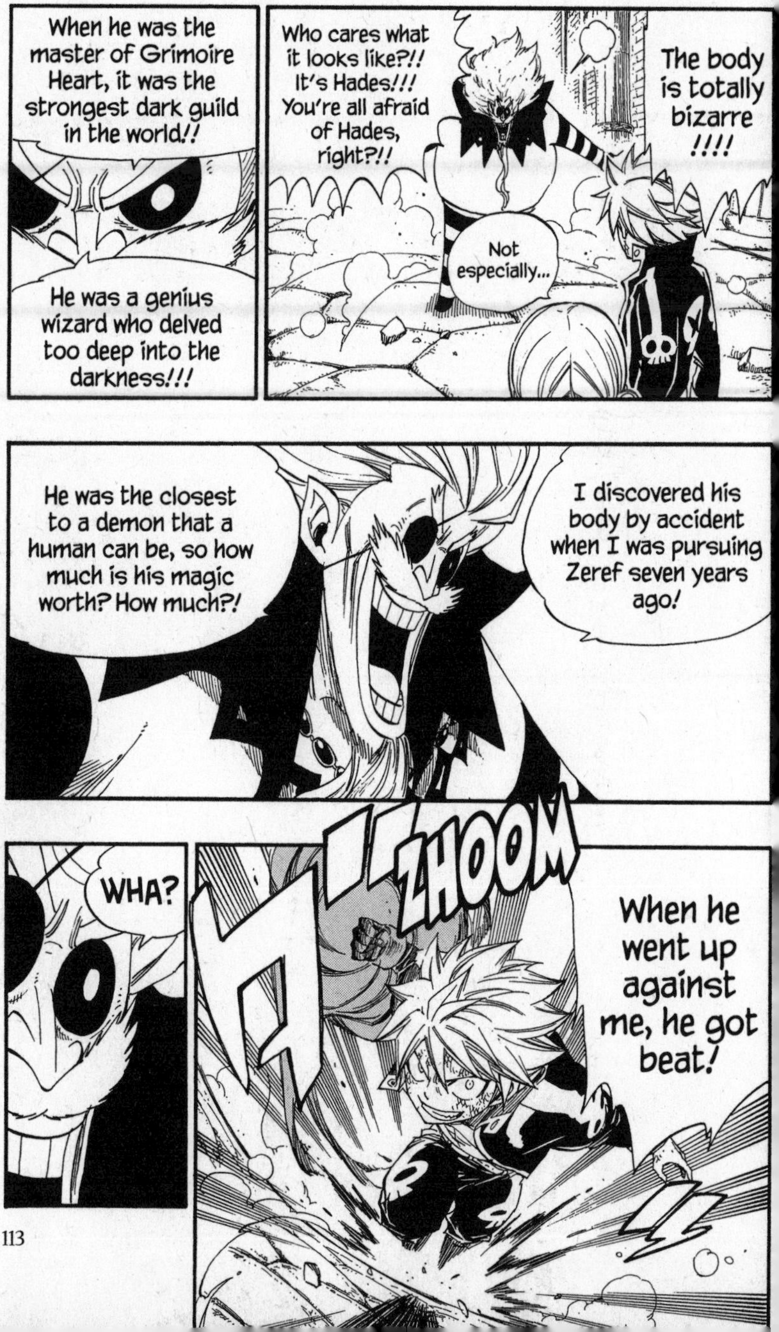
The body is totally bizarre!!!!
Who cares what it looks like?!! It's Hades!!! You're all afraid of Hades, right?!!
Not especially...
When he was the master of Grimoire Heart, it was the strongest dark guild in the world!!
He was a genius wizard who delved too deep into the darkness!!!
I discovered his body by accident when I was pursuing Zeref seven years ago!
He was the closest to a demon that a human can be, so how much is his magic worth? How much?!
When he went up against me, he got beat!
ZHOOM
WHA?

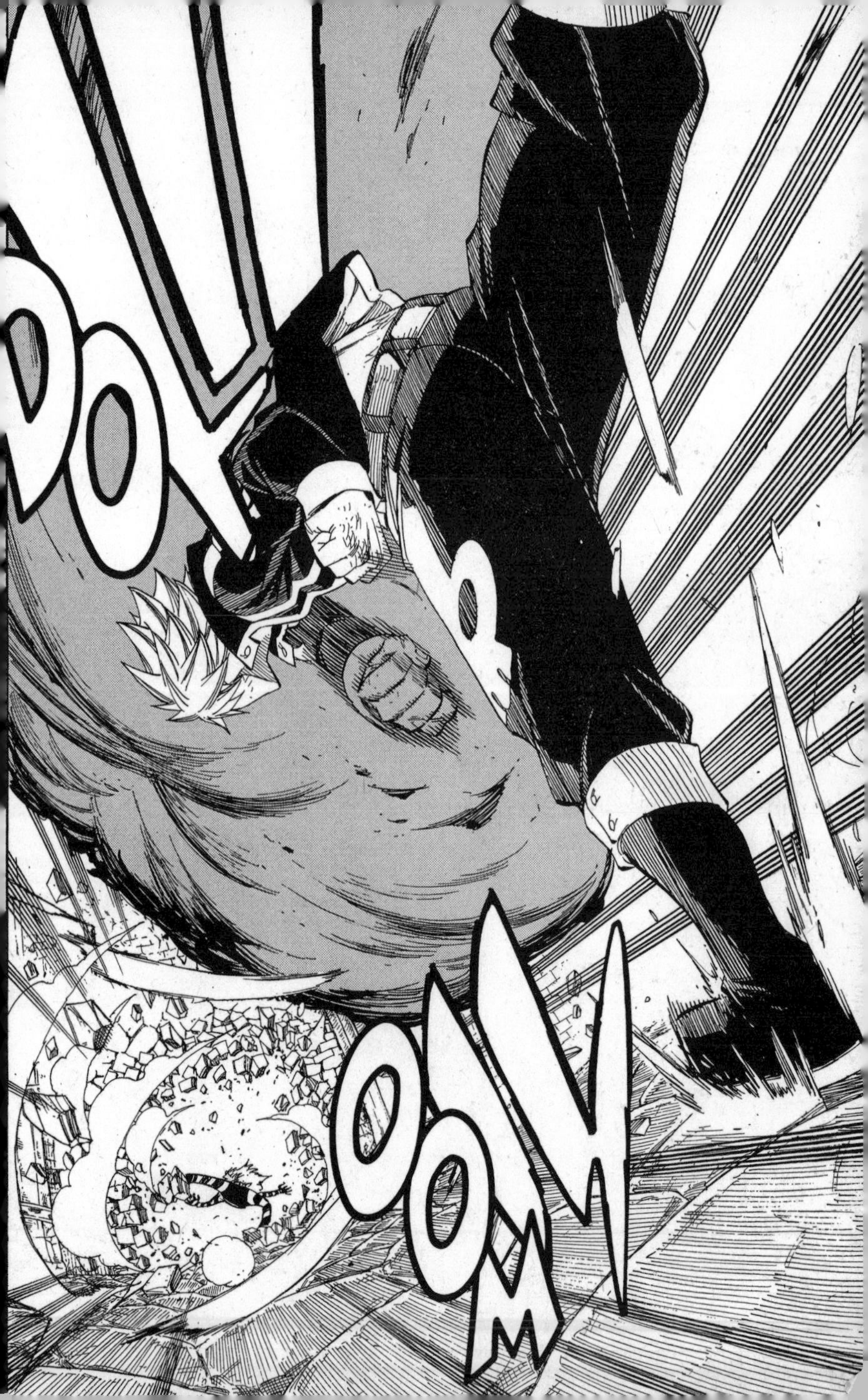

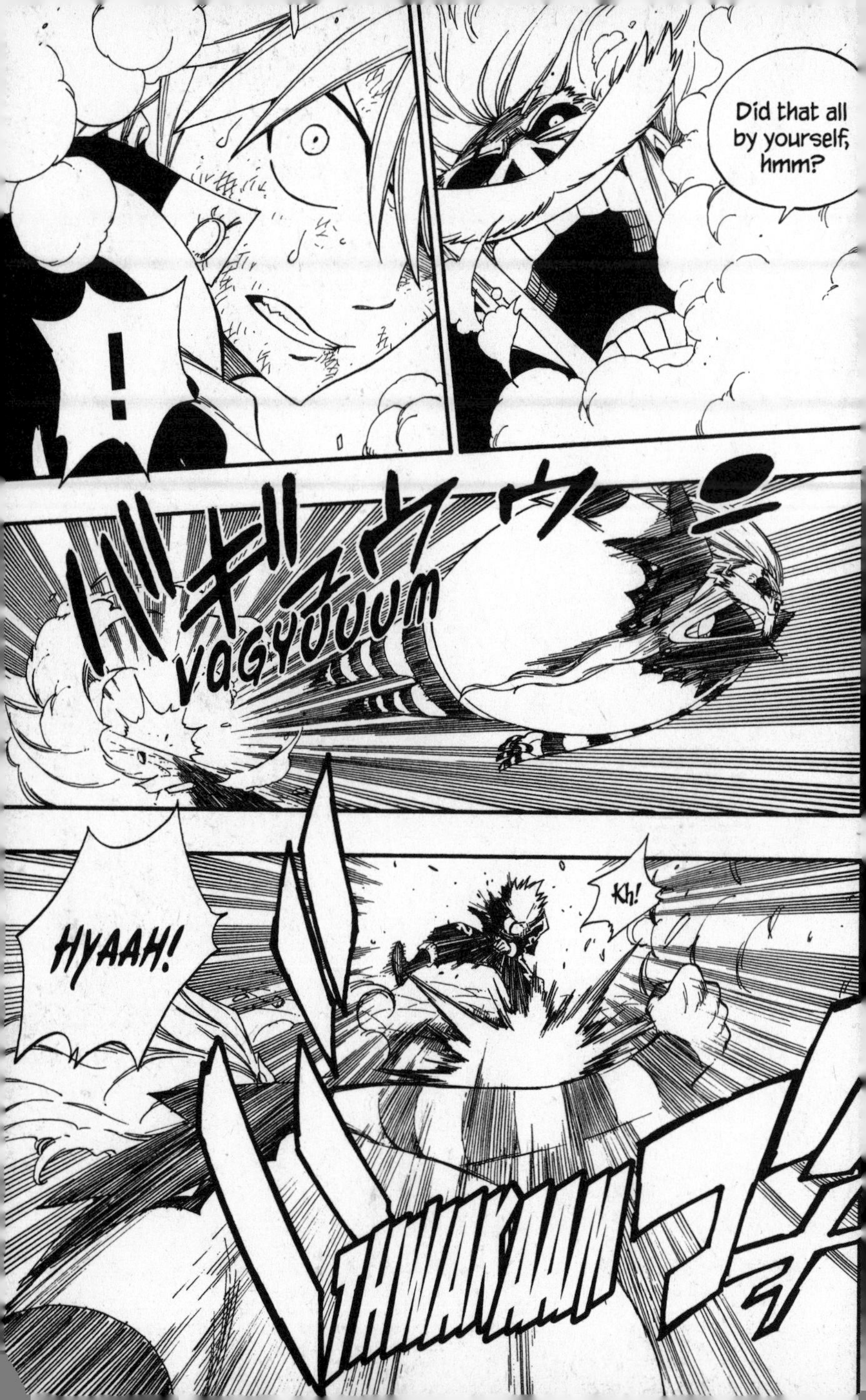
Did that all by yourself, hmm?
!
VAGYUUUUM
Kh!
HYAAH!
THWAKAAM

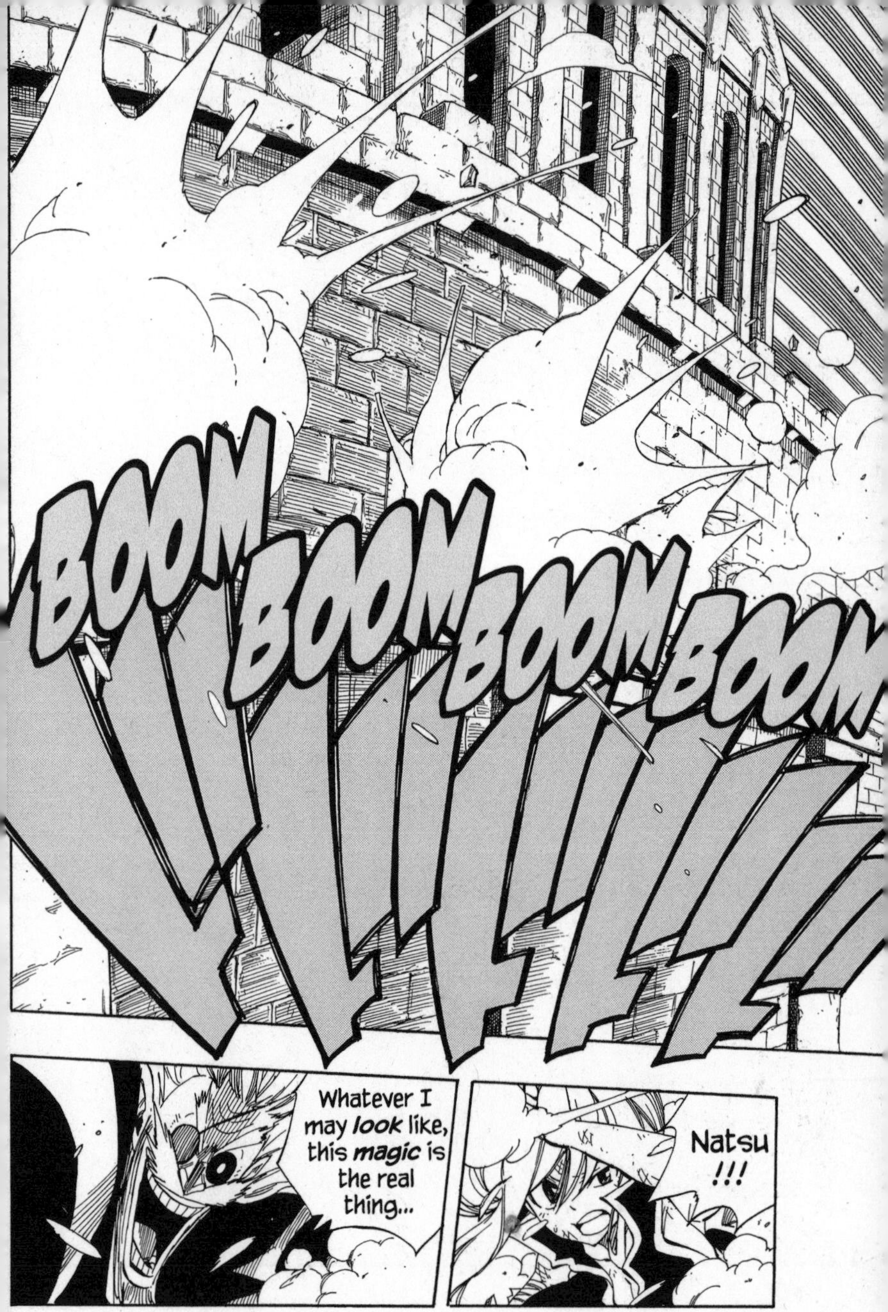
BOOM
BOOM
BOOM
BOOM
Natsu !!!
Whatever I may *look* like, this *magic* is the real thing...

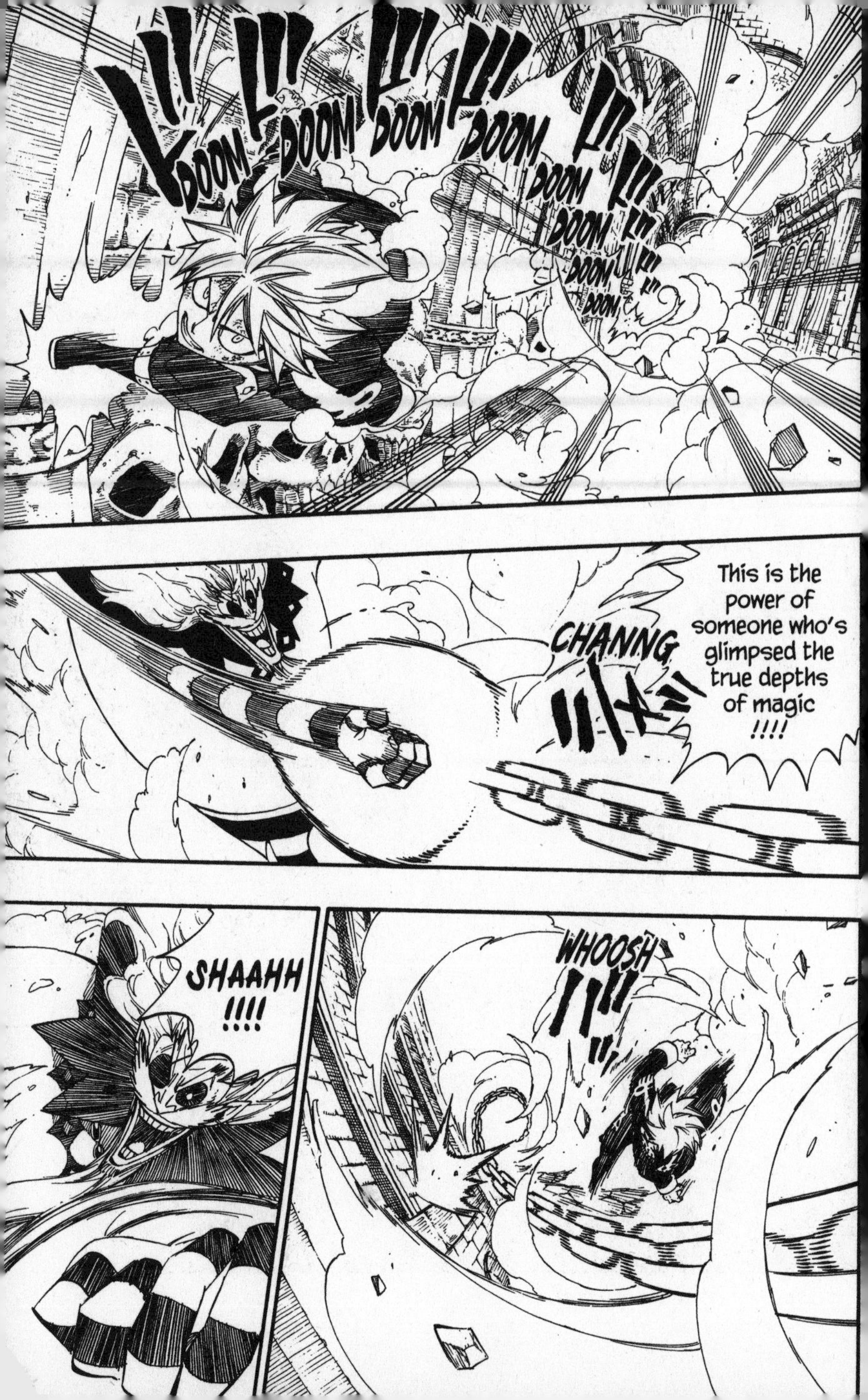
DOOM DOOM DOOM DOOM DOOM DOOM DOOM DOOM
This is the power of someone who's glimpsed the true depths of magic !!!!
CHANNG
WHOOSH
SHAAHH !!!!

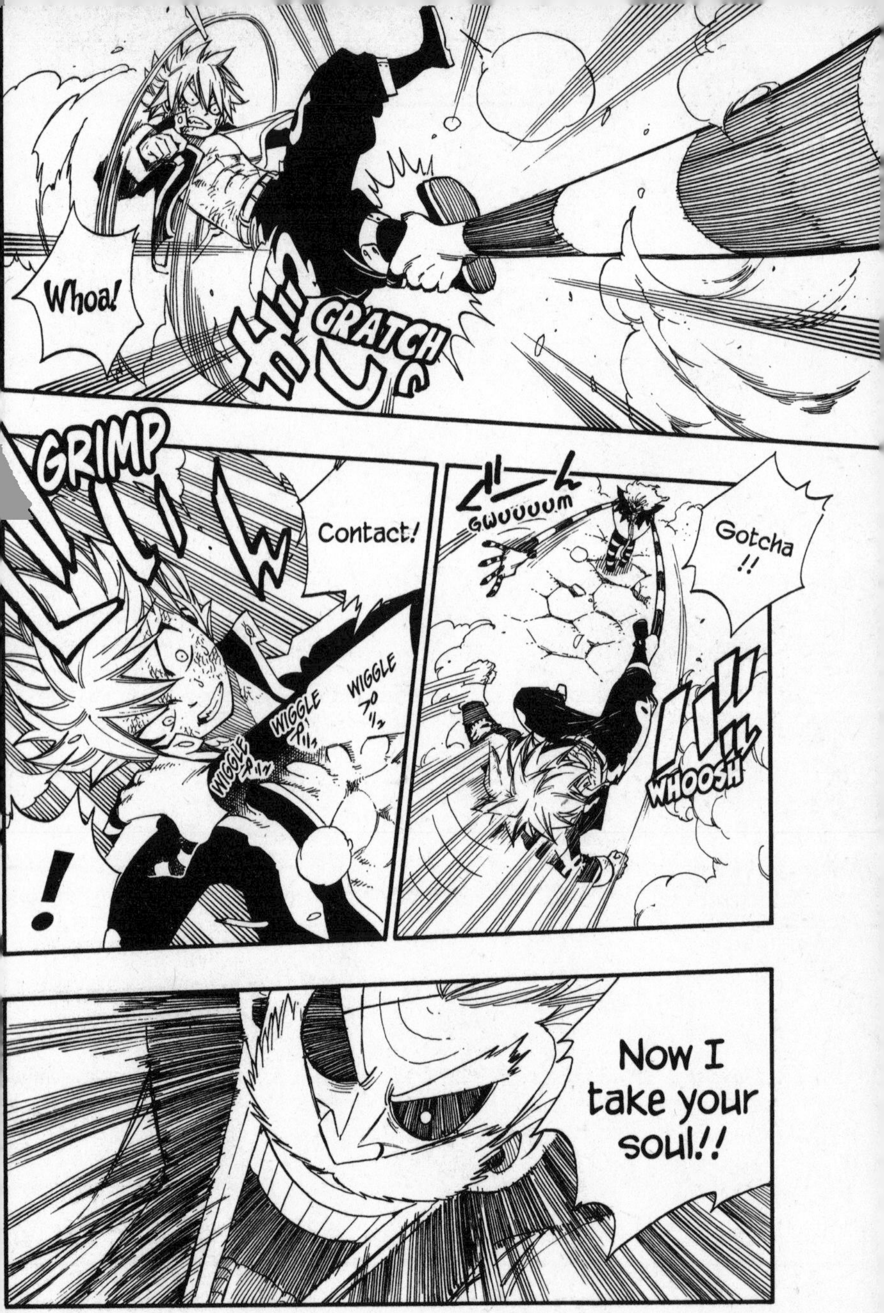
Whoa!
GRATCH
Gotcha!!
GWUUUUM
WHOOSH
GRIMP
Contact!
WIGGLE
WIGGLE
WIGGLE
!
Now I take your soul!!

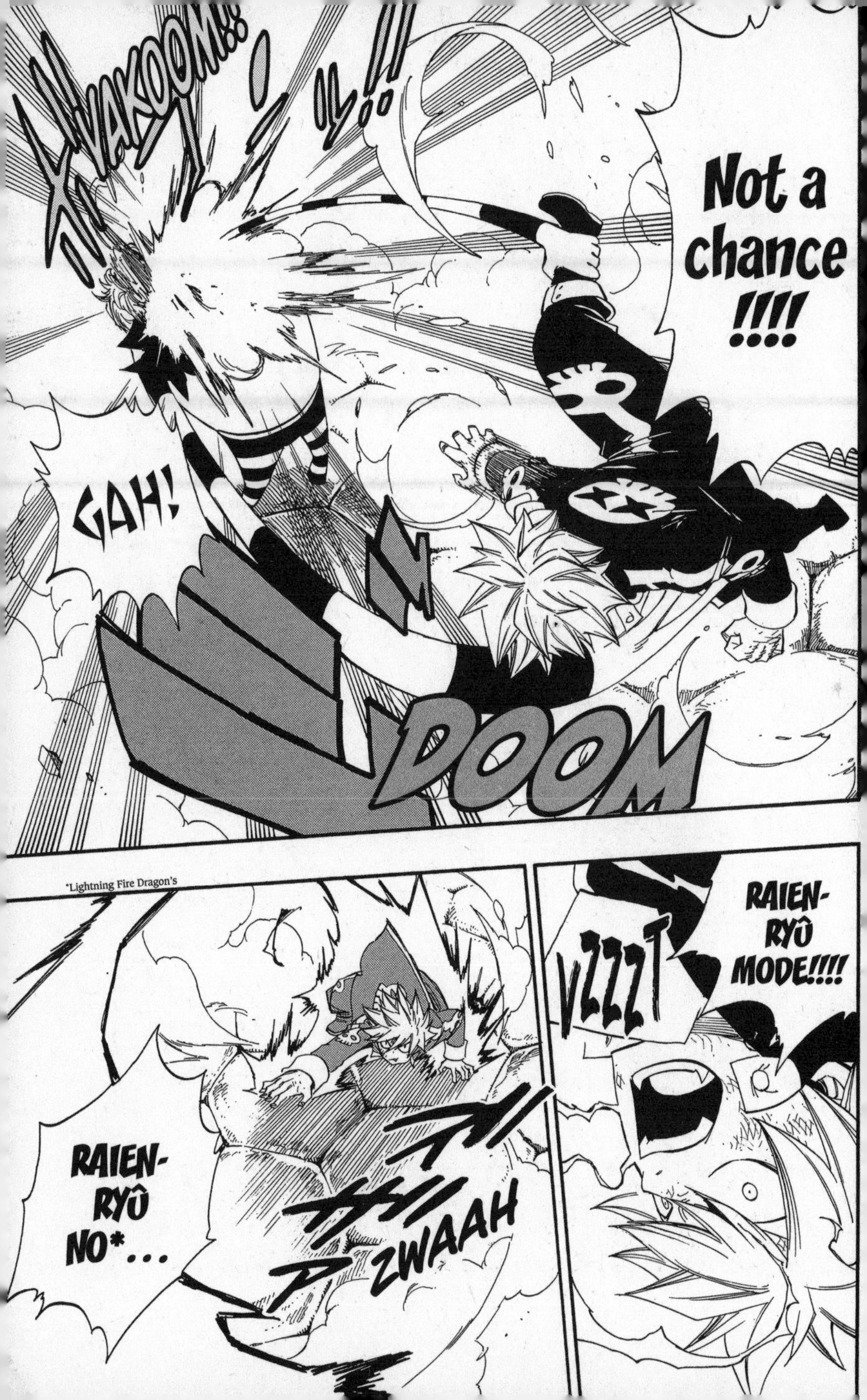

Not a chance!!!!
WHAKOOM!!
GAH!
DOOM
RAIEN-RYÛ MODE!!!!
VZZZT
RAIEN-RYÛ NO*...
ZWAAH

*Lightning Fire Dragon's

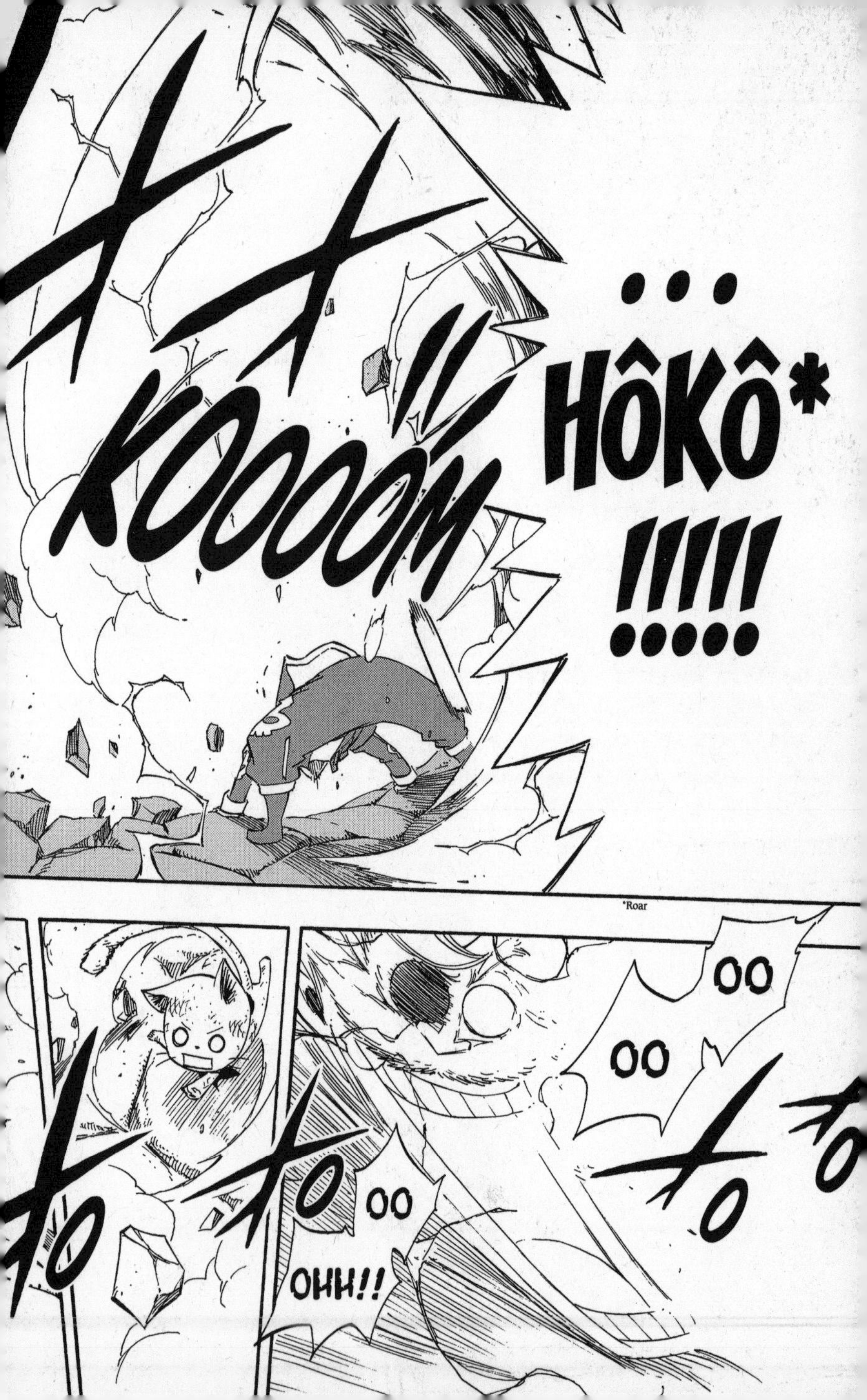
HÔKÔ* !!!!!!
KOOOOM
OO
OO
OO
OHH!!
*Roar

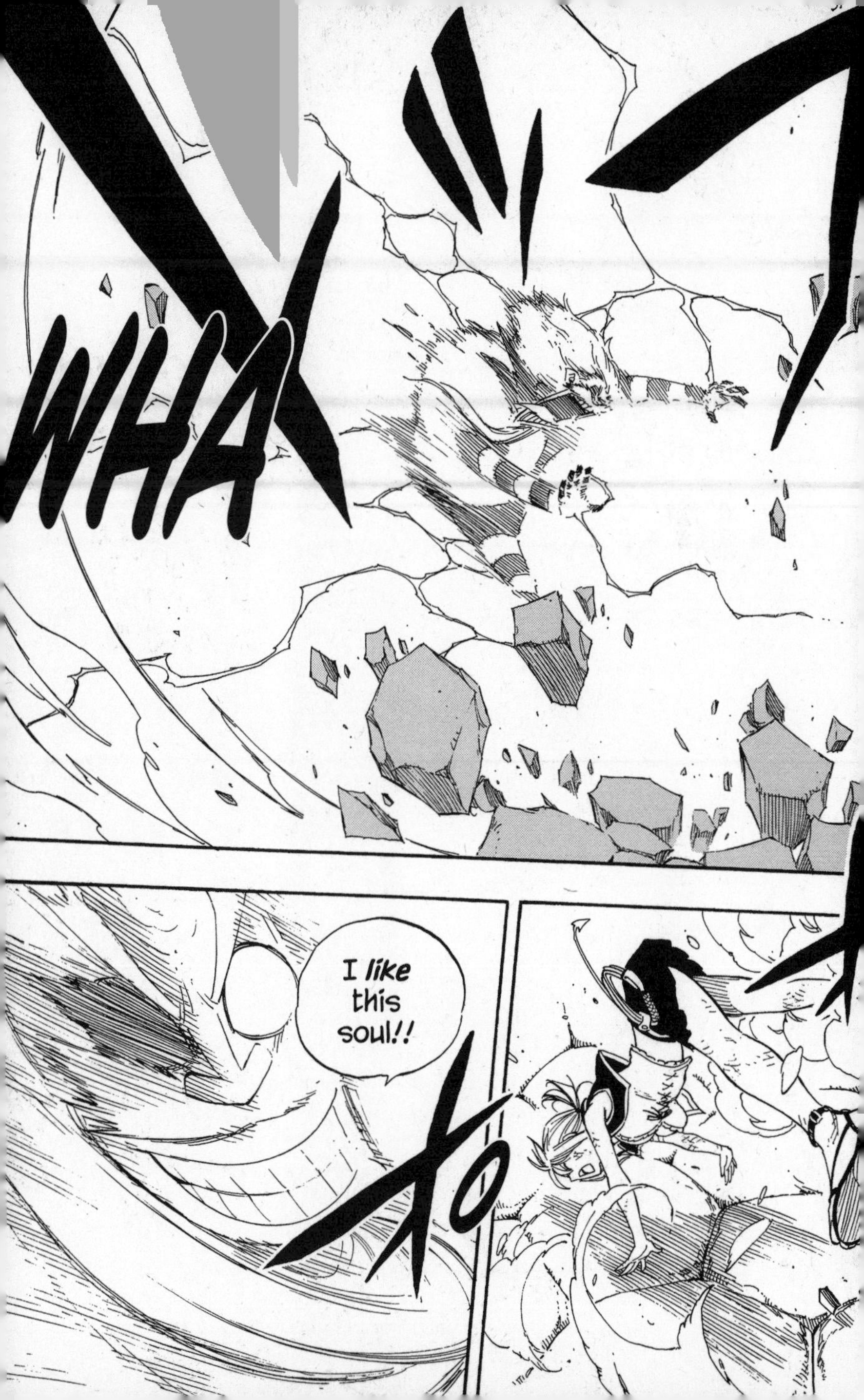
WHA
I like this soul!!

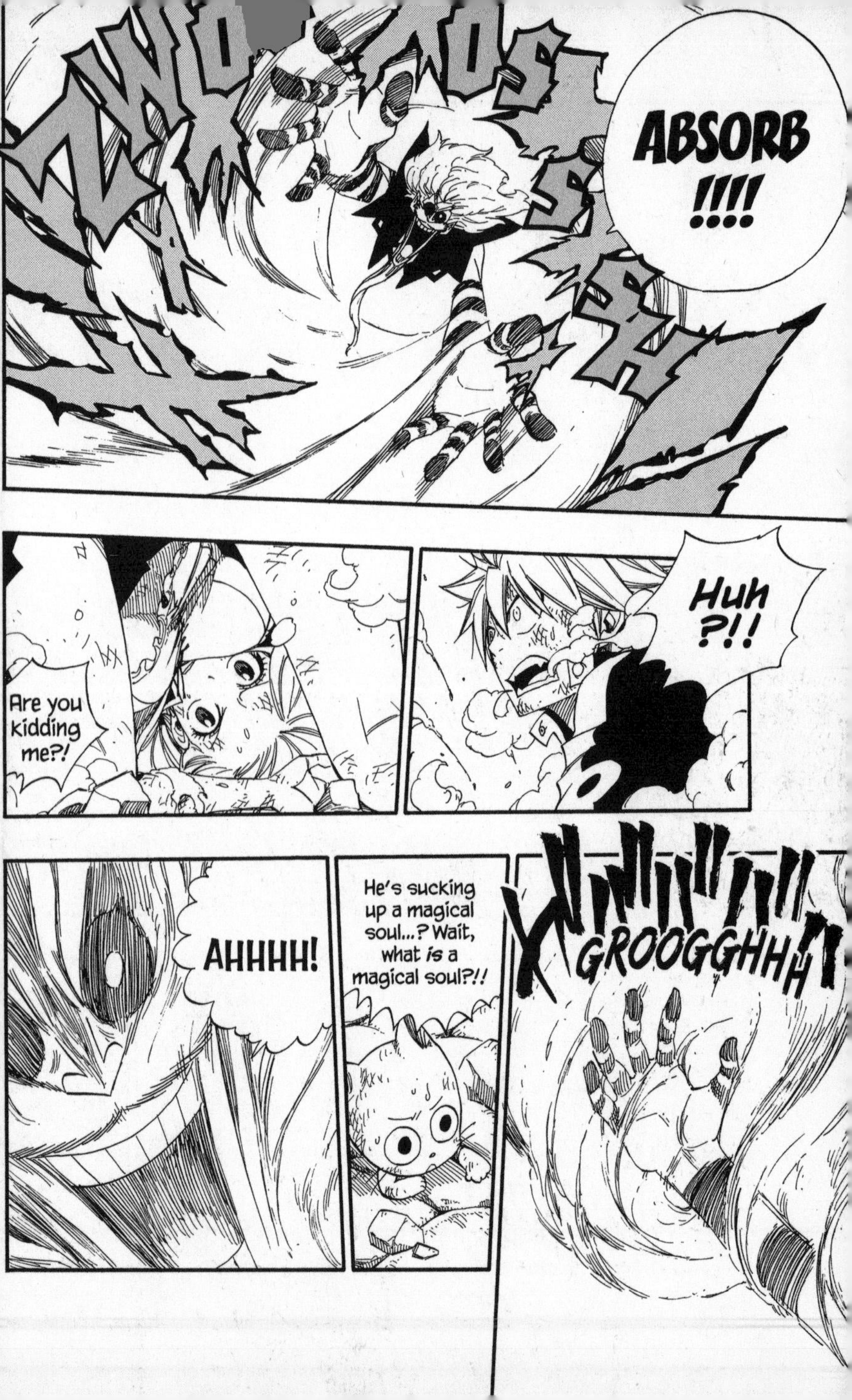
ABSORB !!!!
ZWOOSH
Huh ?!!
Are you kidding me?!
GROOGGHHH
He's sucking up a magical soul...? Wait, what *is* a magical soul?!!
AHHHH!

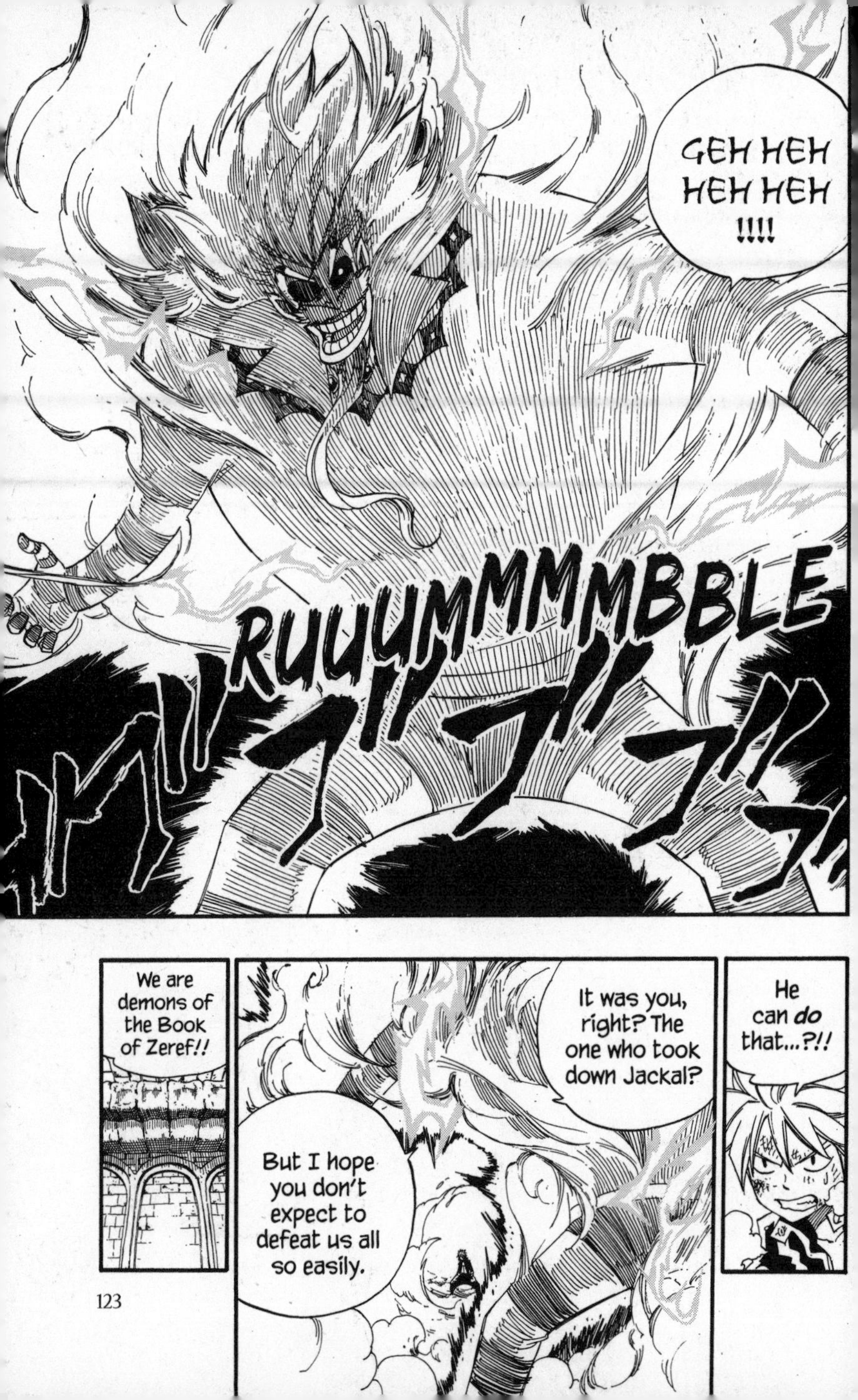
GEH HEH HEH HEH !!!!
RUUUMMMMMBBLE
He can *do* that...?!!
It was you, right? The one who took down Jackal?
But I hope you don't expect to defeat us all so easily.
We are demons of the Book of Zeref!!

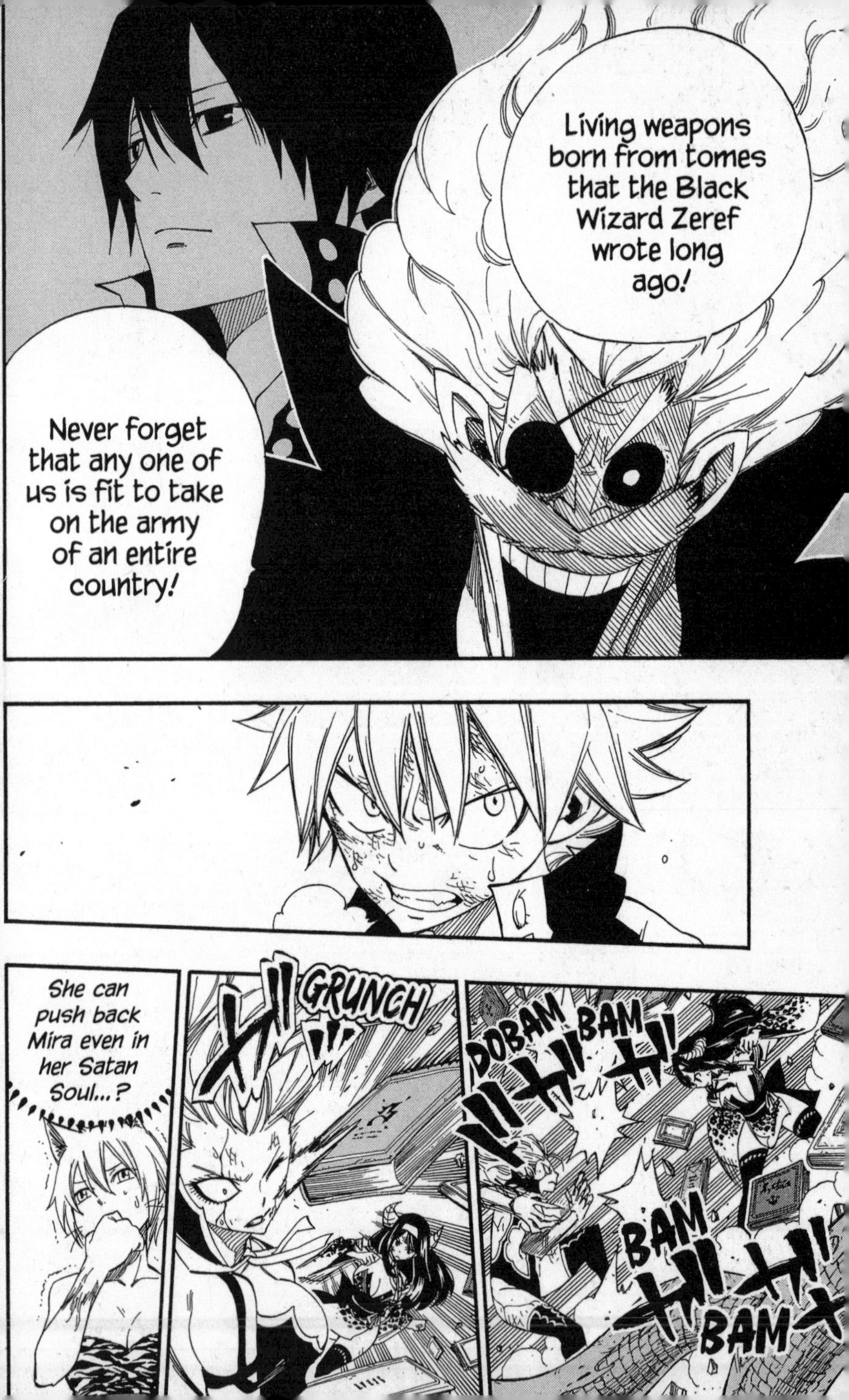
Living weapons born from tomes that the Black Wizard Zeref wrote long ago!
Never forget that any one of us is fit to take on the army of an entire country!
BAM
DOBAM
BAM
BAM
GRUNCH
She can push back Mira even in her Satan Soul...?

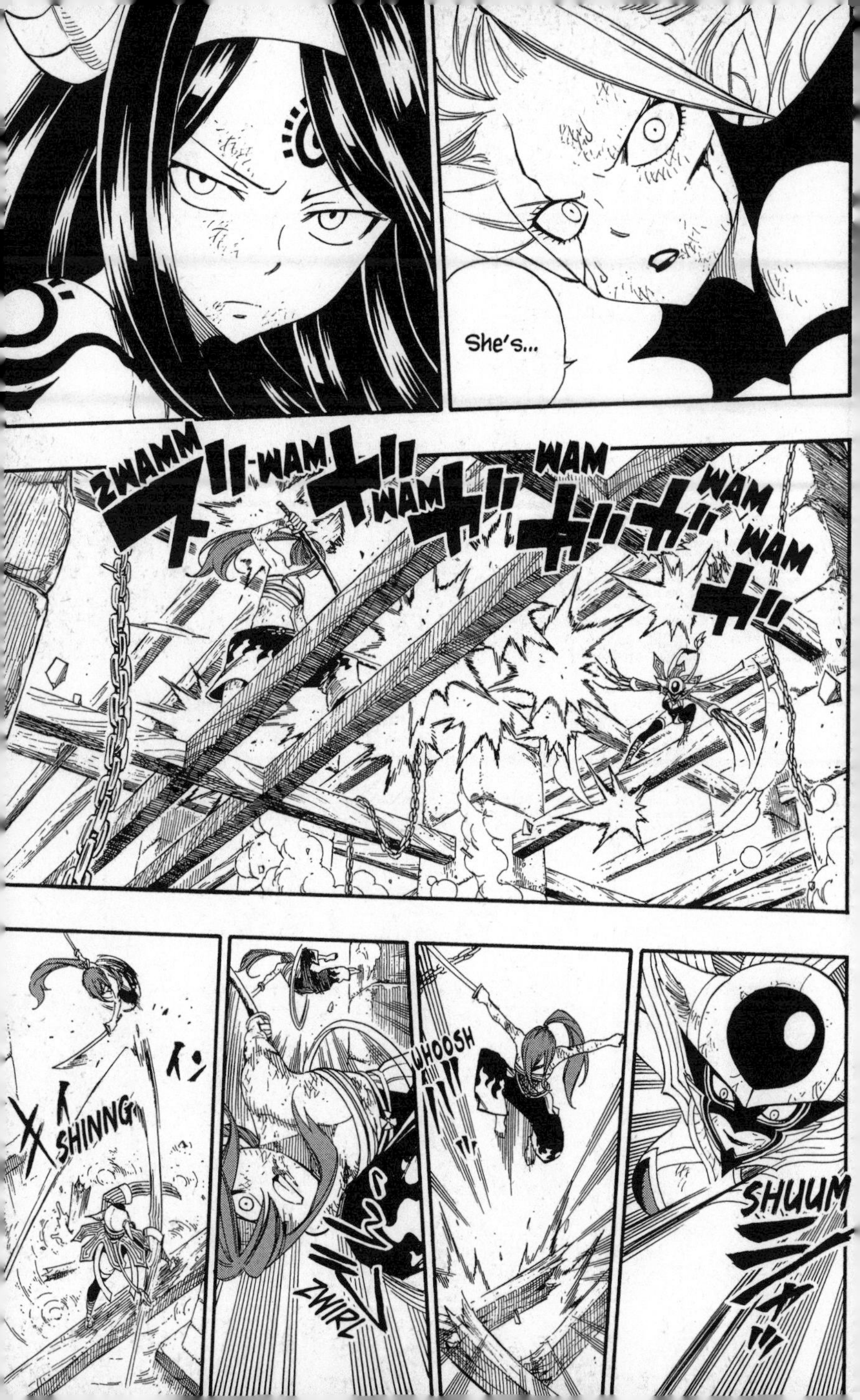
She's...
WAM
WAM
WAM
WAM
WAM
ZWAMM
SHUUM
WHOOSH
ZWIRL
SHINNG

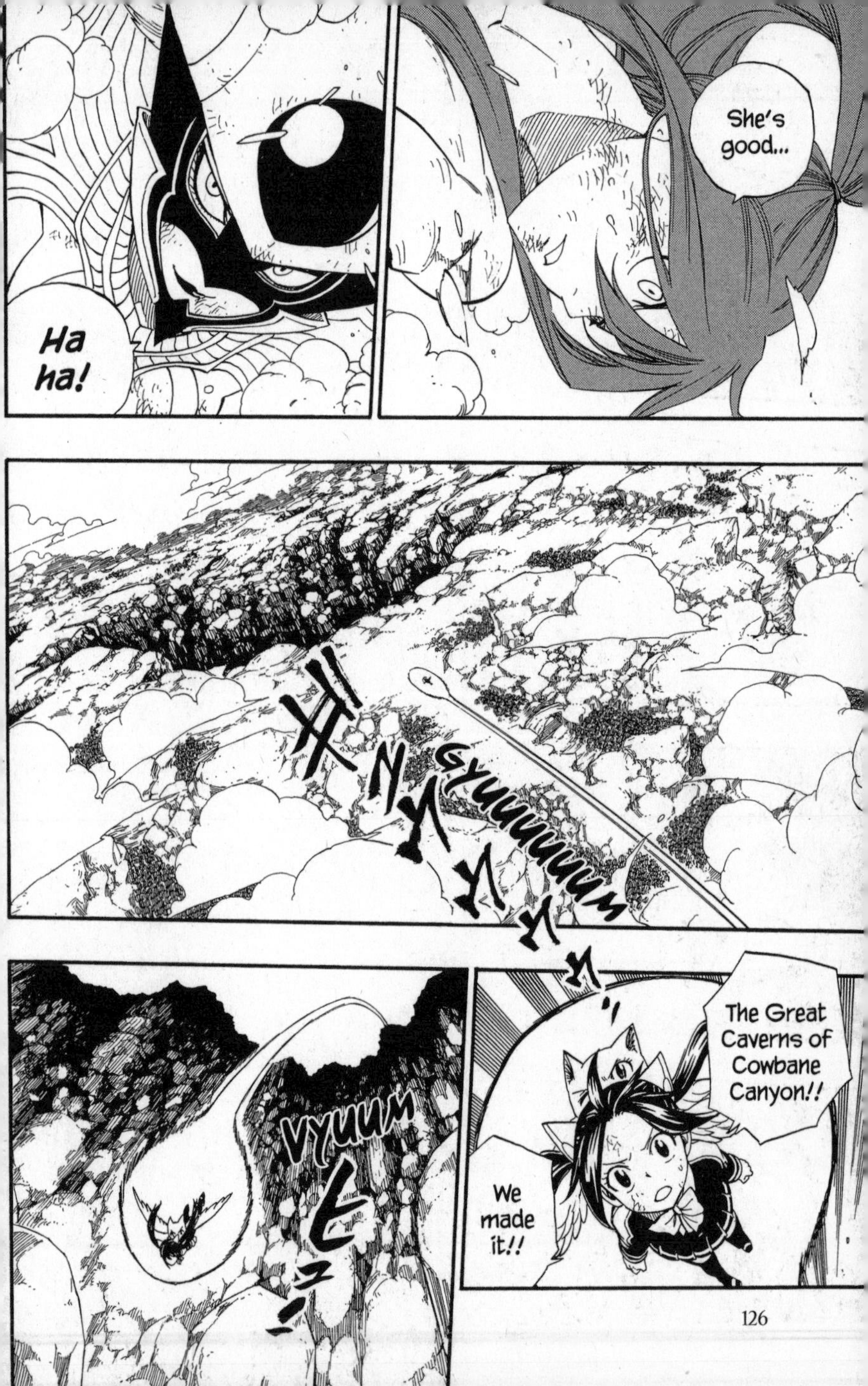
She's good...
Ha ha!
Gyuuuuuuum
The Great Caverns of Cowbane Canyon!!
We made it!!
vyuun

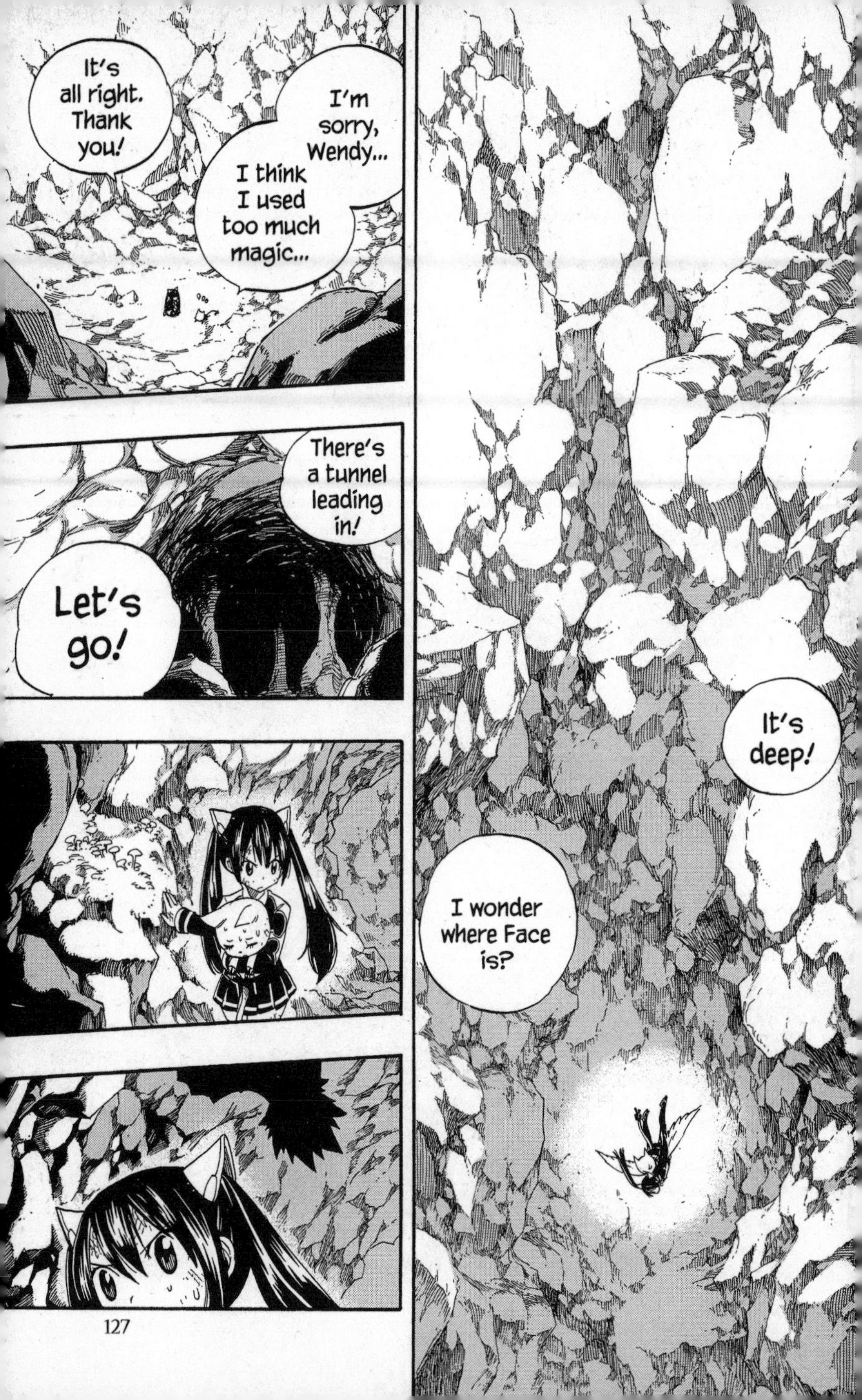
It's deep!
I wonder where Face is?
I'm sorry, Wendy...
I think I used too much magic...
It's all right. Thank you!
There's a tunnel leading in!
Let's go!

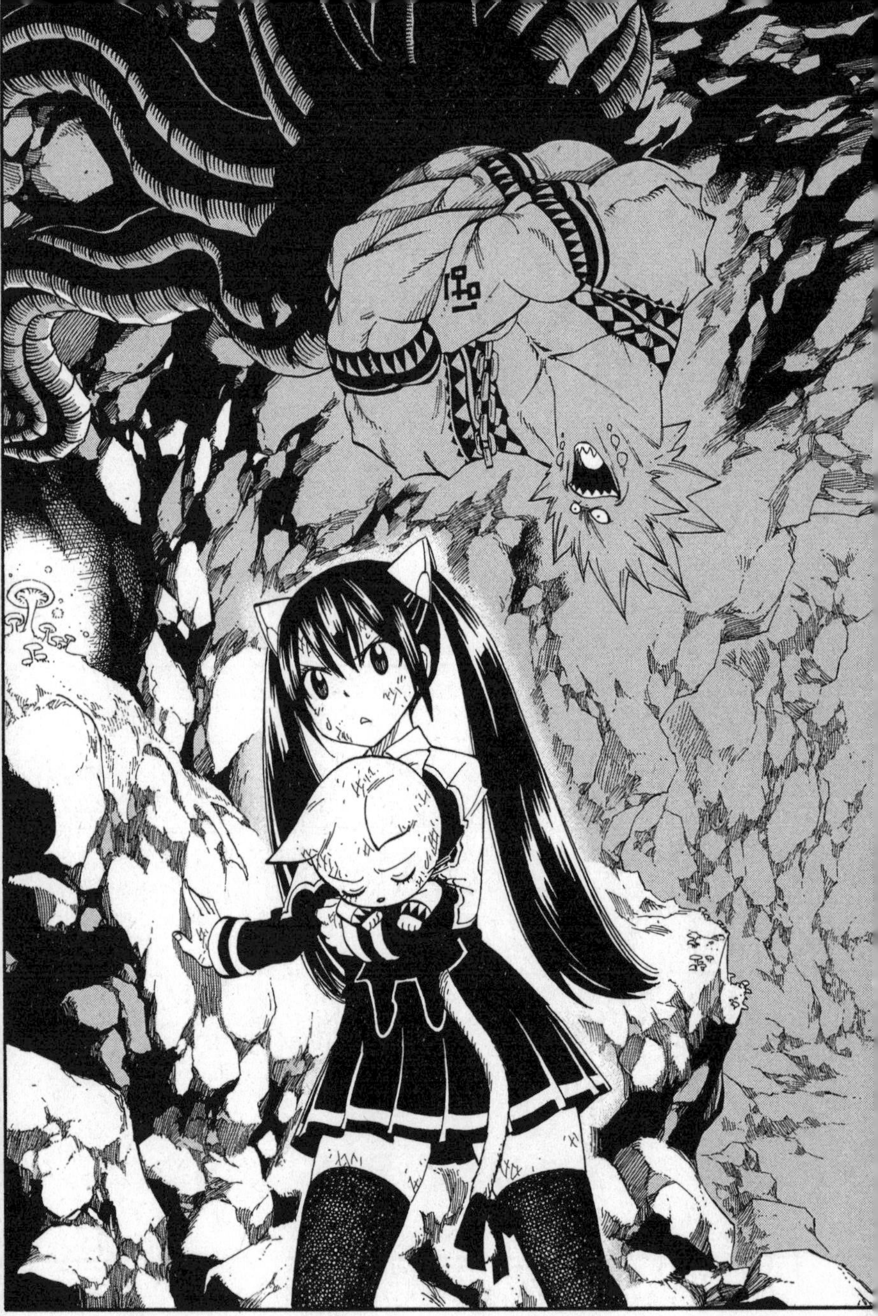

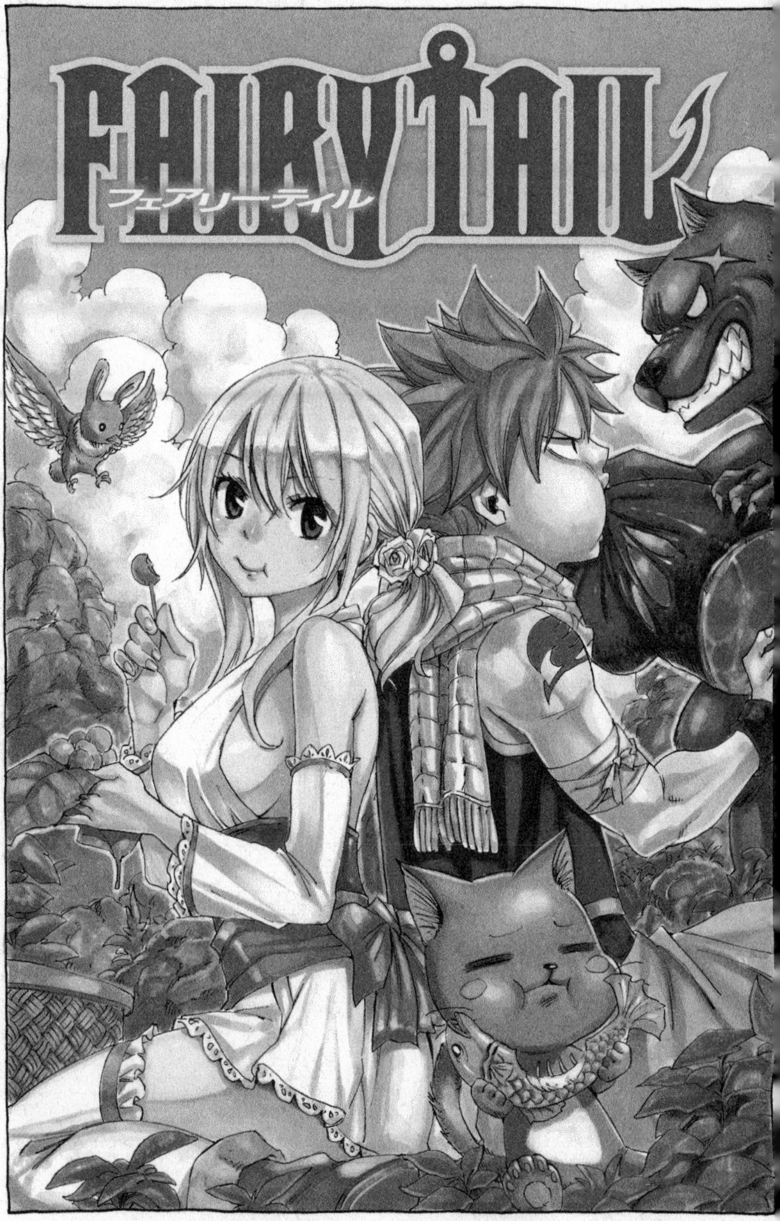
FAIRY TAIL
フェアリーテイル

Chapter 376 Wendy vs. Ezel

The Fairy Tail Guild is looking for illustrations! Please send in your art on a postcard or at postcard size, and do it in black pen, okay? Those chosen to be published will get a signed mini poster! ♪ Make sure you write your real name and address on the back of your illustration!

PART 2 FAIRY TAIL GUILD d'ART

Gunma Prefecture, Orange Jelly

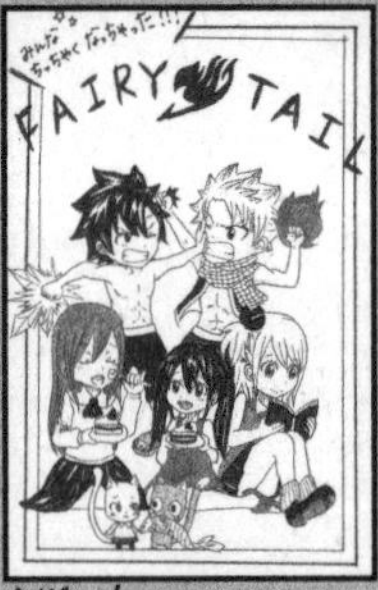
FAIRY TAIL

▲ Whoa! Cute! I'm kinda digging Erza here!

▼ The Tartaros arc is really heating up!! Who will play the next big part?

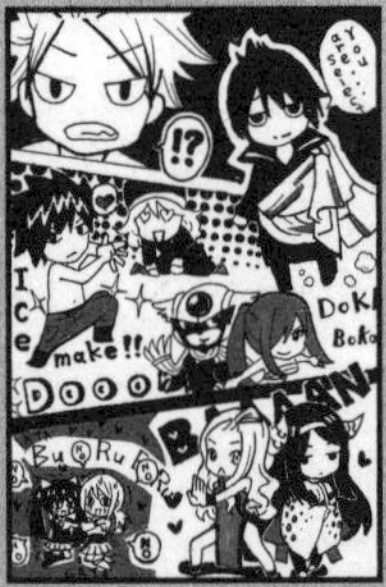
Ice make!!
Doki
Boko
Dooo

Aichi Prefecture, Mayu Matsunaga

▼ This is the volume where Wendy really shows her stuff!!

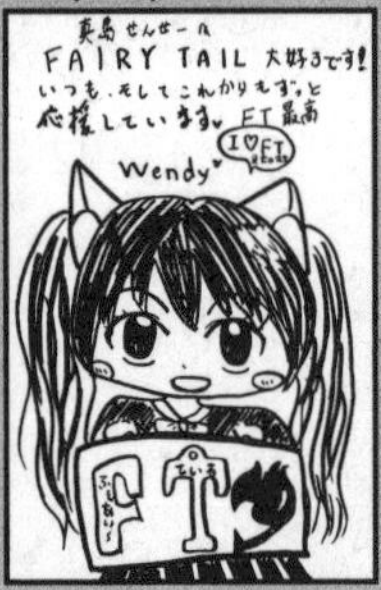
FAIRY TAIL 大好きです!
Wendy
I ♡ FT
FT

Ibaraki Prefecture, Sayaka Kimura

Tokyo, I'm Black Butler!

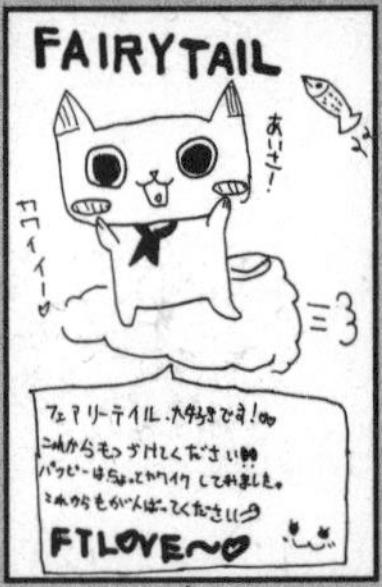
FAIRYTAIL
FTLOVE~♡

▲ Really cute! Sometimes drawing it square-ish is kinda nice!

Hokkaido, Seiya Yokoi

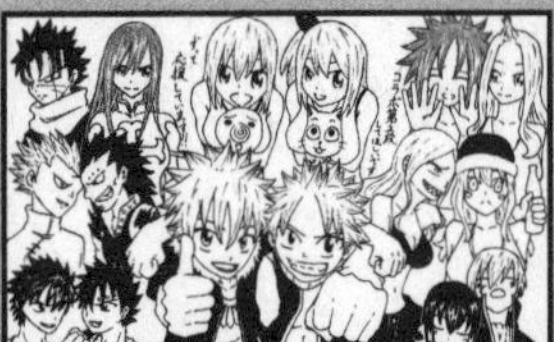

▲ Hey, a Rave/Fairy Tail collaboration! Brings back memories! Thank you!!

Tottori Prefecture, Haruna Sato

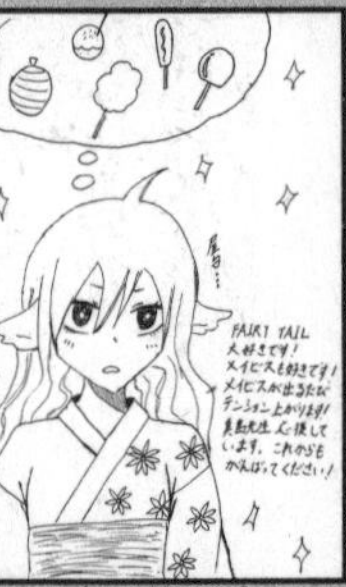
FAIRY TAIL

▲ If you're a Mavis fan, you should check out Monthly Fairy Tail Magazine!!

REJECTION CORNER

Whoa!! ▶ This guy is way over-reacting, but... he's right. The world needs rejections too.

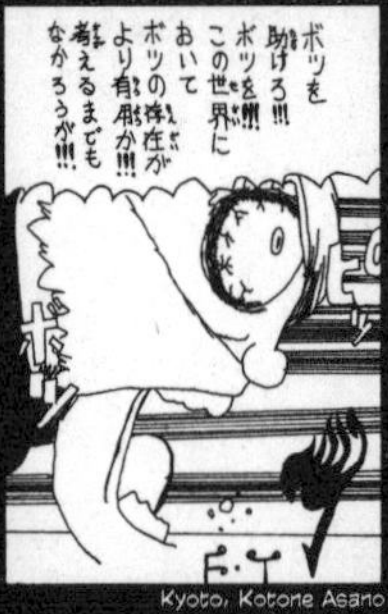
ボツを助けろ!!!
ボツを!!!
この世界においてボツの存在がより有用か!!!
考えるまでもなかろうが!!!
F.T

Kyoto, Kotone Asano

By sending in letters or postcards, you give us permission to give your name, address, postal code, and any other information you include to the artist as-is. Please keep that in mind.

Send to Hiro Mashima, Kodansha Comics 451 Park Ave. South, 7th Floor New York, NY 10016

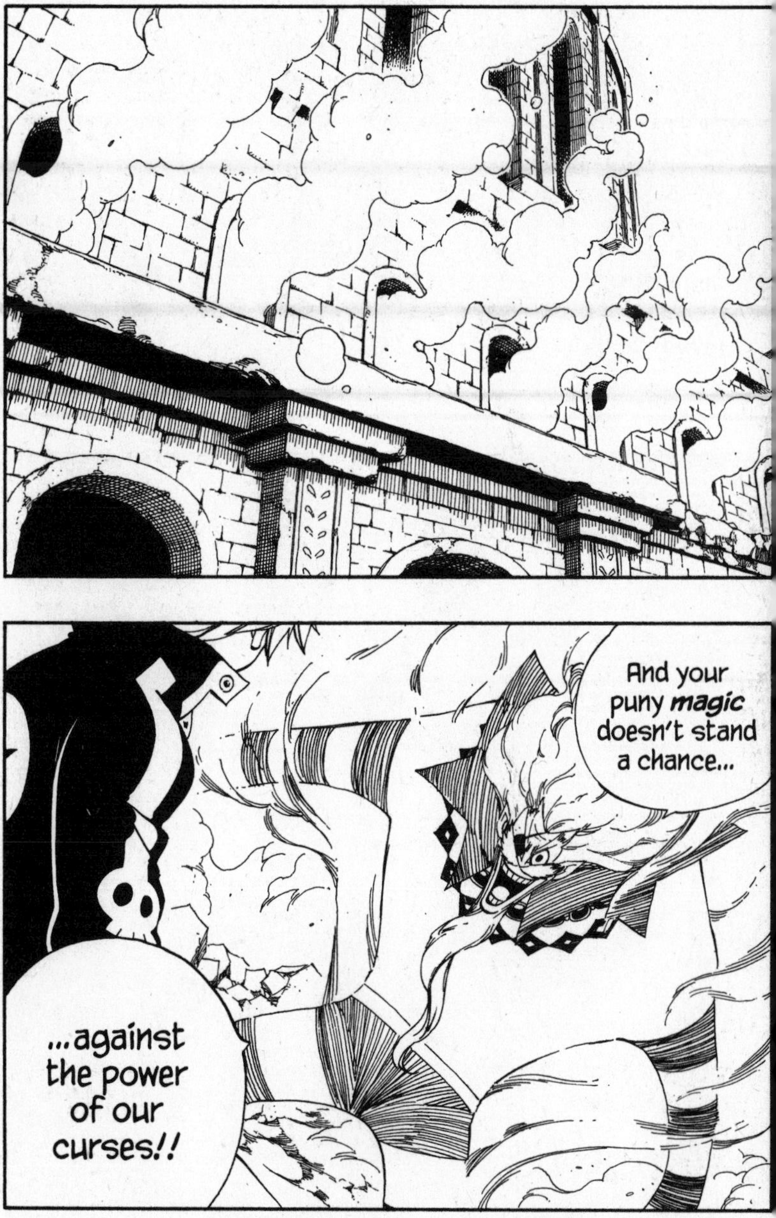
And your puny *magic* doesn't stand a chance...
...against the power of our curses!!

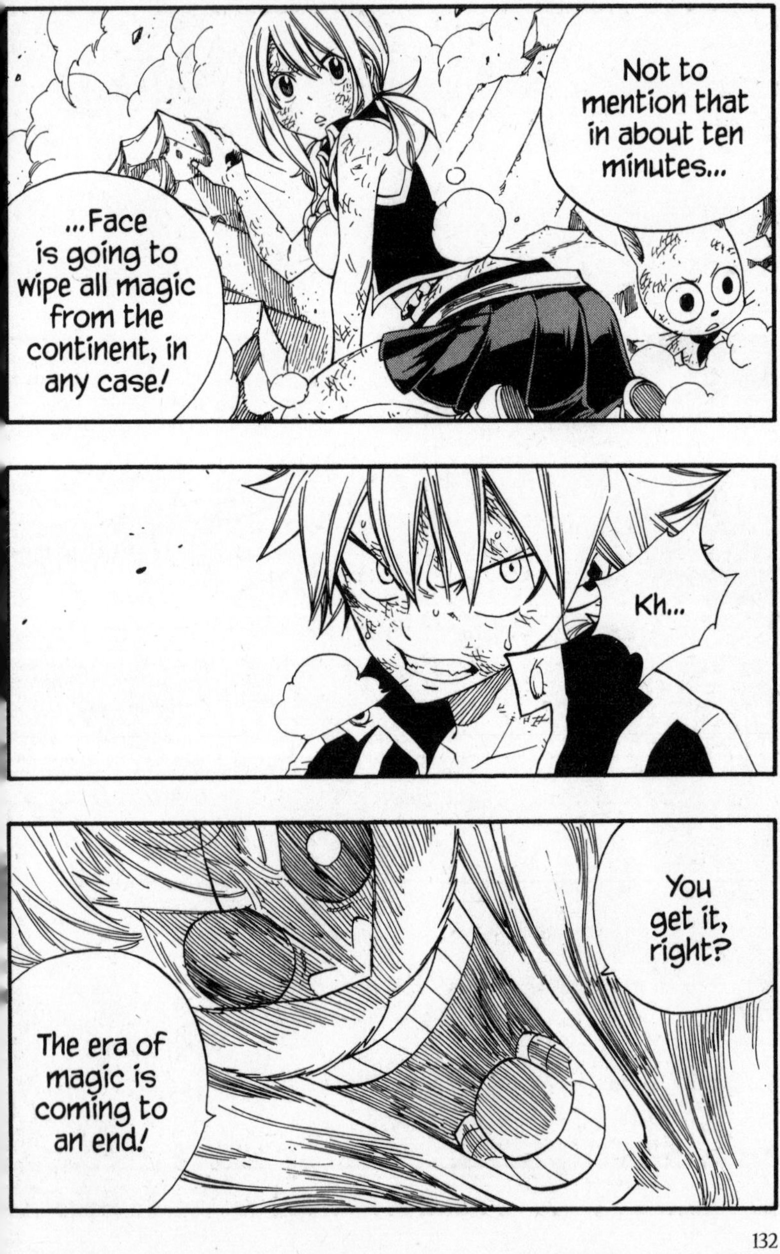
Not to mention that in about ten minutes...
...Face is going to wipe all magic from the continent, in any case!
Kh...
You get it, right?
The era of magic is coming to an end!

All the magic is going to disappear from the entire continent...
I can hardly believe it...
Horologium! Time remaining?
We're down to 9 minutes, 43 seconds, Miss.
PAPOOM
The whole guild is battling Tartaros right now...
If everyone's magic were to suddenly cut out...
Wendy, please...

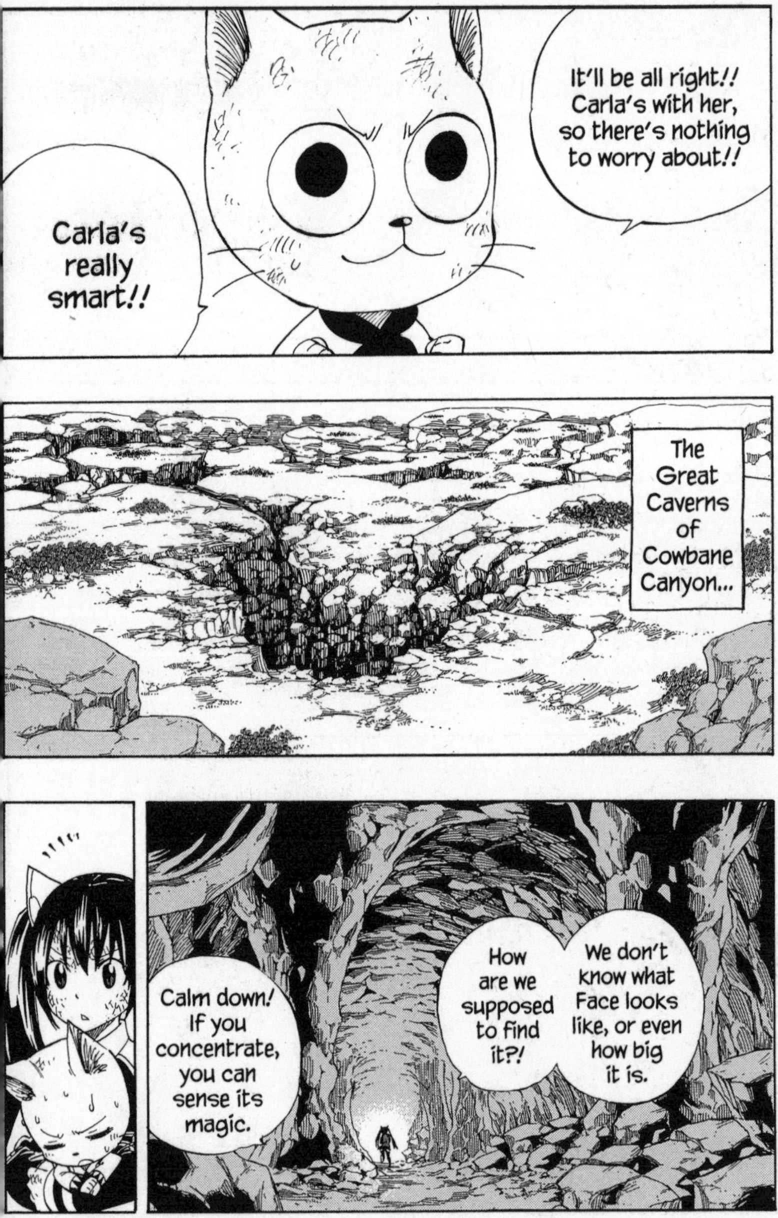
It'll be all right!! Carla's with her, so there's nothing to worry about!!
Carla's really smart!!
The Great Caverns of Cowbane Canyon...
We don't know what Face looks like, or even how big it is.
How are we supposed to find it?!
Calm down! If you concentrate, you can sense its magic.

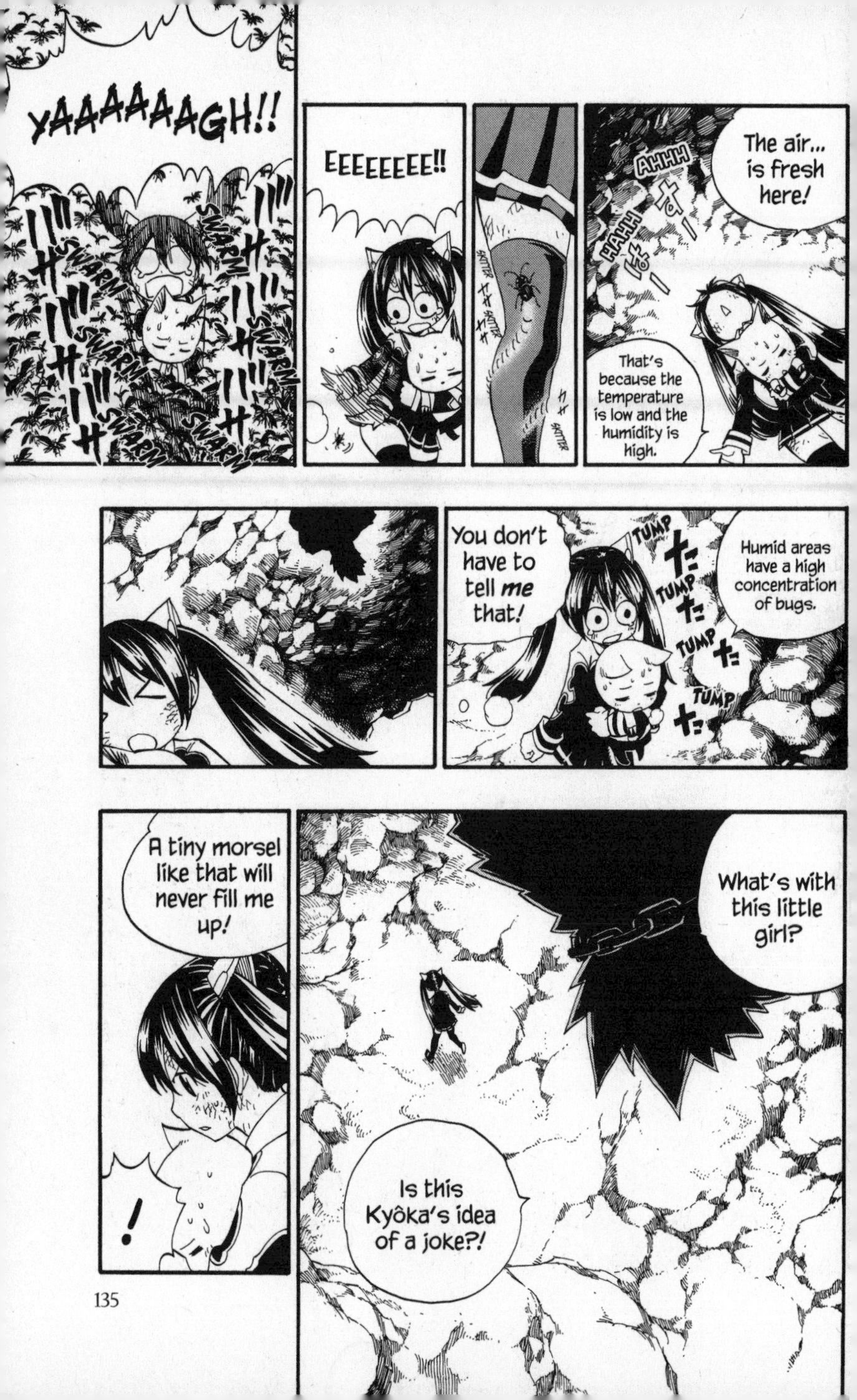
The air... is fresh here!
AHHH
That's because the temperature is low and the humidity is high.
SKITTER
SKITTER
SKITTER
EEEEEEEE!!
YAAAAAAGH!!
SWARM
SWARM
SWARM
SWARM
SWARM
SWARM
Humid areas have a high concentration of bugs.
You don't have to tell me that!
TUMP
TUMP
TUMP
TUMP
What's with this little girl?
Is this Kyôka's idea of a joke?!
A tiny morsel like that will never fill me up!
!

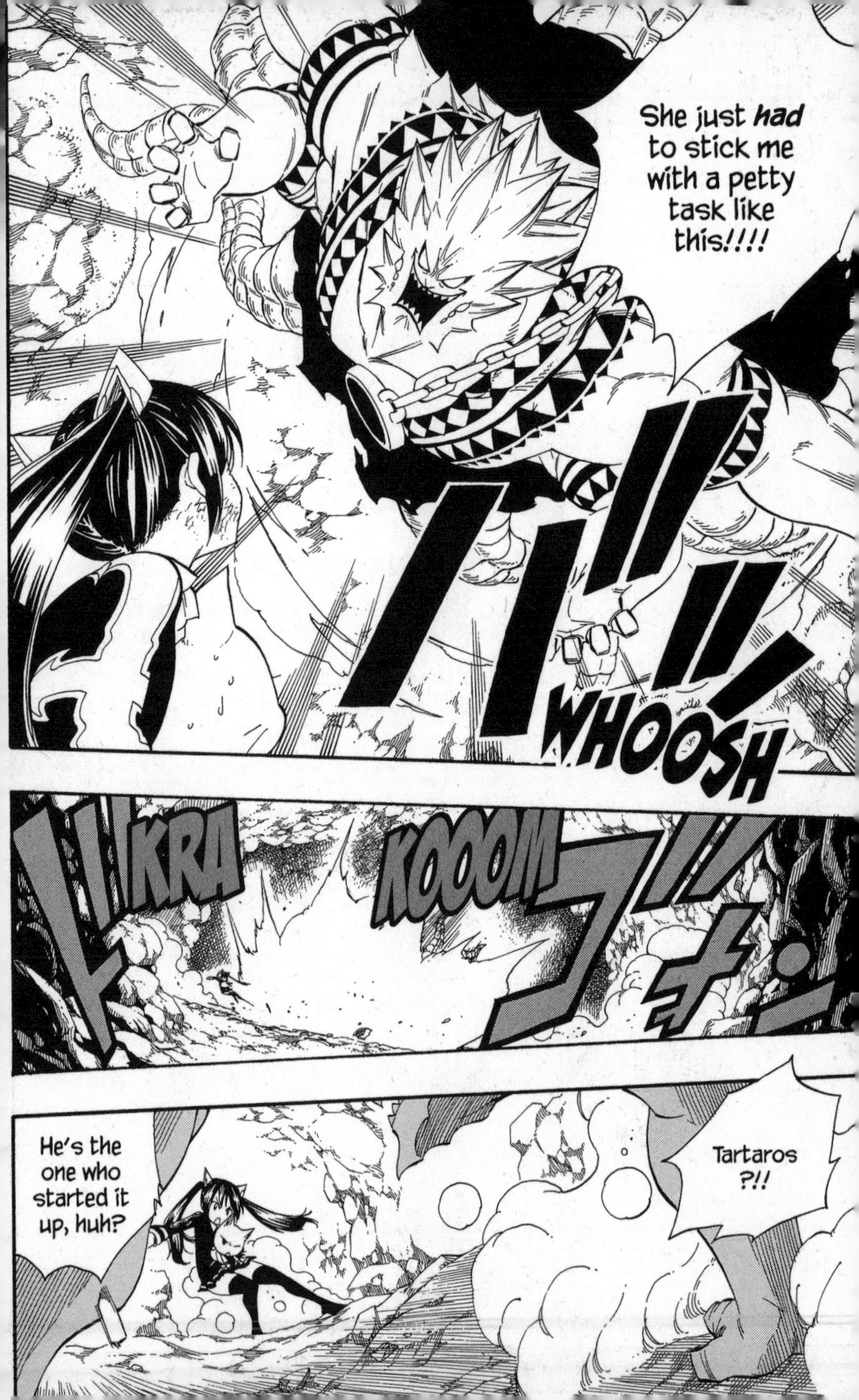
She just *had* to stick me with a petty task like this!!!!
WHOOSH
KRA
KOOOM
Tartaros ?!!
He's the one who started it up, huh?

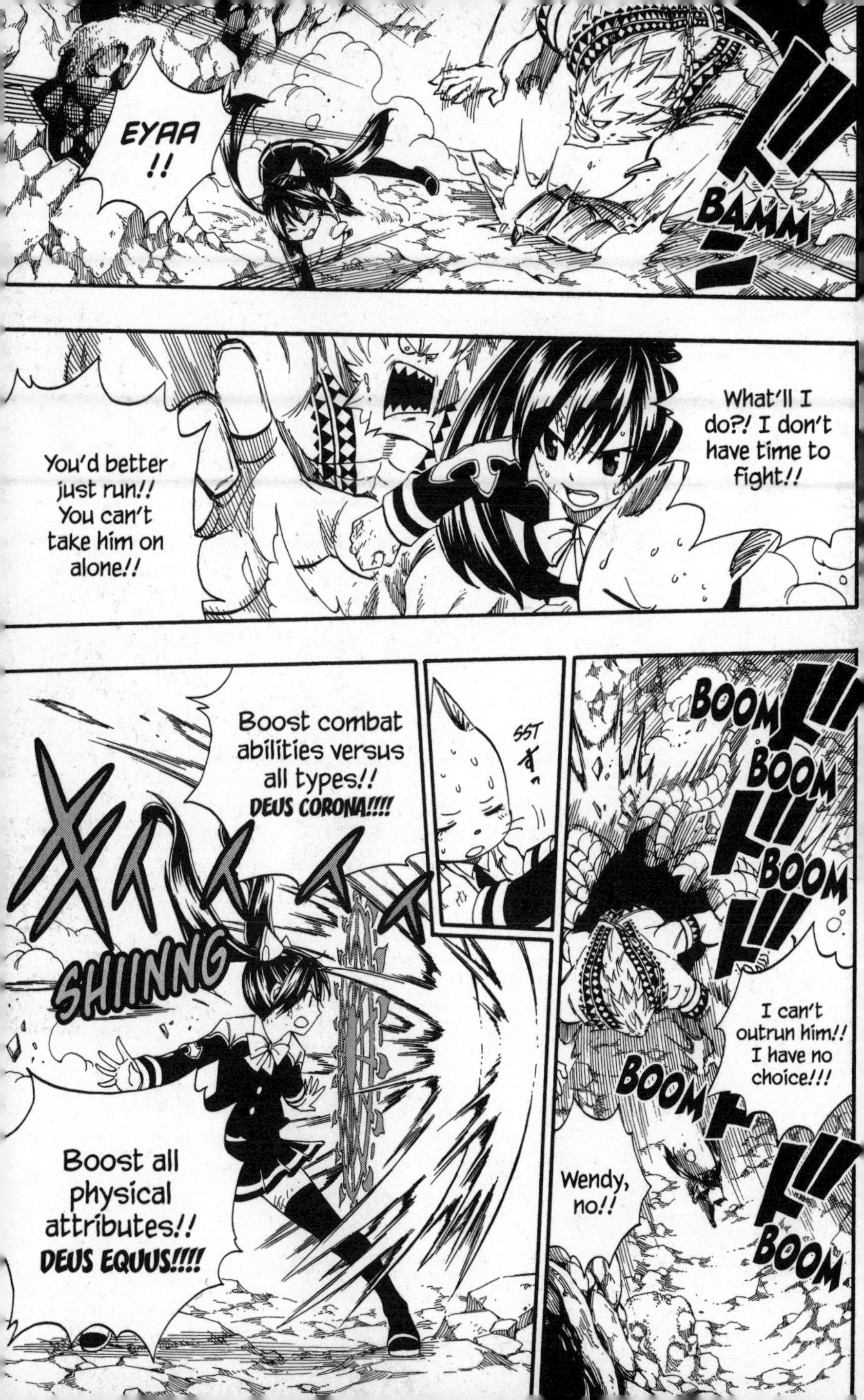
BAMM
EYAA !!
What'll I do?! I don't have time to fight!!
You'd better just run!! You can't take him on alone!!
BOOM
BOOM
BOOM
I can't outrun him!! I have no choice!!!
BOOM
BOOM
Wendy, no!!
SST すっ
Boost combat abilities versus all types!! DEUS CORONA!!!!
SHIINNG
Boost all physical attributes!! DEUS EQUUS!!!!

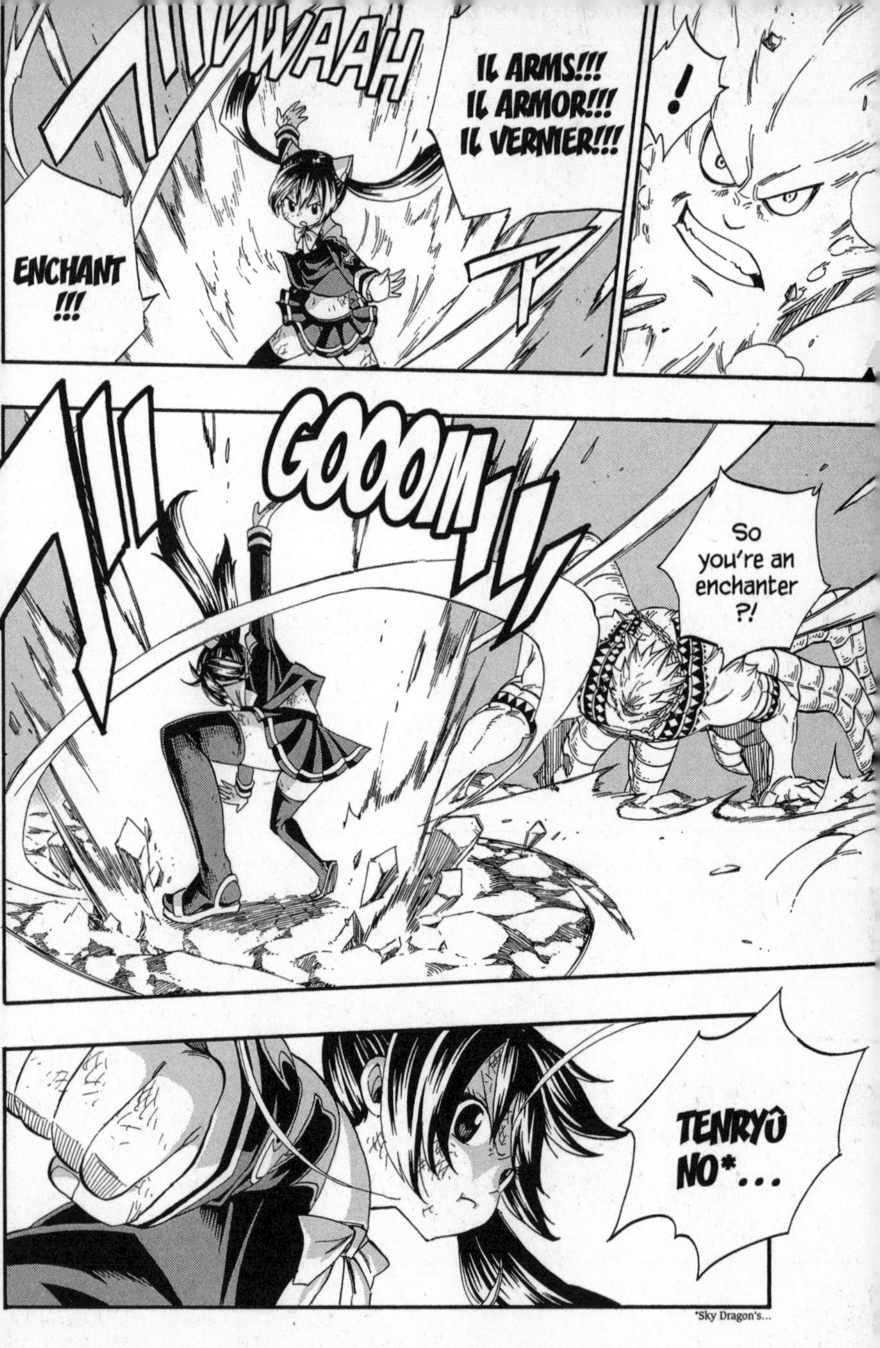
!
IL ARMS!!!
IL ARMOR!!!
IL VERNIER!!!
WAAH
ENCHANT !!!
GOOOM
So you're an enchanter ?!
TENRYÛ NO*...

*Sky Dragon's...

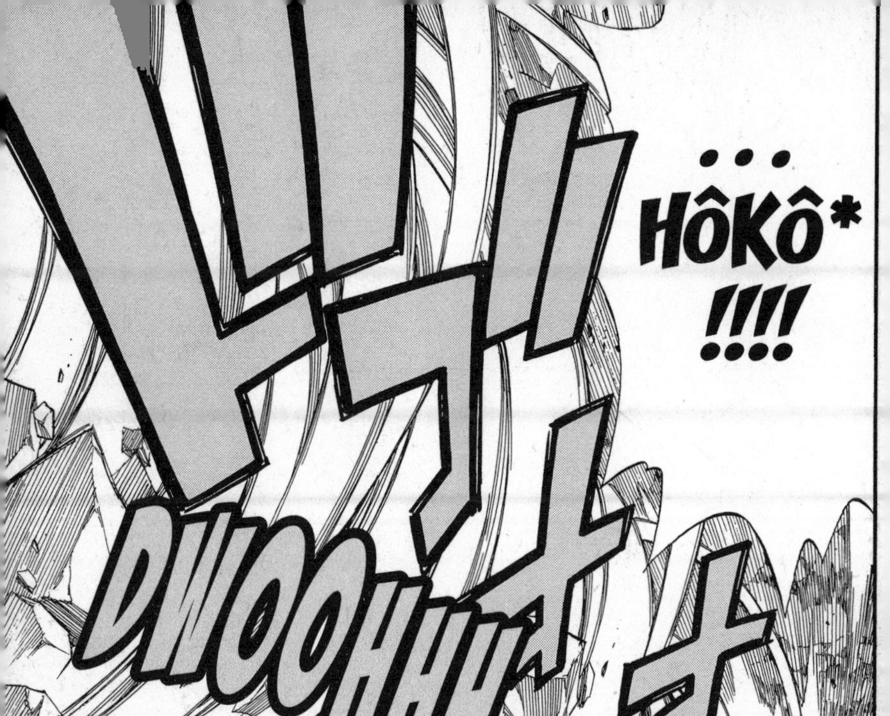
...HÔKÔ* !!!!
DWOOHHH

*...Roar!!!!

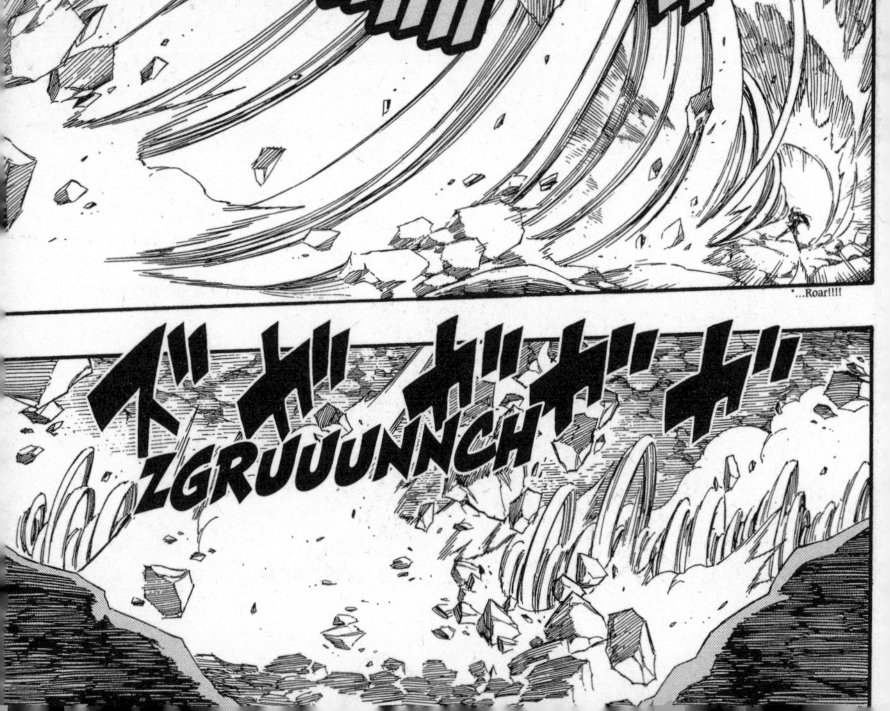
ZGRUUUUNNCH

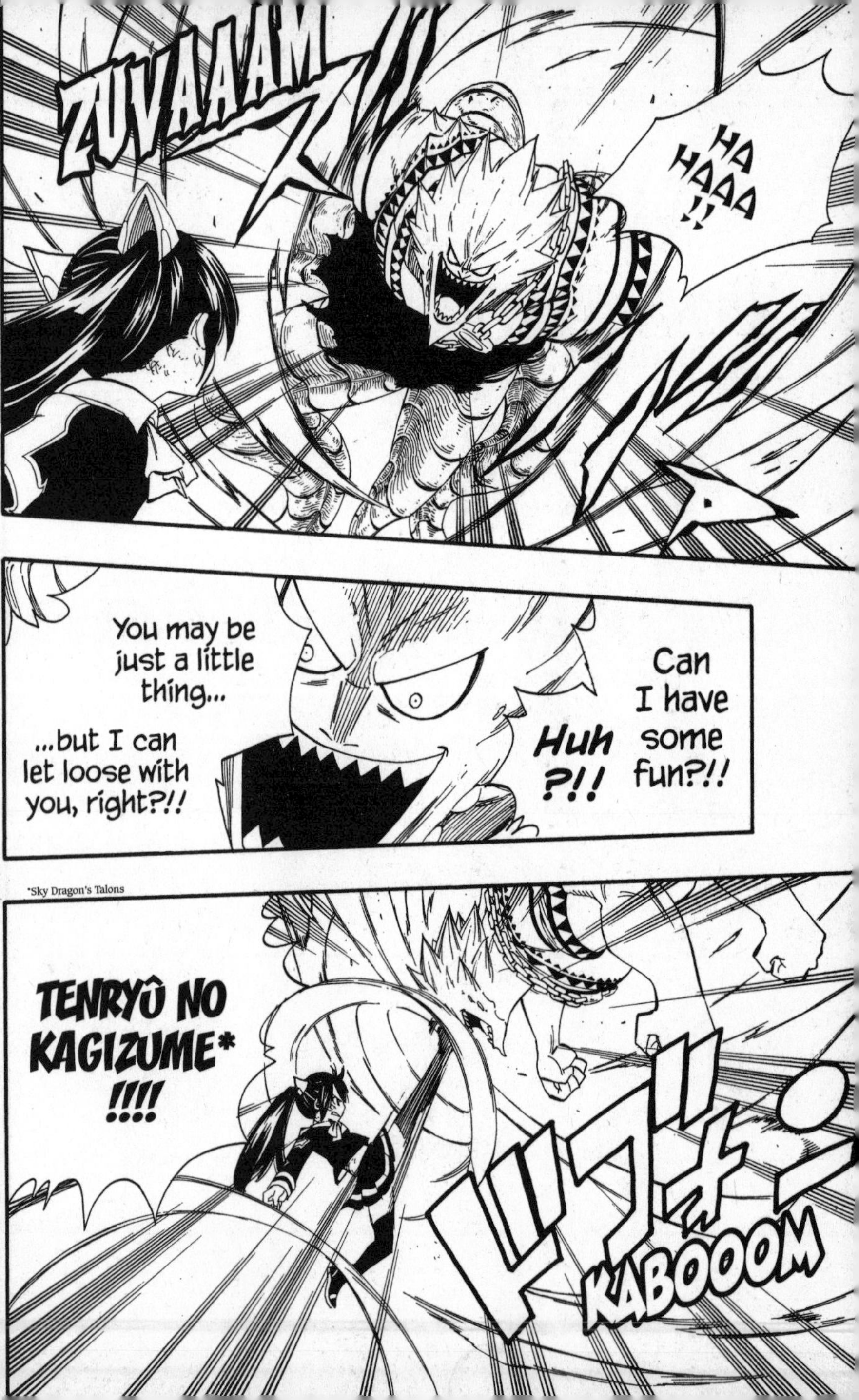
HA HAAAA!!
ZUVAAAM
Can I have some fun?!!
Huh?!!
You may be just a little thing...
...but I can let loose with you, right?!!
TENRYÛ NO KAGIZUME*!!!!
KABOOOM
*Sky Dragon's Talons

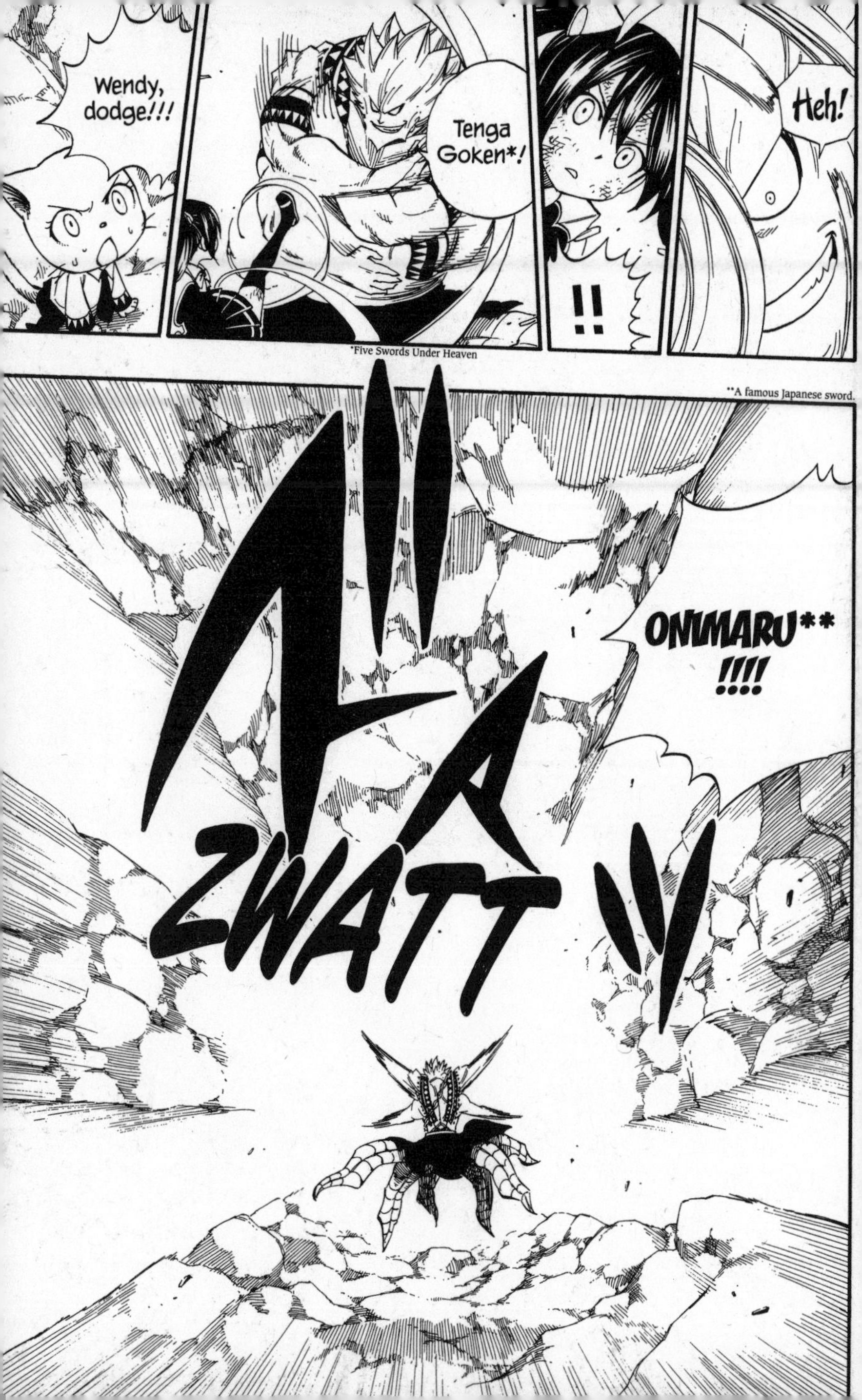
Heh!
!!
Tenga Goken*!
Wendy, dodge!!!
ONIMARU** !!!!
ZWATT

*Five Swords Under Heaven

**A famous Japanese sword.

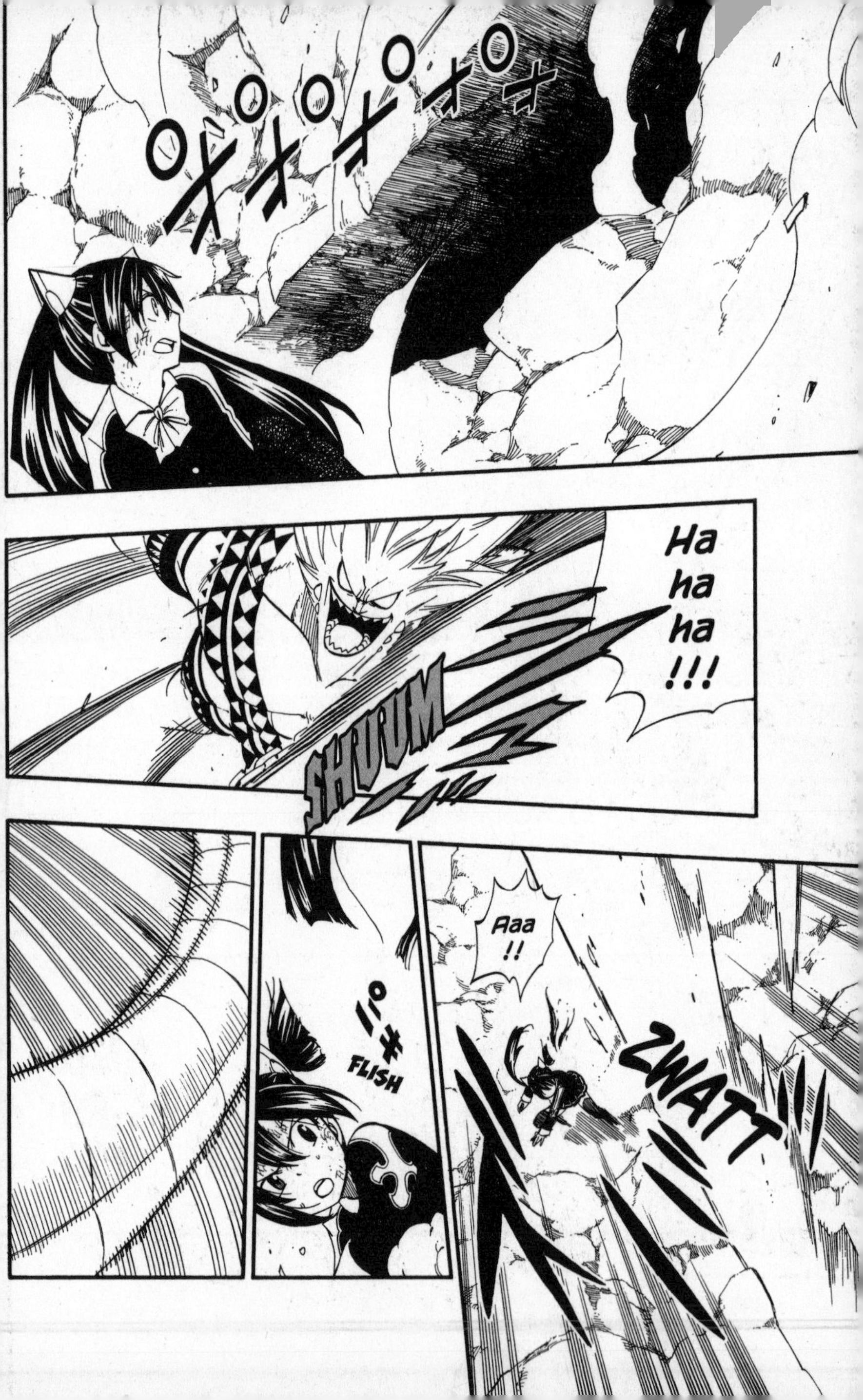
Ha ha ha!!!
SHUUM
Aaa!!
ZWATT!!
FLISH

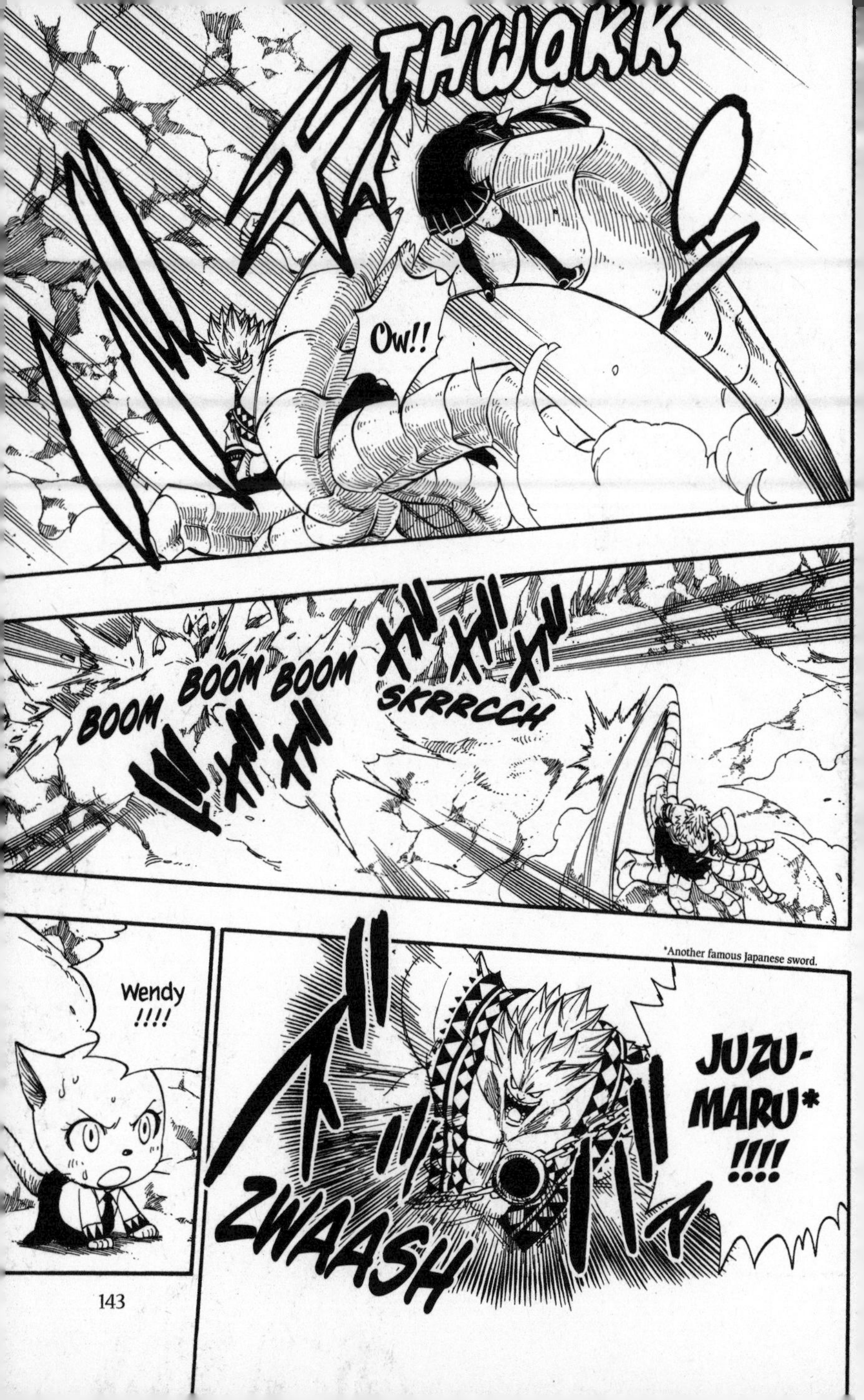
THWAKK
Ow!!
SKRRCCH
BOOM BOOM BOOM
BOOM
JUZU-MARU* !!!!
ZWAASH
Wendy !!!!

*Another famous Japanese sword.

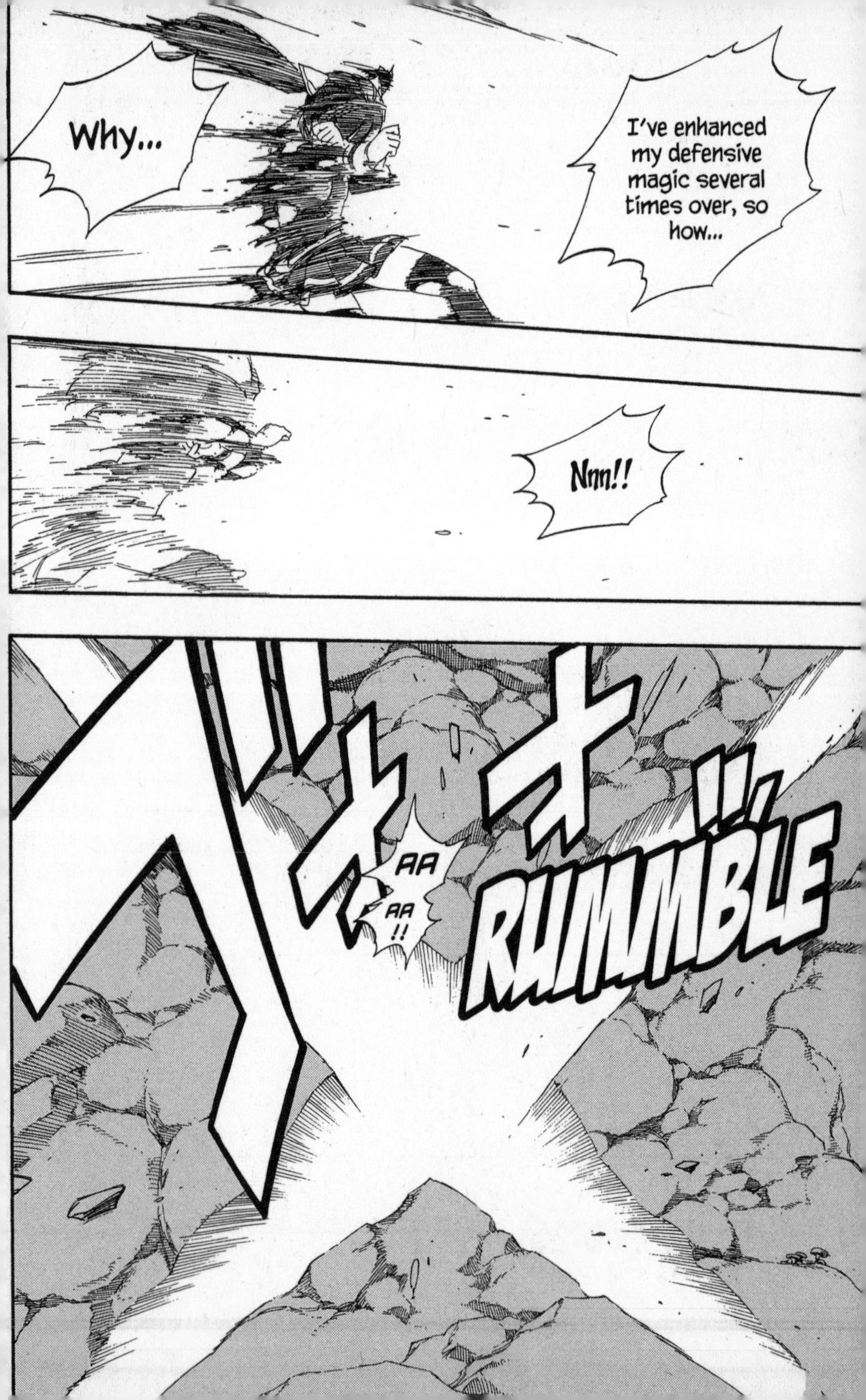
I've enhanced my defensive magic several times over, so how...
Why...
Nnn!!
AA AA!!
RUMMBLE

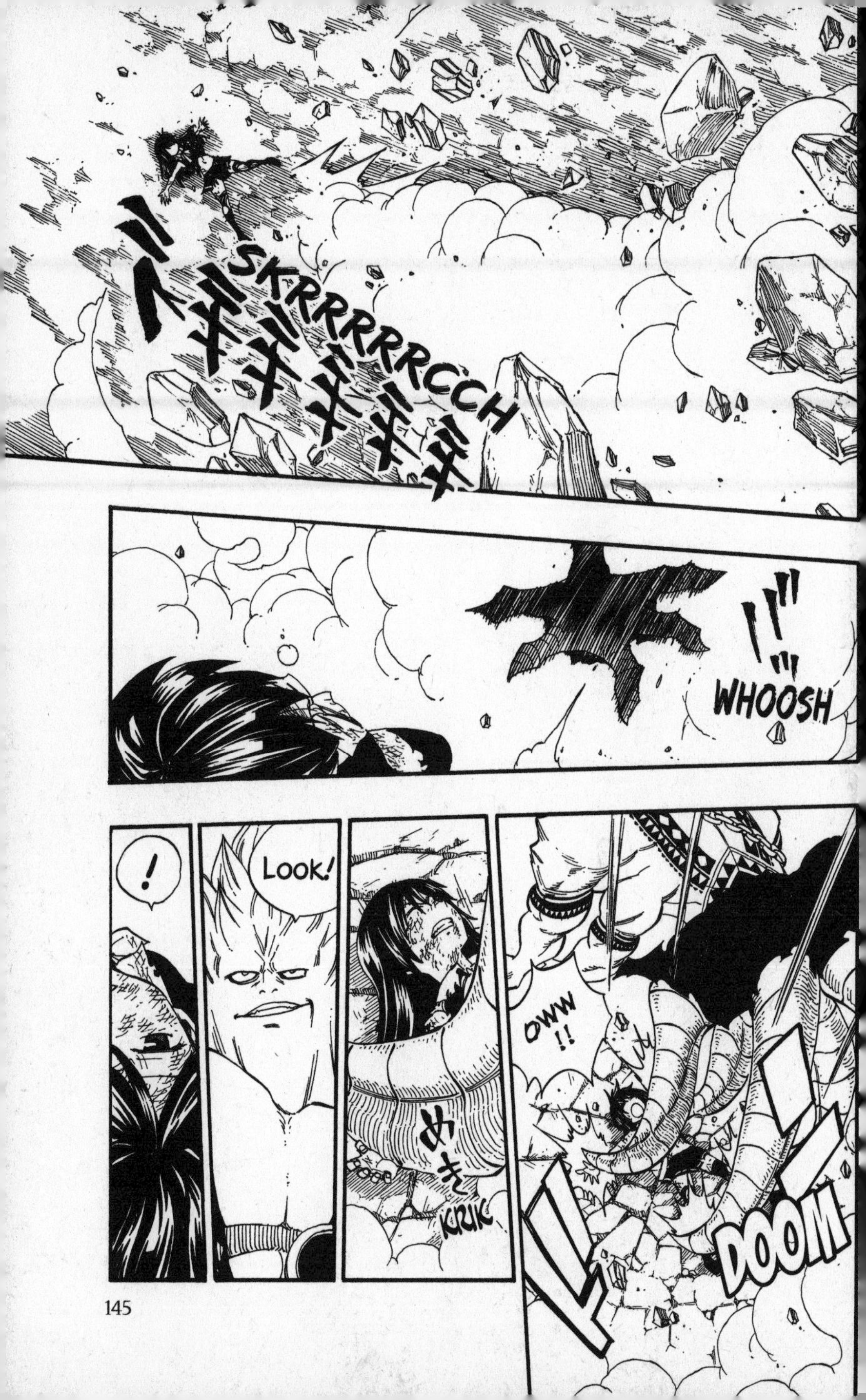
SKRRRRRRCCH
WHOOSH
OWW!!
DOOM
KRIK
LOOK!
!

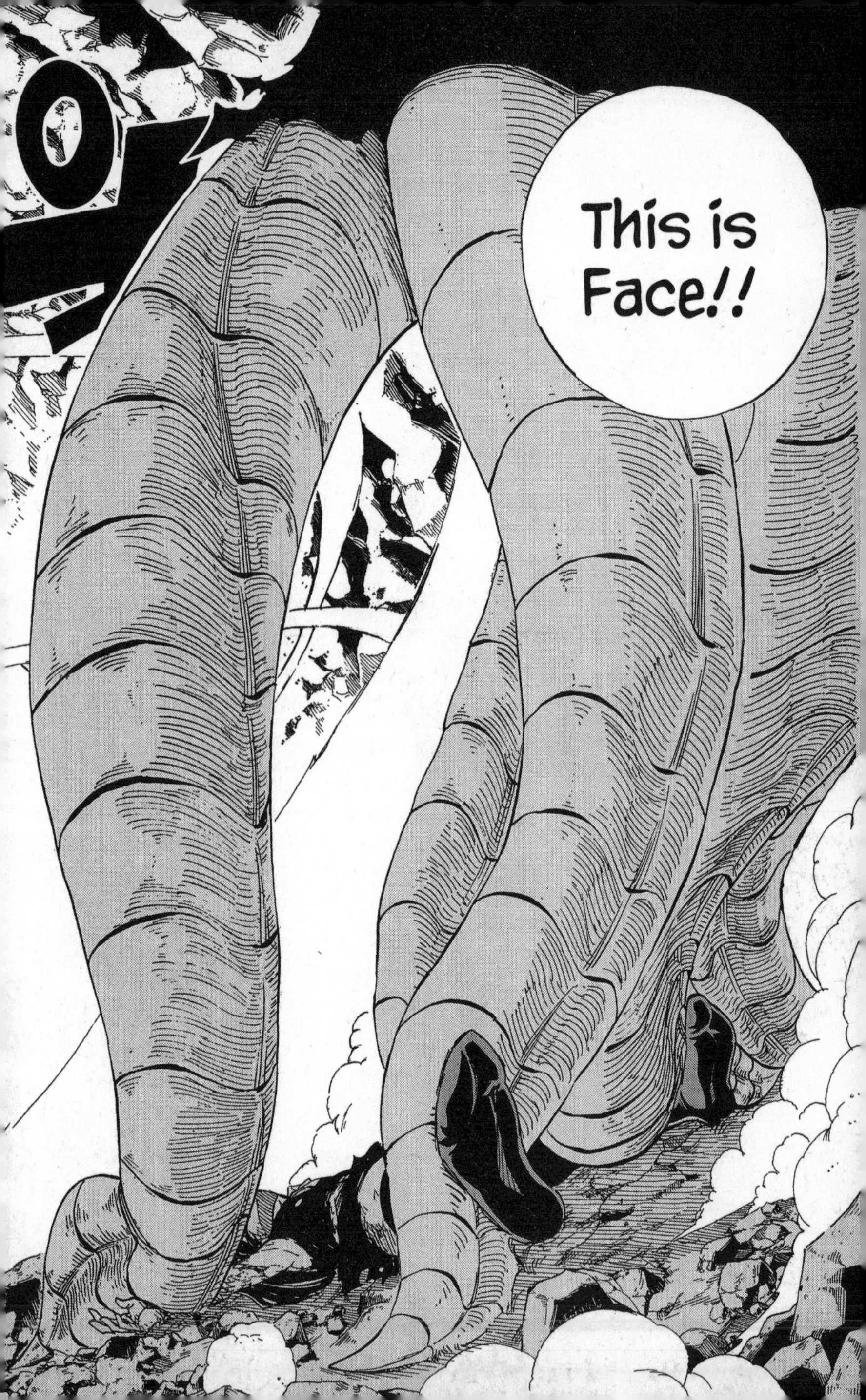
This is Face!!

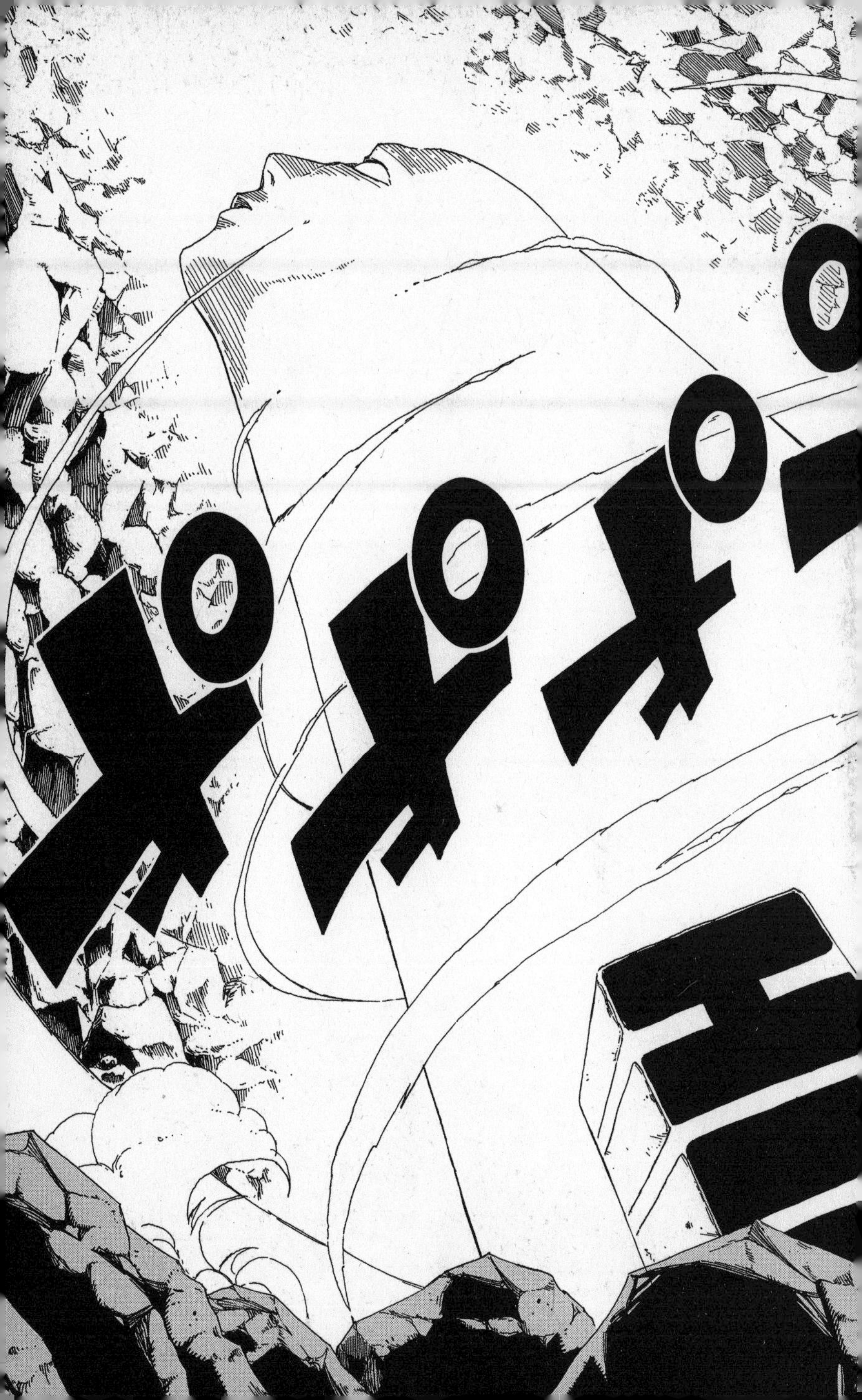

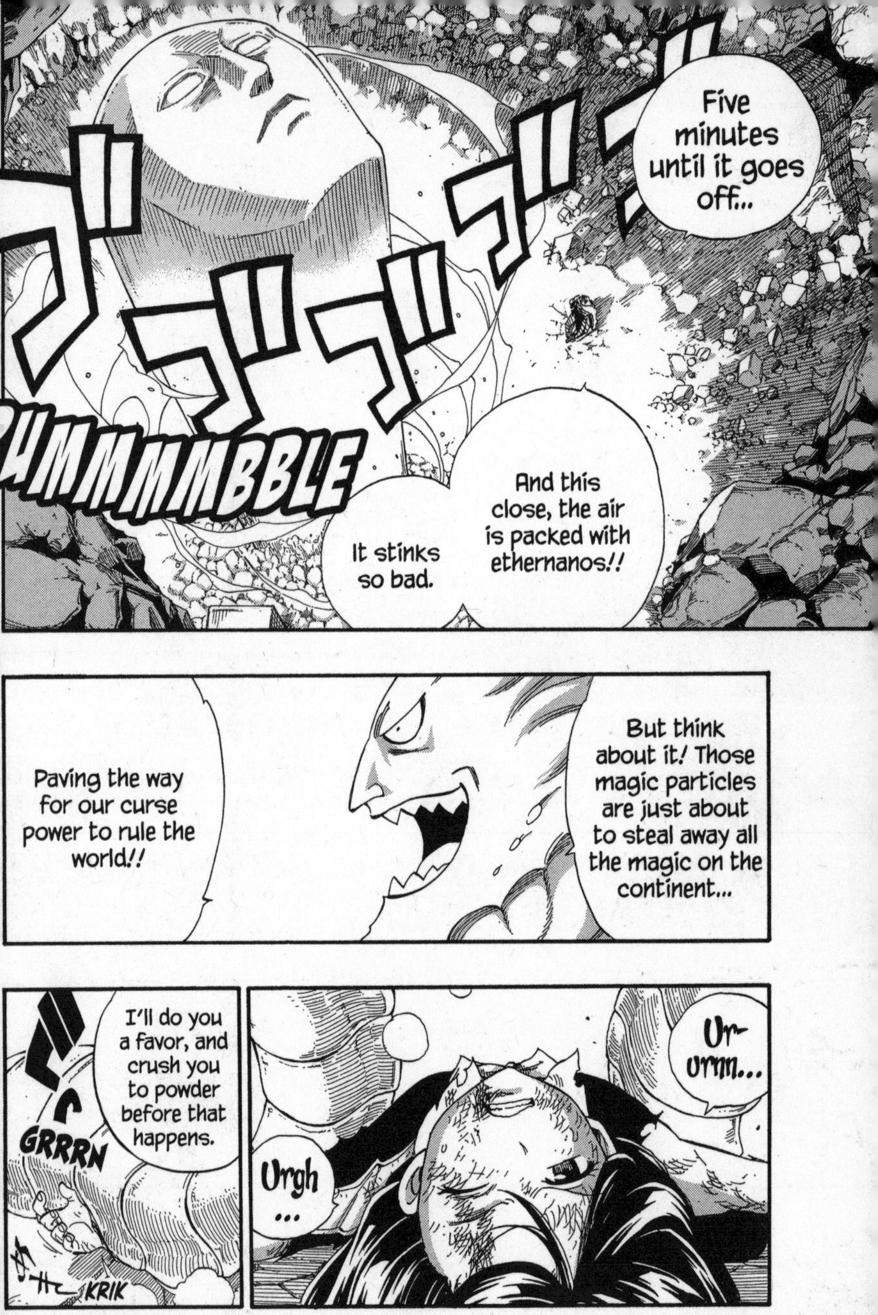

Five minutes until it goes off...
And this close, the air is packed with ethernanos!!
It stinks so bad.
UMMMMMBBLE
But think about it! Those magic particles are just about to steal away all the magic on the continent...
Paving the way for our curse power to rule the world!!
Ur- urnn...
Urgh ...
I'll do you a favor, and crush you to powder before that happens.
GRRRN
KRIK

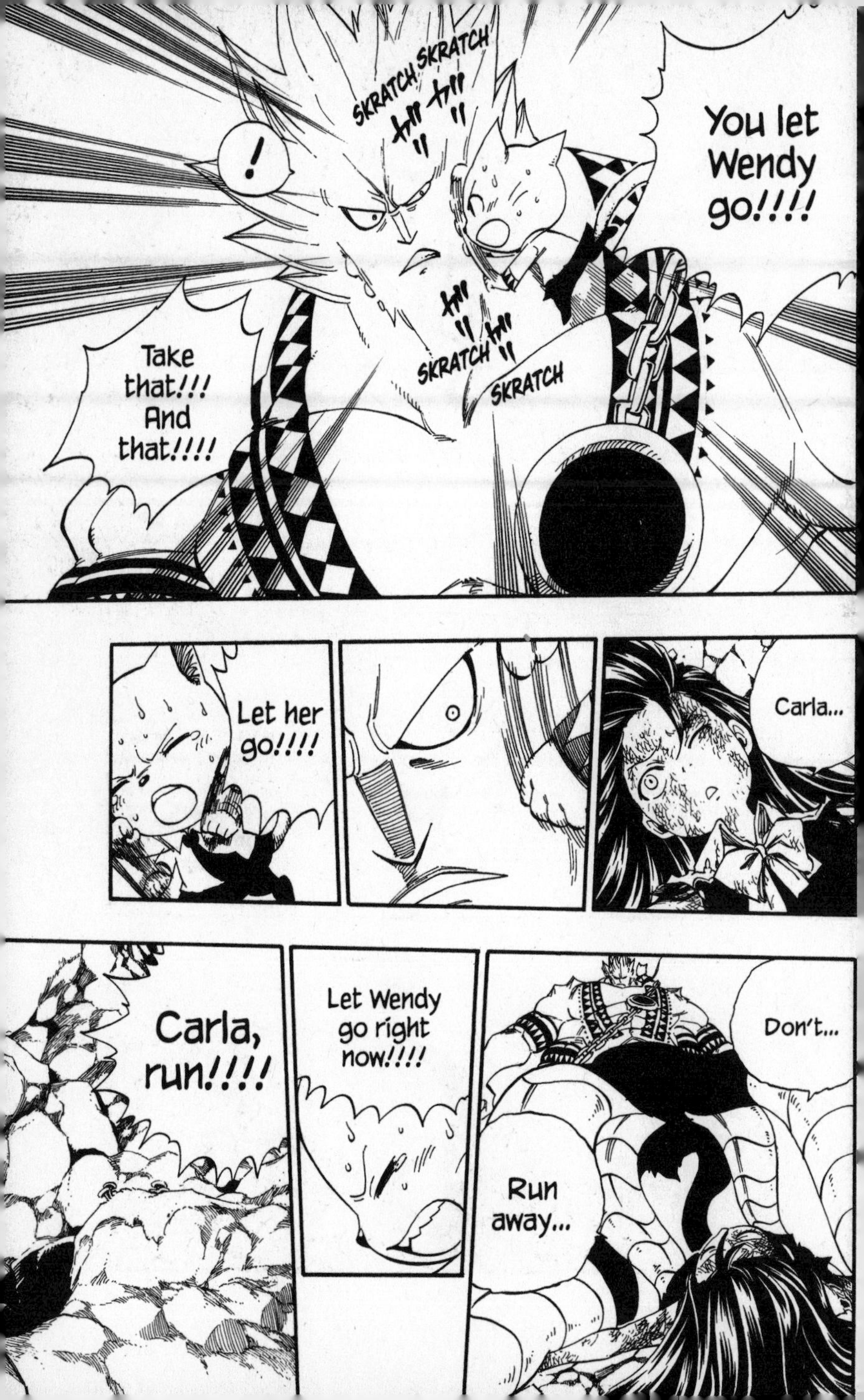

You let Wendy go!!!!
SKRATCH SKRATCH
SKRATCH
SKRATCH
Take that!!! And that!!!!
Carla...
Let her go!!!!
Don't...
Run away...
Let Wendy go right now!!!!
Carla, run!!!!

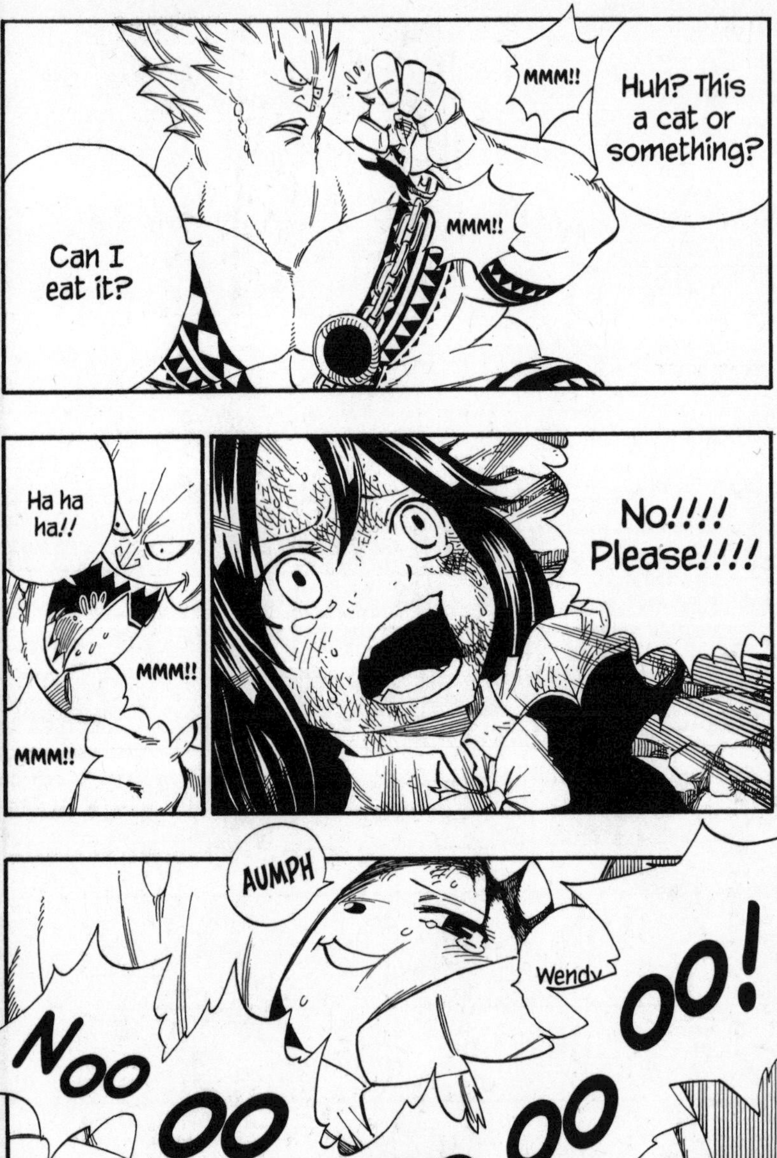
MMM!!
Huh? This a cat or something?
MMM!!
Can I eat it?
No!!!! Please!!!!
Ha ha ha!!
MMM!!
MMM!!
AUMPH
Wendy
Noo OO OO OO OO OO!!

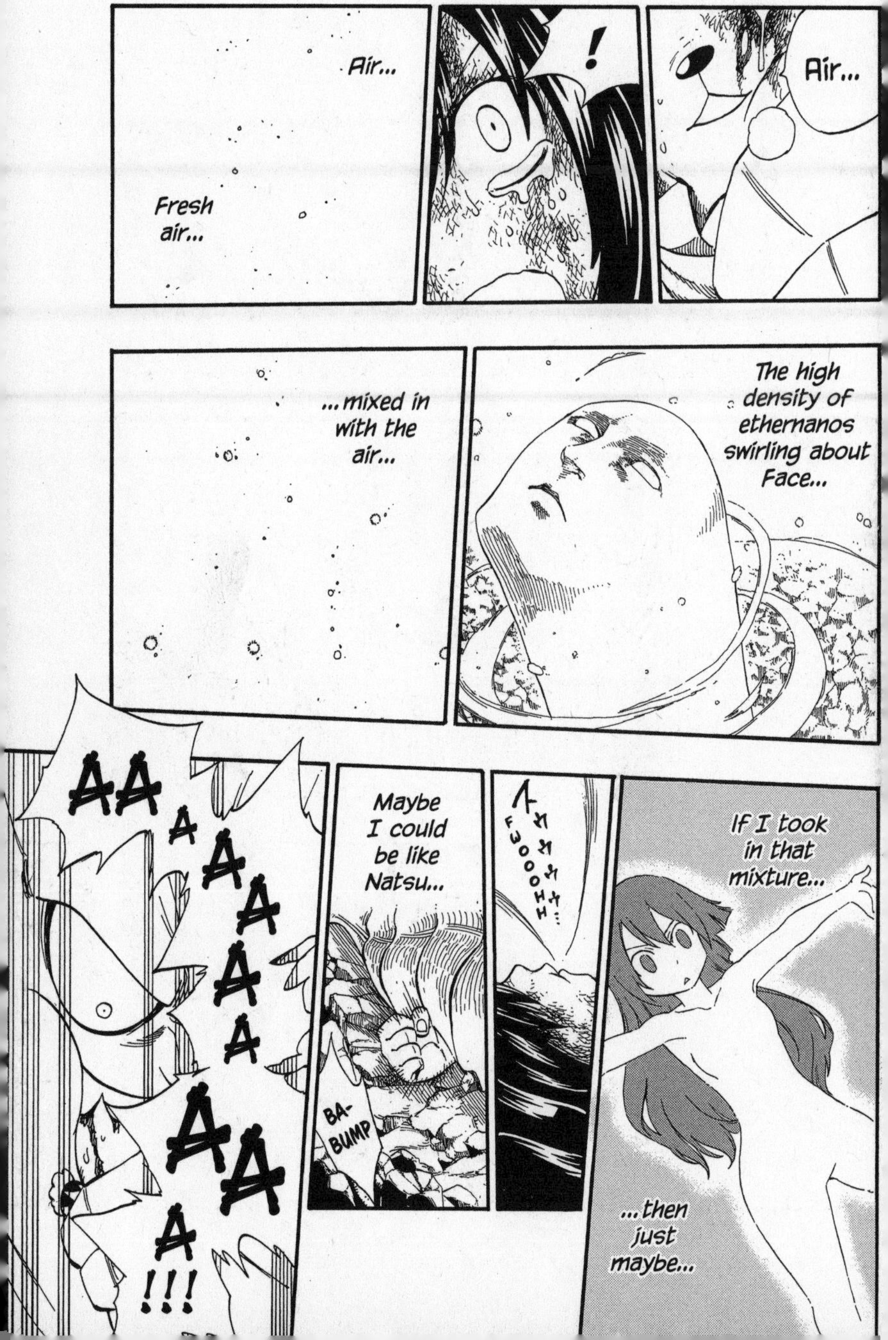
Air...
!
Air...
Fresh air...
The high density of ethernanos swirling about Face...
...mixed in with the air...
If I took in that mixture...
...then just maybe...
FWOOOHH
Maybe I could be like Natsu...
BA-BUMP
AAAAAAAAAAA!!!

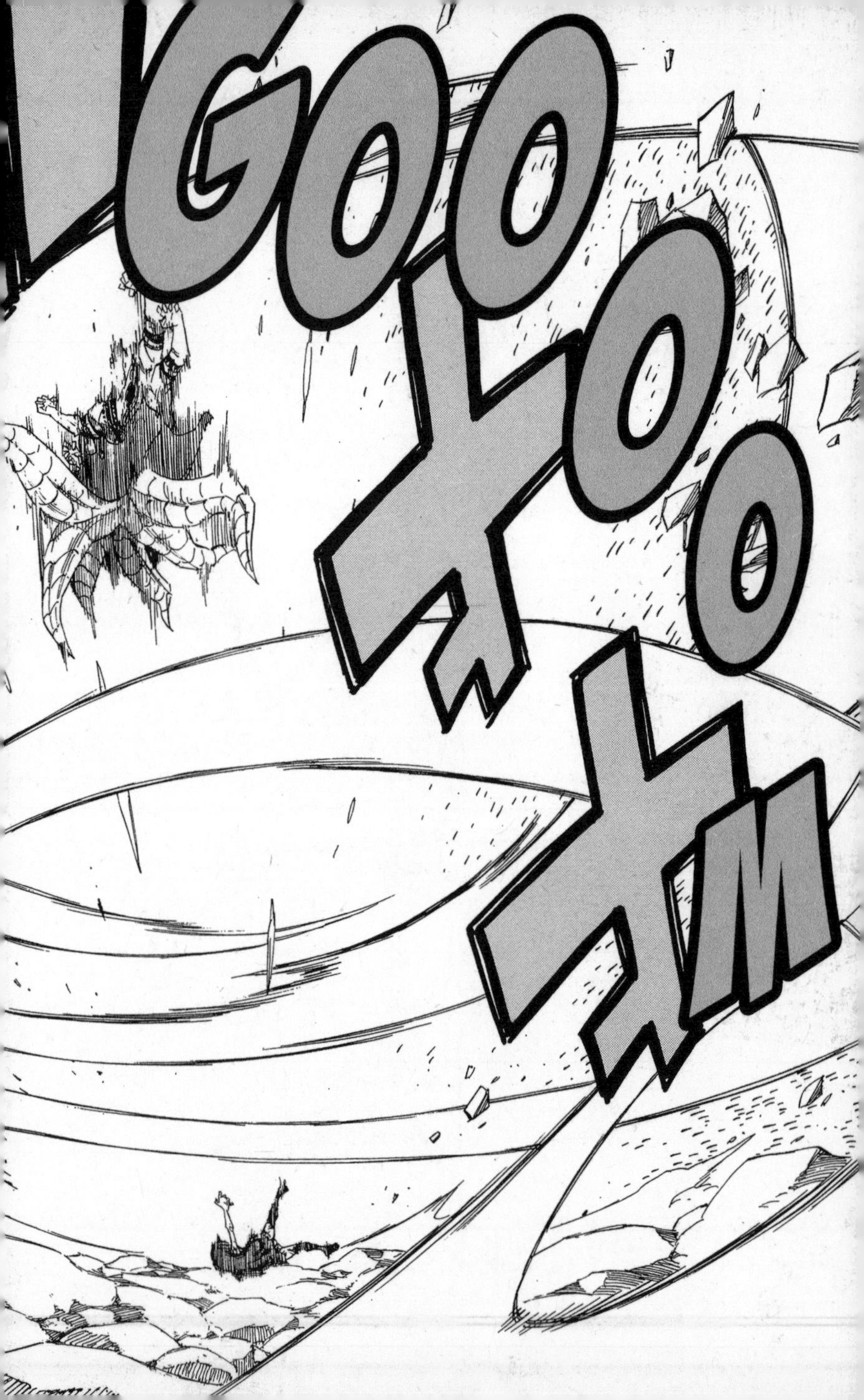
GOOOOOM

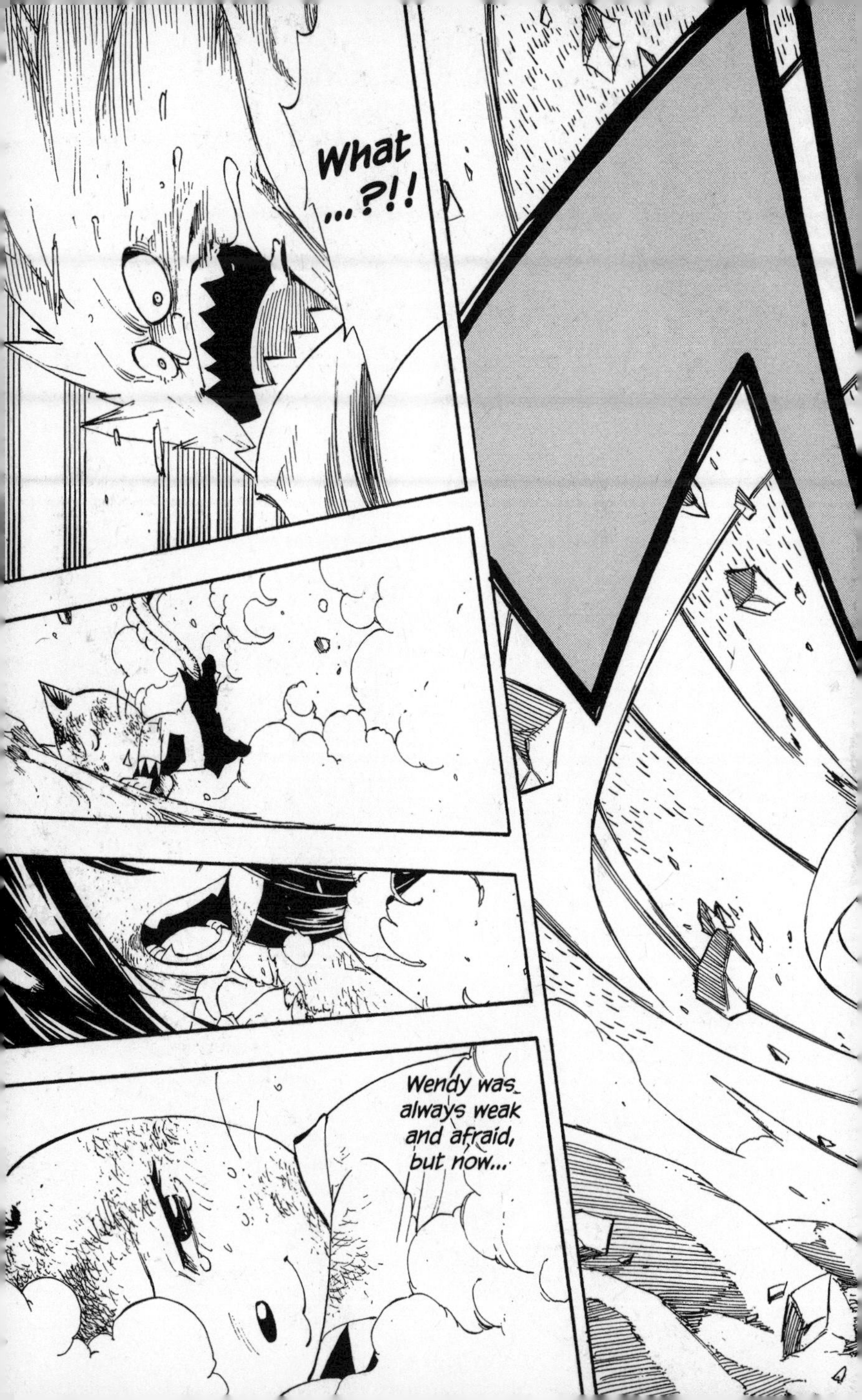
What ...?!!
Wendy was always weak and afraid, but now...

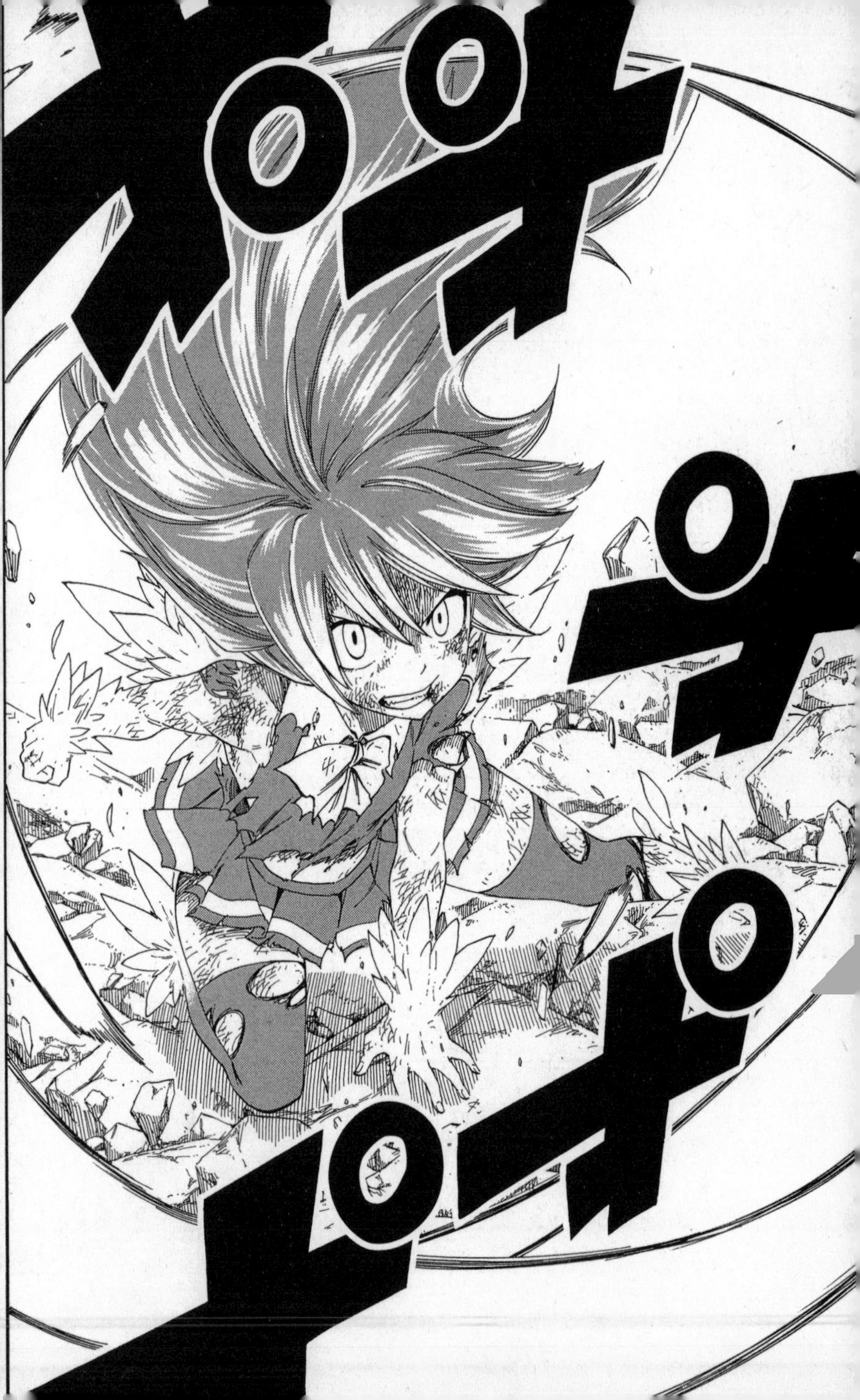

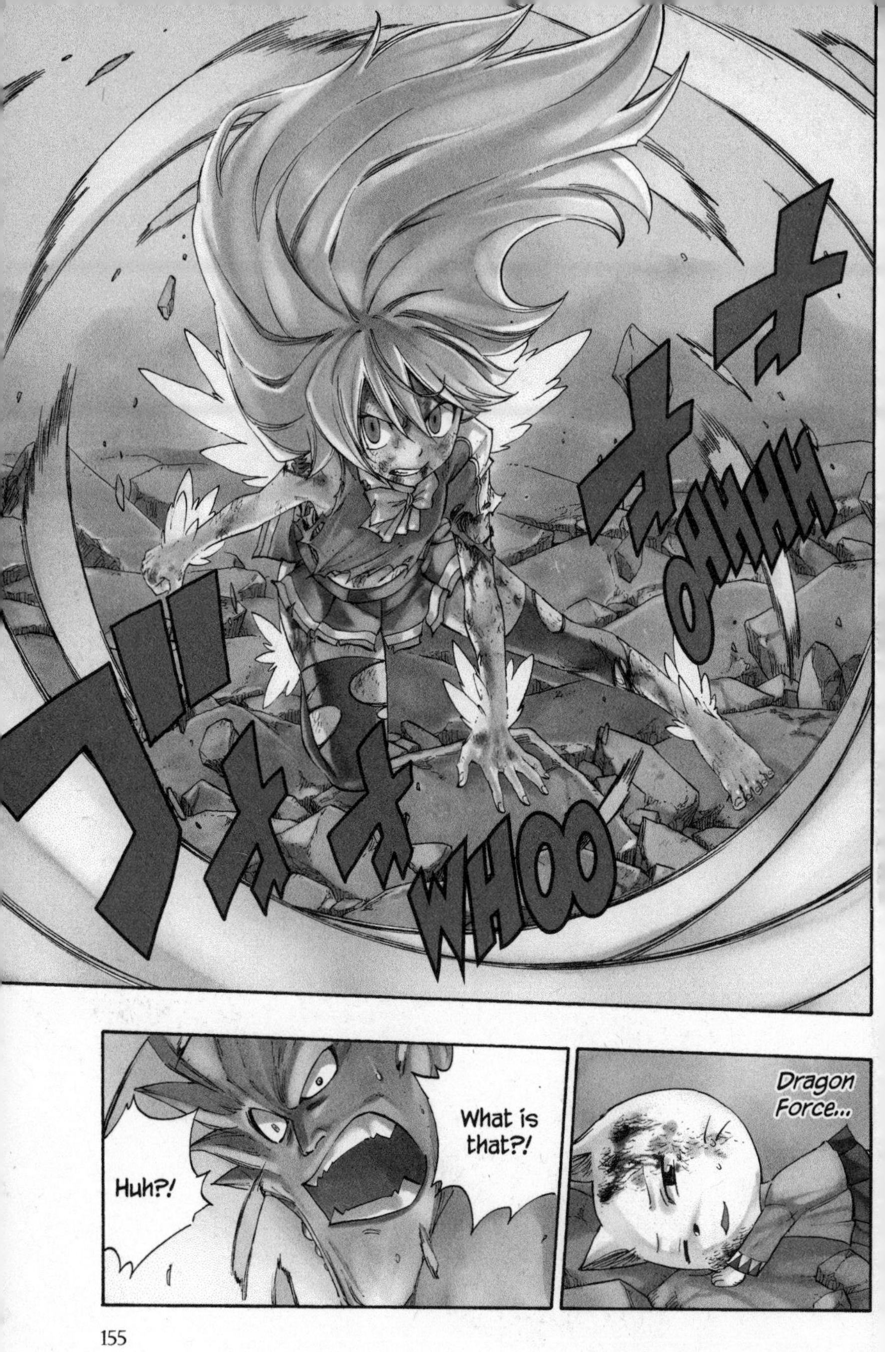
ゴォォォォ
WHOOOHHHHH
Dragon Force...
What is that?!
Huh?!

Chapter 377: The Sky Dragon's Rage

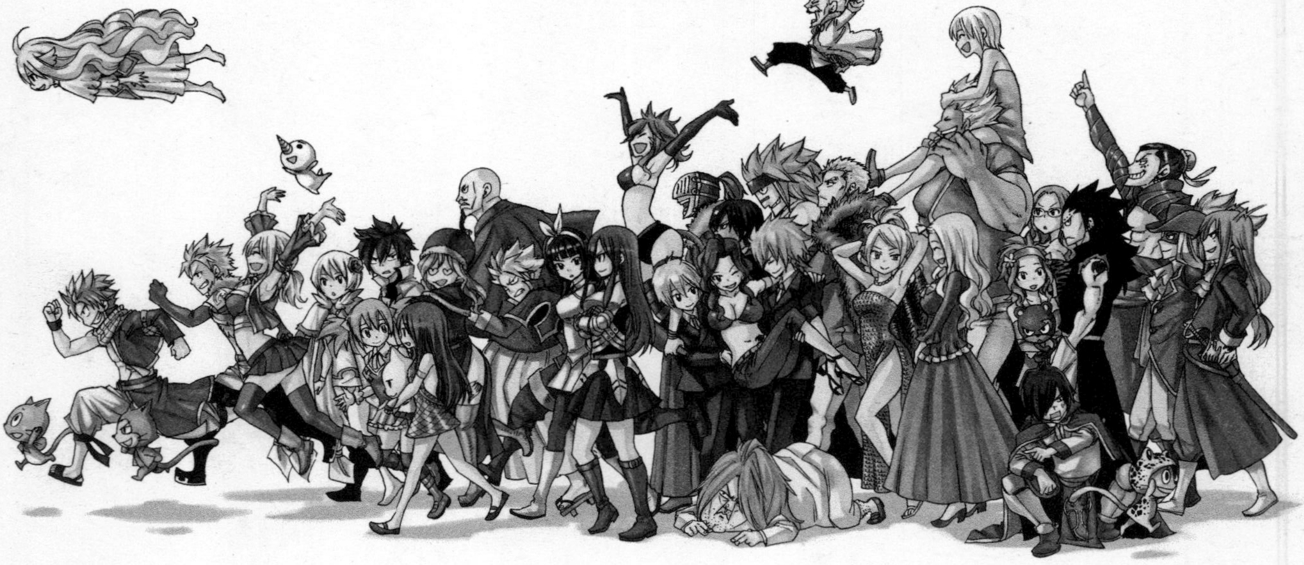

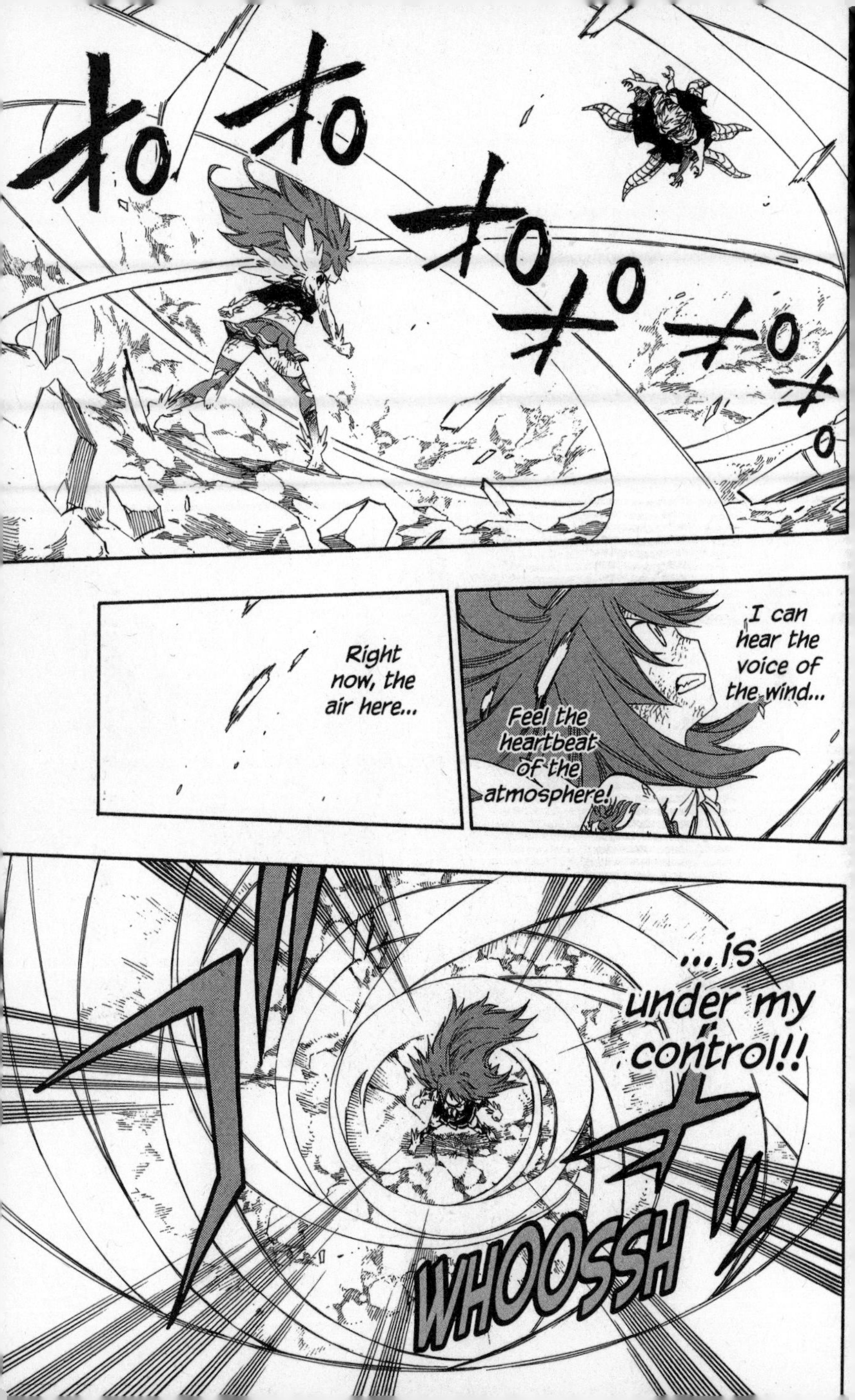
I can hear the voice of the wind...
Feel the heartbeat of the atmosphere!
Right now, the air here...
...is under my control!!
WHOOSSH

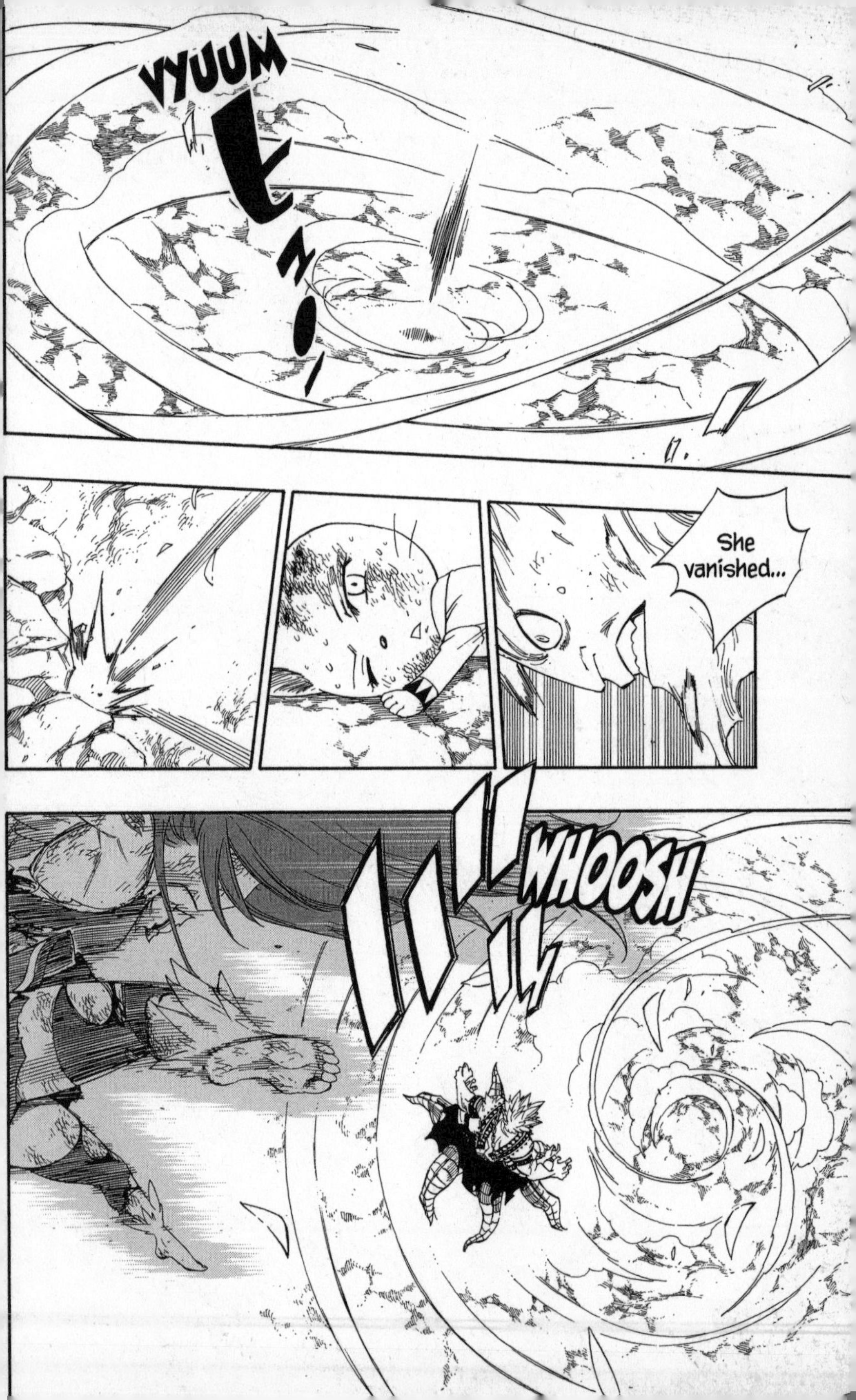
VYUUM
She vanished...
WHOOSH

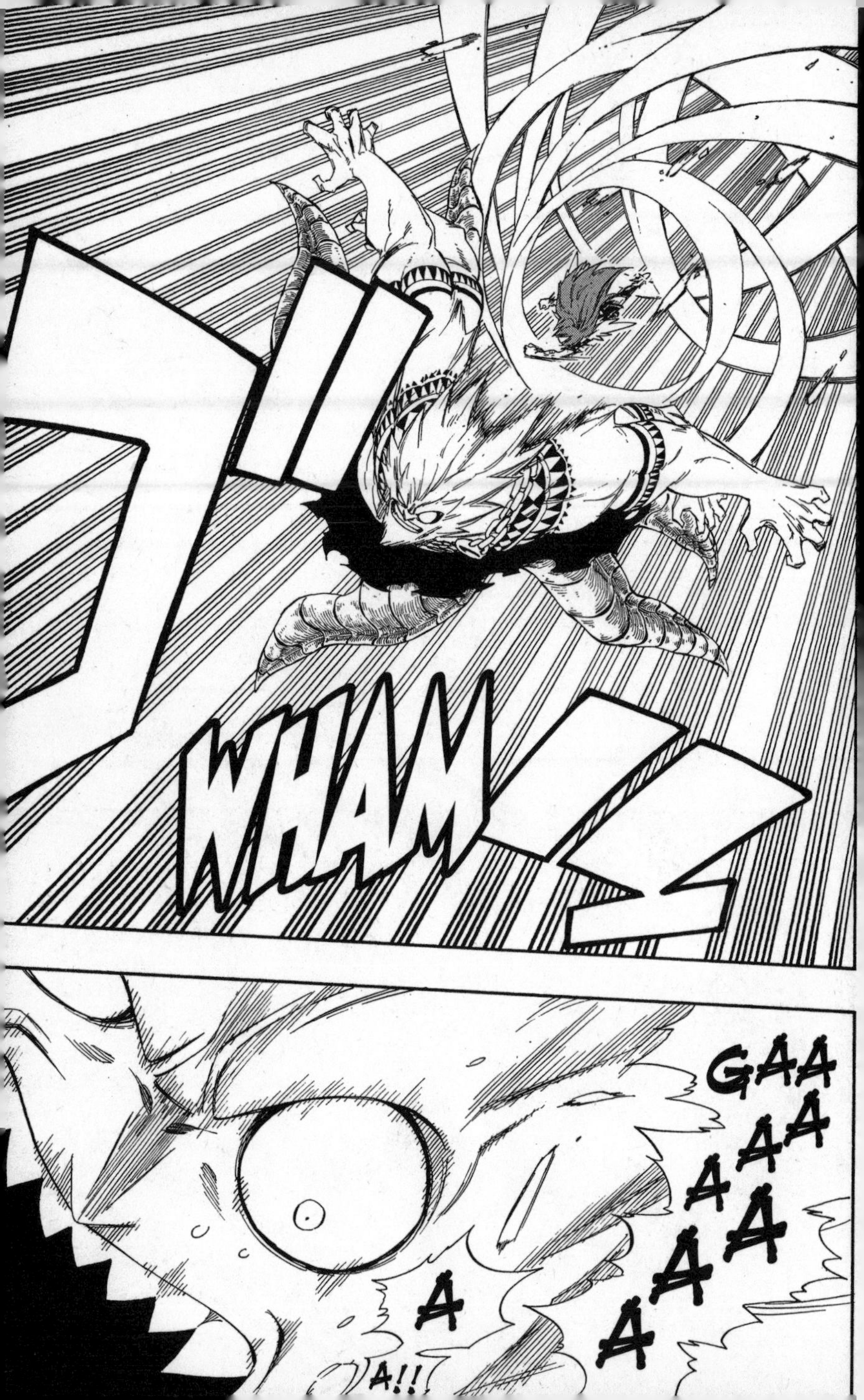
WHAM
GAAAAAAAAAAA!!

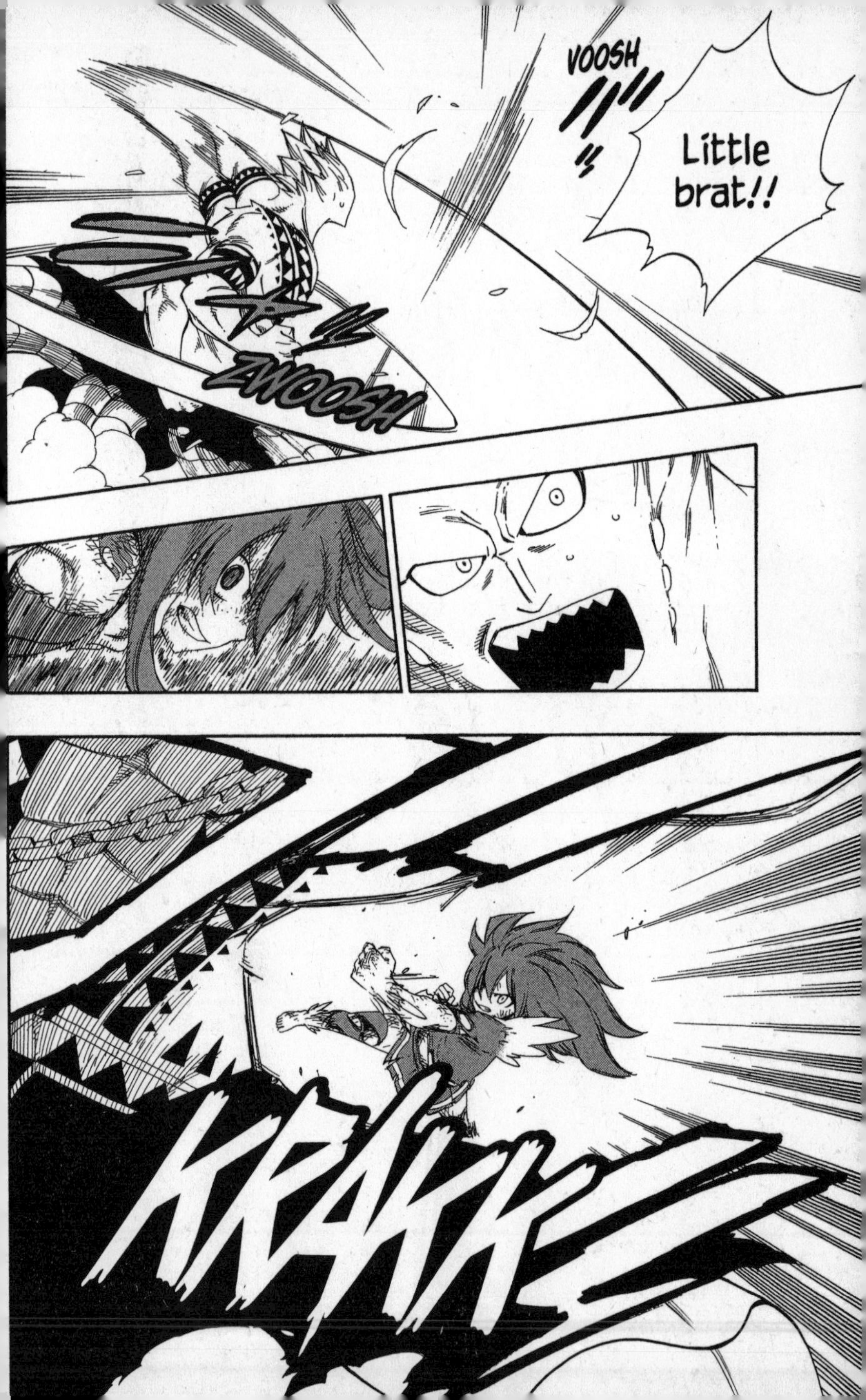
VOOSH
Little brat!!
ZWOOSH
KRAKK

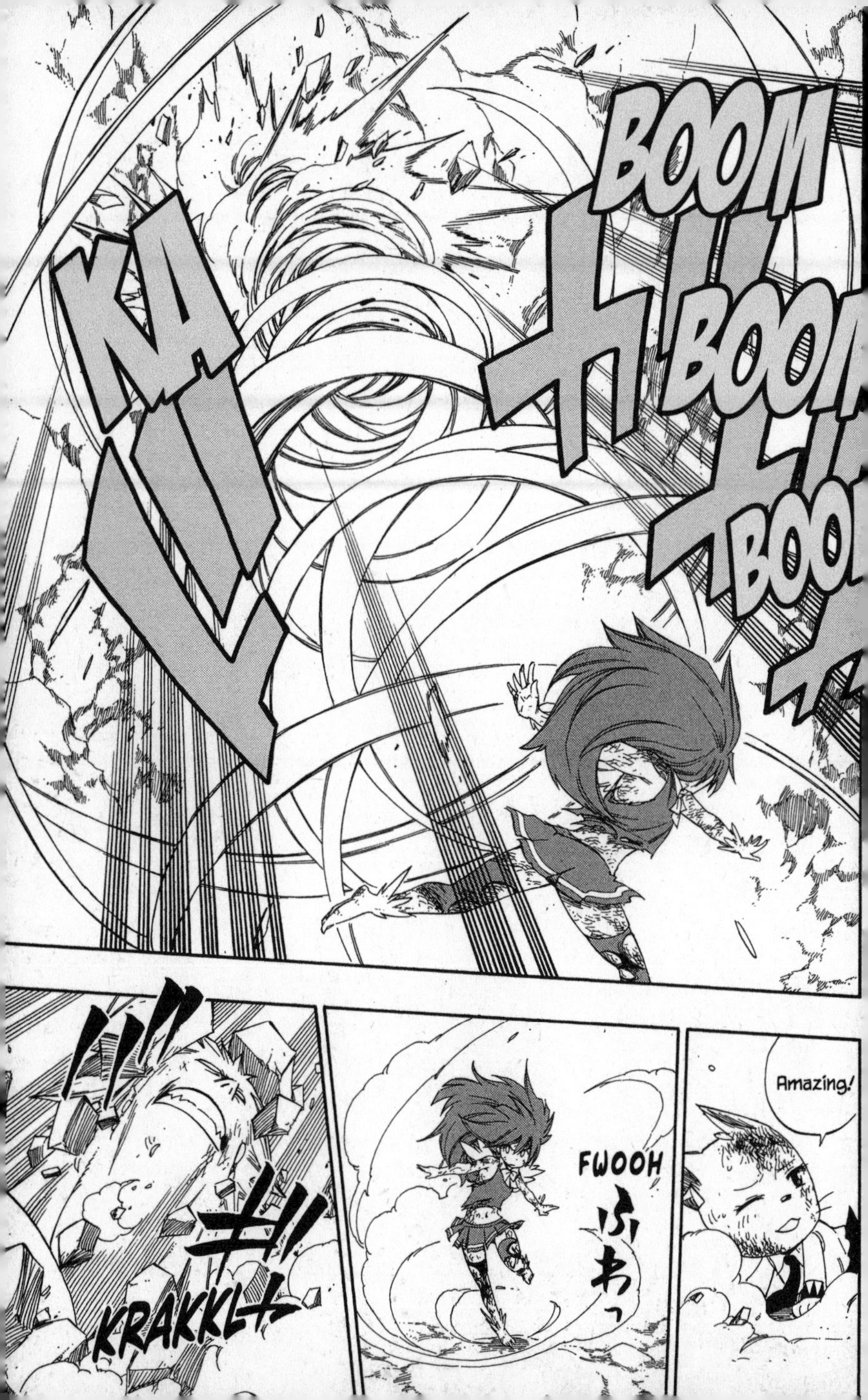
BOOM
BOOM
BOOM
KA
Amazing!
FWOOH
ふわっ
!!!
KRAKKL

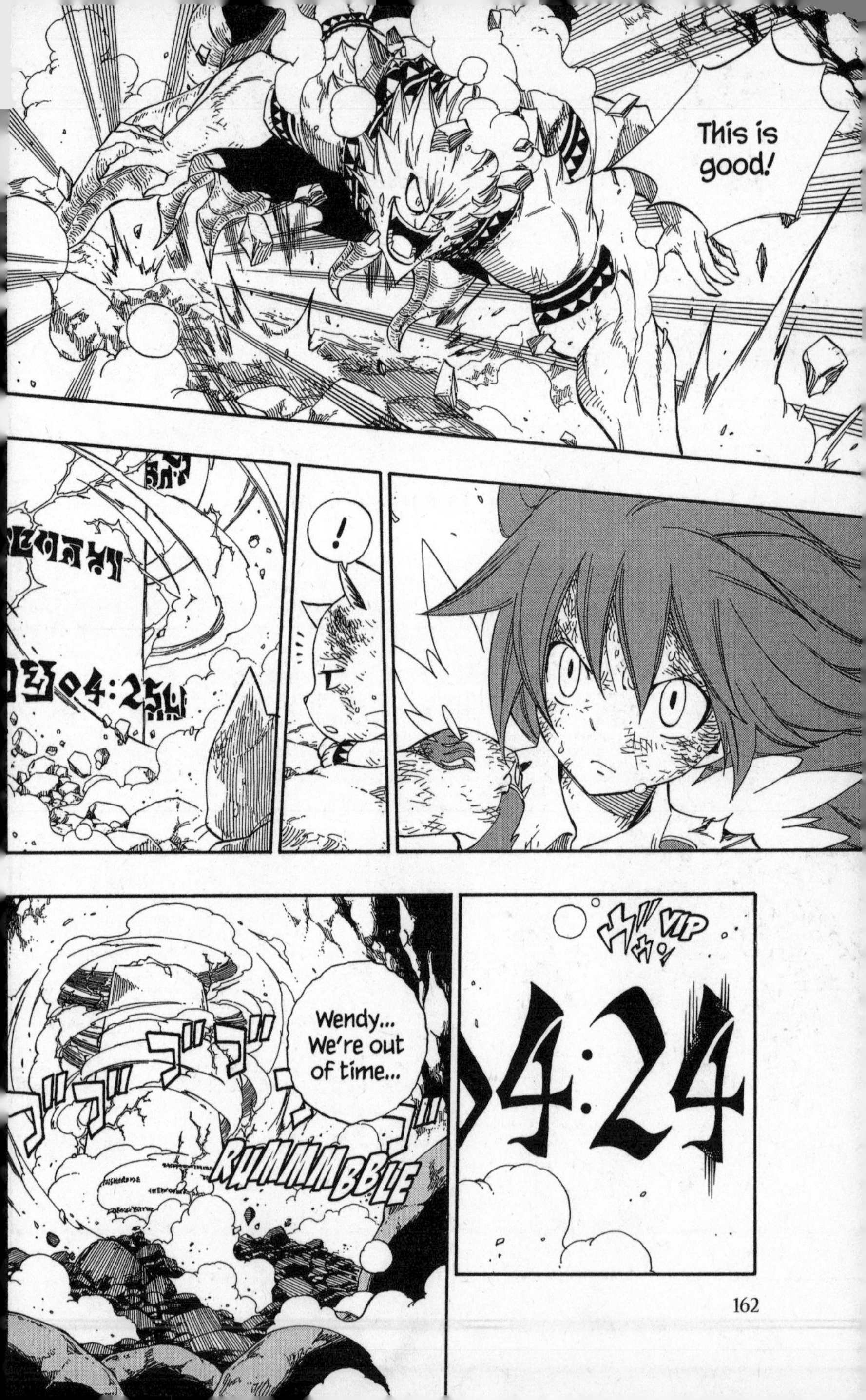
This is good!
!
VIP
4:24
Wendy... We're out of time...
RUMMMBBLE

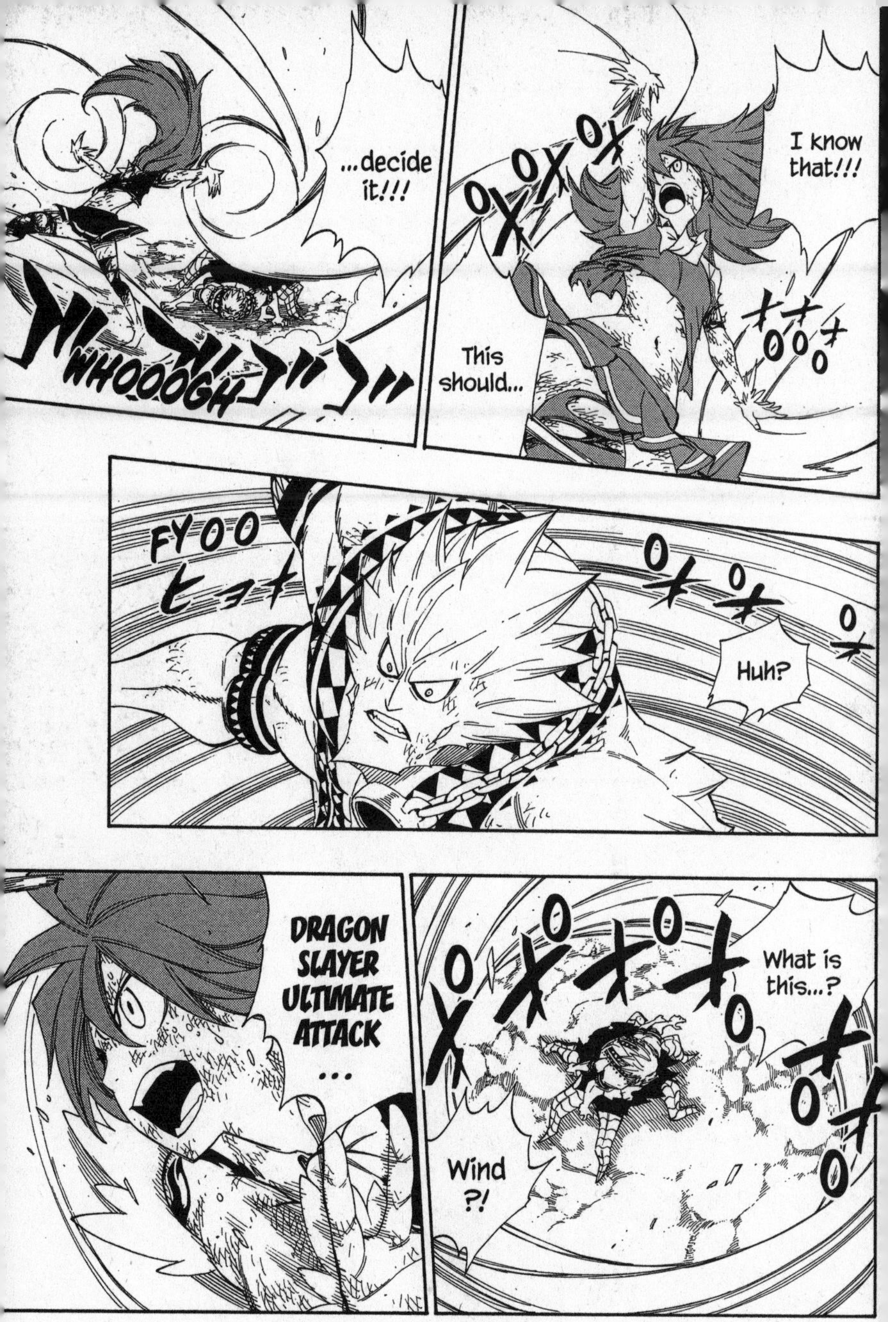
I know that!!!
This should...
...decide it!!!
WHOOOGH
FYOO
Huh?
What is this...?
Wind ?!
DRAGON SLAYER ULTIMATE ATTACK ...

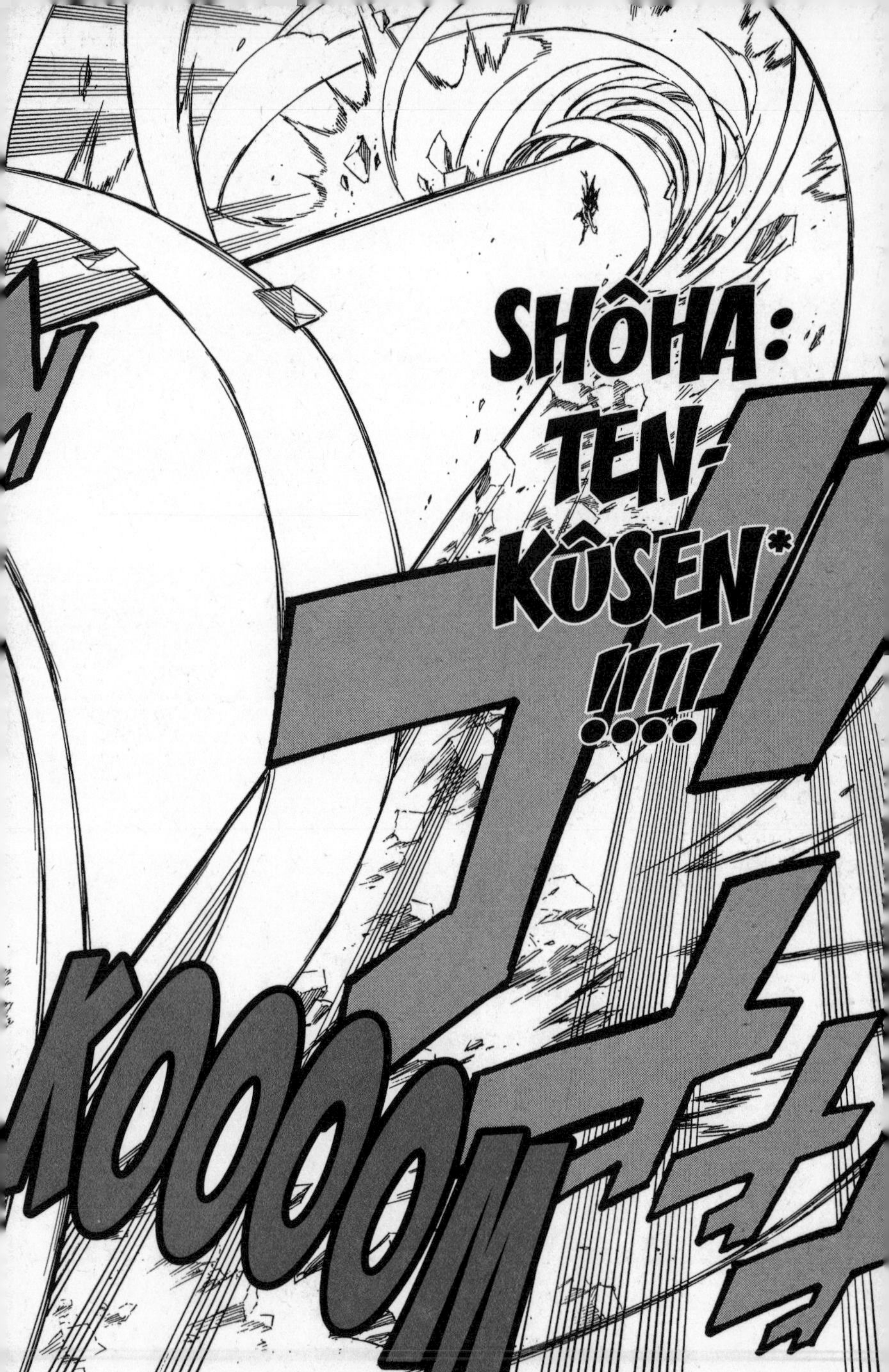
SHÔHA: TEN-KÛSEN*!!!!

*Flare Burst: Sky Drill

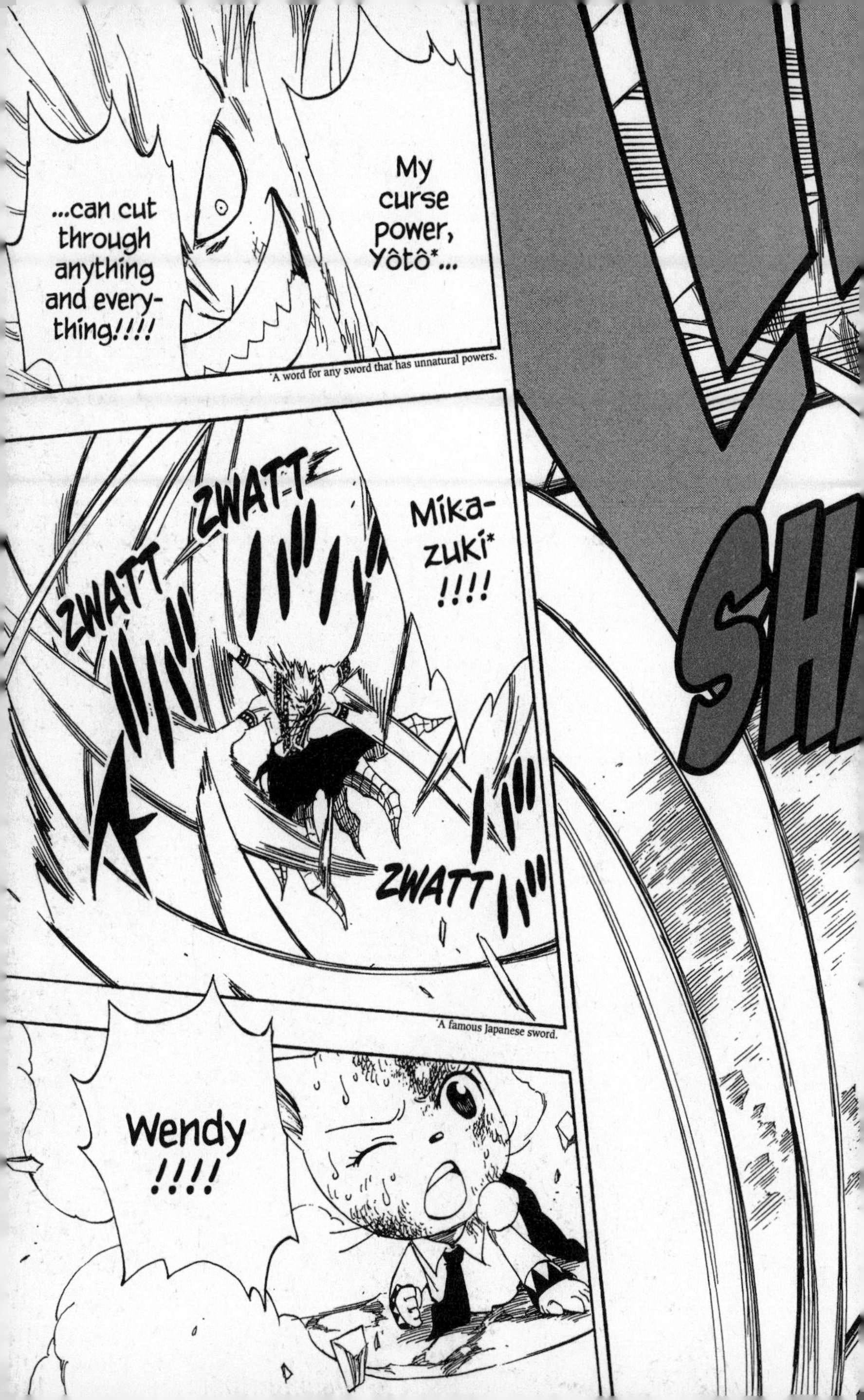

SH
My curse power, Yôtô*...
...can cut through anything and every-thing!!!!
*A word for any sword that has unnatural powers.
Mika-zuki* !!!!
ZWATT
ZWATT
ZWATT
*A famous Japanese sword.
Wendy !!!!

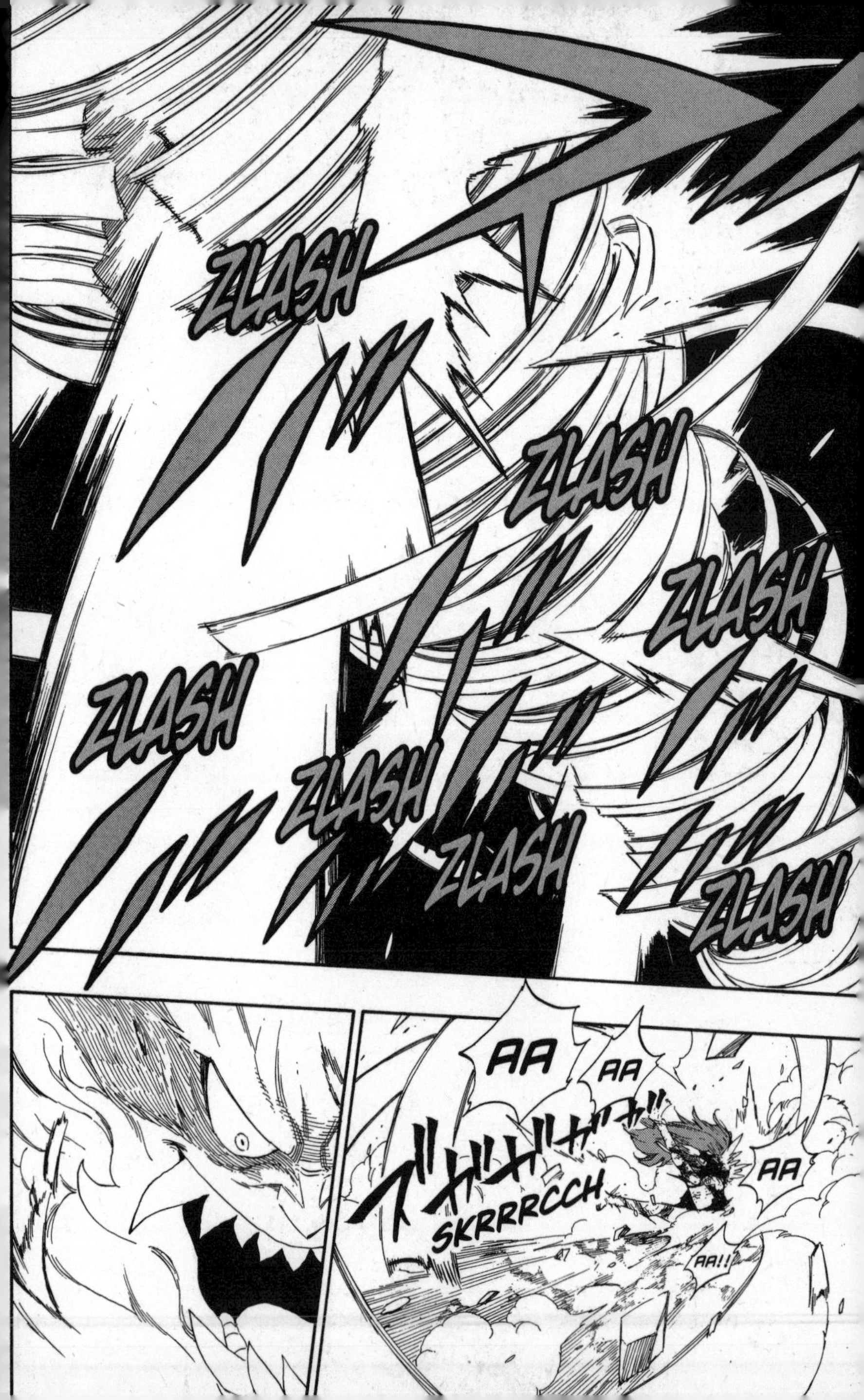

ZLASH
ZLASH
ZLASH
ZLASH
ZLASH
ZLASH
ZLASH
AA
AA
AA
SKRRRCCH
AA!!

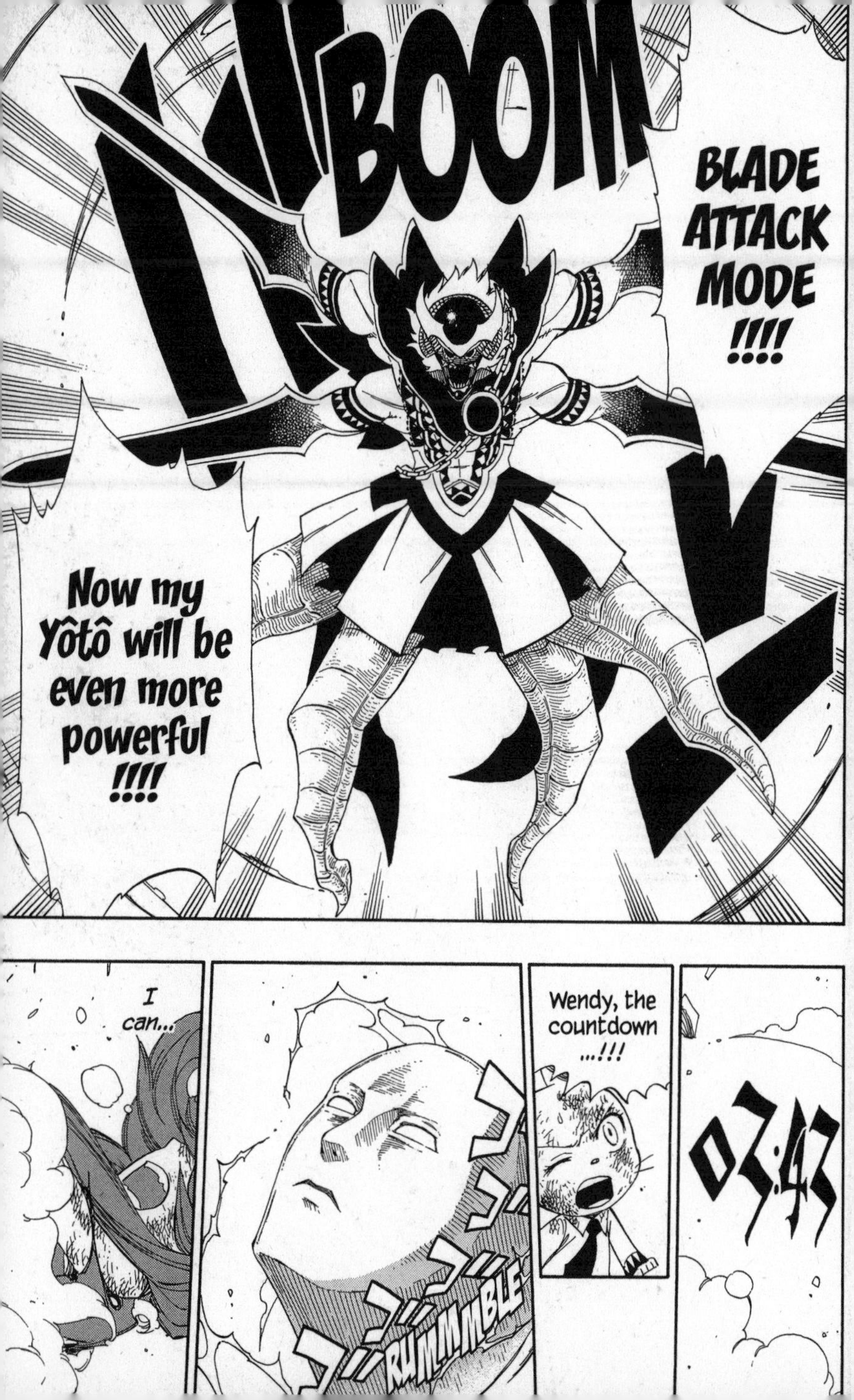
BOOM
BLADE ATTACK MODE !!!!
Now my Yôtô will be even more powerful !!!!
02:43
Wendy, the countdown ...!!!
RUMMMBLE
I can...

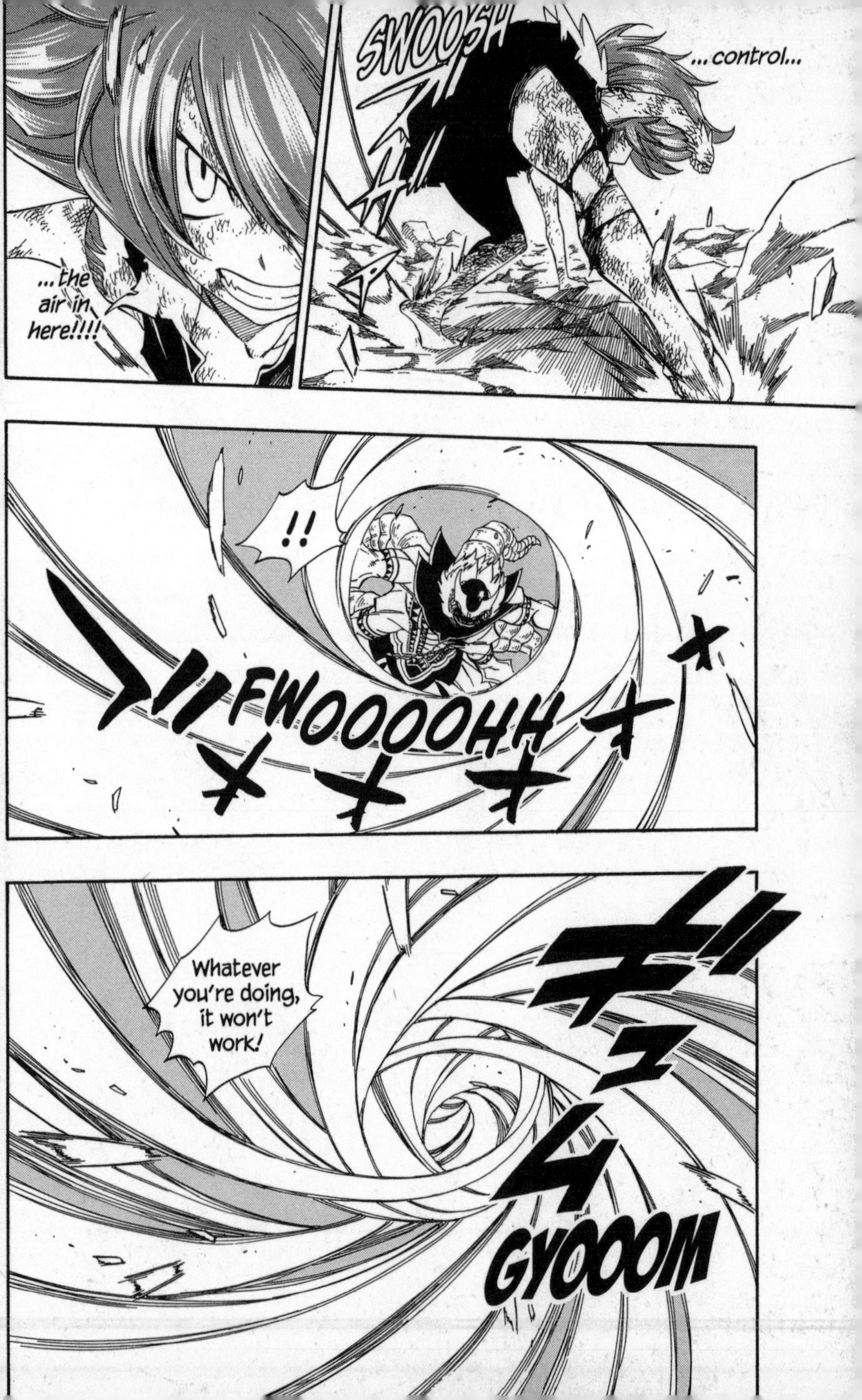
SWOOSH
...control...
...the air in here!!!!
!!
FWOOOOHH
GYOOOM
Whatever you're doing, it won't work!

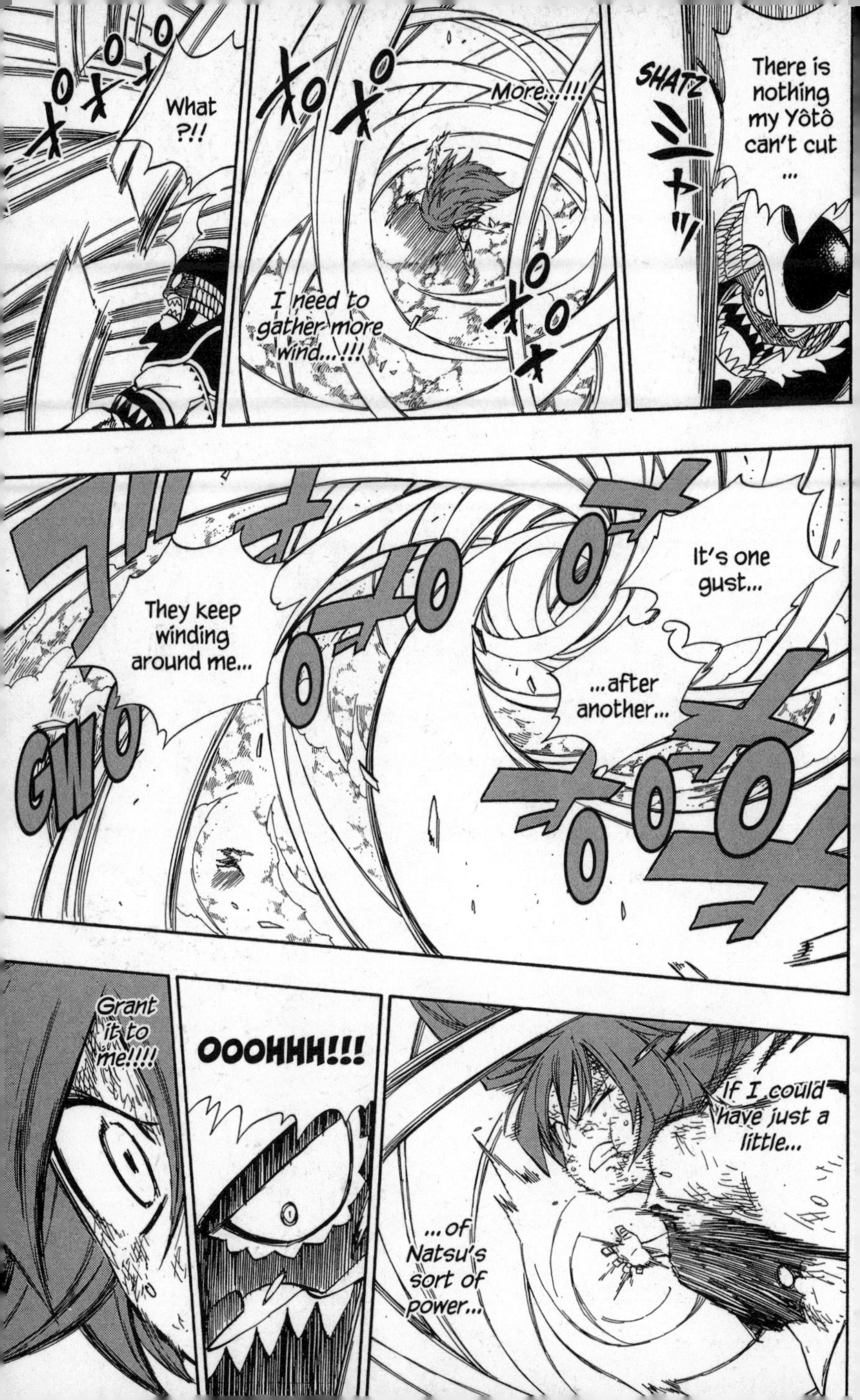
SHATZ
There is nothing my Yôtô can't cut ...
More...!!!
I need to gather more wind...!!!
What ?!!
It's one gust...
...after another...
They keep winding around me...
GWO
If I could have just a little...
...of Natsu's sort of power...
OOOHHH!!!
Grant it to me!!!!

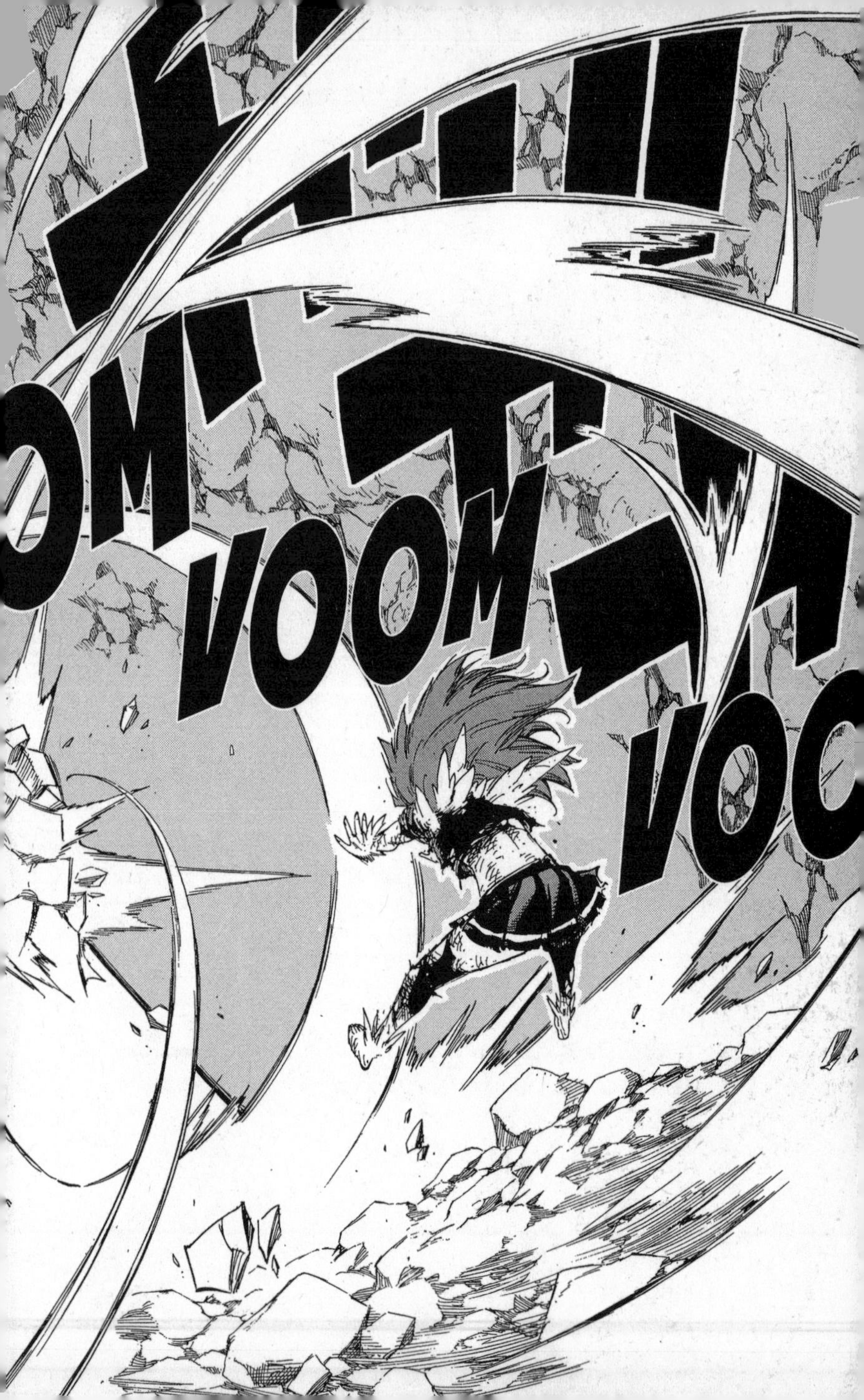
VOOM

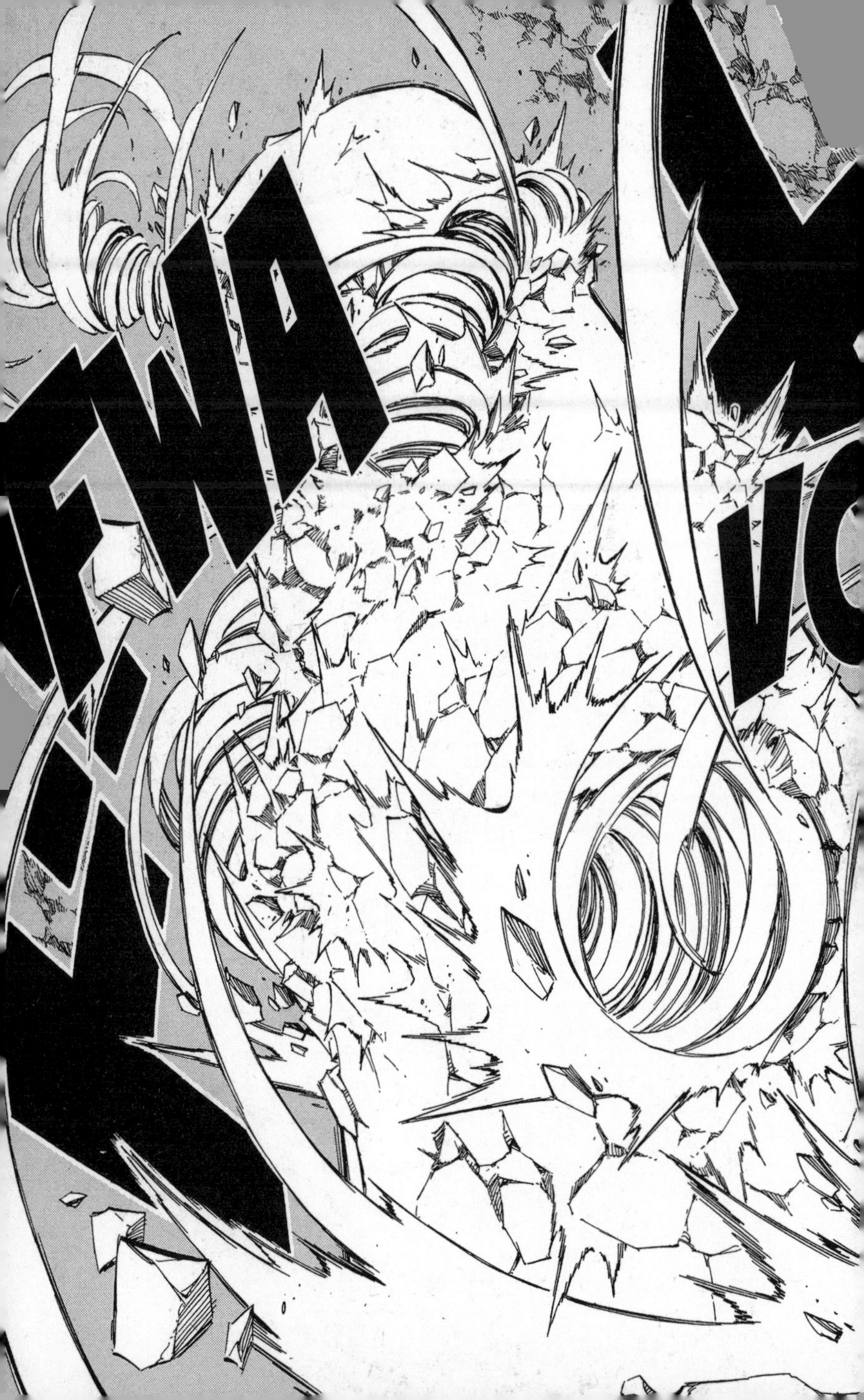

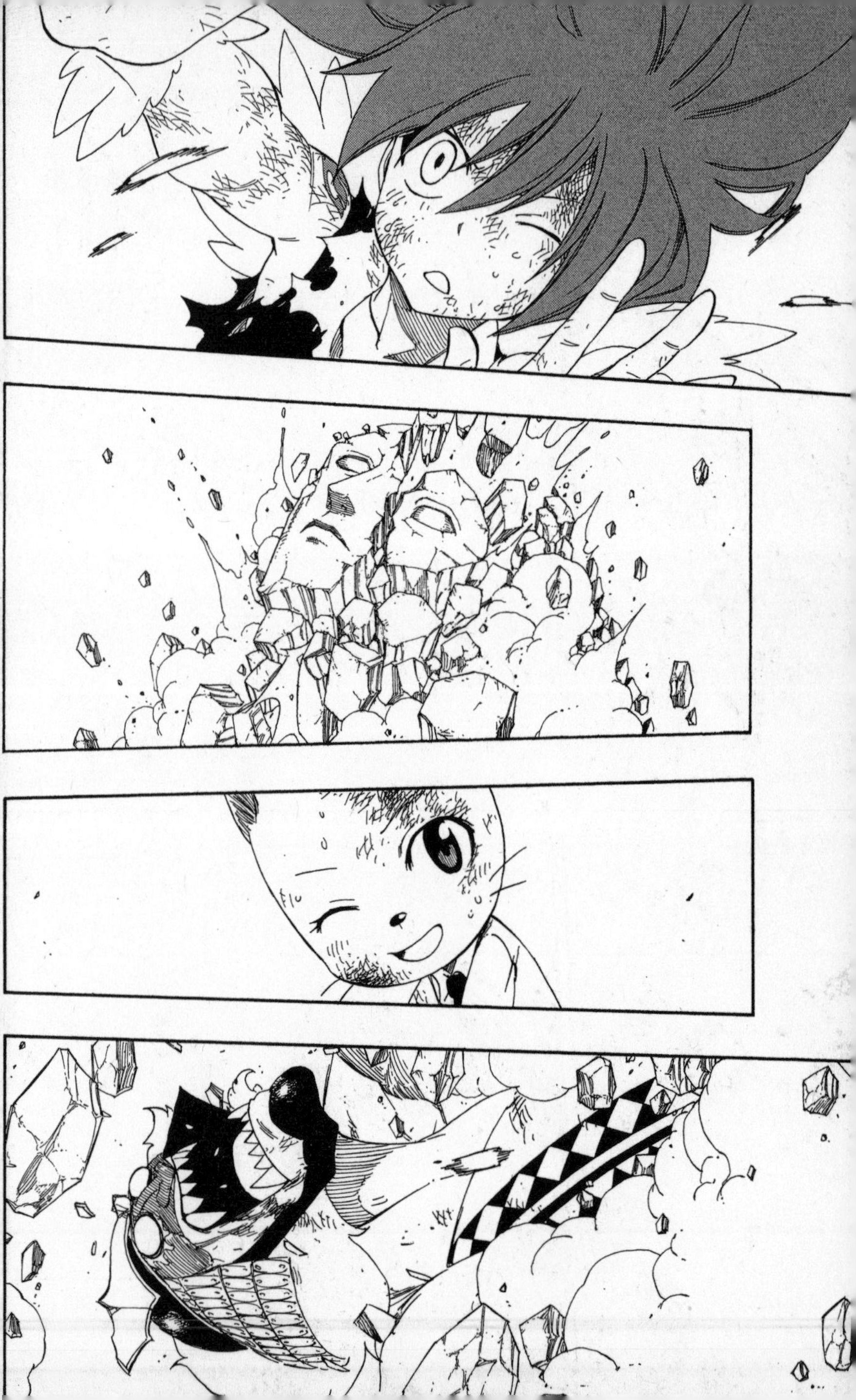

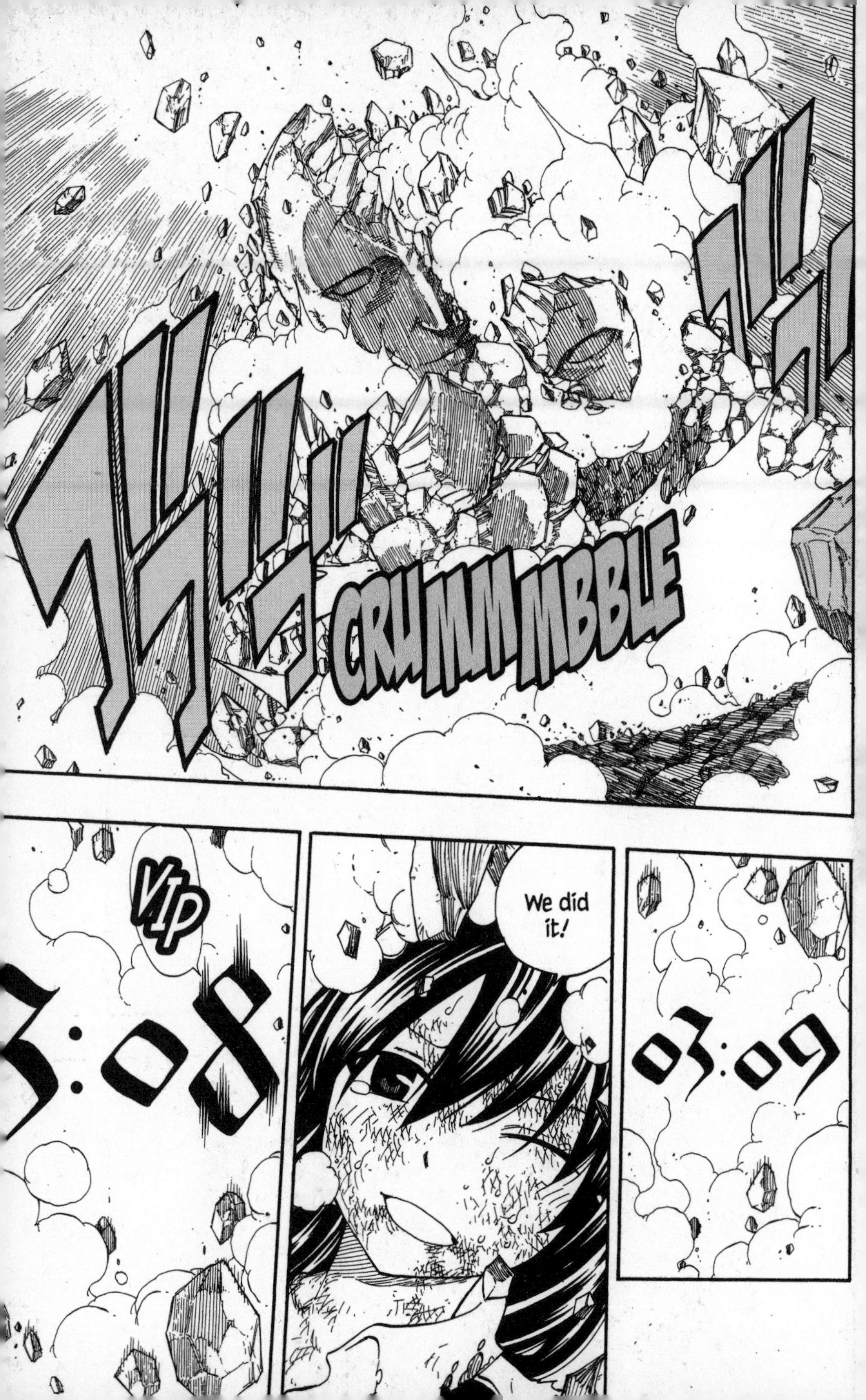
CRUMMMMBBLE
03:09
We did it!
VIP
3:08

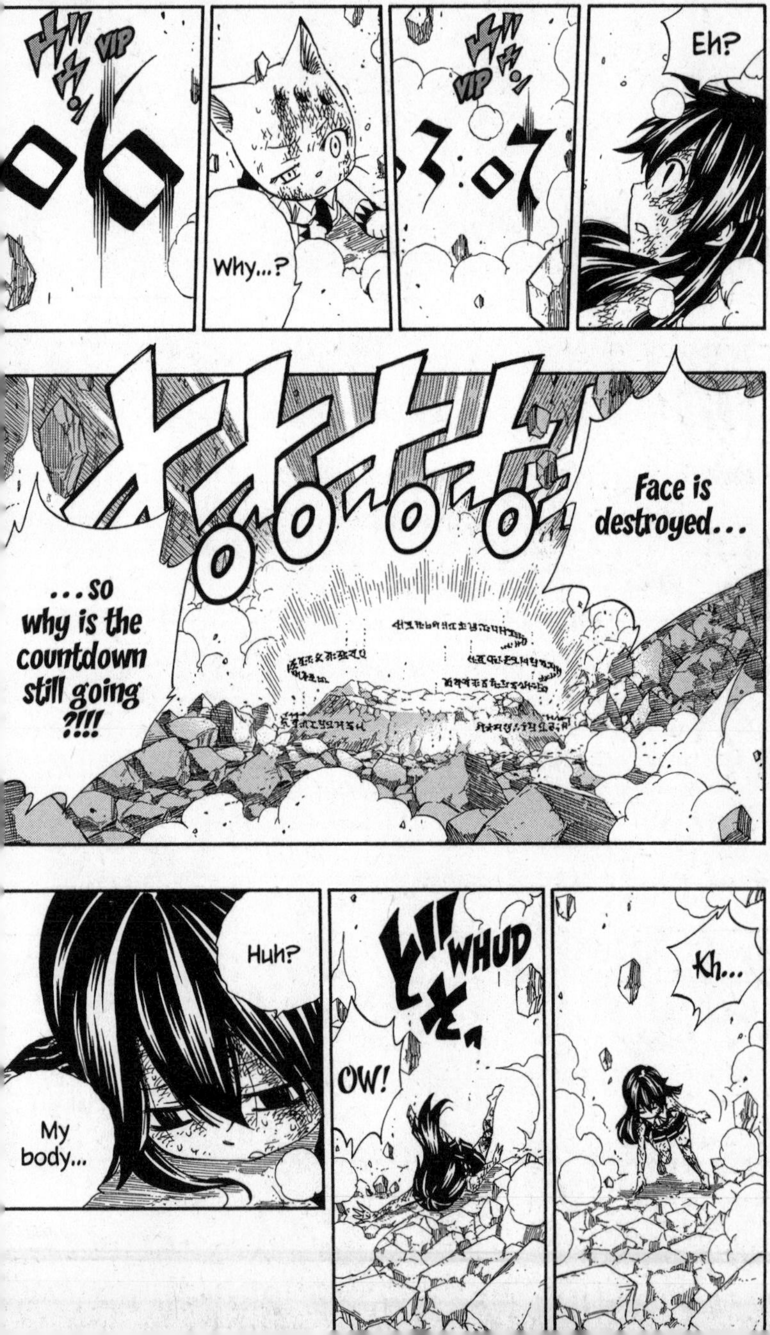
Eh?
VIP
Why...?
VIP
Face is destroyed...
...so why is the countdown still going ?!!!
Kh...
WHUD
OW!
Huh?
My body...

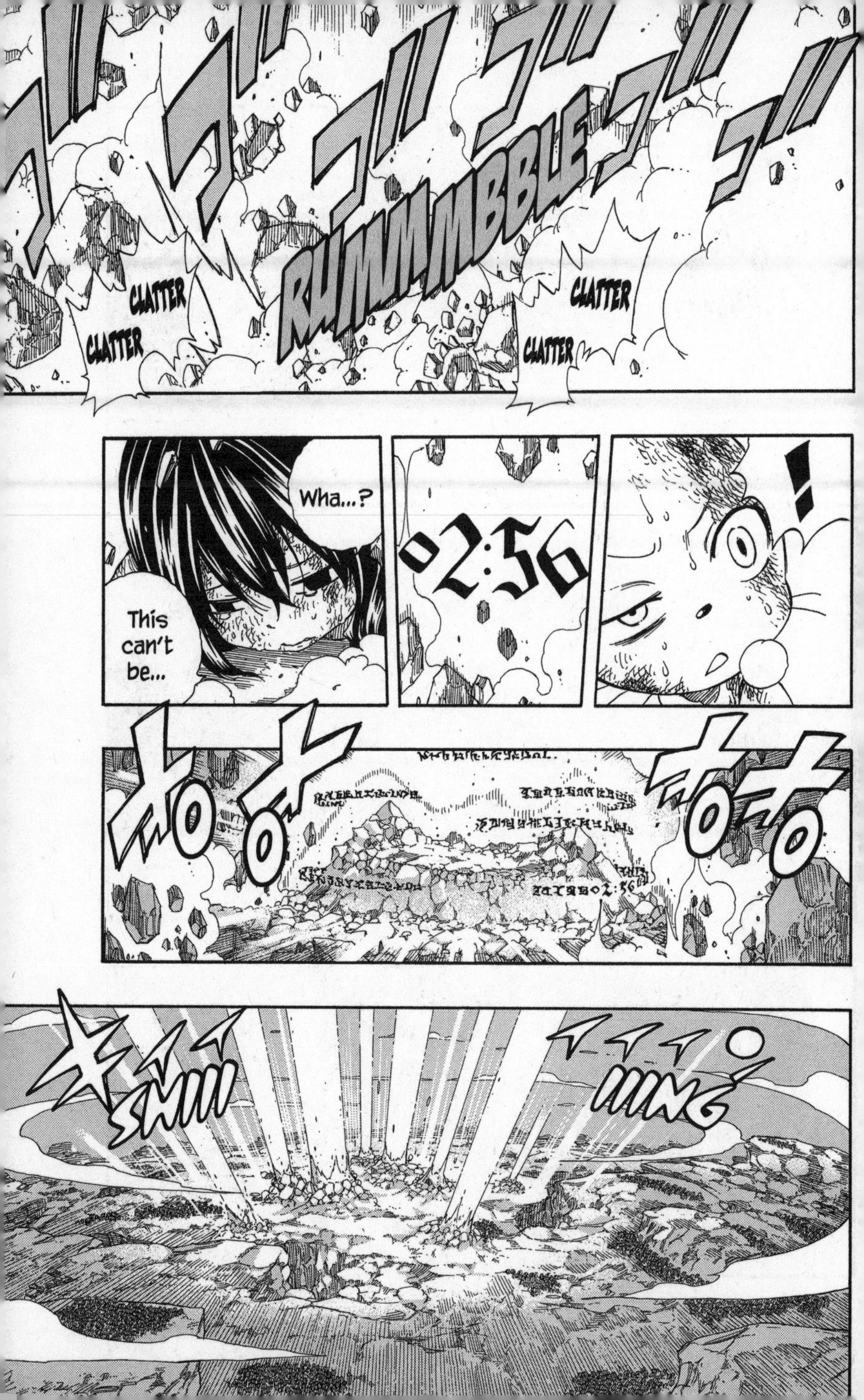
RUMMMBBLE
CLATTER
CLATTER
CLATTER
CLATTER
!
02:56
Wha...?
This can't be...
SHIIII
IIING

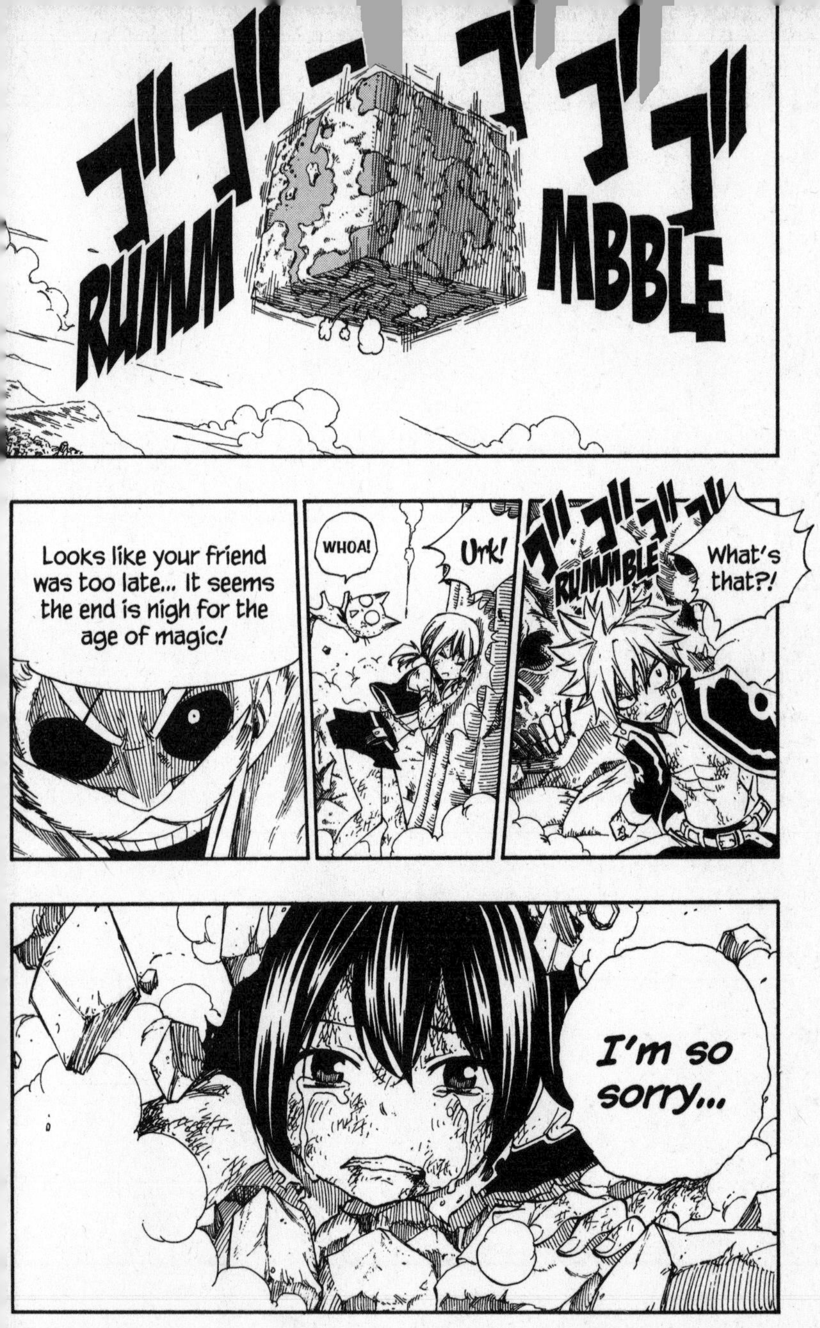
RUMM
MBBLE
RUMMBLE
What's that?!
Urk!
WHOA!
Looks like your friend was too late... It seems the end is nigh for the age of magic!
I'm so sorry...

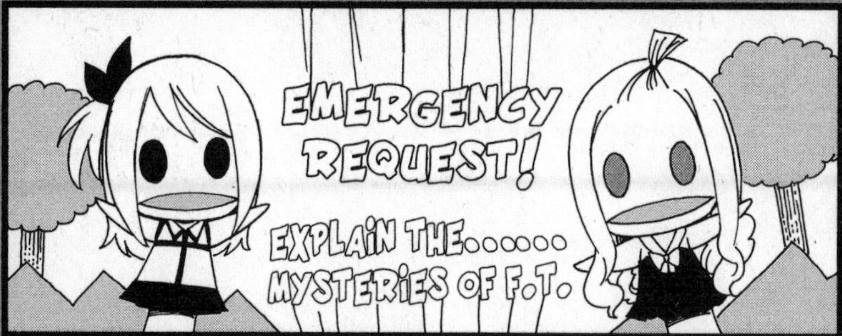
EMERGENCY REQUEST!
EXPLAIN THE…… MYSTERIES OF F.T.

At a gym somewhere...

Lucy: Hey, everybody!! Hi there!!

Mira: Hello!! We only have one page this time, so let's get right to it!

Lucy: Right. First question.

What do Gray's Buns and JuviBuns taste like?

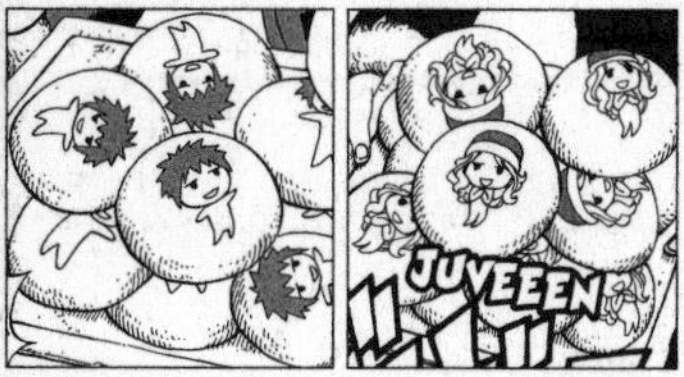
JUVEEEN

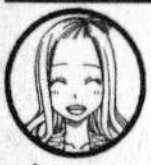
: They look delicious!

Lucy: Juvia's good at that stuff. She's got a lot of feminine power!

Mira: As for what they taste like, they must be filled with the ***taste of love,*** right?

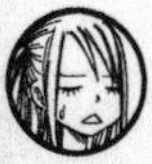
: Yeah, that tells me absolutely nothing.

Mira: Then the taste of life!

Lucy: Let's go to the next question.

In the founding photo for Fairy Tail (?) who is the guy over on the right?

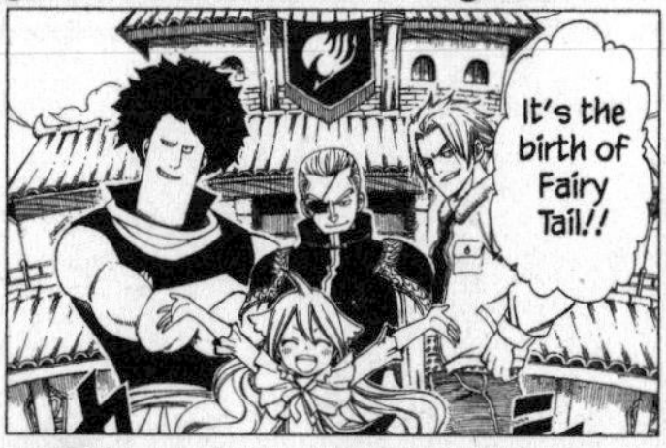
It's the birth of Fairy Tail!!

Mira: We've heard a whole lot of guesswork from the readers on this one!

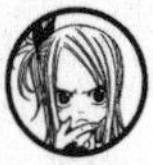
: He looks sort of familiar.

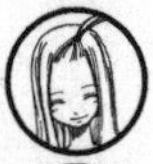
: It's Laxus!! Couldn't it be Laxus when he was younger?

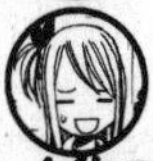
: No, no, no, no... This was taken 105 years ago.

Mira: Okay, the master when he was younger?

Lucy: I don't think the master was even born yet back then.

Mira: Then...

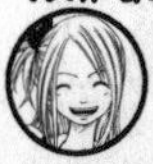
: You'll find the correct answer to that question in Fairy Tail Zero, a series running currently in Monthly Fairy Tail Magazine!

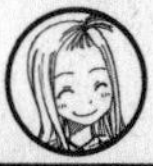
: Wow! That was a really subtle advertisement, wasn't it?

FAIRY TAIL

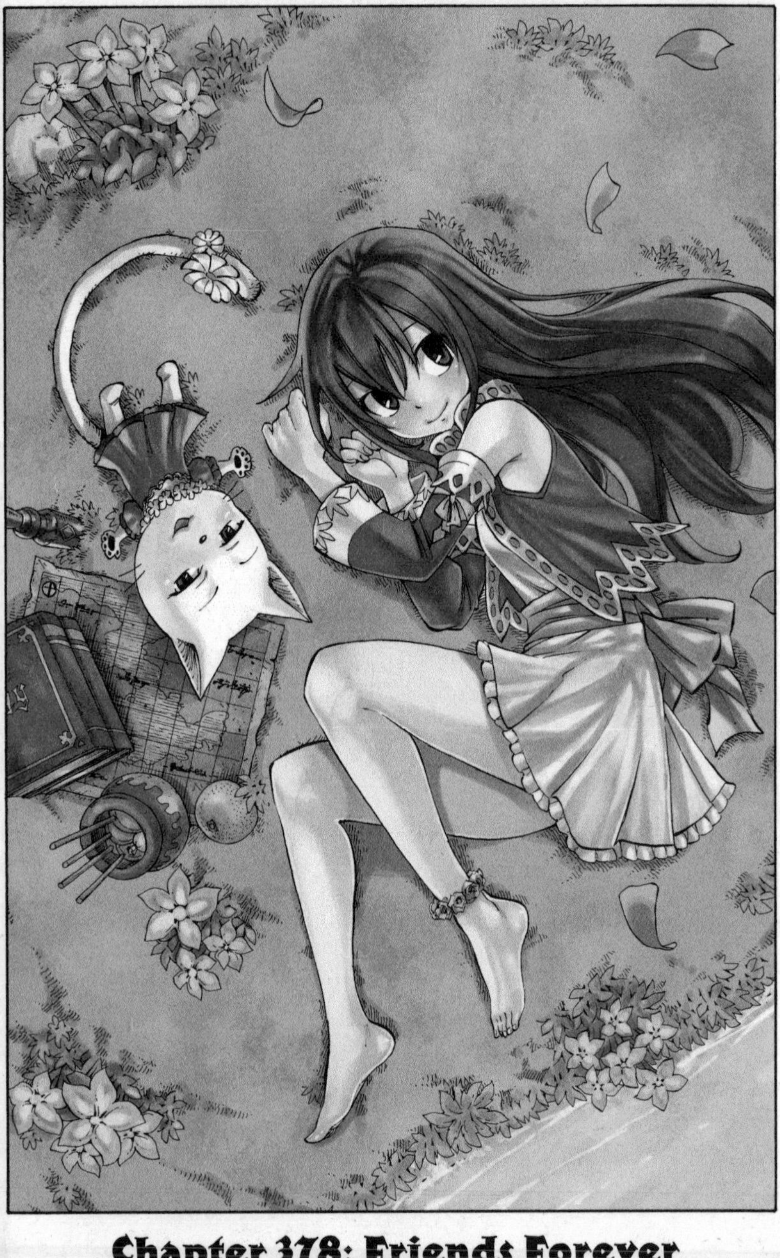

Chapter 378: Friends Forever

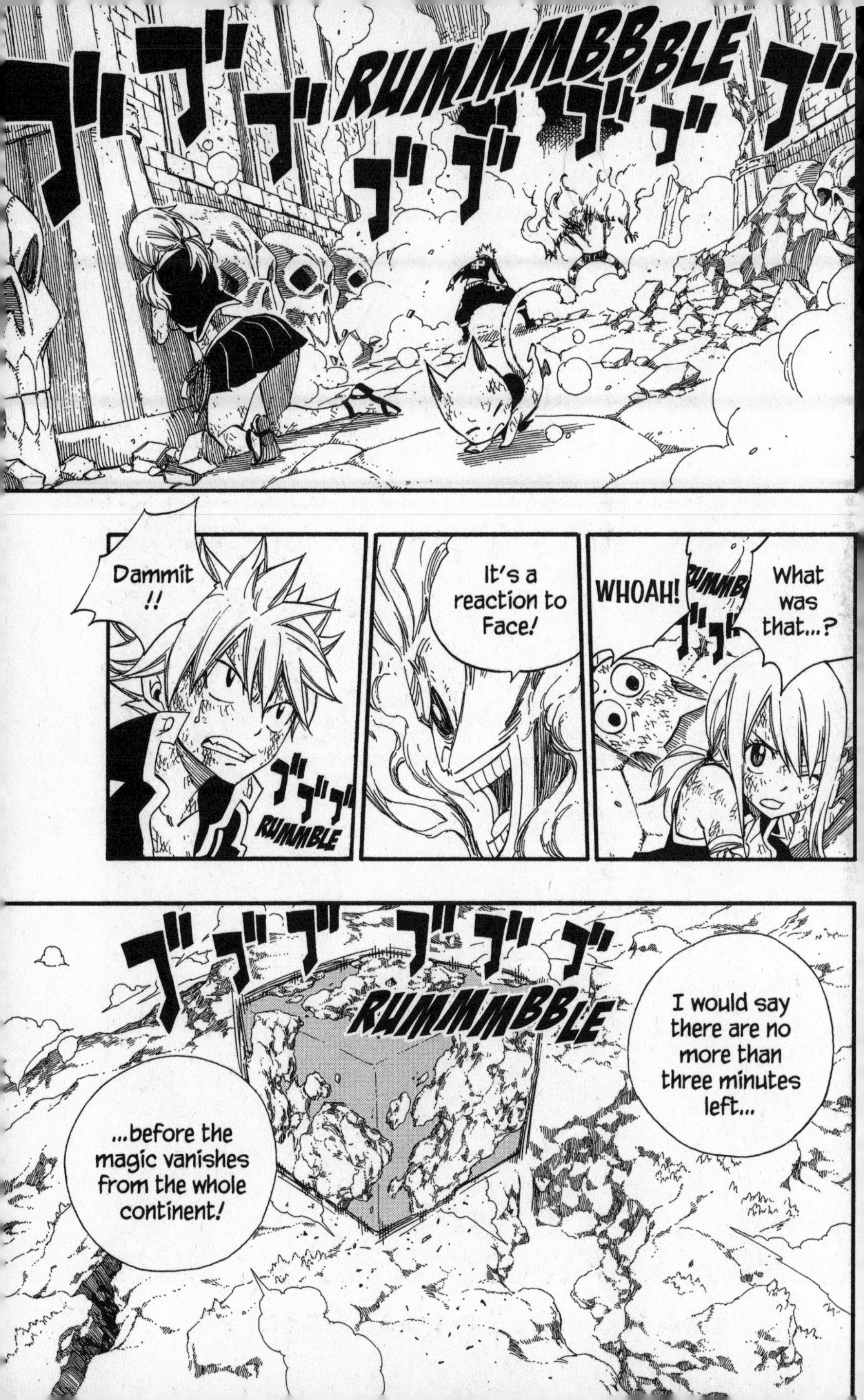
RUMMMMBBBLE
What was that...?
WHOAH!
It's a reaction to Face!
Dammit !!
RUMMBLE
I would say there are no more than three minutes left...
RUMMMMBBLE
...before the magic vanishes from the whole continent!

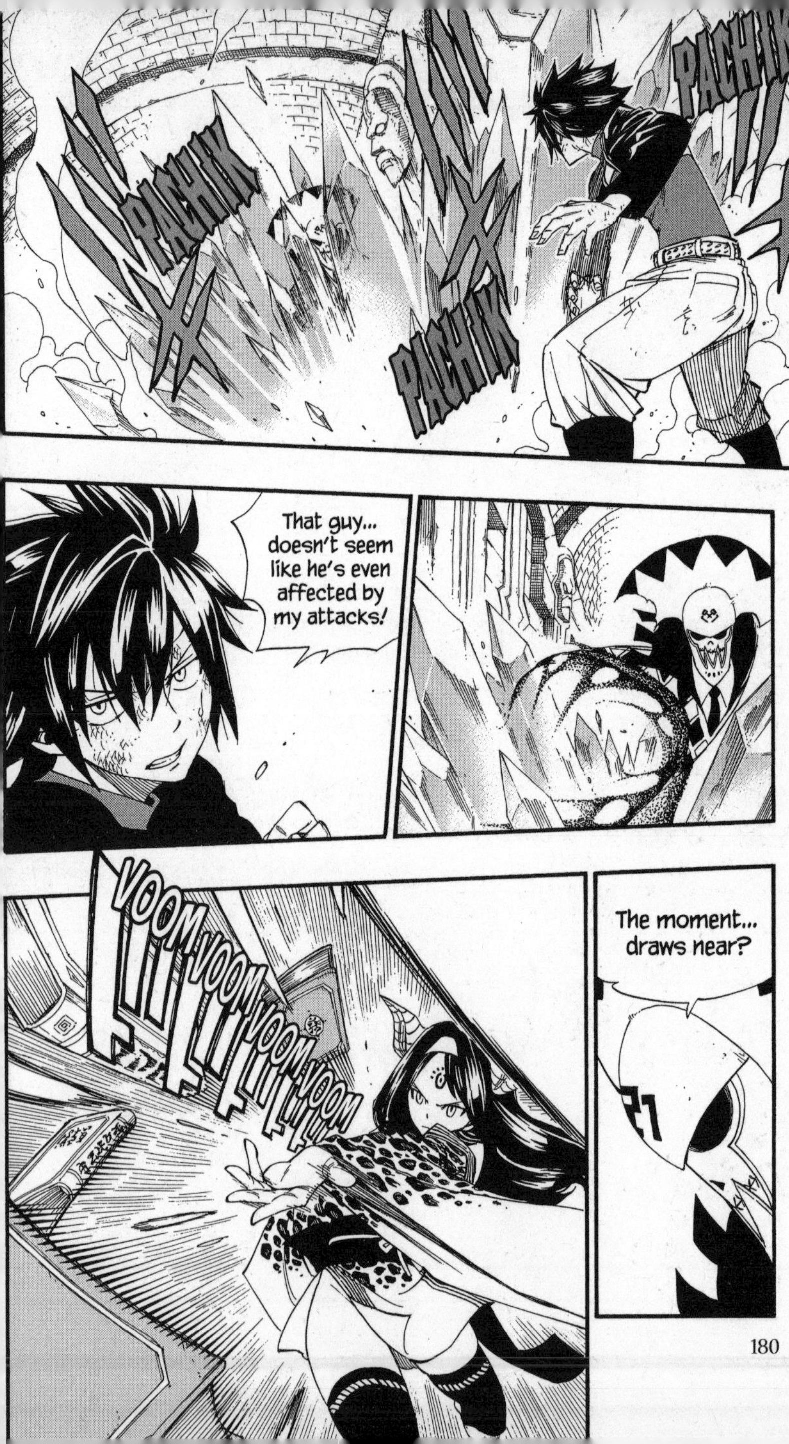
PACHIK
PACHIK
PACHIK
That guy... doesn't seem like he's even affected by my attacks!
The moment... draws near?
VOOM VOOM VOOM VOOM

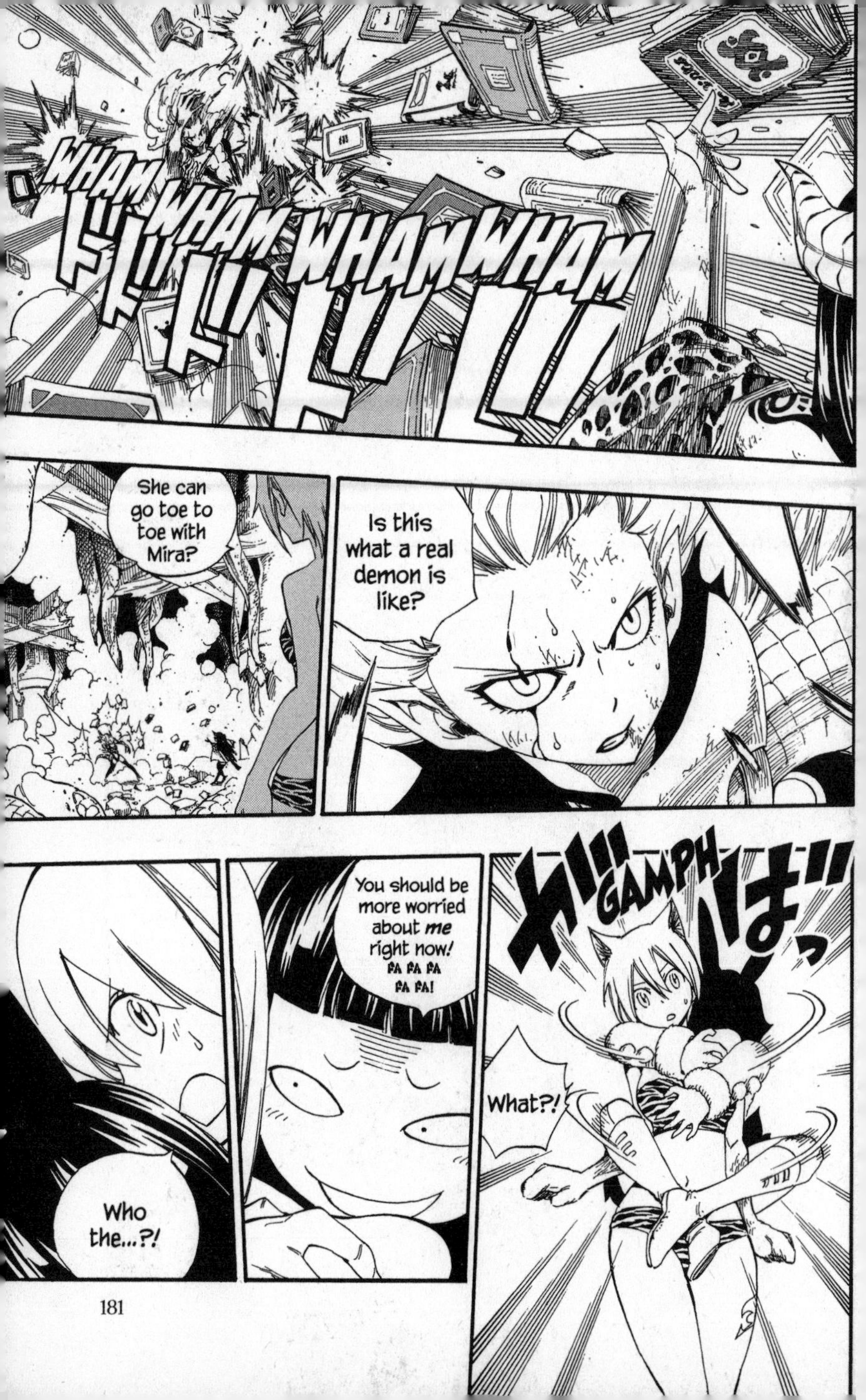

WHAM WHAM WHAM WHAM
Is this what a real demon is like?
She can go toe to toe with Mira?
GAMPH
What?!
You should be more worried about *me* right now! FA FA FA FA FA!
Who the...?!

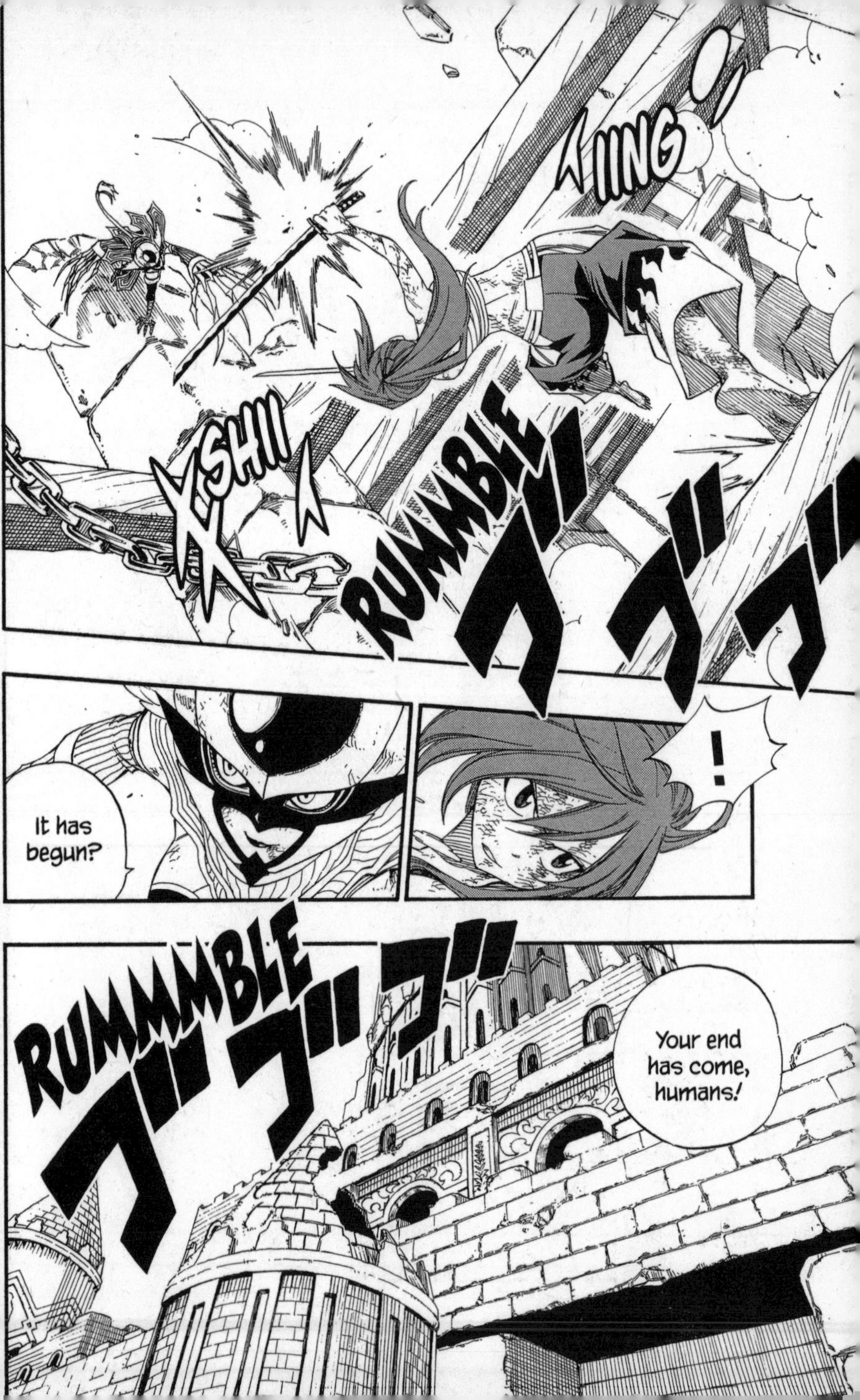

WIING
RUMBLE
SHII
!
It has begun?
RUMMMBLE
Your end has come, humans!

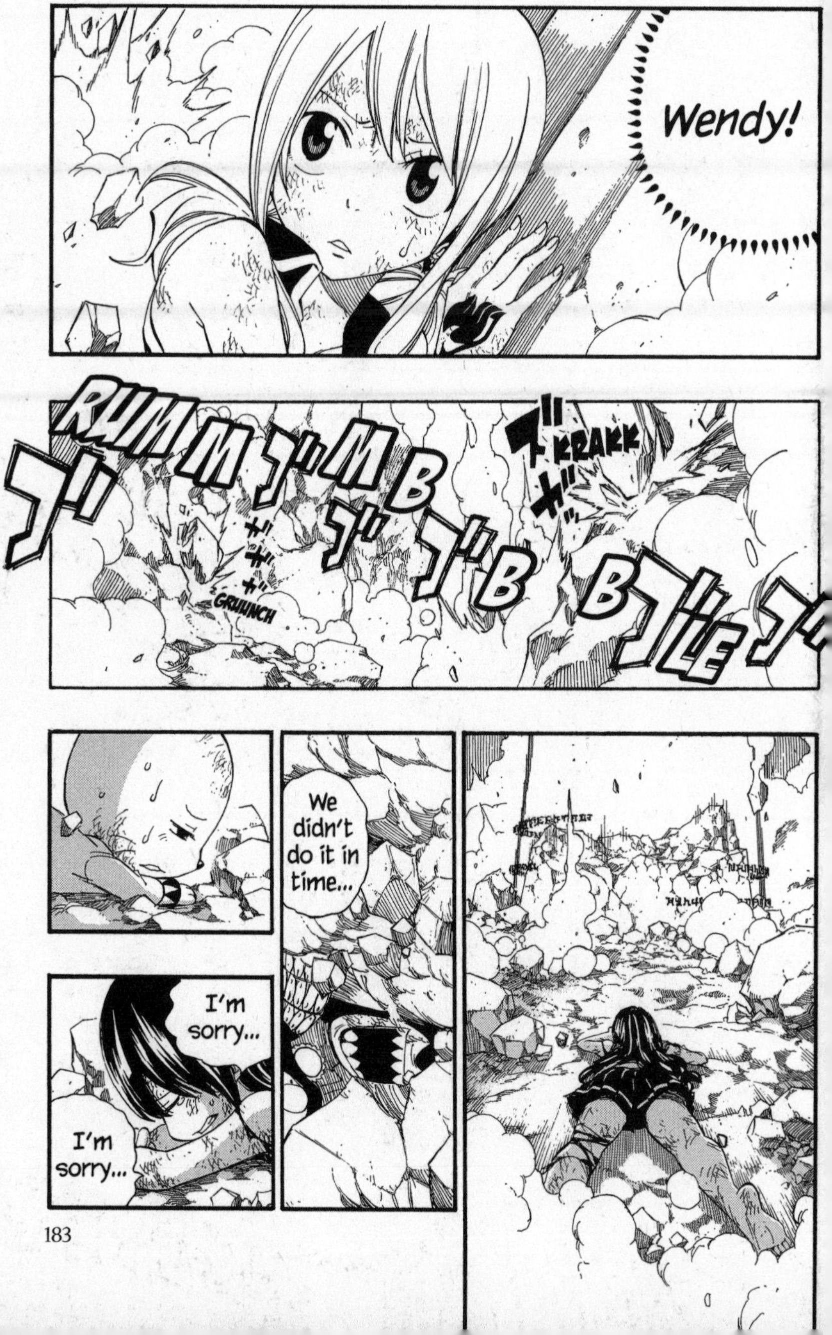
Wendy!
KRAKK
RUMMMB
B
B
LE
GRUUNCH
We didn't do it in time...
I'm sorry...
I'm sorry...

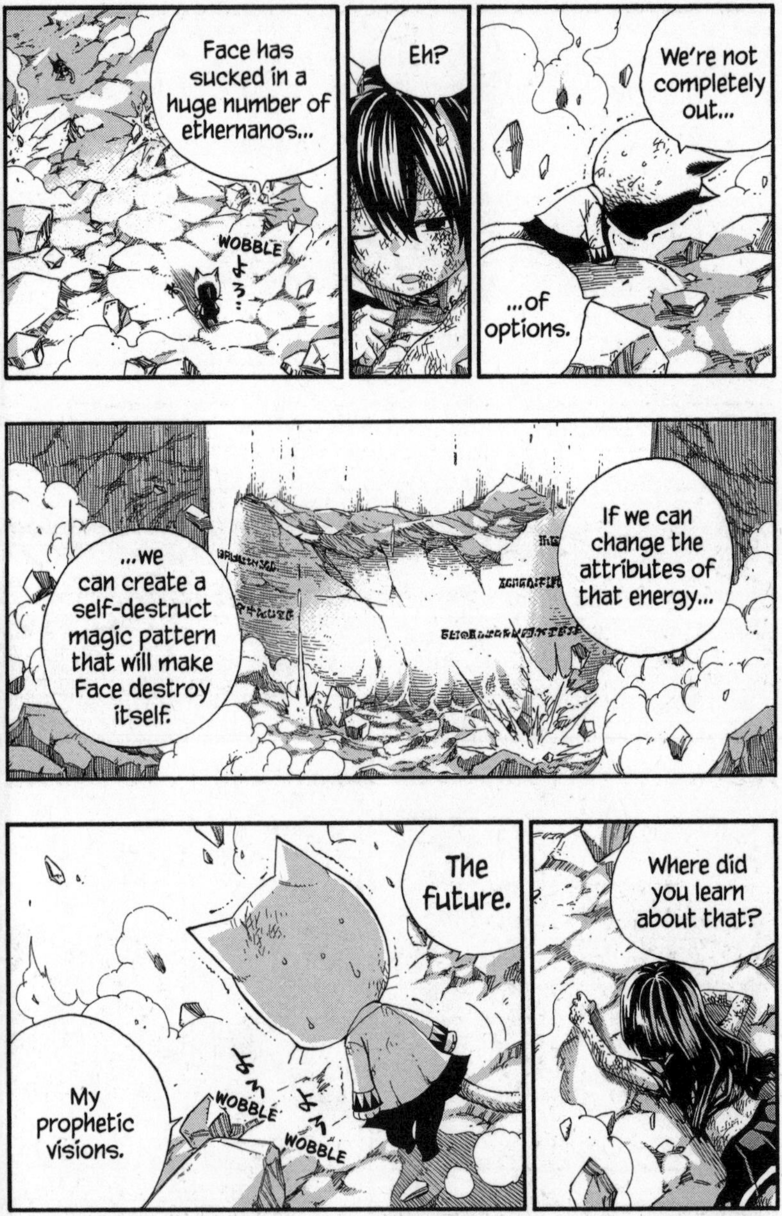
We're not completely out...
...of options.
Eh?
Face has sucked in a huge number of ethernanos...
WOBBLE
よろ…
If we can change the attributes of that energy...
...we can create a self-destruct magic pattern that will make Face destroy itself.
Where did you learn about that?
The future.
My prophetic visions.
WOBBLE
よろ
WOBBLE
よろ

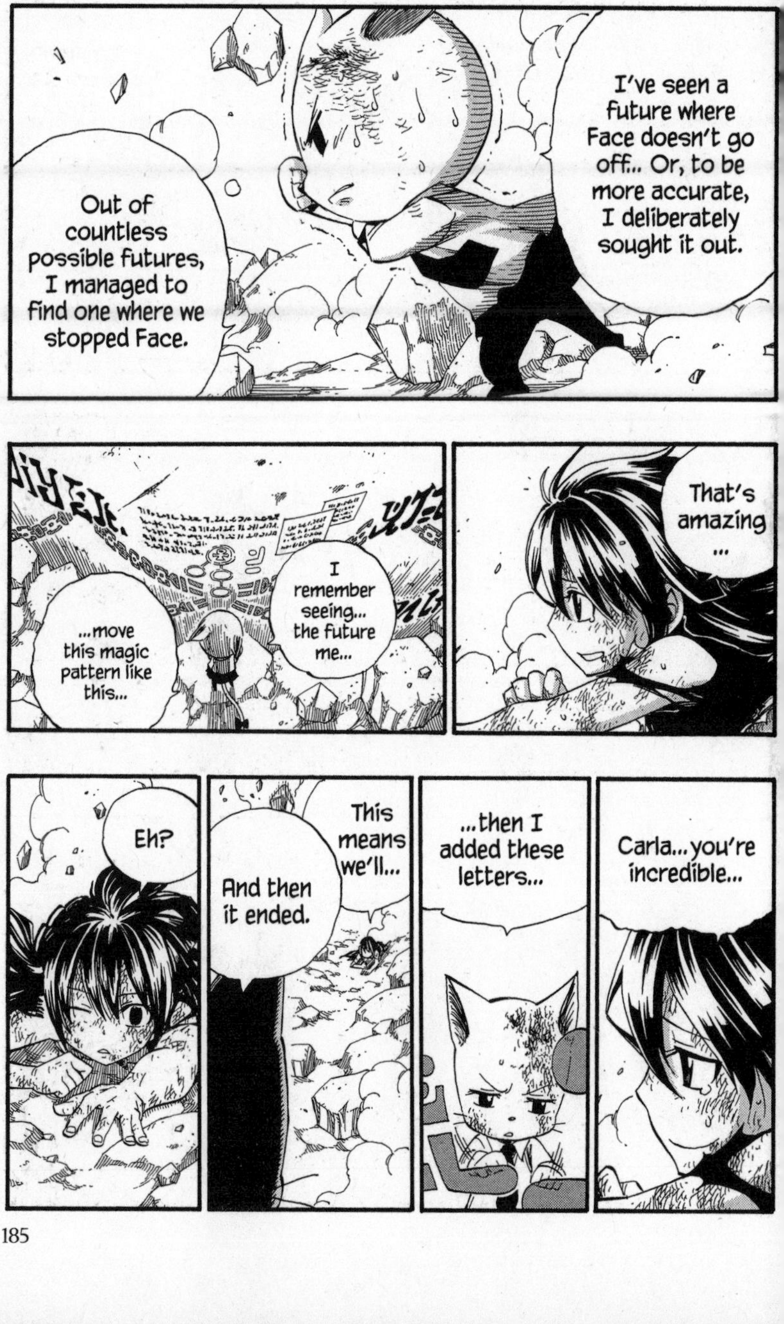

I've seen a future where Face doesn't go off... Or, to be more accurate, I deliberately sought it out.
Out of countless possible futures, I managed to find one where we stopped Face.
That's amazing...
I remember seeing... the future me...
...move this magic pattern like this...
Carla...you're incredible...
...then I added these letters...
This means we'll...
And then it ended.
Eh?

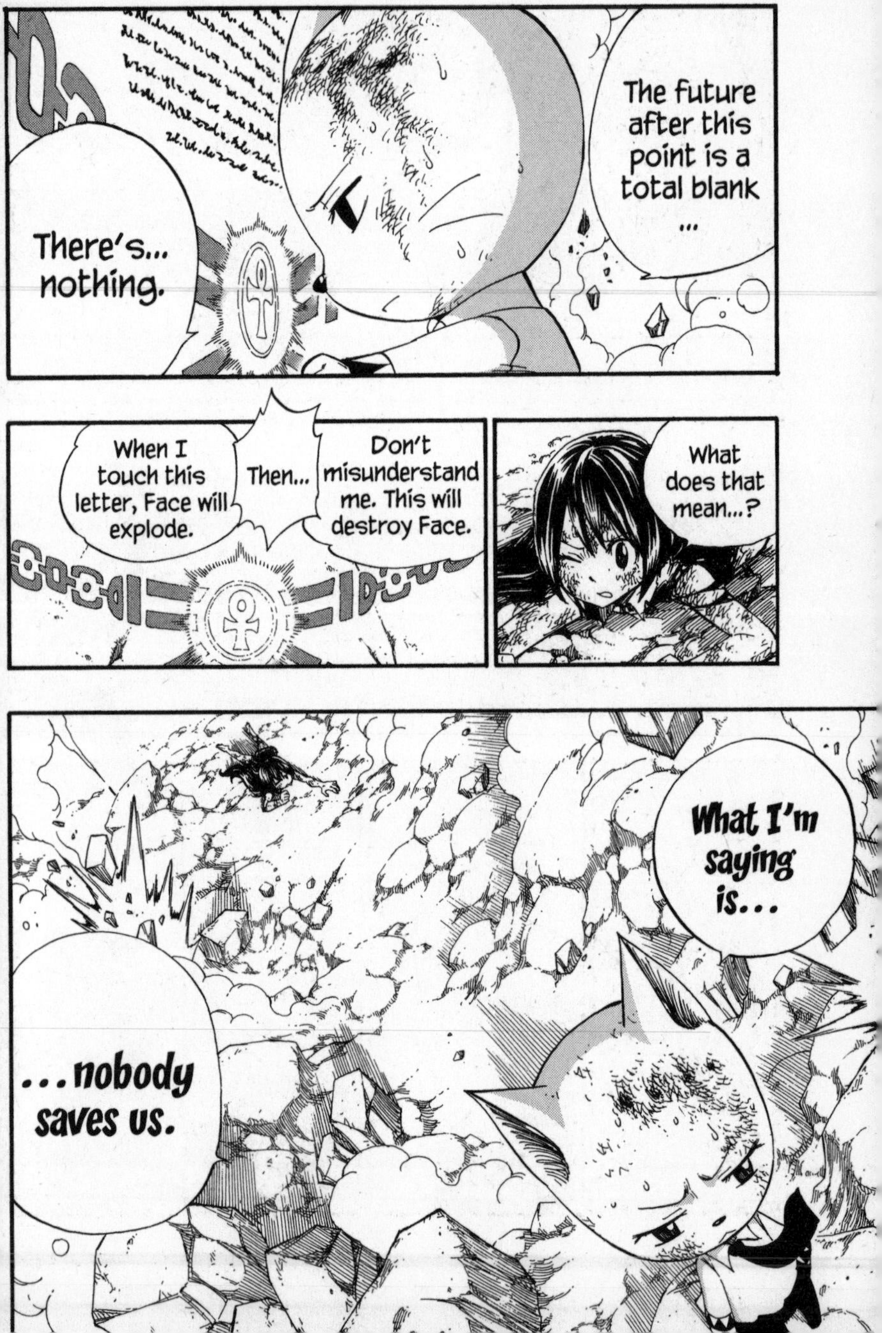
The future after this point is a total blank ...
There's... nothing.
What does that mean...?
Don't misunderstand me. This will destroy Face.
Then...
When I touch this letter, Face will explode.
What I'm saying is...
...nobody saves us.

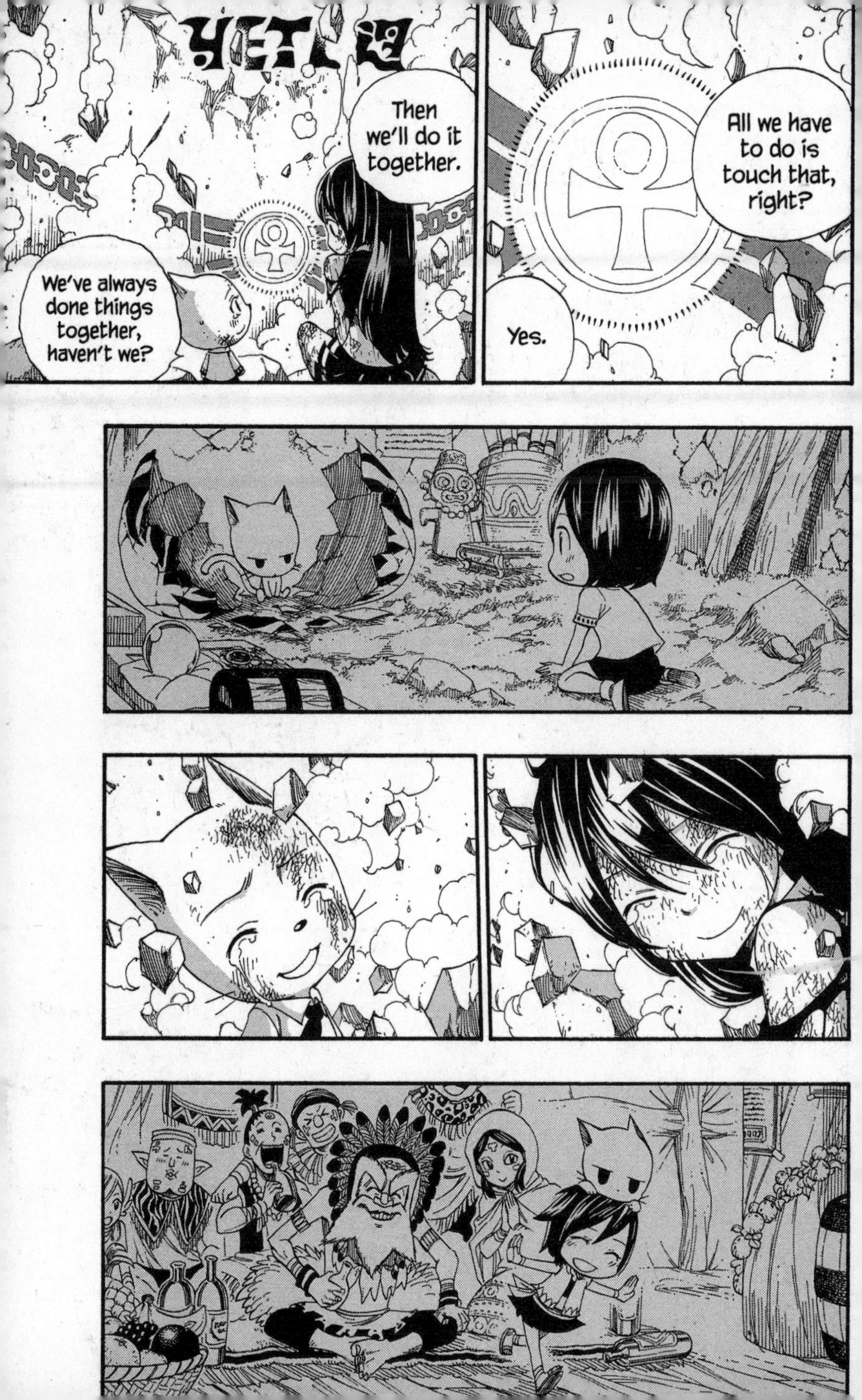
All we have to do is touch that, right?
Yes.
Then we'll do it together.
We've always done things together, haven't we?

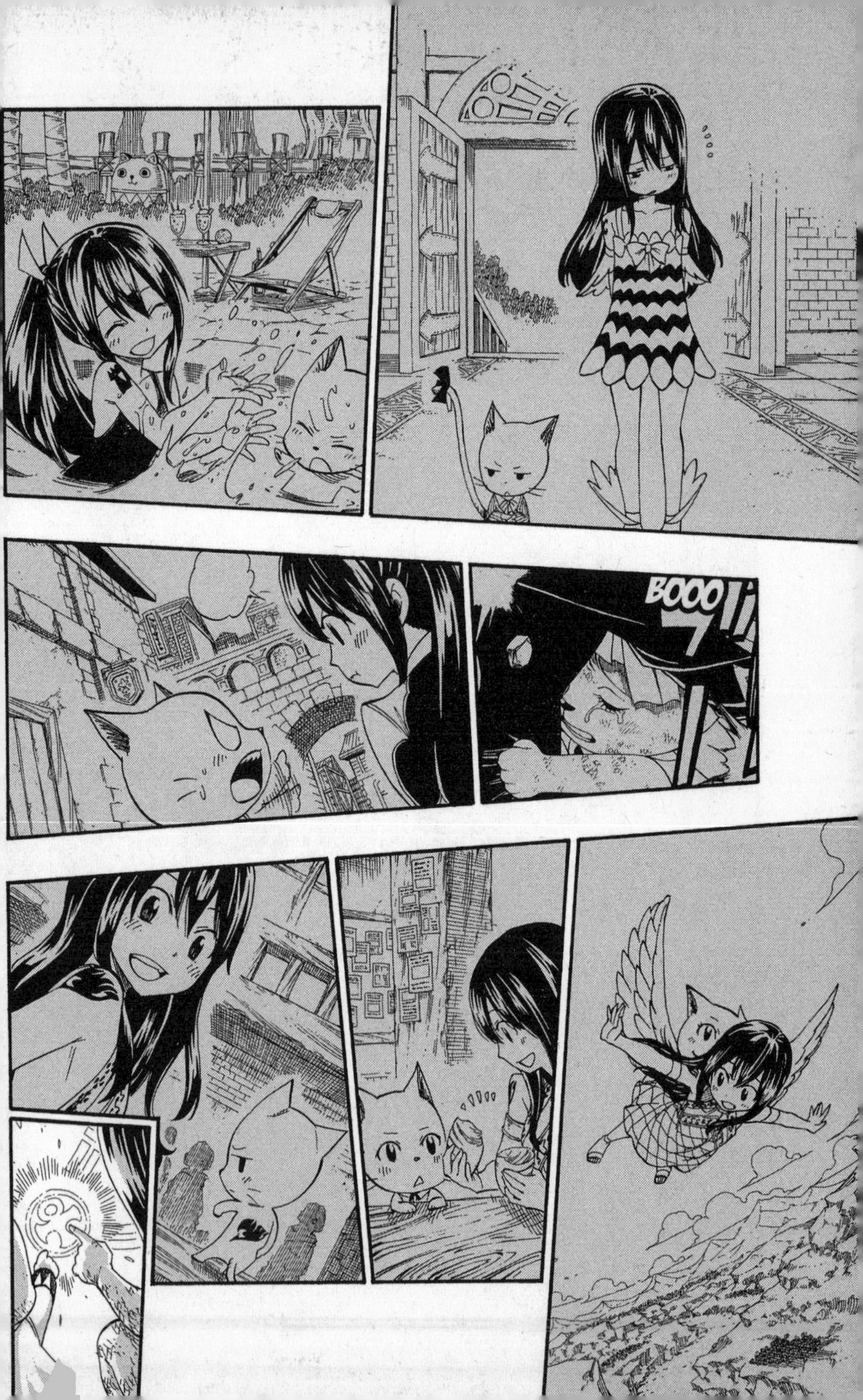
BOOO

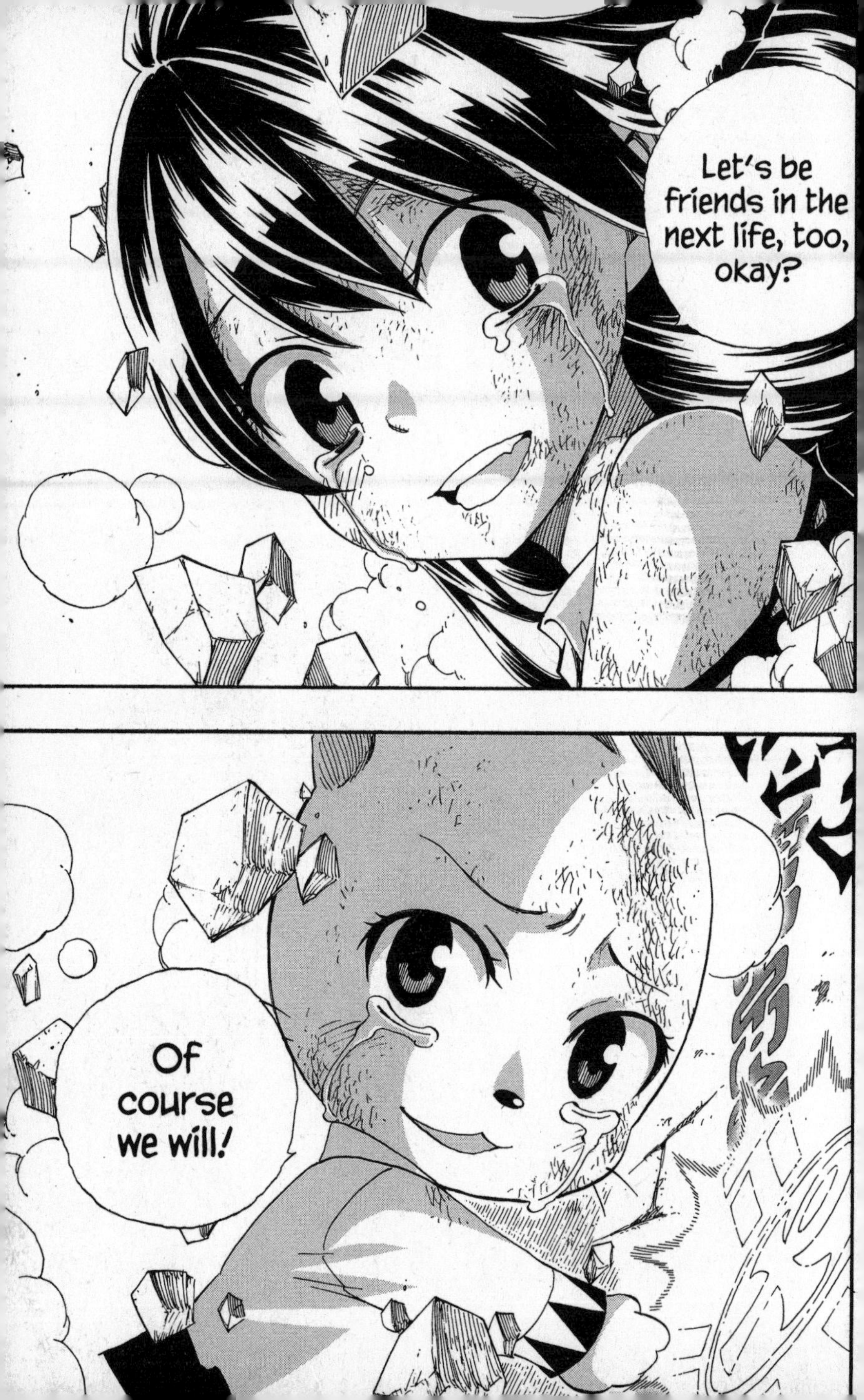
Let's be friends in the next life, too, okay?
Of course we will!

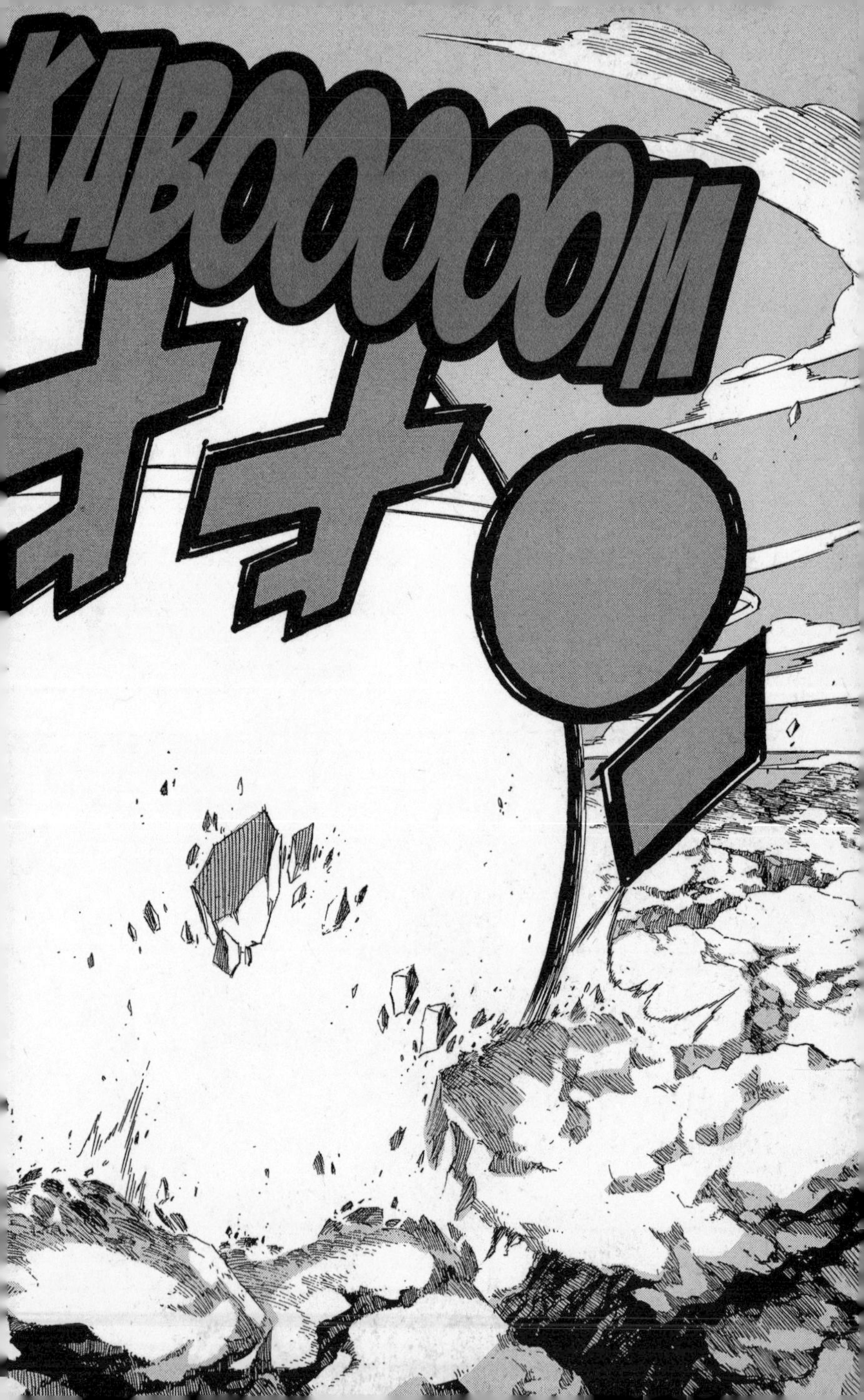
KABOOOOOM

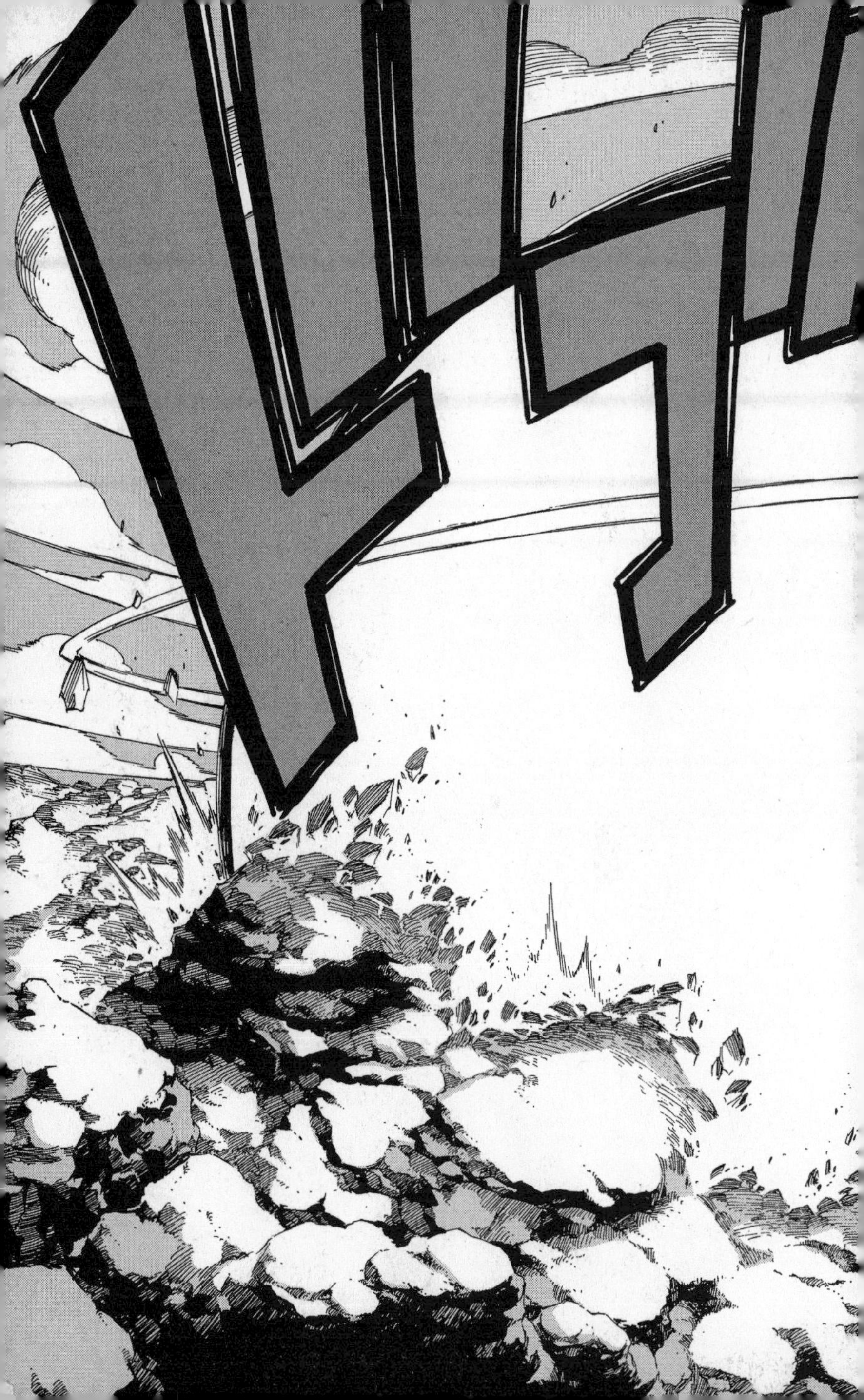

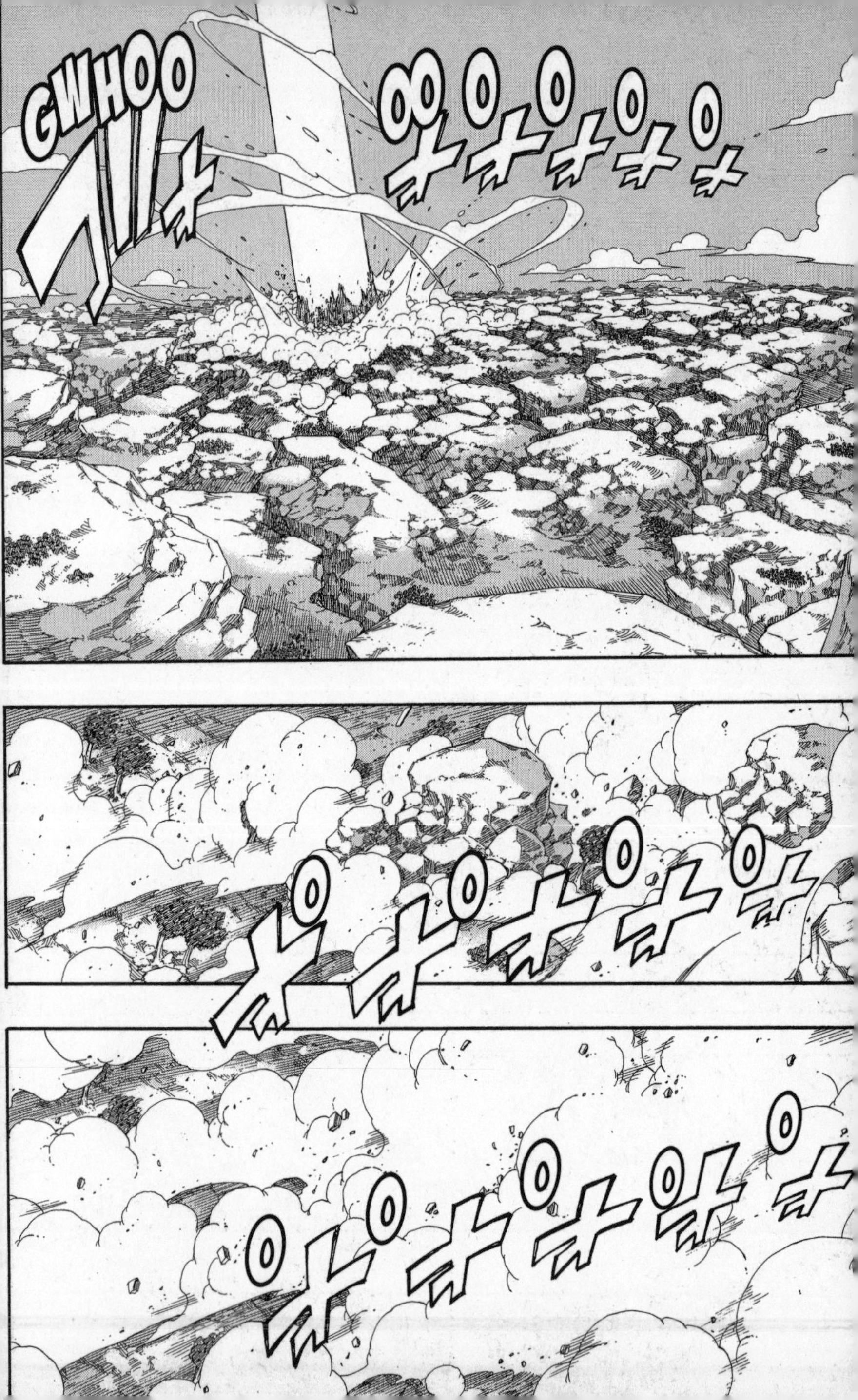
GWHOO

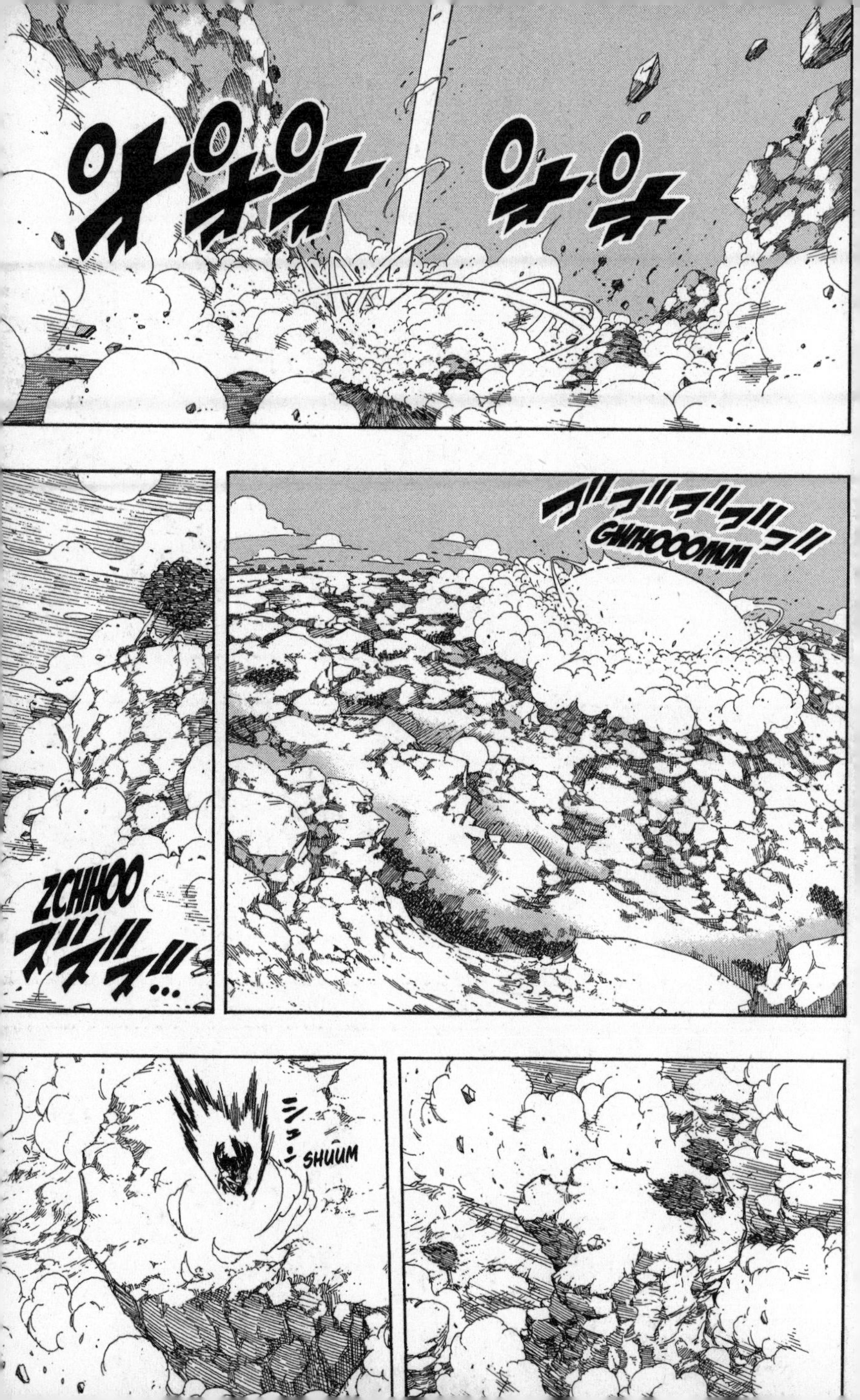
ゴゴゴゴゴ!!
GWHOOOMM
ZCHHOO
ズズズ!!…
シュン
SHUUM

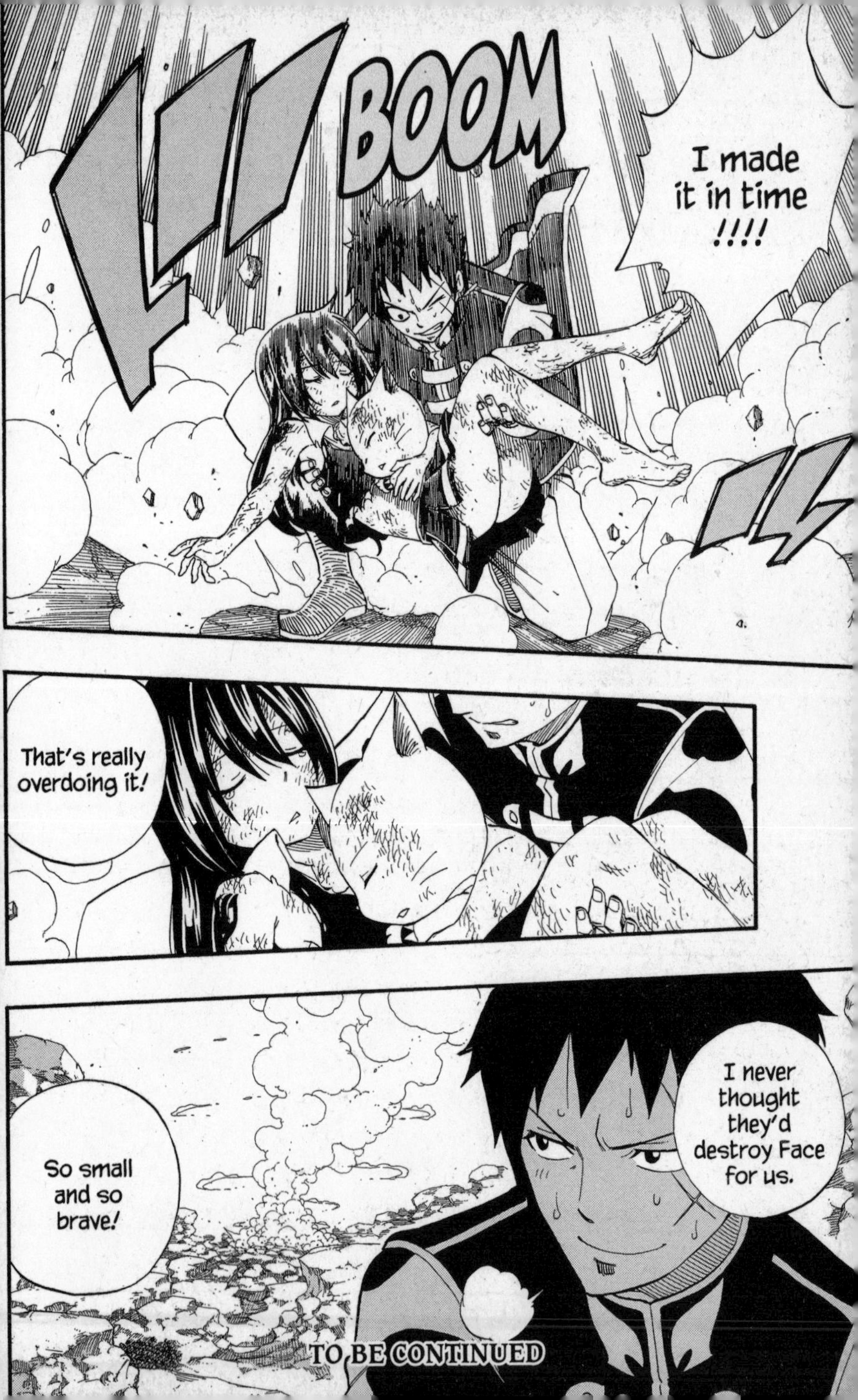
BOOM
I made it in time !!!!
That's really overdoing it!
I never thought they'd destroy Face for us.
So small and so brave!
TO BE CONTINUED

Afterword

Big news!! The first Monthly Fairy Tail Magazine comes out the same day as this volume does in Japan!! Clap, clap, clap!! We call it a magazine, but actually it's a set with a DVD and a fan book, all for 2,759 yen! A new type of product that has never been sold before. The anime DVD includes four episodes of the TV series plus a specially edited bonus feature. The bonus feature has some anime scenes made just for this DVD. That's pretty amazing!!

And the fan book includes a brand-new manga series by me, Hiro Mashima, called Fairy Tail Zero, and it will run every month. As it's planned right now, Mavis is the main character, and it will include the events leading up to the founding of Fairy Tail. There's also a spinoff manga in the magazine featuring Gray. That manga will be a part of a new Fairy Tail world by our great manga hope, Yusuke Shirato!! He's a real worker, so much so that I can recommend him with confidence! You want more? On top of that, the fan book will also include interviews with the voice actors, character rundowns and analyses, and loads of other fun stuff!!

A very large group of people, all with love for Fairy Tail, have gathered to make wonderful DVDs and fan books for this project! So I'd like you all to please take Monthly Fairy Tail Magazine into your hearts!

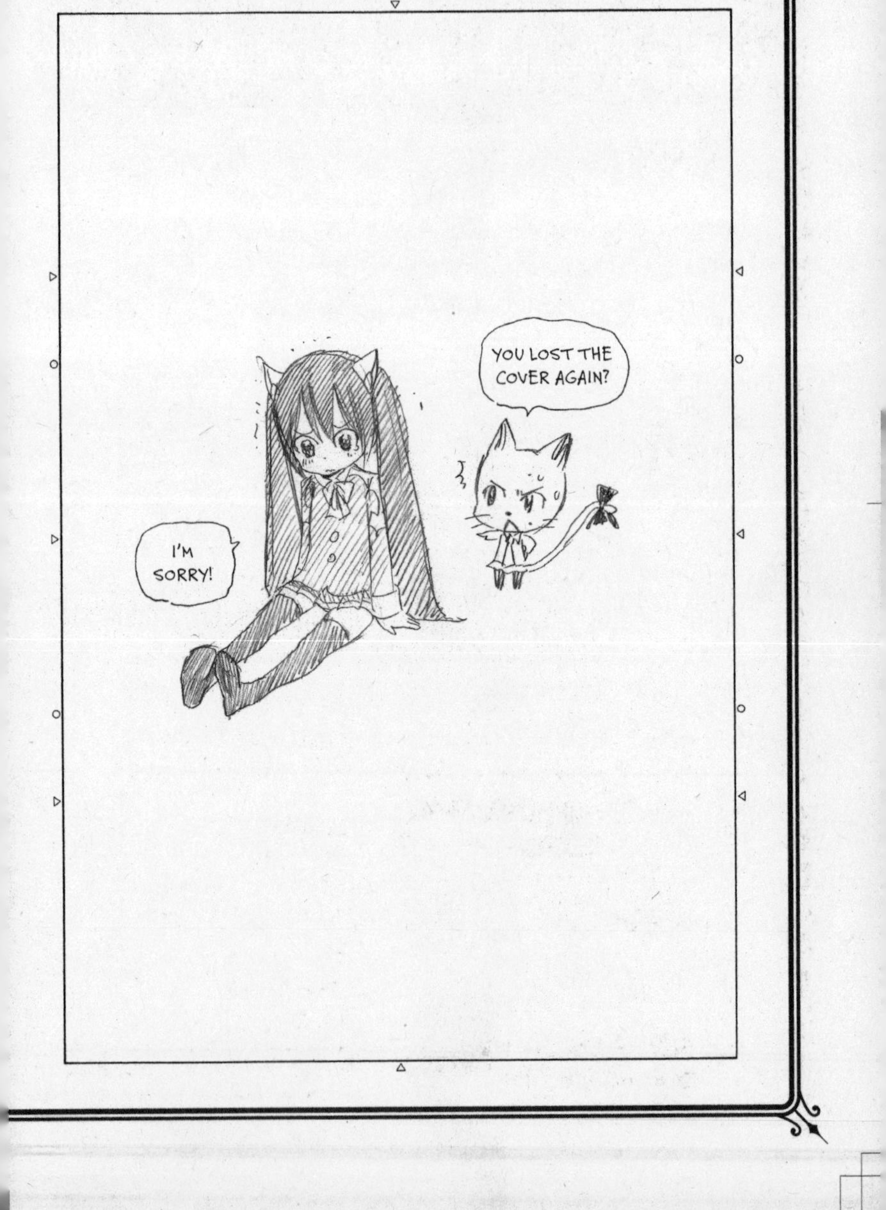
YOU LOST THE COVER AGAIN?
I'M SORRY!

FAIRY TAIL フェアリーテイル 44

TARTAROS ARC

COUNCIL IS BLOWN UP → Council Members All Destroyed

In a highly-visible and shocking way!

They're after Memento

PREVIEW Natsu vs. One of the Nine Demon Gates

Hard battle and Lucy helps

Lahar and Doranbalt are the only survivors

They trade THE SEIS their freedom for information

VS

JELLAL

Seis joins up with the heroes?

Chapter 1 Erza and Mira battle together

They realize this is part of the former chairman's plan

7 or 8 chapters

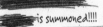

Fairy Tail Destroyed

They're captured and sent to Tartaros

Again...?

Elfman betrays them. Cana betrays as well.

Chapter 2 Wendy and Carla battle to their limits to stop Memento, and they appear to have died in the attempt.

Chapter 3 [redacted] [redacted]

[redacted] is summoned!!!!

Until [redacted]

GAJEEL VS. TORAFUZAR

ERZA VS. MINERVA

GRAY VS. SILVER

Juvia vs. Keyes

Point

Very important to Silver... Link?

HIRO 真島ヒロ MASHIMA

This is the plot from the earliest conception.
Actual names and events have been altered.

FROM HIRO MASHIMA

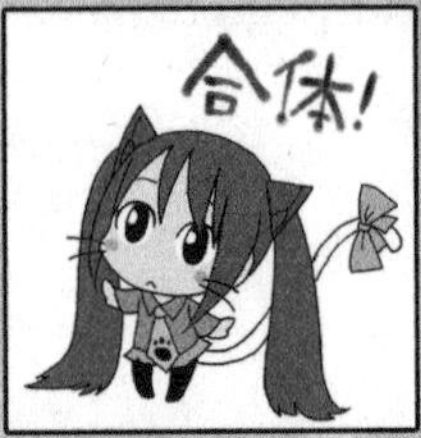
合体!

I went to Nagano Prefecture to have a signing as a part of the celebrations for Weekly Shonen Magazine's 55th Anniversary. It was my first visit back to my home area in a long time, and it was for a signing, so it was really a lot of fun for me. I saw some old classmates and a few school friends who graduated in other years too. Next will be Hokkaido. To tell the truth, this will be my first time setting foot on Hokkaido soil!

Original Jacket Design: Hisao Ogawa

Translation Notes:

Japanese is a tricky language for most Westerners, and translation is often more art than science. For your edification and reading pleasure, here are notes on some of the places where we could have gone in a different direction with our translation of the work, or where a Japanese cultural reference is used.

Page 94, Cowbane Canyon

In the Japanese version, the canyon is called Dokuzeri, which is a type of *Cicuta* plant (water hemlock) called northern water hemlock, also known as cowbane in English. It might be called that because it is highly poisonous but may look to a cow like a normal edible plant.

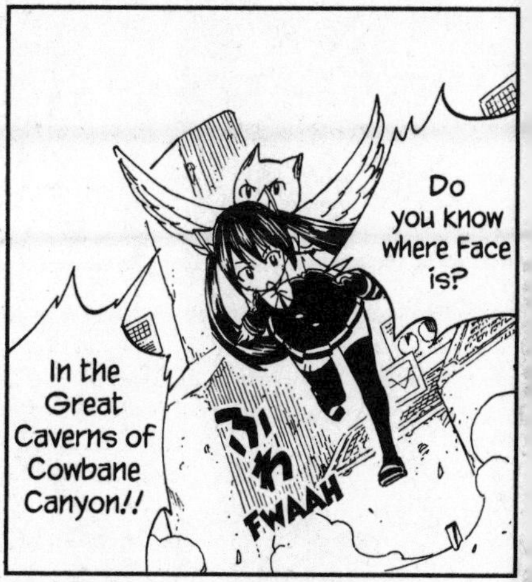
Do you know where Face is?
In the Great Caverns of Cowbane Canyon!!
ふわ
FWAAH

Page 141, Five Swords Under Heaven

The *Tenga Goken*, also called the *Gomeiken* ("Five Famous Swords"), are five swords made by famous swordsmiths from the Heian Era, about a thousand years ago, until the Sengoku Era a little over 400 years ago. Most still exist and are considered national treasures. The five blades include Dôjigiri, Onimaru, Mikazuki Munechika, Ôtenta, and Juzumaru.

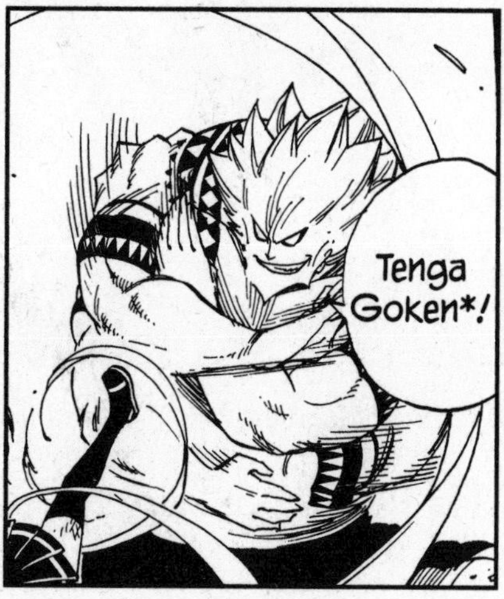
Tenga Goken*!

Page 141, Onimaru

One of the Five Swords Under Heaven, made by the sword master Kunitsuna. Legend has it that it belonged to Tokiyori Hojo, the fifth *shikken* (regent) of the Kamakura Shogunate. When a mysterious illness befell Tokiyori, the sword could tell that an evil spirit was conspiring with Tokiyori's *oni*-shaped hibachi stove. It leapt from its scabbard and struck down the hibachi, saving Tokiyori from his illness and earning itself the name Onimaru.

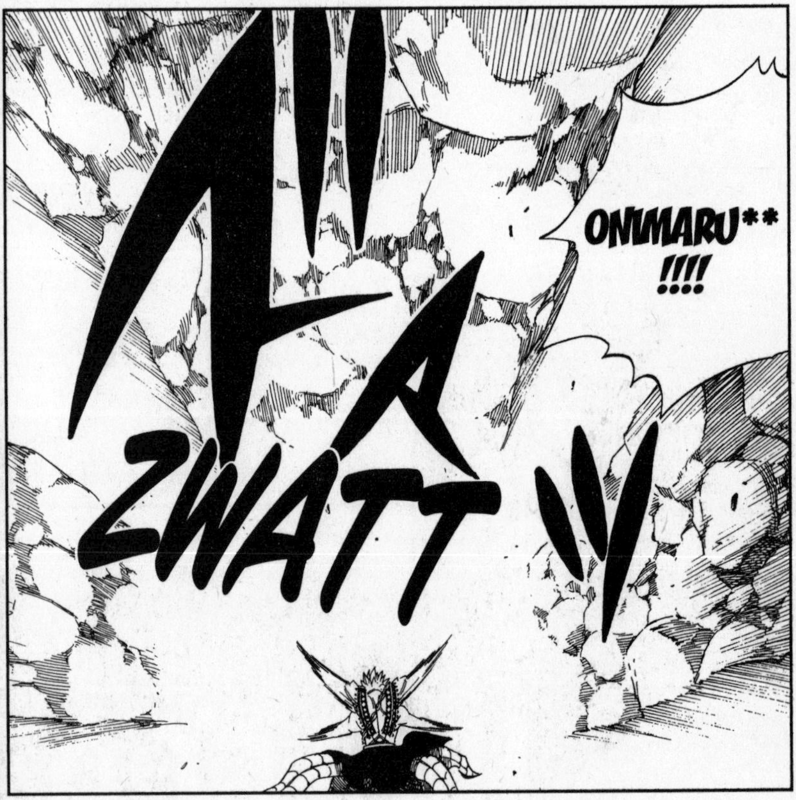
ONIMARU**!!!!
ZWATT

Page 143, Juzumaru

One of the Five Swords Under Heaven, made by the master swordsmith Tsunetsugu of the Bichu school of sword making (named for a region now mostly in Okayama Prefecture). Although it doesn't have quite as imaginative a name as Onimaru, Juzumaru is named after the Buddhist holy man Nichiren, founder of the Nichiren sect of Buddhism, who made his name by predicting the Mongol invasion and the "divine wind" that would wipe out most of the invading force. According to legend, Nichiren wore the Juzumaru sword and wrapped his rosary-like prayer beads (*juzu*) around it.

ATTACK ON TITAN

Humanity
has been decimated!

A century ago, the bizarre creatures known as Titans devoured most of the world's population, driving the remainder into a walled stronghold. Now, the appearance of an immense new Titan threatens the few humans left, and one restless boy decides to seize the chance to fight for his freedom, and the survival of his species!

KC KODANSHA COMICS

A Kodansha Comics Trade Paperback Original.

Fairy Tail volume 44 copyright © 2014 Hiro Mashima
English translation copyright © 2014 Hiro Mashima

Published in the United States by Kodansha Comics, an imprint of Kodansha USA Publishing, LLC, New York.

Publication rights for this English edition arranged through Kodansha Ltd., Tokyo.

First published in Japan in 2014 by Kodansha Ltd., Tokyo
ISBN 978-1-61262-563-8

www.kodanshacomics.com

9 8 7 6 5 4 3 2 1

Translation: William Flanagan
Lettering: AndWorld Design
Editing: Ben Applegate

TOMARE!

止まれ
[STOP!]

You're going the wrong way!

Manga is a completely different type of reading experience.

To start at the *beginning,*
go to the *end!*

That's right! Authentic manga is read the traditional Japanese way—from right to left, exactly the *opposite* of how American books are read. It's easy to follow: Just go to the other end of the book and read each page—and each panel—from right side to left side, starting at the top right. Now you're experiencing manga as it was meant to be!